P9-AFP-198

PANIGÝRI

A Celebration of Life in a Greek Island Village

Alison Cadbury

Art by Alice Meyer-Wallace

Plain View Press
P. O. 42255
Austin, TX 78704

plainviewpress.net
sb@plainviewpress.net
512-441-2452 (phone/fax)

Copyright Alison Cadbury, 2008. All rights reserved.
ISBN: 978-1-891386-86-2
Library of Congress Number: 2008921107

Cover and text art by Alice Meyer-Wallace.

Contents

V

VI

VII

To the Reader
Alíthia and Psémata

I remember that, when I had been living a while in Náousa, a friend, another foreigner, asked me, "How do you bear it, with no movies and no novels?" I replied, "When you live in a village, movies and novels are superfluous. Everyday life is as engaging as fiction." I was referring to the stories people told, histories and gossip, of which there were as many versions as tellers. So common among villagers is the practice of embroidering a tale that a typical response to any story is either (doubtfully) "*Alíthia?*" "Truth?" or adamantly, "*Psémata!* "Lies!" followed by imaginative analysis, speculation, and argument about the "real" events, motives, and so forth.

So it is with this book, which is a collection of stories and essays. Almost all the stories – lives of villagers past and present – are part-fact (as told to me or observed by me) and part-imagination (mine as well as the teller's) to fill in the gaps. However, all the *information* – about customs, practices, and beliefs – is as true as observation and research can verify.

I

Arriving

The Call

Arriving

December 1985

The white ship plows through the sea, blue as ink, laced with small whitecaps. It threads its way past a dozen islands, then more – two or even three dozen. They are all the same – the sea shading from sapphire to jade, the rocks from blue-gray to terra cotta, sometimes furred with the violet of thyme, the dark green of myrtle. The rock of the shore rises up in cliffs, which stretch out to become fields crisscrossed with walls of rock; these rise into terraces and stair-step upwards, becoming mountains. Here and there, white houses are encrusted upon the rocks like the lime-white barnacles that cling to ancient amphóras rescued from the sea bottom. The islands are all the same, whether massive or tiny, inhabited or deserted – all the same except this one to which the ship is heading. To catch the first glimpse of it, the passengers lean on the bow rail, their hearts beating with the throb of the engines. Mouths salt-filled, eyes misted, they strain to make out the jagged blur on the horizon that will tell them they are almost arrived, almost home.

Wherever you were born, in a white iron bed in a village or in a foreign city far away – because, as so often happens, destiny or need has driven you from this place – to return you come by sea. The salt sea bears you to the island as a mother's waters bear the babe.

Wherever you have come from, wherever you have been, however long you've been away (weeks, months, years), to arrive here is to achieve *nostos* – return – and to be away is to know pain, emptiness, *nostalgía* – the ache to return. Here everything is real and right, even the illusions and the lies; there (wherever that is) everything is alien, other, strange – even when you know it well. To arrive is to enter time, real time, where days pass slowly in important weather – there is one word here for time and weather – yet life changes steadily: births, marriages, aging, deaths, births. And everything and nothing is the same.

A group of four stands at the rail, braving the spray from the waves, the leaping and sinking of the deck. They are a seaman tanned by Asian suns, a student red-eyed from writing exams, a godmother clutching boxes of tulle-wrapped *kouféta* for the baptismal guests, and I, a stranger. Earlier we were chatting, shouting above the deafening growl of the engines, exchanging news, discovering we are all bound for the same place. But from the time the ship left its last port of call, each of us has been wrapped in a shawl of silence.

Soon on the horizon appear two towering rocks – not a Colossus but a natural divinity, cloven by an unimaginable force – guarding the harbor. No hour passes more slowly than this last one that we grind through. As the white ship moves past the rocks, more passengers crowd the rail. As the bay spreads out before us, the town, its snow-white houses and shops, its blue-domed churches, a small mountain crowned by a monastery, seems to rise up, grow larger. My companions and I come alive, making out each familiar cliff or beach, lighthouse or farmhouse, cove or bay. "Look! There's Áyios Phokás! There – that's my cousin's house on the Kástro!" With each recognition comes implosions of breath and explosions in the blood like children's Easter firecrackers underfoot.

Past the gigantic rocks, the ship ceases to be a sleek machine and becomes a bumbling monster, backing and filling, turning in half circles, fighting buffeting or capricious winds, trying to match its stern to an impossibly positioned dock. Each attempted landing seems to be its first; sailors on board and harbor officials on the dock rush from starboard to port, yelling conflicting orders, cursing each other, until the great steel ferry door, barely held back by clanking chains, finally smashes down upon the dock.

Even then there is no orderly birth of the enwombed souls, no quiet one-by-one stream of the seahorse's young, but a melee, a brawl. The old ladies, using every advantage of seniority and every weapon from sharp-cornered valises to plastic bags of oozing squid, fight their way to the front. The decks are narrow and slick with spray, the gangway thresholds shin-high and sharp, the ladders steep and greasy. From the maw of the hold growl and roar large lorries, between which we must squeeze, darting and shoving until suddenly, a small phalanx led by the godmother, we break out of the mass of people and machines, panting, whole, almost arrived. "Almost" because this port is the *hóra*, the main town, not the *horió*, the village, where we – the seaman, the student, the godmother, and I – are going. To get to the village, we can board a bus, which would wait and wait until our excitement had dwindled into exhaustion, or we can share a taxi. The taxi drivers stand by their cars, eyes on the ship. Will they go to the village? They are equivocal, they temporize, they seem to be waiting for something – but what? A new transmission, a long-lost relative, or Christ with the seven crowns upon his head, heralded by archangels, rising from the hold to accomplish there in the rowdy port the Second Coming? Whatever they are waiting for – leaning on the hoods of their gray cars, smoking, ignoring the passengers piling into the seats front and back, their baggage (more than will fit in the trunk) strewn on the macadam

– it doesn't happen. Disappointed, the drivers yield reluctantly to the expostulations of the passengers ("Come on! Let's go!" "*Kýrie* Pétro, my son is waiting!"). One by one they sigh, turn from the ship, and slide slump-shouldered behind their wheels.

In our taxi, the godmother's boxes take up so much room that the seaman and I have to squash in beside the driver. But I am glad to be up front, to get a good look at the road. It is almost fifteen years since I first arrived on this island, and five since I last visited. I am anxious to know that every house and windmill and stone wall along the way are still there, still as I remember them.

The journey to the village reveals fragments of the history of the island – not as in the books, era by era, with one event leading into another (mostly conquests and occupations), but as people tell it every day to their children, all jumbled up, triggered by sights or scents. Skirting the civic garden (where the roses seem to sigh for Persia and the royal palms for Egypt, and only the oleander and the bay look at home), the taxi passes the gates of the Panagía. The godmother (not having heard above the roar of the ship's engine that I have been here before) informs me that it is the oldest church in Christendom in which the liturgy is still sung. The church was decreed by Ayía Eléni, on her way home to Constantinople after finding the remains of Christ's cross, over fifteen hundred years ago. When it was finally constructed two centuries later, she says, the builders raised it over a Roman gymnasium whose marble columns and mosaic floor – depicting the tasks of Hercules in many-colored stones – were recently uncovered beneath the church.

More evidence of the ancient past springs to the eye as the taxi passes the small pine woods between the church and the road. There, covered with pine needles and censed with the sharp fragrance, is a litter of white marble sarcophagi. On each the *makarítis*, the blessed departed, reclines on his or her bier, receiving the funeral guests, still after two and a half millennia, with smiles and wine.

After another mile the student points out – in an ordinary rock wall edging a farmer's field, among the medium-sized boulders of schist and gneiss and marble – two or three huge blocks. The archaeologists date them from the Cycladic era, he says, three thousand years or more before the church. It's a mystery how such gigantic stones could, like those of Stonehenge, have been quarried miles away and brought here.

A little farther along the road, a sweet green valley of olive trees stretches up a conical hill. The godmother points it out, saying it is what's left of the estates of the Venetian dukes, twelfth to sixteenth centuries, still farmed by their descendants. (From a hint of pride in her manner, I surmise she carries a Frankish name, Ventourís, perhaps, or Daferéras.). A few minutes later, the seaman, not to be outdone, points to a field full of jumbled stones. Foot-high walls surround marble paving, while carved marble lintels and thresholds stand doorless and open, surreal portals to another world – another church, one perhaps older than the Panagía. The marble pieces were, he says, prudently salvaged from a nearby temple to Apollo, disassembled by an edict of the early Christian church.

For a while the road cuts through fields and orchards: almond trees climbing a mountain on one side (in spring they would be a pink cloud against the dark rock), olive groves and vineyards falling away on the other. Block-shaped white houses and tiny blue-domed chapels dot the fields. The shattered mountains tumble stones into the road; the driver swerves to avoid them, nearly grazing a red tractor emerging from a dry creek bed. (In fall the tractor's trailer would be heaped with grapes.)

The road climbs gradually, mountains on either side terraced to their rocky peaks and crowned with inaccessible chapels or holding monasteries in their clefts. Most of these were built in the seventeenth century, says the student, but on even older foundations, so that beneath their smooth white walls, were you to chip away the layers of whitewash, you would surely discover a column from a fifth-century church, a bas-relief from an ancient temple, or perhaps fragments of the lost memorial to the island's famous poet, Archilochus.

Suddenly the taxi is cresting a rise where exactly at the watershed stands a small church. Today must be its name day, as multicolored flags flutter over its newly whitewashed facade, its powder-blue dome. At the summit the car seems to pause, to hang in air for a moment – a moment when even the taxi driver, bored with the road, bored with the ruins, bored with stones of any kind, sits up and takes in his breath.

For this brief moment, the whole of the *koinótita*, the community of the village and all its environs, is spread out beneath us: the mountain terraces, the valley farms, the vineyards, the wide bay almost closed by pincers of rocky peninsulas, the dozens of small coves scalloping the shore, and, at the heart, the white-white (*katáspro*, they say, "intensely white") village, house upon house, squares and rectangles of chalk white – a cubist's rendering of a cataract, tumbling down three hills, pooling in a level space, flowing into the sea.

We forget about the past; we are rushing toward the present. Swiftly the taxi descends the almost straight road, passing on one side the wheat fields, golden now with stubble, and on the other the vineyards, the citrus orchards, the olive groves. "My great uncle's," says the seaman.

Gathering speed, the taxi roars past the small cypress-guarded chapel of the Holy Apostles, the driver crossing himself with the hand not holding a cigarette. A curve around a massive cliff of dark brown gneiss, a sprint along the sea and over a small bridge, and suddenly, before we quite realize it, we are in the *platía*, the village square, stopped beside a giant eucalyptus tree.

Sitting at the café tables, sipping coffee, are half-a-dozen grandfathers, their canes between their knees, their grandchildren playing around them. Housewives are crossing from bakery to grocery, baskets on their arms. A group of high school boys, tossing a football, is heading for the field beyond the *platía*. The taxi rolls up and everyone stops and turns to see what the ship has brought today.

As the other passengers get out, the bystanders cry, "*Yiánni!*" and "*Mána!*" and rush to fold them into eager arms. "*Kalós ílthate!*" the coffee drinkers and the shoppers and the footballers shout to the godmother and the seaman and the student, "Well come!"

I stand where the taxi driver has deposited me, my baggage at my feet. Memories flood in, jostling each other, conflicting with change. There's a new sweet shop, the hardware store has become a bar. I feel like the stranger I am, ungreeted but an object of curiosity, until I see — late as usual, hurrying to meet me – my old friend. Approaching, he calls my name and says, "You're back, are you?" And then, "*Kalós ílthas!* It's good you've come." And "*Kalós se vríka*," I say, glad to have found him again.

The Call

I arrived for the first time on the island of Páros on the first of September 1971. My arrival was fortuitous and prophetic, even blessed. I had no idea that the first of September is the New Year in both the ancient but still observed Greek agricultural calendar and that of the Orthodox church, the backbone of life in rural Greece. In the villages, time is not reckoned according to the official, Gregorian calendar, but by holy days. "What day is today?" a stranger might ask. An islander would immediately reply, "Ayíou Máma," St. Mamas, "when the sheep are blessed."

Despite my ignorance, my arrival on the New Year coincided with several local traditions. September first is the day when all annual contracts, especially those of tenant farmers, shepherds, and servants, are renewed. Another sort of renewal is described in an old saying: "Earth stops bearing and begins again, becoming pregnant with the new fruit." She lets go her apples and quinces, her pomegranates and grapes, now come to ripeness, their sweetness peaked. She has done all she can for them. They drop as they will, and she turns her energy to germinating the seeds of the new crop. The first of September is a favorite time for marriages; such beginnings, in harmony with Earth's, it is hoped, will result in fruitfulness of the new family.

Looking back on that time, I see that I too made a sort of contract with Greece – specifically the island of Páros and eventually one village, Náousa – to dedicate myself to understanding its unique and beautiful culture. The seeds were sown on a dark blue midnight, scarcely lit by a sliver of moon, when I climbed down the slippery ladder of the Evangelístria, a rusty old tub, and set foot on the soil of Páros. I had come on a kind of quest, but I had no idea of what was in store for me, that I would realize what I was looking for and that I would find it: a new life, a new understanding of the way life should be – austere but joyful, practical but spiritual, based on millennia-old beliefs and practices and yet vulnerable to change.

I came in search of boats and houses. Some months earlier, I had been browsing in the travel section of the public library in my hometown – Eugene, Oregon – when I came across a photograph of six or eight fishing boats half-beached on a sandy cove. The *kaḯkis*, as I would learn to call them, some with masts, others with small motor housings, were painted – each differently but just as beautifully – in two or three brilliant hues. The hull of one was sky blue, its gunwales yellow, its cabin orange.

Another was scarlet and lime green, while a third had red masts and a Bristol blue hull. Across the small waves of the sea, the colors mixed and scattered. Farther along in the book was a photograph of a village: forty or fifty boxy white houses with blue or green windows, piled up like children's blocks. The houses – walls, roofs, and courtyards – were intensely white, *katáspro*. Even the flagstones on the streets were rimmed with white. It looked as though a blizzard had passed over the village, leaving a fine dusting of snow. The light itself had the clarity of sunshine on snow. Again, like the *kaîkis*, each house was different from its neighbor – some angled one way, some another; some were one story, some two – but the village as a whole was a composition no architect could devise, no king or pharaoh order. It had the harmonious randomness only generations of like-minded but free people could achieve.

I took the book to a desk and pored over the pictures. The boats were beautiful, but almost greater than the beauty of the individual boats was the collective beauty of the group. The same held true for the houses. I tried to imagine a group of people – ordinary people, fishermen, housewives, for instance – who shared an aesthetic that encouraged them to build or paint as they wished and that yet resulted in a harmony that spoke of both liveliness and peace. I reflected that the people who built the snow-white houses and painted the brilliant boats must, as the Navajo might say, walk in beauty. I immediately decided to go there – the Greek islands – to discover the community of people who expressed themselves with such creativity.

It was a time in the United States when people I knew were reassessing life itself, trying to find ways to live with the earth and each other. Many were looking to other cultures for wisdom and for models of life. Some went east to India while others chose Japan, but neither of those prospects spoke to me. I was looking for a community, one that valued simplicity and beauty, had energy but used it sparingly, and had a tradition of doing things by hand. Looking at the boats and houses in the pictures, I thought that on one of the Aegean islands I might learn ways to walk lightly as well as in beauty upon the earth.

In my American way, I thought fulfilling my quest would take me about three weeks. I didn't count on falling in love, not with a man but with an island – and, more specifically, one village. I didn't count on having to learn – in my effort to understand my beloved village – a five-thousand-year history of settlement, of wars and piracy, of occupation and abandonment, of generations of gods and saints. I came for three weeks; I stayed, that first time, five years and have returned often. And for the last thirty-five years, I have been more obsessed with this island of Páros, this village called Náousa, than with any demon lover.

II

Lággeri
The Sea and the Village
The Agorá

Lággeri

Spring 1972

The village of Náousa and its outlying farms surround a great bay on the north side of the island of Páros. The village proper occupies a headland, east and west of which two long rocky promontories curve outward like the arms of a dancer. Into this embrace flows the Aegean, creating a wide but sheltered bay six miles across.

At the land's heart lies the village, a dense settlement of perhaps two hundred houses, twenty or so shops, and a dozen churches. The houses, flat-roofed and boxy, are stone-built and whitewashed, two-storied with outside, unrailed stairs of thick marble slabs leading up to wooden balconies. The doors and shuttered windows are painted many shades of green or blue.

The village meets the sea in a little harbor, anchorage for several dozen *kaíkis*, fishing boats, and home to the fishermen's cafés and their *apothíkis*, storerooms where they store and mend their nets. Two parallel streets largely devoted to shops constitute the *agorá* or market, and run inland from the harbor to the *platía*, an open space dominated by a giant, shady eucalyptus tree, around which cluster the chairs and tables of cafés. The village then climbs three hills, the houses stair-stepping upwards so that from some window, veranda, or roof of every house, the sea is visible – blue-green in summer, white-slashed and slate-gray in winter. No house in the village is out of sight or sound of the sea. All the buildings – shops, houses, churches – are as white as foam, as though gigantic waves had once washed over beaches, gull-sheltering cliffs, and all the homes and shops, leaving a chalky residue of eroded shells and seamen's bones.

The harbor is an open rectangle of three moles or docks, partly closed on the seaward side by the ruins of a Venetian tower. Along the three moles are small shops, warehouses, and a few private houses. These back up to the remains of high stone walls that once enclosed the village. Who built the walls? As always, there are several stories. Some say the walls, as well as the now-all-but-ruined tower in the harbor, were built by Venetians, who occupied the island from 1207 to 1566 A.D. Others say the walls are the very ones erected overnight by frantic villagers in 460 B.C. to defend themselves against the vengeance of the Athenians, who attacked the island for having supported the Persian side in the Ionian Revolt. Although Miltiades, the Athenian general, succeeded in scaling the walls, the villagers report with some satisfaction that he injured his leg in the attempt and died of gangrene. Villagers on the other side of the island claim that the walls in question were theirs and take credit for the death of the illustrious general. Nobody seems bothered by a thousand-year gap in the explanations.

The village was lovely, lively, and engaging, but when I first arrived in Náousa, I stopped there only long enough to ask after a road I had heard about. I had been living for about a year and a half in the *hóra*, the main town of the island, but with the advent of the beautiful May weather, I was dying to get out into the country. Hearing from a man in a café that a long road out of Náousa led to a remote and lovely beach, I hopped a bus to the village and inquired in the *platía*.

"You don't want to drive there, do you?" a taxi driver asked, looking like a man in pain. "It's a terrible road. Broke my suspension last year."

"No," I answered, "I want to walk."

"*Kalá,*" he sighed with relief. "Go up the *agorá* to the Panagía, the church at the top of the village. And keep going east. You'll come to a big bay called Lággeri."

"How far?" I asked.

"Two cigarettes," he answered in the island measure of distance. As I turned to go, he wished me, "*Kaló drómo.*"

"Thanks," I replied, hoping it would indeed be a "good road."

I walked along the *agorá*, calling "*Kaliméra*" to housewives sweeping their stairs, hanging out laundry, or watering pots of carnations. They greeted me in return, "*Kaliméra sas!*" I climbed the shallow steps leading up to the churchyard shaded by an enormous, ancient pine tree whose heavy branches were supported by rough marble columns. The church was washed a pale yellow and, with its twin belfries, looked more Italian than Greek. Later, when I would walk into the village from Lággeri, there was a point at the crest of the last hill when the church would suddenly seem to rise up on the horizon, and I would know I had only a mile to go until I could sit in the village harbor, mop my sweaty brow, and sip a cool lemon-ade.

But this day I was thinking not of the road back but of the road before me.

The Countryside

Fanning out from the village proper is the countryside, which slopes gently upward from the sea to the mountains. Here are the farms and orchards, the vineyards and wheat fields, the olive groves, and the pastures with their gentle cattle. To the west and south of the village, bordering a mile-long inlet, are Kolymbíthres of the strange, contorted rocks; flat Kamáres and Livádia with their deep soil easy to cultivate; and Ayioú Andréa, its sloping wheat fields topped by a seventeenth-century monastery now inhabited by a farming family. Another monastery, this one full of monks, perches in a higher cleft of the same mountains, seeming to spread its influence over the valley. Inland to the southeast, Kámpos stretches up from level vineyards to its own small monastery inhabited by a single eremitic nun. Edging the eastern arm of the bay are the areas of Lággeri and Santa Maria; from the latter it's but a short boat ride across the strait to the mountainous island of Náxos, behind which rise the sun and the moon. On the heights of the mountains and on the promontories thrusting into the sea is the dry, stony land where bees hum over the fragrant thyme and sheep graze, nosing among the gorse and thorny burnet for small mouthfuls.

All the land is open to the azure sky, bathed in sunlight. Even the mountains are not high enough to cast shadows. Dry stone walls divide fields, keeping the cows out of the vineyards and holding up terraces built into the slopes of the mountains hundreds or even thousands of years ago. The land is dotted with irregular clumps of boxy, white, one-story houses and barns, often stepping down a slope. Each field or orchard has its square stone *stérna*, a reservoir of water for irrigating, and each vineyard its *patitíri*, a similar stone vat for treading grapes. Here and there in the middle of a field, hidden by stubble, lies a stone-floored, stone-ringed threshing circle or, tucked into a corner of the same field, a small white chapel, a gift of thanksgiving from a family for, perhaps, the survival of a son in a war or of a daughter from influenza.

The Road to Lággeri

All the rural areas in Náousa are beautiful, but to me the most beautiful, the most perfectly, flawlessly beautiful was Lággeri, which I discovered on that day in May. From the church the road meandered about four miles, following and leaving the sea as headlands and coves appeared and receded. It was a striking road, very different from the ones I had walked on the other side of the island, the south side. Few roads on the island, surfaced or not, were wide enough for cars, but others called *monopátia* were stone-walled lanes just wide enough for a mule loaded with panniers to pass. Sometimes, these paths were rocky stream beds, usable only in the dry season. Now, in May, the roads and lanes on the other side of the island were winding around stone-walled fields luminous with blood-red poppies nodding above the new green wheat. Spring lambs and kids were bounding onto the rock walls, returning at peremptory bleats to nuzzle into the warm bellies of their mothers.

But those roads were on the south side of the island, where here and there even a banana tree sprouted in a garden. The north side, I found as I walked along, was not lush. The fields, if they had bloomed, had already dried. But the landscape had a bare-bones beauty, like an archaic statue that, most of its gaudy paint eroded by wind or time, is even more beautiful in its nakedness. The land was bleached to tow, to ochre, to pale tan, here and there hazed with a white veil of Queen Anne's lace or shadowed with the dark green of juniper or *skinári*, mastic bush.

The road was barely graded, its surface one of loose dirt and natural gravel over bedrock, which, once in a while, did project high enough to scrape an oil pan off a car. The dust of the road was a pale yellow. Where the grader had scarred the land, rocks, often white marble, fell from the banks, stained rust-red from the clay that held them. Rock walls crossing and enclosing fields were many shades of gray, charcoal to pearl, crusted with yellow lichens. Papery statice bloomed blue-violet in the dust. And always, as the road curved inland and then out again, the sea appeared and disappeared in flashes of sapphire and jade.

The landscapes the road passed through, if subtle in color, were amazingly various. Beyond the church, the road dipped down to a broad bay with a long, curving sandy beach, shaded by tamarisk trees with pink blossoms and feathery leaves, and honey-scented by a modest little plant called thorny peterium. Here mothers lay on the sand while small children played and splashed in the shallow water. In a field across from the beach, wiry grass and scrub struggled against salt and sand.

Leaving the bay, the road turned inland and climbed a long but gentle hill, passing a pasture where a few cream-colored cows with black-rimmed eyes grazed companionably with a donkey and a mule. The road continued past several headlands, bare rock sparsely dotted with scrub, beyond which the sea came now and then into sight. On the sea side of the road, the land was largely flat, bare, toast-colored country rock scattered with eroded gravel, where it seemed even thistles had a hard time surviving. To the right were fields enclosed by stone walls, but most of these were fallow, and the blond wild grass lay tangled like hair on a pillow. The land seemed deserted – neither house nor barn visible from the road; only the stones of what might once have been a sheep pen or a chapel lay tumbled in a field, two once-walls still meeting at a corner.

About three miles out from Náousa, just as I thought I had lost sight of the sea for good and was wondering where in all this aridity I might find rest for my sun-baked eyes, I breasted a small hill and was shocked into stillness.

From the crest of the hill, the land fell away in a sort of hollow. Five or six square miles of land and sea stretched out before me. The sky seemed to explode into a huge bowl of blue the color of long-buried glass. On the inland side, straw-colored fields cut into irregular squares by low stone walls gently ran uphill and turned into terraces in the distant, blue-gray hills. On the sea side, the hollow was filled with a large bay, perhaps two miles across and roughly round. The bay was enclosed on the west by a steep, rocky headland with so little vegetation that even sheep could not graze there, and on the east by a curving, hilly peninsula of juniper scrub sloping down to a beach whose sand, I would find, as fine as talc, drifted over outcroppings of pink marble. In the middle of the bay sat a tiny, stony islet, joined to the mainland by a nearly submerged sand bar. The pale sand of the sea bottom was so clean it reflected light up through the water, meeting the flashing of sunlight on the surface. And the sea – shading from jade in the shallows to aquamarine to emerald to deep blue, almost violet out towards the mouth – the sea was so beautiful, so present, so alive it seemed to be singing.

From this height, for the first time since I had set out over an hour earlier, I saw habitations. A lone cottage sat on the shore opposite the islet, and two clusters of white farm buildings, like children's stacked blocks, topped the promontory far across the bay. Between the two groups, on the water's edge, was a small, white church with a blue roof, its buttresses standing in the sea, lapped by gentle waves.

The bay and its environs, I would learn later, are called Lággeri. The word has meant many things down through the ages: "clear," "immaculate," "purified" as with gold, "limpid." That day in May it was all of these. Lággeri, with all its brilliance and plainness, its dryness and abundance, its generósity and parsimony, and above all its secrets, was before me.

Descending from the crest, I passed a small, shallow inlet paved with egg-shaped rocks. The waves passing over the rocks tumbled and smoothed them, but their rubbing against each other caused them to growl. Later, coming home on a night with no moon, the muttering of the rocks would let me know where on the road I was passing. First the grinding rocks and then a patch of sand on the road directed my feet away from the sea. The area of the inlet is called Ksifára.

From Ksifára, the road ran beside the shore, first a sandy beach and then, across from the cottage, a rough shelf of toast-colored bedrock, scarred with a number of rectangular troughs that had been cut into it. On the land side, in a field long uncultivated, stalks of wild sesame, yellow-crowned fennel, and purple thistles sprang up along the walls. The house next to the field was shuttered and empty, so I sat on the steps and gazed at the beautiful bay, sparkling in the midday sun.

Across a narrow strait from the house was the islet, reached by a sand bar presently about a foot under water. A dozen or so sheep grazed the sparse vegetation, their dull bells ringing slowly as they dipped their heads. If the sandbar was under water, I mused, how did the sheep, not notable swimmers, get there? And then I remembered seeing, during a voyage by kaíki that had threaded among groups of islands and islets, a shepherd rowing a boat in whose bow sat a single placid sheep, unfazed by the mode of transportation.

Again my eyes were drawn to the farm buildings high on the opposite promontory. Beyond and below them was a long stretch of pure cream sand, edging the immaculate jade green sea. Perfect! I could almost feel the slight chill of the sea on my burning and dusty skin. But how to get there? The road was leaving the shore, keeping east. I would learn that it led to Santa Maria, a wide bay that cuts a scallop into the land, the sea washing in from the straits between this island and Náxos.

To get to the beach, I would have to leave the road and take to the sea's edge. And so I did, hopping the stone wall of a vineyard, wading through the shallows of a tiny cove paved with pottery sherds, and finally all but swimming to a pier under the chapel. I climbed up and found a hilly path leading through scratchy juniper scrub to the beach.

The cove was as perfect as I had imagined: the sand clean and soft, the sea utterly pristine, deep and calm. The quiet was made somehow more quiet by the small faraway voices of children. After a long swim in water so deeply blue it seemed impossible to rise from it without being dyed indigo, I was thirsty. And I had forgotten to bring water.

I knew that in Greece a request for water is always honored, so I climbed the cliff to the farmhouse. No one was visible, but when I called out, a woman appeared in the doorway, followed by the faces of two little girls, peeping around each side of her skirt. I realized they were sitting down to their noon dinner and apologized. Luckily, my Greek ran to simple conversations, especially polite ones. However, without a ghost of annoyance, she brought out from the house not just a glass of water but a large terra cotta jug from which she poured me a second glass as I finished the first.

Lélla was one of the most beautiful women I have ever known, before or since. Her face was somewhat square, with wide cheekbones and firm chin; she was of sturdy build but not at all fat. Her great beauty was her skin, smooth and lightly brown – the coloring of people who work outside but avoid tanning – and her cheeks were rose red. Her hair (partly covered with a white scarf) and her eyes were dark brown, the eyes just light enough to show a ring of black around the irises. Her beauty was both startling and in such harmony with the spare, strong beauty of the surroundings that it took my breath away. The two little blonde girls had by this time dared to come out and stare at the stranger. A tall, gray-haired man I took to be Lélla's father emerged and stopped in the doorway.

I stood drinking and looking out over the bay and the farm with its small citrus orchard, olive grove, and tomato patch, its cows grazing in the pastures, and chickens and turkeys gathered in the deep shade of a giant plane tree in the farmyard. From this height, I could see almost all the way to the village on the west, across the straits to Náxos in the east, and far out to sea to the north. The quiet was palpable. From the pasture came a faint lowing, from the chickens a murmur, but in all the six or seven square miles, no other sound could be heard, save the whispered question of a child to her grandfather. "Yes, child," I heard him answer, "the lady is a foreigner." And he glanced at me in a friendly way, as though we shared a joke.

I was suddenly flooded with the desire to live there, though I hadn't much hope. The whole area seemed very sparsely built up in contrast to the other side of the island, with its plethora of vacant country houses. But still I inquired of Lélla whether she knew of any place to rent. To my astonishment, she replied, pointing downhill at the second cluster of buildings, "My uncle Minás rents out that little cottage down by the well. He lives in the village. Minás Anagnostópoulos. Ask anyone where he lives. "

As she turned to go back to her meal, she smiled and said, "*Kalós ílthate.*" "Well come."

"*Kalós sas vríka,*" I replied. But it would not be for years that I understood exactly how good it was I had found this place and these people.

The Farm

After walking back to the village, full of dreams of Lággeri, I easily found Minás, a tall, rangy, gray-moustached man nearly the twin of his brother Panayiótis, Lélla 's father. Minás and his wife lived in the village and raised fruit and vegetables in a walled garden with a brook running through it. The next day he hoisted me onto the back of a large black mule and hopped up behind. As we rode out to Lággeri to see the cottage, Minás peopled the area for me: where I thought the land deserted, he showed me that hiding behind brakes of cypress and *kalámia*, cane, were perhaps a dozen farms. Anna and Pantelís grew fruit and vegetables for their son's greengrocery in the village. Margaríta and Michális, Bárba Níkos, Epaminóndas, and others all raised a great variety of fruits and vegetables and animals. "Now Stávros," Minás laughed, "lives farther out that *monopáti*. You've got to see his place. He raises peacocks and partridges and crazy-looking chickens with feathers on their feet." Panayiótis mostly raised cows, he said, and the women, his wife Styllianí and his daughter Lélla, used the milk to make cheese. He himself raised vegetables and rabbits in his village garden and tended several beehives on the farm. He told me too about the family living on the farm. "My brother and his wife had no children, so they adopted Lélla and Aristídis. And, what do you know? They married each other. They had another boy, adopted too, but he went on the ships – with the merchant marine – and was murdered in New York." Silence. "You're not from New York, are you? They might not like to have a neighbor from New York." I hastened to assure him that an entire continent separated my home from that city of murderers.

The one-room house was tiny but charming. Its one small, blue-painted window looked out past the church to the bay, flashing blue and gold in the sunlight, and framed the little island. The double doors opened onto a rocky, east-facing farmyard, which afforded plenty of light. There was a cot, a table and a chair, a hearth for my stove, and pegs for my clothes.

"*Toualétta?*" I asked shyly. And Minás, with a twinkle in his eye, reached outside the door, produced what looked like a World War I trenching tool, and nodded toward the adjacent orchard.

The little house was newly whitewashed and smelt fresh as a sea breeze. The quiet was amazing: deep silence emphasized by tiny distant sounds – the tinkle of a sheep's bell, the low grumble of a cow, the voices of the children in the farmhouse. This simple dwelling seemed the perfect amount and kind of shelter needed to live in such beauty and quiet.

Minás took me up the hill to meet the folks in the farmhouse. The radiant Lélla and her tow-headed little girls I had already met. Lélla's husband Aristídis was short and broad-shouldered, brown-skinned with graying black hair and black-olive eyes. Most of the family received me cordially. The little girls came out from behind Lélla and said, "Hárika" when prompted. However, Styllianí, the formidable grandmother, she of the malevolent squint, regarded me with suspicion, as perhaps having my eye on her husband or even having "the Eye," a danger to her little girls, chickens, and baby animals. "Make sure you tell the foreigner how to use the well," Styllianí said to Minás; "she might poison it." But when Minás and I went down to the huge well behind the church, I showed him that I could sink the bucket and not lose the rope, and that I knew not to let water that had touched my body fall back into the well. The water was icy cold, pure and sweet, a miracle for a deep well only yards from the salt sea.

Before we left, Minás took me into the little church, newly white-washed inside and out, its *yiortí* or name day having been recently celebrated. The miracle of the sweet and abundant well was celebrated by the dedication of the chapel to the Zoodóhos Pigí, or the Life-giving Spring, an aspect of the Panagía, the Mother of God. A blue-painted ikonostásis held a painted ikon of the Mother and Child sitting in a fountain from which streams of water spurted into ewers held by tiny people. Several framed paper ikons of the same image sat on shelves. Minás took a slim beeswax taper and handed me one. He lit his, kissed the ikon and crossed himself, prayed quietly, and placed the taper in a bowl of sand. I followed suit, feeling we were somehow sealing a contract for more than the rental of a house.

As we were leaving, Minás said, "Come, I'll show you my bees," and led me to a fig orchard in a sort of hollow where the earth seemed to have fallen away from the hill. Here, housed in funnel-shaped terra cotta hives dug into the bank of the hill, his bees lived and buzzed, harvesting the pollen from thyme growing on the stony fields beyond the farm. "When I come to take the honey," he said, "I'll bring you some." He also invited me to pick figs when they ripened. "But don't eat all of them. My wife craves them!"

Two days later I descended on the village with my possessions crammed into a taxi. Neither that driver nor any of the two or three sitting in the shade of the eucalyptus tree would agree to drive out to Lággeri, but an old fisherman, Bárba Stéllios, brown-skinned and white-thatched, offered to take me in his boat. After piling up my boxes, cases, and folding chairs onto the thwarts of the open boat, we chugged out of the harbor into the bay, Stéllios standing up in the stern with his bare foot on the tiller. It was exciting to approach by sea: we passed headlands where gulls swooped around their nests and pelicans perched on wave-swept rocks with their wings stretched out to dry. As we came into Lággeri bay, I spied another house, far out on the peninsula, very run down, and later learned it housed a shepherd family and their animals. The small flock of twenty or so sheep and a few goats were presently grazing on the seaward side of the little island.

Tying up the boat, Stéllios helped me up the hill with my stuff, carrying my big gas bottle on one shoulder and my suitcase on the other. "Met the folks yet?"

"Yes."

"They offer to sell you anything?"

"Yes, tomatoes, eggs, bread, cheese..."

"Wine?"

"Oh, yes. Why?"

Stéllios whistled. "You're a lucky girl! They're the best folks on the island. And Panayiótis makes the best wine in all of Greece. Also, he's had stomach trouble for a couple of years and hasn't been able to drink, so some of that wine is three years old. I had a few glasses at their yiortí a couple of weeks ago. Mmmh!" He kissed the air, looked off toward the church, and sighed, perhaps remembering the wine. When he cast off, he was still staring blankly and humming a bit.

The rest of that first day I spent arranging the house. There were no closets or cupboards, just a niche for pots and dishes. A small hearth accommodated my two-burner gas stove and bottle. My fanári, a screened cupboard for foodstuffs, I hung from the rafters. Some clothes went on pegs in the wall and others into baskets which also hung from the ceiling. Although the space was small, it was light and uncluttered. I made a cup of tea and took a book out into the farmyard. I meant to read, and I did – Homer, George Seféris, Yiánnis Rítsos – but that evening and many others I simply sat as darkness fell, enjoying the silence and the tiny, infrequent sounds: the lapping of waves, a bird rustling the leaves of a lemon tree, a stone falling from a wall.

As Minás' tenant, I was received politely if not warmly by his brother's family. They were busy folk – irrigating and hoeing, feeding animals, milking, making cheese, and baking bread in a brush-fired beehive oven. But in the evenings they would gather on their veranda, resting from their work. I bought most of my food from them, so if I timed my arrival for just after sunset, they would visit a little. After a year and a half of study, my Greek was adequate for our homely conversations. I was curious about the

31

neighbors, of whom there were many more than I had at first thought, and Styllianí was, though she tried to hide it, curious about some of the friends I was making in the village, where I went every three or four days to shop. We would swap item for item, each believing she was manipulating the other. Styllianí disapproved of my going into the village so much, called me a *gyrístria,* gadabout, but Lélla simply wondered why on earth anyone would leave Lággeri for so much as an evening. The women's contentment with their situation was echoed by Panayiótis, who, although he took his tomatoes, eggs, and cheese into the village every few days, always just turned his mule right around and headed home, rarely even stopping at a café for a coffee.

I have never known people as content as this family. They were much respected throughout the community of Náousa, but their visitors were few, and visits to others even fewer. They were, I think, almost self-sufficient, emotionally as well as physically. As I learned more of the history of the area, I would find that with few exceptions – a bottle gas stove, a transistor radio, a few aluminum pots – they lived and worked much as the Bronze Age people who had occupied the same land over thirty-five hundred years ago. There was at that time no electricity in the countryside; the family's lives were in complete accord with the seasons. In the summer they rose before first light, worked through the morning, dined early, slept in the hot afternoons. When the heat had diminished, they awoke, drank a coffee perhaps, and completed the day's chores. In the evenings, although they occasionally lit a kerosene lamp, mostly they sat in the dark, talking and laughing among themselves.

They raised almost all their own food, including animals and *their* food. They did not irrigate with a gasoline pump – a common practice – but grew all the tender vegetables and trees downhill from the well, watering by gravity, bucket by bucket. Water for the house and the stock they hauled uphill, and plowed and threshed in the old way with a mule. Their Bronze Age predecessors had also dug wells and built cisterns, plowed with ox or mule, baked in beehive ovens, grown grains and pulses. Minás' terra cotta bee hives, I found out later, had a history far earlier than even the Bronze Age, reaching back to Egypt, and yet they were still being made and were for sale in the *agorá.*

I doubt that Panayiótis and his family had many "off-land" expenses – kerosene and clothes, perhaps an occasional tool, batteries for the radio, since Panayiótis was deeply interested in the news. They didn't seem to long for anything, neither the adults nor the little girls. At first, every time I went into the village I would ask if I could bring them anything: embroidery or sewing thread, canned goods, sweets, crayons? But no, they never needed anything. After I left the farm, when I went back to visit, I was always stumped by what to bring as a present. The customary liqueurs and candies they received in a puzzled politeness, as though they had never seen such things before, even though the items came from the village. One of the girls asked me, "Did you bring these from America?" Stylliani was more blunt: "What we eat, we make." The gifts were placed on a high shelf, perhaps to wait for more bourgeois visitors.

"East of Eden" was how I often thought of this farm. Certainly the inhabitants lived by the sweat of their brows; not only did Panayiótis delve, but Stylliani spun their own sheep's fleece with a simple drop spindle. The resemblance was underlined by the relationship of Lélla and Aristídis, as close as brother and sister but, as adopted children, sufficiently distant in blood to be able to marry. "You should find yourself a husband," Lélla said to me one day – a single person, man or woman, being an object of pity.

"Find?" I said teasing, "you didn't even have to look! He was right under your feet!" She laughed and blushed.

Adoptions such as theirs were not uncommon in the village. Generally, the children were not orphans or abandoned children but belonged to a local family, perhaps relatives of the childless couple. The children were usually not infants but old enough to both show character and have a say in the matter. In most cases, they did not break off relations with their birth parents There was no formal adoption as we know it – Aristídes, for instance, kept his birth name. The adopting parents simply signed agreements for the child to become their legal heir. The benefits were clear: the adopted children would inherit, the adoptive parents would gain children not only to love but to work their lands or businesses and to care for them in their old age. All at Panayiótis' farm were devoted to one another.

If the life of the family on the farm in Lággeri was idyllic, so was mine, though less busy and much more solitary. The long, calm hours of the early mornings and late afternoons were given to writing relieved by chores – hauling water, doing laundry and dishes, taking pots to the sea to scrub with sand. Near twilight I would do my "shopping" at the various farms, slowly getting to know the neighbors. Days passed when I spoke only Greek, broken as it was.

In July, when the summer visitors began to arrive in the village, to my delight they were mature and interesting people from all over the world: Athens and Egypt, Rome and Ireland, France and America. A few had been coming to this village every summer for many years; their kids had grown up with the village kids, and both children and adults had special friends among the villagers. Through them, I also began to get to know the villagers, who were more open than the tourist-hardened café owners and shopkeepers of the *hóra*. I would swim with the foreigners at Santa Maria or Lággeri, and, once or twice a week, join a mixed crowd of foreigners and natives to drink ouzo and eat octopus at the harbor *ouzerí* or walk a couple of miles out to a lively seaside *taverna* for *mousaká* and *souvláki*, wine, and dancing.

My real fascination, though, was with Lággeri and its inhabitants, both people and animals. The farmers I visited when I felt I was not intruding, or rather – because there were few minutes in the day when they weren't working – when I could limit the intrusion. I would find some excuse to stand in the doorway of the cheese room as Styllianí dipped curds from an iron pot of milk boiling over an open fire, ladling them into grass baskets. If I saw Lélla heading out to milk the cows in the pasture, I would take my bucket to the well, peering over the wall as she settled her little stool and began squirting the milk into a bucket. Gradually they got used to me, and soon, whenever I would arrive at twilight, Styllianí would hand me a basin full of melon scraps to cut up for the chickens, "so they won't get gas." This would free her hands for spinning.

When threshing time came around, I followed Aristídis and the little girls up to the round stone threshing circle, where he harnessed a mule and began leading it around. As the girls threw sheaves of wheat under its feet, the mule trampled the grain. Soon the father lifted eight-year-old Panayióta (named for her grandfather) onto the mule's back, and with clicks and brrrs she gently urged the huge animal around and around.

Animals

My main company at Lággeri turned out to be animals. The first afternoon I was there, as the sun began to set, I was sitting outside reading
when suddenly the cows from the adjacent pasture started to enter the
yard. These cows were large and angular, with high, sharp shoulder bones.
Like all the island cows, they had skins of a soft, creamy tan color; their
eyes were lined with black as though painted with kohl. And they had
horns – large horns. As they drifted into the yard, I retreated to my house,
peering out the half-door. But they acknowledged me not at all, ambling
toward the gate at the end of the farmyard, where they stood patiently
waiting for Aristídis to come and open the gate so they could wander up
the hill to their stable and their evening meal. The setting sun poured over
the sea in a golden stream, spreading a halo over the cows.

The summer I spent on the farm, I was reading Robert Fitzgerald's wonderful translation of the *Odyssey*. Living on the same land beside the same
sea brought the story alive in so many ways, but my closeness to these
cows brought tears to my eyes when I read how Odysseus' men slaughtered
Apollo's cattle.

> O Father Zeus and gods in bliss forever,
> punish Odysseus' men! So overweening,
> now they have killed my peaceful kine, my joy
> at morning when I climbed the sky of stars,
> and evening, when I bore westward from heaven.

It was only a little fanciful to imagine these cows waiting for the sun
god to end his day and come, like Aristídis, to walk among them to their
stable.

Until that time, I had never imagined I could care for a cow. But one quiet afternoon I was reading when I heard a bellowing coming from the pasture. I ran down and found a cow pressed up against the low stone wall, lifting up her head and mooing piteously. To my astonishment, tears were welling up in her eyes, tangling in her long eyelashes, running down her face. Fearing that she had somehow hurt herself, I ran up to the house to tell Lélla, who just laughed. "Oh, she's crying for her calf. We're weaning it, so we just brought it up here. We'll put him back in the pasture in a week or so." I was about to ask why they had to wean the calf when I figured it out. Still, I felt sorry. I went back down to the pasture and held the grieving mother's huge head in my arms for a while. She seemed to take some comfort in my presence, but I heard her broken-hearted mooing off and on for a few days more.

Besides cows, the farm at Lággeri housed a number of chickens and turkeys, a towerful of white doves, and a large pig who lived in a sort of grotto and consumed all the family's food waste. The doves flew free in a flock of perhaps fifty, gleaning the grain fields all over the area, but the earthbound fowl roamed no farther than the farmyard. In the hot afternoons, they would gather in the shade of the lone plane tree, the small white hens in front, the larger black and white ones behind, and the rust-colored roosters guarding the borders, keeping the silly hens from running out and giving themselves sunstroke. Behind the chickens squatted the hen turkeys, and lording it over all were the great toms with their black and white tails fanned out, their faces dripping with crimson wattles. The colors of the flock glowed richly in the deep shade. They looked as though they were sitting for a group portrait – "The Poultry Night Watch," perhaps.

Panayiótis kept no sheep or goats on this land, but may have owned some of the flock of the shepherd Evstrátios, who lived farther out the peninsula. He and sometimes his wife, called the Polonéza (the Polish woman), tended about twenty sheep. Three goats acted as sheepdogs, keeping their charges in line as they traveled across the sparse grazing land. These goats were extremely smart, which sheep are not, and their expressions always seemed to me to indicate the sort of cynical patience exhibited by those of superior intelligence forced to work with morons. One day, I heard baaing coming from the little island in the bay. I looked out and saw that the flock was being pastured there. The land sloped gently upward until fifty or sixty feet from the water's edge, where it rose in a sheer cliff maybe thirty feet high. This cliff itself sloped down in the other direction. The bleating ewe had wandered up the slope and arrived at the cliff's edge. Looking down, she spied her fellow ovines. Desolate to be separated from them, she was too terrified to jump and too stupid to remember how she had gotten there in the first place. As I watched, one of the goats detached itself from the flock and slowly, slowly, world-weariness in every movement, complete contempt showing in the slope of his shoulders, ascended the hill, butted the sheep in the rear, and turned it around. The goat had to do this three or four times, as the sheep continued to run back to the cliff edge and baa. Finally, after repeated buttings, he managed to get her turned around and heading down the slope, though until she joined her kinfolk with happy cries, she was not truly convinced that the goat was returning her to them.

Of all the animals on the farm, the one I most treasured was the one I saw the least, but whose presence seemed like a kind of blessing: a small, gray-brown owl – small enough that I could have cupped her in my hands if she had come near enough. But she usually perched on a slate shelf above the door of the building across the farmyard. Her cry was a sort of whir or murmur. Whatever she was saying was just a shade too quiet for me to understand. Reading the *Odyssey*, I identified her with wise Athena, and only later discovered that she was indeed called *Athena noctua*.

The Secrets of Lággeri

In the three years after I found Lággeri, I lived winters in Náousa village and summers in a series of country houses – one summer on the farm, one in a semi-ruined house on top of the hill looking over Santa Maria, and two in the fisherman's cottage on the bay. Each house revealed to me aspects of the area. Minás' cabin introduced me to the farmers. The "ruin," the family home of fisherman Yiánnis, who became a friend, overlooked the bay-front villa of Athenians Okeanís and Mímis, a magnet for cosmopolitan company. But it was living in the cottage that made me aware of some of the secrets Lággeri keeps.

A crew of archaeologists was working on the islet. The only shade for miles around was the porch on my house, so they sometimes came to rest their eyes from the midsummer glare. For fear of looters or fellow archaeologists, they were parsimonious with information; but, gradually, as they trusted me, they rebuilt for me the long abandoned settlement of the area.

When I first saw Lággeri from the crest of the road, the entire area had looked deserted, abandoned. Miles of empty beaches rimmed straw-colored, fallow fields that stretched back to low hills. Not even a rowboat had been floating on the sapphire surface of the eight or ten square miles of bay. Only a heap of stones on the beach – a partial wall of a structure eroded by the sea – the lone cottage, and the faraway farms gave any indication of human life, past or present. And indeed, the history of the area, spoken in whispers by the faintest of voices – those of stones, as I learned from the archaeologists – is one of continual habitation and abandonment for over seven thousand years. Even the Phoenicians were here, they say, and were not the first to find and colonize the island. People, presumably Greeks – some say Cretans, some Dorians, and so on – built a village on the islet at about the time Homer composed the *Odyssey*, but even they were not the first to settle – and to disappear. All around the area of Náousa are layers upon layers of settlements – Mycenaean on top of Cycladic or pre-Cycladic, Hellenistic on top of Classical. People lived here two thousand years before Pericles, twenty-five hundred years before Christ. In the first century B. C., Roman soldiers had an encampment in the field next to my cottage. There I found a cubical stone with two round holes in it and showed it to Dimítris, the archaeologist. "Oh," he said, disappointed, "it's only Roman."

Each group of inhabitants that lived here built houses and barns, using the stones from their predecessors' fallen buildings. They all had work to do – farming, fishing, trading. They plowed land, kept cattle and other domestic animals. They ate, slept, coupled, raised children, and disappeared.

This site is so old, so very old. None of the sparse evidence of habitation (besides Panayiótis' and Minás' houses and the church) is newer than the first century B.C. A great gap, sixteen to eighteen hundred years or more, exists between the remains of the Roman camp and the farmhouses and little church at the end of the bay, presumably built in the seventeenth century, though it is not possible to date them with certainty. What happened in all that time? The land like a stern mother keeps her secrets, doling out few clues, making us work so hard, fighting our infinitesimally short life spans, to learn her story.

Some of the clues she has recently handed us casually (so casually we suspect they are distractions from something she does not wish us to uncover) are the stones on the island in the bay, called Oikonómos. I first found them when I waded across the sand bar and walked around the shore. The land was all bedrock and gravel, no soil or only inches of it, barely enough to anchor a thyme bush. There were no trees, just a little scrub and a few scratchy junipers on the top of the hill. Rocks, just the size one could lift, littered the ground. As I walked, I looked up the slope, perhaps wondering what on earth Evstrátios' sheep could find to graze on, until suddenly I saw, among the chaos of tumbled rocks, lines of them running straight – lines pointing north and south with other lines intersecting them at right angles. One stone high. No, there – one short piece of wall two stones high.

One day the archaeological architect allowed me to help her measure stones – that is, measure the distances from one stone to another, to see where they might have fallen from a once-wall.

"Twenty centimeters left. Maria?" I said.

"Mmm?" she replied.

"When were these houses lived in?"

"Roughly? Eighth century B.C., give or take."

"Seventeen centimeters right. Maria?"

"Mmm?"

"What did they look like?"

"Oh," she said, raising her head, finding, across the bay, Panayiótis' farm, the two clusters of houses and barns, my cottage, "like those." Found-rock walls plastered with mud inside and out, cane roofs layered with *phíkia*, the ribbon weed found in abundance on north-facing beaches, and topped with earth.

"Whitewashed?"

"Probably." Exactly like all the country houses on the island, presently inhabited.

"How do you know?" I wondered. She took me to a little dip in the bedrock, maybe once a damp place, lifted a stone, and there in the hard-baked clay, almost fossilized, was the imprint of *phíkia*. A house is abandoned, the roof falls in, cane and *phíkia* fall. Mud falls on top of them. Whitewash flakes away, mud dries and falls off. Then rocks fall, weighting and covering. The sun – the searing, drying sun – bakes it all. Cane and seaweed degrade into dust. Three thousand years in the sun. Turn the stone over, read it like a book.

Other clues, not so easily read, were across from the island. Seaward of a small vineyard was a tiny cove. This cove may not exist any longer because even then it was, little by little, shifting, flattening, undermining a rock wall, and eating into the vineyard. It was completely paved, in and out of the sea, with thousands of potsherds: red-brown or tan biscuitware. Some were crusted with white sea animals; some were as clean as the day they came out of the kiln. Lying in the lapping shallows were curved fragments of terra cotta pots like those the villagers used to bake chickpeas on Fridays during Lent, as well as rims of jugs such as Lélla and Eiríni in the house down the road used for cooling water in a north window. There were many handles; they last the longest.

One day I induced the archaeologist to come and look at my finds. I reached down and retrieved a handle. "Dimítri?"

"Mmm?" Talking to archaeologists, you bring them back from wherever they are – thousands of years away.

"Are these shards old?"

"Old?" Old is not a word much used by archaeologists. "Well, this one, and the one you're holding? Probably early Cycladic. That's between, roughly, three and two thousand B.C.."

"How can you tell? They look just like pieces of the pots and jugs everybody buys off the boat from Siphnos now."

"Easy. Does it glitter? Yes? Then the clay has mica in it, like this piece. That means it was made here, on Páros." He was turning in his hand the rim of a jar. "This island used to have good clay, which contained mica, but apparently it was played out by Roman times. Some of these shards are Hellenistic." At my blank stare, he added, "Alexander the Great? Fourth century B.C.? Kind of late . . ."

I held the broken handle in my hand. Maybe three, maybe five thousand years ago, someone had dug clay, put it to soak, sieved it and kneaded it, built or thrown a pot, then took a little lump in both hands, rolled it into a sausage, and, with the thumb pressing down, pulled a handle. Five thousand years and the groove made by the potter's thumb, the raised edge where the clay squeezed out, remained. I placed my own thumb in the hollow.

There is no certain explanation for the shards. Rather, there are several: the area may have been a harbor where ships were laden with amphóras for export, whether filled with wine or empty. But since a lot of the shards seem to be from household pots and jugs, maybe there was a pottery workshop here. "There is still clay of that kind on Páros," said Dimítris, "in the marble quarries. It's just too difficult to get to." I wonder: On Panayiótis' farm, the large hollow where Minás' beehives are dug into a cliff may be a part of a hill where the earth had fallen away – or been dug out. Could it have been a quarry?

Beyond the cove, Panayiótis' wheat field was itself half soil, half shards. "I keep trying," sighed the archaeologist, "to get that farmer not to plow the field. Every year the plow breaks up more shards, or whole pots perhaps. It would be nice to find some whole pots." Still, as he would say himself, probably they're "only Roman."

Neither was Panayiótis much impressed. "*Kalá*," he said, "let him come and remove all the damn things to the museum. They dull my plowshare." Two-thousand-year-old pots hold no interest. "But let me find a jug of gold *líras* from a hundred years ago?" His eyes lit up.

Every time I passed the cove, wading through the clear shallows, I would pick up and examine the shards. I looked for some clue as to who made them, and why, and when. Once I was walking there in a time of doubt, asking myself, "Why am I here? What am I doing?" My eye lit on something the sea was pushing up onto the shore, wavelet by wavelet: half a little oil lamp, the size of my palm, small as a toy or votive offering, broken through its well, its handle and wick-hole intact. I'd been looking for a sign and took this for one: "Half the light you seek is, has always been, right here, a common thing in plain sight. The other half you must imagine."

Perhaps the land's most teasing clues are the troughs on the shore facing the islet. Long, straight-sided, perhaps half a meter wide and the same deep, they have been cut into the rose-brown rock. Here they run parallel to the shore. As well, a few such troughs appear here and there on the bedrock shores of the village. But in the bay of Santa Maria, a mile or so to the east, dozens of them stripe the sea bed, seven or eight meters under the surface, perfectly spaced, perfectly parallel, perhaps a quarter of a mile long. Flying over in a plane, on a day with no wind, for a moment you can see them: dark lines in the clear green water, lines as straight and evenly spaced as those on music paper.

Here in Lággeri there are also large round holes the same width, and several square ones. The archaeologists can't date them – Cycladic? Roman? Venetian? – and can't explain them. We have all thought and thought: Foundations? Boat slips? Beds for sea urchins or other shellfish? Did the Phoenicians, who were here at some time, cultivate sea snails for their famous murex dye? The snails do live in shallow water among rocks. The most revered archaeologist of this area claims the Romans cut such trenches to plant fruit trees in them. But why so close to the sea, in the teeth of the north wind, when there is sheltered land all over the island? Then there's the issue of the rise in sea levels over the millennia, at least seven meters since classical times. Maybe all the troughs were once on dry land?

The land has given us a glimpse of some folks who lived here, sweated here, chiseling (with what tools? Copper? Bronze? Iron?) into the country rock, but she withholds any other clue, watching us search, wonder, and speculate, moving, day by day, to the end of all thought.

The people who used the mica pottery – cooked in it, drank from it, broke it, tossed it away – lived here eons ago, before Homer, before Zeus, even before his father Kronos. They worshiped the Great Mother. Their effigies of her – plain faced, small breasted, arms crossed over the belly – were sculpted from the translucent marble for which Páros is famous. Some of these images have been found here and taken away to museums in Athens. No matter. In the little church on the farm, there are other versions of the Mother, wood and paint and paper Panagías, over-dressed for the ancient taste perhaps, but we know who she is, this provider of springs, mother of wheat, she with the dove on her shoulder, the babe in her arms.

Where a good spring was, there on Anna's land or Bárba Níkos' or Panayiótis', the ancients would have placed her shrine. Like the present inhabitants, they would have kept her festival days, perhaps walking over fields or rowing in boats, wearing their clean clothes, bringing bottles of oil or bunches of herbs or flowers, and, after paying homage, gathering to eat and drink and dance together. But I imagine also a couple of women, out for a walk on an ordinary day, opening the shrine door to air it out, sweeping the floor, then lighting incense and candles, kissing the image, making simple requests: "Mother, please see that my sister has an easy birthing." "Mother, it's too dry. Please send us the rain we need." Whatever else has changed in this place – houses and villages risen and fallen, peopled and abandoned; the sea itself risen and fallen; the very land constantly re-shaped by winds and water – this cannot have changed.

More Farms

The wells of Lággeri are its greatest treasure. Although the land is at or barely above sea level, the wells, far from being brackish, are sweet and clear and deep. Some say they reach into infinitely generous and ancient aquifers, while others maintain they tap the legendary rivers of snow melt that flow from the Caucasus through the salt waters of the sea. Because of the sweetness and abundance of this water, Lággeri is rich with farms; these riches are well hidden from the fierce north wind behind brakes of cypresses and *kalámia*, cane. There are several kinds of farms – *manávika* or truck gardens; *perivólia* or orchards (*perivóli* means something surrounded, whether by high stone walls or windbrakes), and primarily dairy farms – although few are really specialized. The most lush ones are found in Ksifára, strung along a rocky path leading inland from the beach of egg-sized stones. These are the farms and orchards of Anna and Pantelís, Margaríta and Michális, Epaminóndas, Stávros, and others. All these farmers grow fruits, vegetables, and food for the animals – doves, rabbits, chickens, even a cow or goat or two – that provide them not only with meat and eggs but, more important, with manure. On the farms where cattle are primary, the fields that grow their food and serve as pastures need no protection. A mile or so across the bay, on the promontory, Panayiótis' spread is all but treeless, with its open grain fields and pastures with grazing cows. But there too there are orchards and vegetable gardens, and it's a rare farm that doesn't have an acre or so devoted to the cultivation of the grape.

The farm I most loved to visit was that of Anna and Pantelís. So, on a sunny day fifteen years after I first came to live here, back for the summer, I walk out to see how they are doing. As usual, I pause on the crest of the hill and draw in my breath. The years have not dulled the impact of cresting the rise and seeing all of Lággeri – the brilliant sea, the modest land – spread out before me. At the growling stones, I turn inland and walk up a sandy road lined with cypresses standing tall and dark, their piney smell mixing with the scent of thyme on the dry hill opposite. Soon on my left appears a whitewashed stone *stérna*, a shallow reservoir of water, edged with pots and cans and beds of stock, carnations, roses. I call out.

And there is Anna, on her vine-covered, flower-crowded veranda, drinking a tiny coffee with a neighbor. "*Panagía mou!*" she cries. "Is it you? Come, sit down. Where have you been?" And all the news, whether two weeks or, as now, five years since I'd seen her, I must tell her. "Think of that!" she laughs at something I say. She's over sixty but shy about it, though with her smooth, lightly tanned, unlined skin she looks forty, younger than her son Pípis, the greengrocer in the village. Anna is fair and strong, her slight fatness simply a smoothness over muscles – the easy, flexible muscle of the gardener.

After the coffee and the news, the neighbor departed, we pass together into the gardens. Anna and Pantelís' is the prettiest of all the farms in Lággeri. With its fruit trees and vegetable patches, and Anna's flowers, there is always something exuberant growing. This time it's melons, stretching their sociable arms, sprouting their extravagant leaves, enjoying their long youth before getting down to the work of setting fruit. Last time,

I remember, it was pistachio trees that startled me – mad, rude upside-down "hands" like tiny, green-red bananas. As always I experience a stab of regret: How could I not have been here when the peaches were flowering? The lemons?

We stroll through the grounds. The paths are crowded with boxes of starts. Plants spring up wherever there is a bit of ground to hold them – no inch of soil wasted, no drop of water. Beyond the *perivóli* there is a field of obedient tomato plants, but here and there are parsley in a rusty bucket, cucumber sprawling out of a fish box, zinnias in an orange plastic dishpan. Rabbit cages, too, and cats and kittens ducking in and out of sheds, up and down trees. Somewhere there are chickens and a duck or two.

I have become more knowledgeable about gardening since I have been away, so I have many questions to ask. We discuss rabbits and manure. "You don't keep doves, do you?" I ask. The clouds of white doves floating in waves across the azure sky are an amazing sight. Farmers provide towers for them; from these they fly free and glean the fields, then come home to lay their eggs and leave their droppings, said to be the finest manure.

"Doves? Oh, you wouldn't know it to look at them," Anna says, tucking a curly strand of gray hair into a bun, "but they're quarrelsome, always fighting, and stupid! They push their own eggs out of the nest. And they're traitors! Worse than bees. You feed them good corn all winter and still they're likely to up and fly off to someone else. Rabbits – not as beautiful but much safer. Except when dogs get loose and eat them."

We walk through the orchards. There are no real paths because the sites of the vegetable patches beneath the trees keep changing. Vegetables planted under trees? Yes, to keep them from being sunburned. Plant zucchini and melons in troughs, not hills? Oh yes, to keep the water in. Also to keep in water, vegetable beds are rimmed with shallow dikes. And water at night? "*Amé*," Anna exclaims, "you must water at night, otherwise the sun burns the leaves, and the seedlings – pff!"

I remember how my temperate-climate ideas of gardening led to disaster. When I lived at the cottage on the bay, I wanted to grow some tomatoes and squash. Anna's neighbor Stávros came and dug me some beds under the fig trees. I thought, *They're not going to fruit without sun,* so I dug another in the open. Never have I seen a tomato plant go so quickly to seed. The little fruit got about as big as a five-drach piece and dried up. Stávros kindly did not say, "I told you so." Also, I re-dug the squash beds into little hills . . . but never mind.

In Anna's orchard, the trees are beautifully pruned The mandarins, dark-green with fine shiny leaves, are as smooth and domed as topiaries in a French formal garden. From the branches of many of the trees hang a variety of glass bottle-like objects. A white cat with gray ears, who has been following us, runs up a tree to stare into a bottle where an insect is buzzing; her paw doesn't reach. "They're insect traps," explains Pantelís, coming from ditching around the trees at the far end of the orchard. They do spray, he says, but they wait until a certain number of specific kinds of insects show up in the bottles. "We don't want to kill them all." There was great sadness and anxiety a few years ago when all the island bees died of a disease or perhaps chemical spray. Would the trees be pollinated? They were, but whether there were enough immune wild bees to do it, or whether other insects filled in, nobody's sure.

Everywhere around the orchard are square beds of edibles diked with earth, as well as boxes, pots, and buckets of starts and cuttings, not only of vegetables and flowers but also of fruit trees. Pantelís is over seventy, but he's rooting peach trees that won't bear for nearly ten years.

I love to see the June flowers of the vegetables: the white potato, the yellow tomato, the blue eggplant, the large fragile yellow horns of squash. "You could almost put them in a vase," Anna laughs, but she is passionate about real flowers – her cans and pots of intensely fragrant plants: jasmine and stephanotis climbing the porch posts; brilliant carnations, pink streaked with rose; gardenia and rose balsam and green domes of basil. She begins, as always, to cut a bouquet for me. This time it is classic: carnations, roses, basil, a little mint – the fragrance indescribable – rich, sweet, spicy.

Pantelís joins us on the veranda, his work over for today until evening watering. Tall, slender, and stooped, he is a handsome man, striking with his white hair and black eyes and eyebrows. Anna and I seize the chance to share the news with him in antiphony, each one adding to the other's stories. Anna and Pantelís savor news from the village; they almost never leave the farm now. When the new socialist government brought electricity to the rural areas, Anna and Pantelís immediately closed their village house, bought a heater and a television, and moved out to the farm "winter-summer." The electricity, Pantelís says, was about two steps ahead of his rheumatism and saved him having to buy another gasoline pump. "Oh, I am so luxurious now," laughs Anna. "In the winter, I jump out of bed and put the heater on, and get back in. Then, when it's warm I make the coffee." Of course, it is still five o'clock when she is jumping out of bed.

Life wasn't always so "easy," but they were younger and stronger, Anna says. "And the children helped." Children can do so many small but important tasks – sowing, pricking out, watering starts. The garden was not more than four acres, with another acre presently fallow to be planted in a couple of years. Pantelís inherited the property from his father, but he also inherited five sisters. The four or five acres fed them all, dressed them, but didn't provide five dowries, so he did the only thing he could do, in the economic climate of the thirties – he went to sea. He sailed mostly to America, remembers well New York, Boston, Galveston, San Francisco, Oakland. He dowried his sisters even in those lean years, but was an "old man" of thirty-five before he himself could marry. And these few acres have sustained them in comfort, built large modern houses in the village for their children, their daughter Konstantína and their son Pípis (who is tall, handsome as his father, and fiery-tempered because he is always quitting smoking).

It's a puzzle: how is it possible in Greece to raise a family in comfort, endow it with property, on the proceeds of four or five acres? In the United States, with its endless water, virgin soil, and so forth, a hundred acres can hardly support a family. A prosperous island farmer's daily produce may not be more than six or eight bushels of assorted vegetables and fruit, a few cheeses, some eggs. It's only recently they've had farm subsidies, and those are to encourage them not to sell farm land for development. Americans have had such subsidies for decades.

Some answers may lie in attitudes toward time and money, and machinery. The young farmers – often left alone to work the family land, the others having emigrated or opted for city life – look to the tractor to replace missing labor. To afford this machine, more expensive than a house on this island, many will go to sea for a few years. It's true, the tractor is faster than the wooden plow, but its advantages, one old farmer told me, are temporary. "The worst thing about the tractor is that it won't plow close to the *mandras*, the stone walls. And so the weeds get a hold and keep on going to seed. Also, the tractor doesn't plow deep enough, and the weight of it compacts the soil. All the soil it's not turning over is getting hard and sterile. So what to do? Use chemical fertilizers?" He sighed, "We're only living on a meter of earth, but we've been living on it for thousands of years." American agriculture, as Louis Bromfield noted, went from virgin soil to Dust Bowl in less than two hundred. How long will Greece produce the delicious fruits and vegetables it is famous for if its soil continues to be compacted by tractors and burned by chemicals?

Pantelís has a rattly old contraption, a half-rototiller, half-truck with a motorcycle engine, which he uses to plow and to take produce to market. The noise of it wakes up the whole village in the early morning, but at least it is light on the earth for the rough plowing of the orchards, which keeps the insects down, and for the field. But all the beds are built and weeded with a mattock, so Pantelís owns several of different weights and sharpnesses. With these he hoes by hand all the basins around the trees and the irrigation channels, which have to be opened in a pattern, a man with a mattock rushing ahead of a stream of water, building and destroying little dams, directing the water to the small diked beds or channels. The water flows directly from the well and sinks immediately into the soil, so almost none evaporates off.

Something I say puzzles Pantelís deeply: American farmers are locked into a debt system by having to buy seed. "*Buy* seed? Don't they save it from year to year?" I explain about hybrid seed, sterile like mules. He replies that the farmers who let the scientists or industrialists lock them into a money economy based on the future are stupid, clearly not practicing *noikokyrió*, good husbandry. "Borrow against the *future?*" Pantelís exclaims, disbelieving. "Farmers? Impossible." I wonder if it's partly a matter of time; Americans always want to make money fast and will take big risks to do so, but only for short periods of time. I can't imagine a seventy-year-old American farmer starting trees from cuttings.

A wonderful quality of island farmers is that they can be so thoroughly *noikokýri* – which can be translated as "holistically, organically economic" – without being fanatic. Perhaps it is the blessing of heritage. Americans seem to acquire ideas, even about farming, as lumber barons used to acquire castles from Europe – all done up, every stone numbered, "authentic." We haven't had millennia to test and refine; we have had to reason it all out backwards. We want instant change, instant structure, every new idea or theory breeding a kind of manic energy. Several seasons of this and we're burned out. Still, every movement leaves its trail – Buddhism, pacifism, organic farming . . . Maybe in a thousand years we'll get to be *noikokýri*. If we don't devastate the world first.

It is time to go. I politely refuse anything but the flowers. "You're the first, but I want to see some of the others. They'll all give me something, and I'll have to walk back loaded like a donkey with eggs and cheese and zucchini!" But, says Anna, Michális and Margaríta are in Athens seeing the doctor.

"The diabetes?" I ask.

"No, just a check-up. After losing a few toes, he's being more careful. Going to Stávros?" She is just suppressing a laugh.

"Not right now. Maybe later." Stávros loves to have visitors, loves to break out the wine, and loves to slaughter, so it is better to visit him with some notice.

"Time to clean up the blood?"

"And the feathers."

As we walk down the path, Anna's hands are as always busy, deadheading the marigolds, tweaking a sprig of mint to taste, shifting a pot of basil into the sun. Stopping at the stérna, she says, "Goodbye! Come again! Send me some seeds. But not," she calls, "those mules!"

I do want to visit Iakoumís. So I turn back towards the sea, passing the cypresses, matte green-black against the transparent sapphire of the sky. A little way along, the path forks and I follow it to Iakoumís' garden. Iakoumís is in complete contrast to Pantelís. A few acres of sandy seaside were all he inherited – not a tree on it, nothing but beach grass. His life was anything but easy: poverty, war, then twenty-five years living alone in Piraeús, working at the Papastrátos cigarette factory, sending money to his family, and putting away what he could. At last, freedom and a pension! Away he rushed to the island, and began with American haste to build up his garden from nothing – with dreams. "Until two years ago," he said, when I first met him, "I wasn't even sure there was water! But Yiórgos the dowser found it, swinging his key chain." Hurry, hurry! Plant *kalámia* all around it – no time to wait for cypresses when you're sixty-five! Scour the countryside for any sort of compost: soil, manure, straw, garbage. Pay for it. "Pay? Iakoumís, you're crazy!" the other farmers laughed. Inconceivable to pay for waste. But in a year he was planting vegetables, a year later, trees – apricots, citrus, pears – and a vineyard as well.

Iakoumís' was a busy, open little garden, fruitful and self-congratulating, neater than Pantelís', but lacking the serenity of the old trees. Iakoumís' watering system was his pride and joy: a modern miracle of black plastic pipes everywhere, evidence of seasonless city years solaced with catalogs. He was so happy and proud the first few years he had to be convinced not to give everything away! Or maybe even then, he was a little too susceptible to female attractions, overloading my baskets with tomatoes, peaches, melons, grapes. Huge, bumbling Iakoumís with his raggedy gray mustache, so sweetly urging me to have a glass of his wine, to come some evening and drink in the garden, under the moon, and sing. How guiltily I always brought with me a friend, a child, a ready excuse. How, when we ask so much charity, can we give so little?

So here I am. The garden has matured. Even the dwarf fruit trees are over my head. But Iakoumís is not here, or maybe he is having a siesta in his tool shed. Anna will give him my greetings.

Then I walk along the sea road to the cottage I lived in – can it be thirteen years ago? Next to the cottage was a small garden of two or three acres, surrounded by *kalámia* and terraced into the hillside. A huge stone well head dominated the upper terrace. How fruitful and serene it seemed! There were a dozen or so fruit trees – orange, pomegranate, peach – a few beds of tomatoes, okra, and peppers, and a vineyard. Hanging from the trees were braids of garlic or onions drying. Of buildings there were only a tool shed and a tiny hut for napping in between work and work. When I came to live in the cottage, Bárba Níkos, although in his eighties, was still working the garden. He would ride out on a donkey, sidesaddle, a straw hat protecting his head and eyes. He'd hoe, prune, or harvest, sit under a tree and have lunch or a snooze, go back to work, then fill up the donkey's panniers and head for the village. This was just a family garden; all the lemons, onions, peaches, and artichokes, along with the wine from the grapes, were for his children and grandchildren, his nieces and nephews, although he urged me to help myself.

The day I moved in, Bárba Níkos came to greet me and to invite me to draw water from his deep, clear well. "Your well," he said, "is brackish, and anyway it will dry up in the summer." An exception to the generous sweet wells of Lággeri, and something my landlord had not thought to mention. In the kitchen, Bárba Níkos noticed the green and yellow cans of grape leaves on my shelf. "What are those?" he inquired.

"Grape leaves, for *dolmádes*." I was proud of my skill in rolling the rice-filled treats.

"*Canned* grape leaves? In spring?" He laughed, and took me to the window, outside of which stretched his vineyard.

Oh. I felt like an idiot. Outside, among the vines, kindly he showed me: the white grapes, the tender leaves, the ones less lobed. The cans stayed on the shelf.

I peek through the rattling cane. The vineyard is still there, the fruit trees are still flourishing, although no onions hang from the branches. But where there were once beds of tomatoes and peppers and okra, there is merely weedy ground. Over by the tool shed is a big tub for mixing cement and a pile of concrete blocks. I hear later from Bárba Níkos' nephew, the taxi driver who formerly wouldn't risk his transmission to come out here, that the place is being "fixed up." Whether for a summer place for the family or "bungalows" for tourists, he doesn't say. Changes, some for better, some for worse. But this area is a paradigm of change and endurance.

As it turned out, my visit to Anna and Pantelís was the only one that day. I would not be going out to Panayiótis'. Three years ago at Christmas time, on arriving in the village, I had spotted the notice of the forty-day memorial service for the old farmer pinned to a light pole. I had just had time to climb up to the church and offer my condolences to Lélla and Aristídis. They had seemed confused at my presence, and I realized they did not remember me, one foreign tourist out of hundreds perhaps. Later I found that both Styllianí and Minás had preceded him in death.

Changes had come with the deaths. Minás' son had taken over his father's land, "fixed up" more tourist quarters, and sold off acreage for development. So some of the pastures where the gentle, dark-eyed cattle had grazed were now spotted with villas and scarred with driveways. Even the naked hills could not escape the building craze. I wonder what happened to the bees . . .

And so I sit on the steps of the cottage, looking out over the still beautiful bay, remembering the times of my life when I was, I believe, the happiest.

The Sea and the Village

Náousa is a *parathalassinó horió*, a village beside the sea. The sea – with its presence, its power, its uses – not only dominates the village but defines it. The sea feeds the village, cleans it, plagues it, pleases it, causes it to weep and to rejoice.

The sea has many names: *pélagos, póntos, yialós, thálassa* – three masculine, one feminine. *Pélagos* and *póntos* are for maps and poetry; no one uses them otherwise. *Yialós* is the familiar sea of the village, the useful sea where you go to fish, bathe, scrub pots, or toss garbage. But *thálassa!* *Thálassa* is her name as a force, as something greater and more beautiful and more terrifying than . . . I am tempted to say "God," but she is far more present than God: she is here, there, everywhere – she has color, form, movement, power. You can see, smell, feel, hear, even taste her – parts of her, that is, while the whole of her is too great for your imagination, even for the imaginations of the poets.

This sea is a sea like no other. She is saltier, they say, and thereby more buoyant than the oceans and seas that surround her, and though she storms and rages, she rarely kills. In the memory of the village, no seaman has ever been drowned, though many like Odysseus have floated to shore after a boat has broken up in a sudden *fortoúna*. But elsewhere, boats have gone down and men have been lost. Thrilling sad songs show a constant awareness of the treachery of the sea. Here, a loved one cries to a sailor:

> I've told you, I'll tell you again.
> Don't go to sea.
> The sea makes storms. It will take you,
> And you will be lost . . .

And here, one seafarer sings with bravado:

> If I die on the ship,
> And the black fish eat me...
> Say that I died a "levéndis,"
> One who celebrated Life.

This sea is shallow. Winds that would seem like breezes to a Gloucesterman here roil the waters up from the very bottom. And the winds are capricious, now soughing down cold and steady from the

Caucasus, now bursting in chaotically from the South like a truckful of gypsies, bringing heat, headaches, and red sand from the Sahara. Such a *sirókos*, a south wind, can overturn a good-sized *kaíki* in a moment.

The village lives by the sea and from the sea. Fish, octopus and squid, lobster and crab, and *thalassiná* – sea urchins, mussels, winkles, and other shellfish – are the foods of choice even for the mountain-dwelling farmers and shepherds. Olives and other vegetables may have been first preserved in seawater; even now the test of brine to cure olives or cheeses is whether it matches the saltiness of the sea. Human and animal life depends, on its most basic level, on the sea's most elemental gift: as a sultana might toss gold coins to a ragged, faceless crowd, the sea carelessly splashes her precious water onto rocks at the shoreline, where it is caught and evaporates, leaving sparkling crystals of salt. On the other side of the island, in man-made ponds, salt is more systematically derived, but anywhere there are rocks, the sea salt can be scraped up with a spoon. No one need go without it.

Seawater and sand can clean anything: a burnt pot, a barnacled boat, a rag rug, last year's wine barrel. Also, until recently – until plastics – the sea itself was the best dump: whatever had lost its usefulness – bottomless baskets, stubs of brooms, old chairs, vegetable scraps not fed to chickens – was tossed into the sea where the action of waves reduced it to microscopic fragments, food for fish. The sea also cleanses the sand, taking it out and laundering it, tossing it back, pure and crystalline, to dry on the shore. After a storm, the waves leave another bounty on the beaches: *phíkia*, ribbon weed, which when dried becomes roofing for houses, stuffing for mattresses, bedding for cattle, and mulch for fields.

The sea is an age-old means of communication. For millennia (the island has been occupied off and on for seven thousand years), the sea has linked the villagers to the world – the near world of other islands, the far ones of the mainland, Europe, the distant continents. Given a worthy ship, there is nowhere in the world you could not sail from this small island: ancient Greek burial sites have been found in Scandinavia, and boats arrive daily with messages and goods and visitors from faraway countries. In Greek there is no word meaning alone, lonely, cut off, that derives from the root for "island." Where the sea surrounds, no one is alone. A fisherman once said to me, "The Greek idea of a nation is not a continent surrounded by water, but a sea surrounded by people speaking the same language." Where this pertains, communication, trade, exchange – of news, goods, brides and grooms – takes place with ease.

To see this network for yourself, climb the highest mountain, always everywhere named Prophítis Ilías for the prophet who ascended to the sky in a chariot of fire. If you do this on his name day in mid-July, you will understand the symbolism when, with other visitors, you arrive panting and heat-struck at the tiny chapel. But in the summer the atmosphere is hazy, so for the best view, you must go in autumn, when the air is clear as glass. Then you will see a panorama of a dozen or more islands, and more islets, floating in a round dish of blue sea. Face to the east and see Náxos, green with farms and orchards, behind which the sun and moon rise; rocky Amorgós; tiny Skinoússa and Donoússa. Face south and make out Ios, and maybe with magical sight, Santoríni and Astypálaia. Turn to the north and see Mýkonos of the beautiful architecture; Dílos, the ancient holy center of this world; Tínos, the present "holy island" with its thaumaturgical ikon of the Panagía; perhaps even Andros, so much closer to Piraeús. Then face west and see the near neighbors on that side: Antíparos only a ten-minute sail away; tiny, one-house Despótis bobbing up in the strait. More distant but only a sea-hour away are Sýros, capital of the Cyclades and seat of its bishop; Síphnos of the potteries; and castle-crowned Sérifos.

Between all these islands, see the white lines of wakes in the sea of maybe a hundred boats and ships: the huge white ferry heading for Náxos, the bottle-gas boat arriving from Piraeús, a cargo *kaíki* threading its way back home to Ios through a dozen islands; innumerable fishing *kaíkis* laying their saffron nets; an outboard motorboat carrying in its bows a priest in his black robe and stovepipe cap, bent on a collegial visit with a priest on a neighboring island; Phíllipas going out to fish alone in his red-sailed, gaff-rigged boat; Andónis, two hands on the oars and one bare foot on the tiller, angling for his dinner. The wake lines, appearing and disappearing, form a fragile but timeless network between these islands, and between this group of islands and every other island, and eventually to mainlands from Turkey to Italy, from Albania to Egypt, where on all shores, after thousands of years, Greek is still spoken.

Historically, the Greeks (including all the Homeric tribes, Minoans, Ionians, Dorians, Athenians, Spartans, and Byzantines as well as the present speakers of the language) have been interested only in lands bordered by the sea: all the Greek settlements around the Mediterranean and Black seas have been shore-hugging, not reaching far inland. Only the mountain-born Macedonian, Great Alexander, was eager to conquer and colonize interior lands; ironic that one of the greatest cities on this greater sea is named for him.

You would think that the reason for living close to the sea was to feast on its bounty, but the archaeologists say the Bronze Age settlement across the bay from the village has produced few remains – bones and shells – of sea life. What attracted the colonists, they say, was the protected harbor with its clean sand beaches for careening boats, used not so much for fishing as for communication and trade with settlements on other islands. And, certainly, they settled there, backs against the mountain and faces to the sea, because they were enchanted by the beauty and power of the sea itself.

Above and beyond its usefulness to everyday life, the sea is a constantly changing conundrum that sharpens minds like the study of mathematics, competing in this respect with politics. You cannot dwell by the sea, live by its quixotic bounty, without constantly thinking about it: what causes it to rage like a demon one minute (or in one place) and lie as demure and flat as a wedding sheet an hour later, a sea mile farther? "We were about an hour out of Chíos with a cargo of bricks stacked on the deck," Spíros remembers, "when we ran into a storm the likes of which I'd never seen. I was only a boy, an apprentice, but Kapetán Linárdos had been sailing for forty years, and I could see he was terrified. 'Dump the bricks,' he yelled, 'or we're done for!' Working like madmen, we dumped a thousand bricks overboard – our entire cargo. Ten minutes later, the storm had blown over and the sea was like oil. How could it happen? We talked about it for years: 'You ever know this to happen?' Linárdos would ask any captain he ran across. 'About an hour out of Chíos . . .'"

Lifetimes are devoted to the science of the sea: a seafarer begins by absorbing the knowledge of his mentor and continues over fifty, sixty, even seventy years of gathering his own. But just as, perhaps, he has some handle on it, some answer, some vision in a dream, he reaches the end of his voyage, looks his last upon the fascinating face, and steps into the boat of Háros the Ferryman, bound for darkness.

The village meets the sea most intensely in the little north-facing harbor, built eight hundred years ago during the sovereignty of Venice – not to shelter the natives' fishing boats, which being beachable did not truly need a deep water harbor, but the Venetians' own trade and warships. The Franks, as they (and all Roman Catholics) were called, built well: the harbor is an unclosed rectangle of four moles or docks. Three were built out in a U from what must once have been a beach, and the fourth, the north side, is all but closed by a breakwater ending in a tower, known locally as the Kástro, leaving a small opening for boats to sail through. Gigantic blocks of dressed marble formed and still form the edges of the moles. Behind them, rubble and compacted earth (now concrete) created a *platía*.

On one mole, the seafarers have built two small churches – one to their official protector, Áyios Nikólaos, who with his white beard seems a more charitable Poseidon, and the other to the Panagía, the Mother of God who hears all prayers for help, regardless of occupation. Along the other two moles, beneath the old and new two-story houses of village notables, are found the ground-floor store rooms where the captains store their cargoes of wine and bricks and the fishermen mend their nets. Here also are the mariners' special *kafeneíos* and *ouzerís* where they congregate when not on the sea. Sitting upright and barefoot on straw-bottomed chairs, nursing tiny glasses of coffee or ouzo in their weather-roughened hands, the cargo captains receive orders for *porseláni,* a fine clay from Santorini to smooth on walls; sapling olive trees from Crete; even tricycles and canned goods from Piraeús. Here also groups of fishermen sit to mend their nets and discuss the weather, always in sight of the bobbing crowd of wooden *kaíkis* with their blue or green or white hulls striped with yellow and orange gunwales, surmounted by crimson cabins and masts, decorated at the prows with carvings of fish and dolphins, and, each one, protected by an ikon of Áyios Nikólaos.

The high, double-gated walls enclosing houses and churches, the harbor with its Kástro guarding its entrance, raise the question of why the Venetians went to so much trouble to fortify this tiny village, protect it from the infamous pirates, the Vikings of the Aegean. On other islands, the inhabitants survived the pirate eras by building their villages high in the hills, leaving only a few shacks on the beaches below for the fishermen to store their gear. But this small village has existed for hundreds of years bravely or brashly facing the piratical sea.

Or was it not bravery but knavery? From time to time, it seems, the village was home base to pirates! It was so during the fifteenth century, until the Frankish duke Somaripa, he who built the Kástro, kicked them out. Four centuries later, the Venetian warships long sailed away, a pirate named Avgoustínos operated out of the village; he is reputed to be buried in the ruins of a church near the harbor.

However, there may have been other reasons for fortifying the village. To the west of the old part of the village is a mile-long, deep-water bay. The harbor of the *hóra* on the west side of the island is both relatively shallow and extremely wide, vulnerable to the tricky west and south winds. The long, deep bay of the village, however, is both open to the steady north wind and protected by a mountainous peninsula – perfect anchorage for large ships, warships or traders loaded with wine and cedar wood, waiting out the storm before sailing off to Venice or any of her colonies or trading partners. Even now, when dangerous winds blow and ships cannot dock in the port of the *hóra* or even continue on the open sea, they'll brave a rough sail round the rocky northwest cape of the island to anchor in this bay. In a bad storm, ten or a dozen ferries or cruise or cargo vessels may shelter there, prows to the wind, lined up in twos and threes like cows at milking time.

Perhaps another reason the tiny village was so protected was that the Venetian dukes – and one duchess – who ruled this island also ruled Náxos, the large island always visible from the village harbor. The governors lived in elegant houses (some still standing) in the *hóra*, but their duties took them often to Náxos. Although the sea passage from the *hóra* to the village, round the high cliffs of a headland, is notoriously rough, the overland passage is gentle – a couple of hours' amble on a good mule – and the sea crossing from the village to Náxos generally calm. If I'd been governor, I'd certainly have chosen to ride to the village through the hills, fragrant with broom and thyme, then sail out of a harbor from whose tower my brief voyage could be continuously observed.

The Venetians officially withdrew in the sixteenth century, although some remained to govern for the conquering Ottomans, thus saving the island a violent invasion. Over the centuries the threat of attack diminished, gates rotted and rusted, walls were slowly incorporated into houses and churches, and the Kástro, exposed to the north wind and the sea, crumbled into little more than a memory of itself. But the well-built harbor, a valuable heritage, was long ago appropriated by the fishermen and the cargo sailors.

As well as a *parathalassinó horió*, the village is a *psarohóri*, a fishing village. Yes, there are farms where wheat is grown, animals are raised, and cheese is made, and from which come olives and wine, not to mention vegetables and fruits – but these are only food. Fish are not just food, and fishing is more like a religion, a mystic fraternity, than an occupation. It may be the oldest work in the world, predating even agriculture, and the only hunting-gathering still widely practiced.

Fishing is characterized by almost Biblical uncertainty. In this island-dotted sea, fish on their journeys (from where to where?) school in one place, then another – off Santa Maria one day but not the next, off Donoússa in February but not in March. The weather and the season seem to have little to do with where the gypsy fish make their watery camps. Where the fish are, what kind are where and in what quantity (and what prices one might get for them), are the constant topics of conversation among the net menders on the moles. Such conversation is guarded because fishermen are like horseplayers: they may have an instinct, a theory, a tip, even information, but they are choosy about sharing it and chary about receiving it. Vangélis, for instance, may be sincere in telling Achilléas that the *palamída* are running like rivers on the west side of Ios; on the other hand, he may just want to get a rival out of his chosen territory north of the lighthouse. Among ancient observers of the fascinating fish was the polymath Aristotle, who only recently was proven wrong in his theory about the migration of tunny. Or may have been proven wrong: tunny are cleverer than dolphins about eluding capture for scientific purposes, so their true migratory paths are still largely deduced rather than actually charted.

The kind of fishing used depends on the habits of the fish. Do they, like the blue-fin tuna, migrate from South to North, to the Black Sea, streaming across the surface in silvery-blue schools? Then either drift nets or *paragádi,* a long floated line with many hooked lines depending from it, may be appropriate. Are they bottom feeders who come to the surface at night? Then *pyrofáni,* fishing with a strong flare or carbide lamp attached to the side of the boat, is the way to go. Lightfishing is usually practiced in small, one-man boats; a version of it called *gri-gri* involves several larger boats shining their lights in a circle. Fishing with light is best on still, moonless nights, when the traitor lamp plays moon to the unwary fish, sending its beams down through shallow water in the bays. It is very beautiful to watch: on the almost black sea, the small boats are visible only as shadows against the blue-white lights, while the sea around them shines transparent as pale-green glass.

Some kinds of fishing are more geared to the capability of the *kaíki* than to the habits of fish. One such is *tráta,* or trawling, in which a weighted net is dragged along the sea bottom. *Tráta* needs a biggish boat with a strong motor: When the *tráta* (the name of the net and of the boat as well as the method) is drawn up, it has snagged everything in its path, a complete hodge-podge from lobsters to mackerel to spiny little specimens fit only for soup. *Tráta's* advantage is that it can catch bottom dwellers in the daytime, without having to use light. Its disadvantage is that it decimates and destroys every form of life in its path and so is now, fortunately, illegal.

If the fish are elusive and deceitful, the fish broker, who comes around in his truck from the *hóra* every day to deliver ice and buy the catch, is more so. The island fishermen have no way to ascertain the prices being paid in Piraeús, which rise and fall constantly. They have to hope that the kind of fish of which they have made a significant catch, let's say the prized *barboúnia*, has not been caught in great numbers all over the Aegean. If it has, then the price goes down and what looked like a windfall at the dock may turn out to be great labor for little profit. Of course, fish spoil easily, so there's no other real way to dispose of the catch than to sell to the broker. The locals are almost always cheated, being told such-and-such a fish is a glut on the market, can't be sold for cat food, and so forth.

"Why don't you form a co-op, like the farmers have?" I asked Pános. "You could send one of your own to Piraeús every day."

"We did," he sighed. "Whoever went cheated the rest. It was better to be cheated by an outsider."

Before the truck-driving fish broker, a ship called a *psaropoúla*, the "fisher girl," circled the islands buying fish. In the summer, many families would move out – boats, kids, and furniture – to a house on a remote bay. Because it brought ice and news and messages from the village, says Yiánnis, the *psaropoúla* was a welcome sight. "Probably she cheated us too, but it was a lot friendlier."

Maybe the situation was better in ancient times. An inscription found in the third-century B.C. city of Akraiphia seems to have been an edict controlling the price of fish, and it is known that such price controls existed at various sanctuary sites such as Delphi. But these controls more than likely capped the profitability of the fishermen, who, Thomas Gallant estimates, rarely made more than one-half of the daily necessities for their families. The situation is considerably better now: tourism and prosperity have brought more people to the village, and several fishing families have opened their own shops. And demand and prices have risen in the larger markets as well.

The faces of the fishermen, after they have been working for four or five years, acquire from the sun and the wind a ruddy color neither age nor death can pale. Into their rose-copper skins are etched deep lines, especially around their eyes, which, though it cannot be so, seem always to be blue or blue-gray, and always searching (looking up from the nets they are mending) beyond the here-and-now to horizons only they have seen. The work of fishing, with its many and varied jobs on land and shore, is demanding but not brutalizing, and it makes them graceful; they are always the best dancers, lithe and witty. Their diet of fish – many will not touch other flesh – makes them, they boast, intelligent. They are more social and political than the farmers, and more philosophical: they deal with the vagaries of nature with a certain ironic merriness, compared to the farmers' eternal pessimistic reserve, and even in misfortune the fishers are rarely bitter.

Fishing runs in families. Sometimes boys from farm or trade families become fishermen, but it is rare; the skills must be learned day after day, season after season, by working on the *kaíki* with an elder – father, brother, grandfather. By the time a boy is grown, he has all the skills to fish on his own and most likely has become a valued member of a family crew.

"You learned from your father?" I asked Pános, although I knew the answer.

"Yes, and my grandfather, before he died."

"What about your great-grandfather?"

"Was he a fisherman, you mean? Probably. All my family – my uncles and great-uncles, my cousins, my brother – everyone of our name: we're all fishermen."

Sometimes a fishing family will produce another kind of mariner: a ship's captain or engineer, a man of wider seas than the Aegean, but these, while admired for the fortunes they make sailing cargoes to Africa and Siam, Miami and Caracas, are pitied for their loneliness, the months and years they spend away from the village, away from the only sea that matters. Their anchors, as it were, lack a firm bottom; they drift.

Not all the fishers are men. Though rarely, women do fish. Usually they are partners with men in their families. Eléni has been fishing with Sarándos since she married him twenty-five years ago. Margaríta inherited a share of her father's boat and decided to work it rather than pay her brothers to do so; of Margaríta's three children, only her girl, the youngest, loves going to sea.

The fishermen, their *kaíkis*, their nets, and the fish are like partners in a dance, a *syrtós* – a line of entities holding hands, moving together, spiraling in time. The round of work, day after day, is the same and not the same. Much of it centers on the nets, as the fishermen handle them constantly: mending, loading, paying out, hauling in, cleaning, and mending again, always mending. Even when the weather is good, if his nets are full of holes, the fisherman does not go out to sea. Mending the nets, they sit in sociable groups around the harbor on good days, in their storerooms on cold or wet ones. They sit on the ground or floor on very low stools, using a bare toe to stretch the net taut so they can cut away the damaged threads and, with small shuttles, join the intact parts together. The net, like the village itself, is a construct of old and new, beautiful and useful, vulnerable and strong. When the net is finished – holes mended, weights and floats replaced – the fisherman coils its hundred meters or more into a round "snail" which will unroll evenly into the water. As the time approaches to go to sea, whether dawn or evening, the men carry the coiled buns of nets out to the *kaḯkis*, some jauntily balancing flat baskets piled with nets on their black-capped heads.

In the old days the nets were made by women using a shuttle and flax thread, not quite as fine as that with which they crocheted lace for curtains, tablecloths, and pillow edgings. The women worked mostly in white: the nets were white and their needlework white – a legacy perhaps of the Venetians, who for hundreds of years, traded out of this village, lived here, intermarried, assimilated. Walk along the *agorá*, or in the cemetery, and look at the names: alongside Petrópoulos and Kritikós, you'll see Ventourís, Viónis, Alifiéris, Aliprántis, even Barbaróssas. In the *hóra* are Malatéstis and Daferréras. The Venetians left a lot of names, a few walls, a harbor, and a tradition of embroidery. All over the village are windows hung with flat white cutwork curtains through which light pierces (sun from one side, lamp from the other), disclosing delicate patterns of cupids, roses, or peacocks. Also there are windows – and sometimes doorways – still hung with panels of white, small-eyed fish netting onto which patterns, perhaps a vase of flowers, have been darned.

The women made the nets, then the men dyed them, boiling them in caldrons with a dye made from pine bark. I remember seeing these old nets stretched out along the mole, the newly dyed maroon, the fading pink, drying in the sun.

"Why dye them?" I asked Sarándos, who was sitting among piles of the newer saffron-colored nets with Eléni. "Do fish see colors?"

He was polite about this. "No," he said without laughing (Sarándos who laughs all the time), "the dye kept the nets from rotting. But it was a chore. We had to dye them four or five times a year. And look, on every trip we take forty nets, a hundred and ten meters each. We were always dyeing and dyeing."

"Very tiring work!" exclaimed Eléni. "These nets are much nicer." With the hand that held a shuttle, she gestured to the net she was mending, made of fine, silky, synthetic thread. "These are stronger," she says, "but still the dolphins rip them to shreds," and she held up a portion of a net with a hole two feet wide: "Look, this one's almost a dead loss," she tch'ed as she cut away the damaged parts with a little knife. "Oh, if it weren't for dolphins, we'd be rich," she laughed, but there was no malice in the laugh. Dolphins are dolphins; you set a table with their favorite food and they'll attend gratefully.

No one admits to ever killing a dolphin, only a few to frightening them with shotguns. Pános and Stávros had for years a pet dolphin who would join them most days on their outward journey as they rounded Donkey Island. They have photos of their feeding him, he leaping high into the air to catch a *melanoúri* or other tidbit.

"Did he then tear up your nets?" I asked.

"Well, we think it was other dolphins," Pános said, "but . . . it doesn't matter."

If the fishermen play a radio or cassette player, the dolphins will follow for miles. "What kind of music do they like?"

"*Rembétika*," says Pános. "*Bouzoúki*."

"*Nisiótika*, island music," contradicts Stávros. "They like to dance. They go away when the news comes on."

The fishermen's attitude toward dolphins reflects their attitude toward life in general and fishing in particular: always unpredictable. One winter the tuna will appear by the thousands, straining the nets, inundating the little boats, filling all the wooden fish boxes the village can find; then, a fisherman with a strong *kaíki* will bypass the broker and sail the fish straight to Piraeús to get the best price. Yet, another year at the same time in the same place, under almost identical conditions, the nets will be full of small, scrappy specimens even a harbor cat would refuse. This unreliability is not new and not attributable to over-fishing – although that, says Pános, is certainly happening.

When the nets are strung out to dry along the moles, the harbor is a work of communal art few individuals could compose. Against a background of snow-white buildings, with their light blue and lime-green doors and windows, blaze the carmine and orange, the emerald and Bristol blue, of the *kaíkis*. The border of saffron nets echoes splashes of the same yellow on the boats: a cabin, a gunwale, a rudder. In the harmony of their clear, bright gold with the blues and greens of the *kaíkis*, all brilliant against the bright white buildings, the nets seem so astonishingly Greek, so deeply native, that it's a surprise to find out they come from Japan.

Each net has three layers, all of the same twisted thread a little thicker than that used on buttons: the two outer nets have "eyes," spaces between the threads, about four inches square; the inner one is denser, with eyes of one to two inches, depending on the size of the fish to be caught. The common edges of the three nets are sewn to two ropes; on one are strung small lead weights and on the other cork floats.

Unlike the heavy rope-and-cable nets of ocean fishers, which trap dolphins, these nets are as fragile as tulle – indeed, new or mended, when they are gathered up in pleats and hung over a chair or a balcony rail, the gauzy nets look like tutus hanging in the dressing room of a corps de ballet.

Once on the sea, at the place the fisher has chosen, the nets are paid out from carefully laid coils spaced along the gunwales and left to float just below the surface, weighted side down. Fish get caught as they swim through the large eyes of the outer nets into the finer one and attempt to leave through the opposite outer net. Each trapped fish creates a little packet outside the large-eyed net. The clever dolphin swims by the nets much as we stop at a *souvláki* stand for a snack on our way home from work. The dolphin tears the net, frees the fish, and darts after it, leaving the net in tatters. The fisherman takes home what the dolphin leaves him.

The nets are left to float anywhere from a few hours to overnight, each crew having preferences for specific kinds of fish and places to look for them. Pános' father, Kóstas, who fishes alone now that his son has gone in with his cousin on a large new boat, likes the tiny silver *marídes*, easy to handle for a man nearing seventy. Sarándos and Eléni go for *kathará*, "clean" fish – bream, gray and red mullet, lobsters – large, rare, and expensive. The couple likes to cast their nets off the neighboring island of Náxos, perhaps for sentimental reasons, since it is where, over twenty-five years ago, they met. Sarándos, then twenty years old, was fishing with his father and older brother. One evening after casting the nets, they anchored in a cove on a small island off the northern shore of Náxos, looking for a little company other than their own. They brought a mess of small fish for a *kakaviá*, fish stew, hoping to find someone to cook it for them. Sarándos – short, stocky, fair-haired – has always been welcome wherever he goes because of his beautiful singing voice and large repertory of songs old and new. The village was small – only two or three *kaíkis* drawn up on a beach, with no real *taverna*, just a grocery store with a few cans of this and that, a single barrel of wine. To accommodate the three strangers, the storekeeper borrowed some chairs from a neighbor, who herself offered to boil up the soup. A very small village, twenty or thirty houses at most, with even fewer people, mostly old, a few sheep, more goats, and one beautiful, dark-haired, dark-eyed seventeen-year-old girl.

Their meeting would not have been strictly accidental. A mother of such a girl in that place and in those days must have been frantic. Perhaps her daughter was too closely related to marry any youth in the village; perhaps few remained anyway, since the years after the war were the times of massive emigration. Her mother must have fussed and puzzled over the alternatives: send her to work in a larger village, where she might be taken advantage of by an employer? Advertise in the newspaper? But, a girl without much of a dowry – what could you say about her? That she was lovely and strong, a hard worker with a mind of her own? Even the go-between was baffled. And then suddenly, like an angel in a dream, a neighbor came running: "There're fishermen from across," she panted, nodding at the neighboring island, "down at Manólis'. And one of them's young – and with such a voice! A gift of God! Maybe Eléni should go down and help Vangelió serve the *kakaviá*."

And maybe she did, staying for the singing, washing pots and plates that were perfectly clean, sweeping the floor until not a grain of sand remained, hearing him sing over and over a love song about "golden chestnut-colored eyes." After that night, his *kaḯki* anchored many times in the little cove, though not too many, for within the year they were married.

The first time she sailed across to visit Sarándos' village, Eléni helped haul in the nets. As well as with the fisherman, the girl fell in love with the sea, with fishing, and from the time they married they fished together alone on the *kaḯki*. Only during the last months of her pregnancies and in the forty days after childbirth would Eléni let Sarándos take a helper in her place. The babies went with them, one after the other, cradled on the nets in good weather and on the bunks in the cabin in bad. So that Eléni's mother would not lose her only child, they continued to anchor in the cove, netting her kin to his across the straits between the islands.

In the old days, the fishermen found fish by lore and observation. Fish need rocks, Sarándos says, and each young fisher would learn from his father where the rocks were, where which fish went in which seasons, the habits of each kind of fish, whether they fed on the bottom or in the shallows in the day or the night, where they came from and where they were going in their endless migrations. The fishermen fixed the locations in their memories by triangulating landmarks: line up a lighthouse on one island with a mountaintop on another, a church belfry with a promontory shaped like a sheep. Nowadays they have bythometers – some that just describe the bottom of the sea, some that actually locate fish – but the fish are still just as wily, and practical knowledge is as important as ever.

When the fishermen judge the nets are full (depending on the kind of fish they are after, this may take a few hours, overnight, or several days), they haul the nets in hand over hand, with a motorized winch drawing up the ropes. Unlike in ocean fishing, here the nets are paid out and taken in only once. Back in harbor, slowly, slowly, the fish are removed, each one untangled separately. Broken, dead, or inedible fish are tossed back into the sea, or to the waiting cats who know before anyone else when the boats are coming in. The fish are then sorted by type, packed into flat boxes of ice, and delivered to the broker or to the local fish shops – or sold to the villagers, men and women, who come down to the harbor to buy directly off the boats. Villagers are so choosy about fish that some will not eat in the evening fish caught in the morning, but most will give it a day. Heedless of the value, the fishermen frequently reserve a portion of the catch for themselves, and occasionally their relatives and friends, sending a mess of *kefaléo* or *marídes* out to a farm by taxi or motorcycle. These favors are often returned in the form of bottles of wine and oil, baskets of eggs, sacks of potatoes and onions.

When the fishing is done, the nets cleaned not only of fish but of seaweed and flotsam, the fishermen stretch them out to dry along the mole of the harbor. When they are dry, they are gathered up and the mending begins again in the endless cycle.

Fishing is changing. In the last few decades, technology and political-economic alliances have made it an increasingly profitable occupation, perhaps for the first time ever. Although fishing itself has not changed a great deal since ancient times (the kinds of fishing and nets remain similar), two inventions, the gasoline motor and the various sonar devices, have affected the amount of fish being caught. While the latter have augmented orally transmitted knowledge, the former has replaced increasingly scarce "hands." The motors can pull in the ropes of full and teeming seine nets that formerly required many men. One kind of fishing that has all but disappeared needed perhaps twenty boats to set a huge net across the mouth of a bay to catch migrating tunny, and sixty men to haul the net onto the beach. As enormous as the catch may have been, each man's share was small. Still, it was part of the complex pattern of life for farmers to take an occasional day off from farming to fish, and fishermen to take time off seasonally to harvest wheat, olives, or grapes.

The engines not only take the place of hands, they also allow the boats to go out farther from their native shores to seek the pelagic or ocean species. With only oars and sails, the old-time fishers stayed pretty close to home and concentrated on the in-shore varieties. This ability to go far away, to stay out for more than a night or two, and to be free of the immediate necessity of ice, combined with the demand for fish from the European Economic Community, has led to both serious overfishing and greater profitability for the fishermen. The greater wealth of the general population since Greece joined the EU has itself contributed to what in some circles is being regarded as the decimation of the Mediterranean fish population: As the islanders have more money to spend, they drift away from traditional ways that recognized and attempted to alleviate scarcity. In the old days ("Oh, years ago!"), most people observed over a hundred fast days a year, abstaining from meat, milk, eggs, and fish with scales. In one of many seeming collaborations of nature and the church to provide for man in perpetuity, some of the longest fasts on the Orthodox calendar more or less coincide with the spawning seasons (as others do with the drop in egg-laying in August and the birthing and nursing of animals in the spring). A fisherman then had to be flexible, going for swordfish, shark, or red and gray mullet in the summer; tuna in winter or fall; and in the long, fifty-day Lent, octopus, squid, and cuttlefish. He might even abandon his nets during Lent to gather sea urchins and other shellfish, which were not prohibited.

Nowadays, few people observe fasts, and more fish are sold directly off the boats or in shops owned by the fishermen themselves, so demand both at home and from Europe is making fishing a far more profitable occupation than it ever was. Ironically, now there is a shortage of hands even to man the motorized boats, and these are being hired seasonally from other countries, especially Egypt. Not only have the Egyptians come to fish here, but the first crew, who showed up one winter in their own boat, married village girls – sisters who worked at the harbor *kafeneío*. Strange as it seemed at first to see Muslims unrolling their prayer mats on the mole between Áyios Nikólaos and their *kaíkis*, their work and piety have earned them respect and acceptance.

Next to his nets, the fisherman is closest to his *kaíki*. In the harbor are all sizes and kinds, from four- or five-meter open boats, perhaps with a single mast for a lateen sail, to fifteen-to thirty-meter ones with one or more masts (or none), and large or small cabins. Most are beamy and double-ended, though here and there bobs a transom, often carved with leaping fish or dolphins. Although many *kaíkis* may have started life (human lifetimes ago) as sailing vessels, all the *kaíkis* are motorized now, except a few rowboats, pleasure craft for the most part, for spare-time fishermen.

The Turkish word *kaik* originally meant a light skiff propelled by one or more rowers, but the term has become a catchall for most small fishing and trading boats in the Eastern Mediterranean. Here, I think, it might be locally defined as a wooden boat under a certain, or rather uncertain, size (beyond which it would be a *karávi* or *plío*, ship). One boat in the harbor, no larger than any other, was made of steel. Modern and sleek, it was used mainly for ferrying tourists to distant beaches and sometimes other islands.

No fish ever tainted its pristine deck. It was painted pure white without trim, and I noticed that the fishermen referred to it (in quotation marks) as a *kótero*, or yacht. A true *kaíki*, whether rowboat, sailboat, or motorboat, should be wooden, probably double-ended, with various designs for stem and stern, raked or curved. Although there are many traditional designs for *kaíkis*, the favored one is the *trehandíri*, a beamy, heavy-keeled, shallow-draft, one- or two-masted ship of any length from twenty to seventy feet. (In the heyday of sail, many trading *trehandíria* were much larger, carrying up to 250 tons.) Its design was dictated by its use, fishing boats being narrower in the beam than cargo sailors. Those used for long trips often had commodious cabins on the afterdeck.

A traditional two-masted *trehandíri* would have flown up to five sails, the two main ones would be rakish lateens with their yards slantwise across the mast, with others – lugs, sprits, gaffs – tucked between and above, with a jib stretched to the bowsprit. Tradition has it that the *trehandíri* first made its appearance in Greek waters when a crew of Hydriotes escaped after being captured and impressed (in the nautical sense) by pirates. Although the Greeks hated their captors, they loved the ships and, when they got back to Hydra, set about building ones of the same design. Tradition has not a word about where these pirates called home – Morocco? Syria? the Barbary Coast? – so the true origins of the *trehandíri* are unknown.

Whether they still carry a mast or only a memory of one, whether they sleep two on short, hard bunks or accommodate a crew of six, the majority of the village's fishing boats are most probably *trehandíria*. But the most striking characteristic of the boats in the harbor is the glorious way they are painted. Each part is a different bright color: the hull perhaps light or deep blue, the gunwales orange or red, the cabin lime green or sun yellow, the deck orange, the mast crimson, and so forth, all according to the owner's taste. When all the *kaíkis* of the village are crowded into the harbor, the hulls bobbing and the masts and stays weaving with the motions of the sea, the bright colors flash from the surface of the water as though tropical fish were swimming around the boats.

It is impossible to tell how old these *kaíkis* are; most are inherited, and great care is taken to preserve and maintain them. Generally, they are careened annually; there is a boatyard across the bay with both a beach for small boats and adequate scaffolding for larger. But the really big ones would probably go to more sophisticated boatyards on adjacent islands – Sýros or Ikaría. Although they all now run with motors, many retain masts, hinting at a launching in the early part of the past century. Here and there a sail is kept cinched up on the booms, perhaps to use in an emergency, if the engine conks out, or just to save gas.

"Do you ever use your sails?" I asked Kapetán Linárdos, sitting and drinking his first coffee in the post-dawn sunshine of a summer day.

"Illegal," he huffed, sucking in the coffee, "since the war. Government says, use motor."

"Why?" I asked.

"*Sto diáolo,*" he growled. "Who knows?"

I found it hard to believe that Linárdos, the *árchon* of the harbor, owner of the biggest, most beautiful *kaíki* in the fleet, with its two masts, raked stern, curved stem post, and long bowsprit – a sailing vessel if ever there was one – would let the government tell him what to do. I said as much.

"Hrmmph," he said, wiping the coffee from his large, piratical mustache, "maybe sometimes, out of sight of land . . ." His eyes sparkled as he spoke.

Linárdos was less a person than a force: as fierce and ruthless, as mild and agreeable, and as changeable as the sea – his mistress and equal. In his prime, which lasted well into his seventies, he and his large blue *trehandíri* dominated the harbor. Not as tall as he seemed, he carried himself with an exuberant pride that gave him the air of a colossus. A trader rather than a fisherman, in fine weather or foul Linárdos strode about the harbor or sat outside his favorite *kafeneío*, accumulating orders to bring olive saplings from Crete, nets and rope from Piraeús, bricks from Chíos – or, conversely, to take barrels of wine, olives, or oil to *tavernas* on the mainland. Whether he strode or sat, a bird perched on his shoulder. Two birds, first a dove and after its demise a gull, had flown straight from the open air onto his shoulder and remained there for years. He had done nothing to attract either one, though when they claimed their human roost, he petted and fed them.

Linárdos' wife, Aspasía, was just as formidable in her own way. With the profile of the Aphrodíti of Milos, abundant wavy gray hair, and the bearing of a queen, she was a long-suffering but not resigned Hera to his scapegrace Zeus. Her constant struggle with Linárdos concerned not minor goddesses but *papoútsia*, shoes. Linárdos was opposed to shoes in general and his own in particular. Barefoot he went on the *kaíki* on his voyages to Ikaría and Chíos, Pérama and Ios, and barefoot around his own harbor he saw as his right. But Aspasía's mission in life was to keep shoes on him. Once he was about to sail off to Piraeús to be godfather to a child, decently clad for once in a dark suit. He made it to the *kaíki* tied up at the far end of the mole before Aspasía discovered the damnable shoes tucked under the bed. From her balcony – they lived in a house in the middle of the harbor – she hailed him: *"Ta papoútsia!!"* As all the fishing *kaíkis* were out, Linárdos simply sailed his boat into the harbor so close to his house that the bowsprit touched the balcony. Up it he ran, grabbed the shoes, kissed the irate Aspasía with a resounding smack, and sailed away.

The early morning when I was drinking coffee with Linárdos in the harbor, Aspasía appeared on the balcony above us and tossed a pair of boots at his feet. *"Ta papoútsia!"* She waited while he put them on; then, of course, when she went back into the house, he took them off.

Their daughter-in-law, who lived next door, said they had been warring about the shoes for her lifetime, forty years at least. "Neither of them ever gives up."

Linárdos had made a good thing from cargo sailing. Not only had he built his Aspasía a modern house in the harbor, he dowered four daughters and a son with both homes and businesses. Everyone knew he was a man of property, but you had to know it to believe it. In the harbor his usual costume was a worn blue-striped undershirt and black wool trousers, always rolled to the shin. In the winter, he might deign to wear a white wool *fanélla*, handknit for him by Aspasía, and a wool cummerbund to protect his back and kidneys. And, of course, the seaman's black cap. His feet – grimy, horny, callused, snag-nailed – were bare. He never appeared clean-shaven, but always seemed to be wearing two days of stubble on his wind-reddened cheeks. His only vanity was his luxuriant mustache, silvery as a fish, large and bushy as a Cretan's; if he had to trim it (or his hair) and Aspasía couldn't catch him with the scissors, he would just chop it off with a knife.

Despite this lack of pretension, Linárdos, while universally acknowledged to be an *árchon*, a powerful elder, was not universally admired. He was a canny – *ponirós* – businessman, and never hesitated to seize an advantage. Rumors about how he had profited during the German Occupation would surface, even from those who preferred to have it all over and done with. He would, it was whispered, somehow obtain supplies of food – flour, rice, a few kilos of chickpeas or beans – and sell them to the starving villagers at exorbitant prices, taking anything of value in uneven exchange.

He was not the only one to do this. "There's a woman in the village," said Mersiniá, "who wears my grandmother's necklace. During the war, my mother had six children to feed. We were always hungry – always. The woman traded us three pounds of potatoes for a gold necklace and earrings. Some who made such trades gave back the things when the war was over. But not that woman." Mersiniá's mother, whose young husband went down in the first Greek ship torpedoed in the war, managed to hold on to a small plot of land, but many islanders traded away even their fields for a loaf of bread, a cheese, some beets. Thus, rightly or not, some of Linárdos' many holdings were attributed to profiteering.

A profiteer he may have been, but not a collaborator. Some of his war-time activities brought him into conflict with the German military, which, catching him at some of his prohibited trading, towed his *kaîki* out to a distant inlet and machine-gunned it. And that was that, they must have believed, sunk, gone, a dead loss. There was nothing on the island that could have repaired the boat: no wood, no nails, no caulking, no tar, no paint. Linárdos, however, was not called *ponirós* for nothing. Knowing the salt water would preserve the boat, he avoided suspicion by never going near it, but over the next few years he searched and asked and bullied and traded – a nail here (crooked but it could be straightened), a piece of wood there (an old stable door or a broken plow), a bit of string, rope, cable. And when peace came and the eagle-eyed occupiers were gone, he raised the boat and began repairing it. Within months he was back to sailing and trading.

What there were no rumors about, oddly enough considering Linárdos' wealth and charisma, was any sort of infidelity to the goddess of the shoes. She was sixteen and he twenty years older when they were married. She was so lovely at sixty-some, the last time I saw her, with her strong cheek-bones and hair knotted in classical fashion, that it is hard to imagine how much more beautiful she could have been as a girl. Her daughter Tzanétta at the same age had her mother's luxuriant wavy black hair, black olive eyes, and commanding bosom, but she had her father's devilish character, while Aspasía's temper was equable, although perhaps from long practice. When they were married, Linárdos sailed her off on his *kaîki* to another island for a honeymoon. In the port they were met by an acquaintance who said to the groom, "Ah! I see you've brought your daughter this trip." Linárdos never tired of telling this story, even at nearly eighty proud of his young and beautiful bride.

Linárdos, striding about the harbor with his bird or a grandchild on his shoulder, chaffing the fishermen, harassing the housewives, doing deals, shouting on the telephone in his son's grocery, was a colorful figure, an ikon of a disappearing past. But, again, not everyone loved him. Yiórgos the bar owner as a youngster had sailed with him as apprentice, thinking to learn the trade. "It wasn't the yelling I minded so much, or the occasional cuff," he said, pouring a couple of ouzos. "You expected that from a master in those days. But the first time we anchored in Piraeús – it was afternoon – off he goes to his *kafeneío*. He'd promised to bring me supper – we'd had nothing since leaving the island before dawn – but midnight came and went. I was so hungry I cried, curled up in a blanket on the deck. When he finally rolled in, he threw me a couple of pieces of bread and fell into his bunk. The next day – another eight, ten hours without food. When I got home, I ate like a seagull. Glok! Glok!" After a few such voyages, although fortified with *paximádia*, rusks, and cheese from his mother, Yiórgos gave up his dream to be a captain the old-fashioned way and went to marine school instead. Making his fortune, he settled down to run an *ouzerí* on the harbor. "The old bastard never had any intention of training anyone other than his son to sail with him. All the so-called apprentices were just cheap labor." Then the only son was injured and had to give up the trade. So Linárdos was left with no one to even keep him company. "Serves him right, old pirate."

Although Linárdos looked like a pirate, if he had engaged in any illicit activity it was more likely to have been smuggling than piracy. Trading and smuggling in the Mediterranean, especially in the Eastern Aegean, are all but synonymous, or at least they were in the old days. While the distances from island to island, island to mainland, even mainland to mainland are short – in some places less than an hour by small boat – a number of governments claim territory and, somewhat futilely, national waters. Governments being famous for control of imports and taxation, it is not surprising that one government may tax or otherwise control what the other doesn't – the one cigarettes, the other salt, for example. As well, as in licit trade, one place produces or has a surplus of necessities or luxuries another doesn't. This might be pottery in Mytilíni and eggs or beef in Aivalik, whatever can be bought for little in one location and sold for a profit in another. Both opportunities can provide an excellent living for those with initiative and good *kaíkis*.

William Travis discovered in the 1960s that on Sými, an island close to the Turkish mainland, "Many fishermen . . . go out and set lines and attend nets every night of the year." They never caught a single fish but engaged in smuggling, taking over Nescafe and bringing back Turkish coffee! "A seemingly ridiculous trade on which a smuggler can live, and yet it is so. Apart from this they bring back eggs, nuts, tobacco, livestock, and, of all things, antique furniture. . . and they take matches, cartridges, paint and kitchen utensils."

Nearly twenty years later, when I lived in Turkey, the situation was the exact opposite: Nescafe we could get by standing in line at the government store for several hours on certain days, but Turkish coffee was not to be had, except on the black market at outrageous prices. This lack was grievous to the ordinary Turk. Old Seyyid, the night gatekeeper of the school, occasionally accepted a cup of instant from my colleague Ruth, but he would sigh deeply. It was not *coffee*. When, after taking my winter break in Greece, I brought back (legally!) a shopping bag full of the right stuff and presented him with a couple of packets, tears welled up in his old eyes. Such a scarcity is the very font and soul of smuggling. I would not have been at all surprised if an acquaintance of mine, an elderly Turk who spoke Greek and presided over a café in a seaside village in view of the islands of Sámos and Chíos, had been able to offer his favorite customers a tiny cup of "*glyko-varí*," hot, strong and oh so sweet to the deprived Turks.

Fishing, trading, smuggling – the sea has always provided a living of some sort. A means of communication, it is also a means of escape and a safety valve. Even though families on this island tend to be small – there are few in the present with more than three children – the land has never, not even in Classical times, been able to support all of its children. In times of severe economic depression, millions of Greeks have emigrated. Archilochus, the first classical poet, in the seventh century B.C. led Páros islanders to colonize a more northern island, Thásos. The colonies of Magna Graecia were located first on the shores of Italy and Asia Minor, especially around the Black Sea, then in North Africa and southern Europe, and millennia later other parts of Africa, America, and Australia. The losses of loved ones, even when seen as opportunities for prosperity, are heartbreaking to the villagers. Emigration – exile – is such a common phenomenon that there is an entire genre of folk and popular music devoted to it. In one chantey, the chorus – "*Éyia móla, éyia lésa*" – indicates that it is a seaman's working song, but it is his wife or mother who cries, alternately cursing and flattering the means of his exile:

> *O Sea! From all waters and rivers you drink*
> *And leave us none of our menfolk.*
> > *Éyia móla, éyia lésa*
> > *Sea, you deceiver!*

Curse you, Sea! What have I done to you
That you keep my man so long in the foreign land?
. . .

O heavenly Sea, with your bright blue waves,
Bring my love back to me so I may sigh no more.

It is quintessentially Greek that this song of desperate longing is a lively *syrtós*, danced by the singers with their arms around each other, the mourning and vitality both acknowledged and comforted in the communal embrace.

But the sea that takes some islanders away beyond the Gates of Hercules never to return is generous enough to offer an alternative: Greece is probably the font and source of most of the world's commercial shipping, whatever flags the ships fly. A great many young men "go with the ships," as they say, in the maritime or commercial navy. Some go for a few years – to gather capital, perhaps, for a tractor or a piece of land or a sister's dowry – while others study in the maritime academies to be officers – captains, engineers, pursers. These seafarers travel the world's oceans, but in their hearts and those of their families they have not left home. For the years of their traveling, the slim resources of the village are spared. However, both seamen and families hope that their wanderers make their fortunes, come home, and settle down, and all pray daily to the Panagía that the men will not be food for "black fish" in foreign waters.

This Sea, this magnificent, more-than-goddess of jade and sapphire, holds in her watery embrace her hundreds of children, her rocky islands crusted with white villages and teeming with life – animal, human, and vegetable. She is a fascinating but willful mother with immense power to birth and to drown, to enrich and to impoverish, to isolate and to join. Like her winds she is capricious, one day a bountiful mother filling nets with silver riches and the next a Fury, a *maenad*, seeming to take revenge on those who live by her and on her, just as they take her for granted, just as they believe that she loves them. Yet, despite her willfulness, if anywhere in the world there is an island-born Greek living out of sight of the Sea, of any sea (though the others are not the same, never the same), in his heart he yearns to return, to ride on her bosom to his native isle, to be rocked by her waves, to taste once again her salt, gaze on her mutable beauty.

The Agorá

In the summers, I lived in the countryside and bought my food from the farmers: Lélla for dark, chewy bread and Panayiótis for strong light wine; Anna and Pantelís for tomatoes and peppers and onions; Iakoumís for melons and mint. In the winters, I moved into the village. Then my delight was to shop in the *agorá*, or marketplace, a dozen or so shops concentrated along two or three streets that stretched from the *platía* to the harbor.

The *platía* was the commercial center of the village. Here were located the police station, the telephone office, a couple of tobacco kiosks, a bakery, a sweet shop, a dry goods store, and a china shop, some of which had homes above them. Here the buses and taxis coming from the *hóra* discharged their passengers; here trucks just arrived from Piraeús on the ferry unloaded their cargoes, which were then trundled by hand truck to homes and shops, or loaded onto the green taxi trucks to be driven out to the farms. A large eucalyptus tree shaded the *platía*, and under it, when the weather allowed, those with leisure sat on straw-bottomed chairs, sipping coffee, exchanging views on the events of the day – prices for grapes and olive oil, engagements and scandals, taxes, aches and pains, and above all the government.

Houses in this village are two-storied: traditionally, the family lives in the upper story and the bottom is an *apothíki* or storage place, often opening beneath an unrailed stone staircase. This space can easily be turned into a shop, *magazí* ; in fact, both words mean "storehouse." As well, many families, forgoing the *apothíki*, had refurbished the street-level room as a *salóni*, living room, or kitchen. In the days before tourism (before every ground-floor room turned into a boutique, travel agency, or gewgaw shop), probably every other space in the *agorá* was a private home opening directly onto the street, so a walk there was a social as well as a shopping event. A shopper was never too busy to greet Lemoniá sweeping her porch or to stop to admire (but not too much) Chrissoúla's new grandchild. Only a few stores were purpose-built or remodeled with large glass windows; even these were used more for light than display, since everyone knew what each store stocked.

Most shops were very simply furnished with a few shelves, a table or counter, a refrigerator case if necessary, and always a chair or two for storekeeper and customers. The simplicity allowed people to open and close shops fairly easily. When Soúla's daughter in Athens was expecting a third baby and needed her, the grandmother almost overnight closed up her produce shop and rented it to a fisherman for his *apothíki*. When she later rented it to a jeweler, still no alterations were necessary.

Shops were (and are still) small, but space for goods is expanded by using the outside, even the streets. Dresses, feedbags, and buckets may hang on hooks beside the door of the shop. A *pezoúli*, a stone bench built into the street side of both houses and shops, offers a place to display baskets of potatoes or oranges, toys or sports shoes. At my favorite greengrocery, Pípis, the son of my Lággeri friends Anna and Pantelís, would pile his produce crates up a stone staircase on the street, creating a step-pyramid of pale green winter melons, white cabbages, and yellow lemons nesting in their black-green leaves. Sun-sensitive lettuces and greens and feathery fresh dill he would place on the *pezoúli* of the little church of Ayía Ekaterína opposite, taking advantage of its shade.

In the days before tourism transformed the village, and most severely the *agorá*, to walk with basket or bag in hand through the market streets was to feast your senses. First to strike the eye were the *mánavika*. Most of the common village names for market shops and jobs are derived from Turkish: *manav, hasap, bakal* – greengrocer, butcher, grocer – although the signs above the shops are in pure, old-fashioned Greek. (In Turkey, to balance things out, most of the names of fish are Greek!) At the *manávika*, perhaps Manólis' or Pípis', the displays of brilliant vegetables – scarlet tomatoes, emerald beans, purple eggplants, rose-blushed blood oranges – heaped up in baskets lined with glossy green lemon leaves and backed by snow-white walls, were as beautiful as any Cezanne, more ephemeral and more delicious.

Hanging over the baskets in which the farmers had that very day brought their produce in on mule or donkey, the shoppers – I among them – would draw in fragrances of orange, dill, celery, and mint. Not only was sniffing the produce perfectly acceptable, but the *manávis* would often pick off a leaf and crush it under your nose, or tap a Crenshaw melon for your judgment. Greens and spinach, leeks and scallions, were perky and crisp, dusted with good soil; eggplants were sleek as slipper satin. Was any vegetable or piece of fruit the least bit wilted, the *manávis* would hear about it from irate housewives.

When my basket was full, it looked like a painting and was a joy to carry. Sometimes I would be stopped by a villager and my basket examined: "Who has these small carrots? How much? Does he have any fennel?" Part of the thrill was the seasonal nature of the produce. What consolation for the waning of the strawberries was the arrival of the delicious peaches!

How our sorrow for the peaches' passing was assuaged by the discovery of the luscious melons, and in their turn, the ruby-red grapes, the pomegranates, the quinces, the mandarins, the blood oranges! How exciting, after a summer with no greens, to come upon the first spinach, the first lettuce! I'll never forget how a friend pounded on my door one October day to tell me, breathlessly, "There's cabbage at Manólis'!" I grabbed my purse and ran!

After heaping your basket with produce, you might make your way to the *bakáliko*, the grocery store. Up a few steps from the street, the large one-room shop was crammed with wonderful things. Wooden shelves were stacked with shiny, red-and-gold-enameled cans of tomato puree, tins of olive oil in gold and green, cans of peaches or figs with portraits of the fruit on the labels, half-kilo cakes of green soap impressed with cameos of classical gods or olive trees, and salt herring packed in tins hand-painted with scenes of boats and fishing. Around the shop would be wicker or rope-bound demijohns of *soúma* (the local *ouzo*), barrels of "cognac," boxes of *halvás* (if it were Lent), wooden crates of salt cod. Pickled vegetables and olives filled shiny twenty-liter tins, while salted capers were visible in huge glass jars. Flour and sugar and legumes of all kinds, from lentils to *gígantes* (dried beans), were housed in bins. Most things were sold loose, poured into copper measuring cups, scooped up by tin or wooden scoops, or plucked out by tongs cut from cane.

Anything you cast your eye on you were invited to taste, from olives – fruity green ones, pointed black Kalamátas, bitter-rich dried *throúmbes* – to cheeses of many kinds from creamy fresh *mitzíthra* to piquant oil-cured *graviéra*. You bought exactly what you needed: a hundred grams of butter, a few tablespoons of tomato paste, just enough baking powder or soda or sugar to make your cake. You brought your own bottles for oil or cognac. Your purchases were weighed on small cast-iron scales where the weight was equal when two dragons kissed! The grocer accurately added up all your items – ten, twenty – in his or her head, only using an adding machine for verification.

Your next destination in the *agorá* might be the *hasápiko*, the butcher shop. Traditionally, the wooden parts of an *hasápiko* were painted in shiny, pale blue enamel, and the butcher himself wore a long red apron. Rose and white joints of meat hung from hooks in the ceiling of the open, unheated shop, so scrupulously clean that only the faintest odor might remind you of what you were buying. Anything you chose would be laid out on the olive wood block for your close inspection, then cut or ground especially for you. Most likely, the animals would be local, raised under the close supervision of, and slaughtered humanely by, the butcher himself in a practice similar to the kosher and *halál* traditions.

If it was fish and not meat you were after, you would wend your way to the harbor, to the *psarádiko*, the fishmonger's, where lying on ice in the wooden boxes the fishermen had packed their catches in only hours before, you would find myriad silver, silver-blue, and rose-colored fishes, all giving off not a "fishy" smell but the tangy aroma of the sea. What you would never find for sale were the shellfish – sea urchins, winkles, even lobster – for these were the fisherman's perks, given as gifts maybe but never sold.

At the end of the *agorá*, across from the new church, you would walk into a cloud of one of the most heavenly aromas on earth – that of baking bread. This was the neighborhood of the *foúrnos*, or bakery, where bread and rolls were baked twice a day in a wood-fired oven and tumbled into baskets set in the doorway. The bread was so crusty and delicious that it was a discipline to get it home un-nibbled on. If it was nearly midmorning, you might be jostled by people bustling toward you on the narrow streets, great round or long loaves of crusty bread under their arms. Others might be rushing past you, holding pans of chicken and potatoes or stuffed tomatoes and zucchini, to be baked in the residual heat of the wood-fired stone oven after the last bread was removed. I loved taking food to be baked in the village oven. Whether it was a casserole of stuffed manicotti, an oregano-rubbed chicken, or a yoghurt and almond cake, everything was always perfectly cooked.

If sweets were what you had in mind, you went to the sweet shop in the *platía* where Grigóris and Evangelía made and sold not only traditional Greek pastries such as *baklavás* and the shredded-wheat-like *kataífi* but French-type millefeuilles and napoleons. There you could also buy sheets of freshly rolled-out *phýllo* to make your own spinach or cheese pies. If you hungered for yoghurt or *kréma*, a sort of pudding, you went to Chrístos' milk store, but you had to go early. Chrístos, a quiet, rotund man with a complexion rosy as an English milkmaid's, made only so many small containers of each and, smiling sweetly, refused all bribes to either make more or save one or two for late risers. To the astonishment of tourists, he took off every August, seemingly untempted by the thought of cashing in on the "season." If you missed out at Chrístos', you might double back to the harbor café, where Yiórgos and Margaríta made rice pudding so divine that, when Yiórgos' varicose veins finally forced them to sell the café, mourning was universal. Margaríta was generous with the recipe, but, somehow, the pudding others made from it was never more than a memory of hers.

Two shops catering to women occupied spaces in the *platía*: in one you could buy soft goods – embroidery supplies, nightgowns, and baby clothes; in the other, china and glass. This last was considered a *príka* or dowry shop; it carried only fancy goods, but most households, *kafeneíos*, and *tavernas* all over the island used the same common faceted glasses and plain white plates. Tariffs at this time were too high for ordinary people to afford imported items.

At one time there was also in the *platía* a dark little hardware store, where every square inch from floor to ceiling was jammed with mattocks and adzes, files and nails, bins of seed and bags of fertilizer (chemical, with no instructions in Greek), paints, rope, nets, hooks, and other gear necessary to farmers and fishermen. It was run by an elderly man who might once have been a sponge diver, as he was deeply bent. The shop was very much a male preserve. Once, when I went in to buy some nails, the conversation of the owner and his half-a-dozen cronies, their rheumy old eyes glued on me, stopped dead as he counted out my nails and wrapped them in a twist of newspaper. As I left I could almost hear the group exhale.

Another sort of store was the *pantopoleío*, or "everything store." At the end of the *agorá*, on the street ascending to the Panagía, the old church, was such a store that sold "everything" from groceries to fancy lamps to yard goods to heaters. The owner was famous as a *tsingoúnis* – not a miser exactly, but what my down-Maine friends would call very "near." Anxious not to lose out on any possible purchase, he was always asking a customer, "Where did you buy that? How much?" Once, when I'd been away for some years, I went in to get some cookies. While I was choosing, I could see him staring at me, wringing his hands. As I approached the cash desk, he burst out with it: "That friend of yours, Alda, left owing me money." I was a little startled: it was at least five years since Alda had left, very ill, in a hurry. However, she was a dear friend and I readily offered to clear her account. "One jar of Nescafe," he said. Fearing I wouldn't believe him, he reached under the desk for his large, cloth-bound ledger, leafed through the pages, and showed me the account. "I'm only charging the original price," he said, "not today's price." As I handed over the drachmas, about three dollars worth, I remarked that he had a prodigious memory. He seemed pleased.

Greeks have the habit of tapping their wine glasses on the table before drinking; this is because wine "looks good, feels good, smells good, and tastes good" but doesn't make a sound! The *agorá*, however, with the same good qualities of wine, had plenty of sounds: the oooling of the wind on a winter morning, the crash of the waves against the jetty, the good-morn-

ings and how-are-you's from everyone you passed: "*Kaliméra! Ti kaneis?*"
In the early morning, you could hear the musical calls of the itinerant
manávis as he and his sloe-eyed donkey clip-clopped their way through the
streets: "*Melitzánes ého, domátesého, sélino kai ánitho! Ola frésca, óla órima!
Fáte to ároma!*" "I have eggplants, I have tomatoes, celery and dill! All
fresh, all ripe! Eat the aroma!"

The *agorá* in the *hóra* was much larger than the one in the village. Its
main street was nearly a mile long, and several shorter ones diverged from
it. It wound slowly down streets fronted by elegant Venetian and neoclas-
sic houses with marble staircases and balconies railed with wrought iron
griffins and held up by marble scrolls. The offerings of this *agorá* were
more varied and numerous. However, before Greece entered the Common
Market, it was rich with objects typical of Greece, even specific to the islands. Hanging from poles outside the shops would be canvas bags, white
or pieced from multi-colored scraps of awnings or sails, ostensibly to carry
masons' tools but useful for shopping and storing dry foods such as *paximádia*, rusks, and lentils; red-and-black striped goat-hair bags for farmers
to carry their lunches or their mule's to the fields; and odd bags plaited
of rope that turned out to be donkey muzzles. Leaning against the whitewashed walls of hardware stores were rectangular, slant-sided washtubs,
skáfes, of wood or galvanized steel, and the trapezoidal wooden washboards
that fit them. On an adjacent *pezoúli* you might see olive wood mortars and
pestles and many sizes of the round baking pans, *tapsiá* (aluminum, alas,
the superior copper ones having already disappeared in the war or into antique stores).
Nearby on the street would be stacks of nearly conical metal buckets
and coils of hemp rope. Inside were wooden kegs of nails sold by the gram
(you needed five nails, you bought five nails). Tools were there in plenty,
including several sizes of the most characteristic farm tool, the mattock,
which required skill to use and did a hundred jobs well. For these and all
other tools, there were replacement handles. I remembered this recently
when, back in the States, I broke the wooden handle of an expensive
shovel; there was no way to replace it, the less durable part of the tool, and
so the steel blade and shank went sadly, wastefully, into the landfill.
When you entered the largest grocery store, that of Yiórgos Marínos
(called by the natives "George the Foreigner" because his father had come
from Sýros forty years before), your eyes were drawn immediately to the
ceiling, where from the rafters hung baskets in sizes from tiny to enormous, wicker or rope-covered bottles in sizes from one kilo to demijohn,

short-handled straw brooms, and the once-familiar string mops. Yiórgos was especially friendly and helpful. When I entered, he would pull out a chair for me, and then rush around filling my order, dipping olives, slicing salami, weighing flour. Sometimes – from a foreigner – such orders were confusing. Once after consulting my dictionary, I asked for *dáphni*, bay leaves, and was surprised when Yiórgos looked puzzled. But after a moment's hesitation, he leaned out the door and called to one of the old men who were always sitting on chairs in the street outside the store. One man got up and went away, and returned a little while later, to the amusement of the street sitters, with a large tree branch covered with – bay leaves! "Next time," Yiórgos said, "you can just go and pick them yourself in the public garden!"

If it was wine you were in search of, you went to the wine shop, where wooden barrels of black, red, and white native wine, resinated and unresinated, rested high on scaffolding near the ceiling. There you also had to bring a container (one of the wicker-handled green glass bottles was best for carrying). The shopkeeper would climb up a ladder to draw the wine, using a copper can, and, after offering you a mouthful in a small glass, measure your choice into your own bottle. Buying bottled wine (it was possible, but not there) was a sign of ignorance. In the village, there was no wine shop as such; you simply found out who was selling, maybe Andónis of the tobacco shop, and made a private arrangement.

A shop in the *hóra* that I loved to browse in specialized in pottery and terra-cotta ware brought from Síphnos, a neighboring island. There were conical, pie-crust-edged flower pots; *stamniá*, flat-bottomed cousins of the classical *amphóras*, decorated with designs in whitewash, in which to store and cool water; large and small *youvétsia* for baking casseroles; and the special narrow-necked pots for the overnight cooking of chickpeas on Lenten Fridays. A mysterious four-foot-long truncated cone of terra cotta turned out to be a beehive, one to be set laterally into a stone wall or bank, a holdover from Graeco-Roman days. Also, one could order (with no certainty of ever receiving them) *píthoi*, hand-thrown storage jars large enough to stand in.

Another favorite was Michális Pólos' fabric store. There you could buy the colorfully striped island sheet material (you had to hem it and make the pillow cases yourself) and choose among a wonderful array of dress fabrics – from flannel-backed cotton for the plain housecoats called *róbas*, worn by every housewife on the island, to elegant wool challis. Michális also supported local weavers and knitters, so it was there I bought my still-prized handspun, handwoven wool bedspread, or *hrámi*.

The *agorás*, both village and *hóra*, were treasuries of craftsmen and artisans; almost everything an islander needed was made and sold there. One found tinsmiths, tailors, shoemakers, blacksmiths, saddle makers, furniture makers, carpenters, butchers who made sausages, café owners who made fresh yoghurt and rice puddings, bakers of bread and pitas, and bakers of pastries. (Oh, the delicious *galatoboúreko*, a farina custard surrounded by *phýllo* and soaked in honey!) Numerous barbers kept the men well-shaven and shorn, and hairdressers kept women well-coifed. Since not every home had hot water, a shampoo or shave was a much-appreciated small luxury.

While some ready-made clothing was available, it was cheap and unstylish, so most people, men and women, had their clothes made either by tailors, who cut and sewed in their shops on the *agorá*, or by dressmakers who did the same in their homes. Tailors were plentiful in both *hóra* and village. I remember, when I was new to the island, how struck I was by the general nattiness of the men; a retired *kaíki* captain looked to me like a banker on holiday, with his carefully trimmed snow white hair and mustache, white hand-knit sweater and socks, well-fitting black pin-striped flannel trousers. To work in, not just bankers and bureaucrats but builders and fishermen wore wool suits that fit. Soon I realized that nowhere in *hóra* or village could a man buy trousers or a jacket ready made. If he wanted clothes, work or dress, he went, like an English lord or the mayor of San Francisco, to a tailor, who made him clothes that would last long enough to be buried in, if he didn't gain too much weight.

These clothes were, as they aged, carefully mended; if patches were needed, they were done with such care in the matching of fabric as to be unnoticeable. Imagine the astonishment of the islanders when the hippies came through, with their deliberately torn and ostentatiously patched jeans and raveling sweaters. And imagine the puzzlement of generous landladies whose offers to trim and hem ragged cuffs and darn holey sweaters were rebuffed. "It's the style," I tried to explain to Kyría Marína. "It's a waste," she replied, unimpressed. The native young men, however, looked so elegant in their tailor-mades that, if a male tourist stayed long enough, he inevitably crept off to a tailor to bespeak his first (and possibly only) made-to-measure trousers and maybe a matching vest.

To clothe women there were seamstresses in every street and lane. Like the tailors, they had been apprentices, learning to draft patterns with ruler and T-square. The packaged patterns with their "standard" sizes the foreigners sometimes brought them were a great puzzle to these gifted women; they started from the customer's own measurements and perhaps a photograph of a suit or dress in a fashion magazine, which most could copy exactly. Like the tailors, however, they were dedicated to fit, especially around bust and waist, and would have none of the smocklike evasions I favored. "They'll think you're pregnant," Koúla would say disapprovingly.

"Well," I would reply, "let them wait nine months and see." But I always lost the battle, winding up with a dress beautifully cut and finished (rows of tiny buttons with a rosebud centered on each one, or a border of handmade lace) but definitely tight-waisted. "Now that," she would say with satisfaction, "is a Greek dress."

As well as dressmakers, there were semiprofessional knitters, crocheters, lacemakers, and weavers, though these latter were by no means as numerous as they once were. I visited a farm woman who showed me an assemblage of wooden dowels plastered into the wall of a stable. "What do you suppose it is?" she asked, mystified. I immediately recognized it as a warping board, a very clever one which could wind possibly hundreds of meters of thread for yardage or rag rugs. But for some reason, the war perhaps, the woman did not recognize one of the basic tools of weaving. And when a skill skips a generation, it is most likely lost, unless it is revived as an art form. The eremitic nun Antonia, who in a pre-monastic life had studied design, was the only weaver left in the area of the village, and she sold her products mostly to sophisticated tourist shops. Village women did knit, however; every toddler was completely knitted up from booties to pom-pom'ed cap, every school child wore a handmade sweater under jacket or school uniform, and it was a rare outdoor worker who wasn't wearing "next the skin" a fanélla, a tough but delicately decorated sweater made from handspun wool whose sleeves are knit from the shoulders out so that, when the elbows wear through, the sleeves can be unraveled and knit up again. Passing into obscurity even then was the light wool zóni, a knitted cummerbund wrapped over trousers and shirt to protect back and kidneys from the cold.

The agorá of the hóra boasted several workshops of workers in metal: tin, iron, and gold. Yiórgos the tinsmith, or fanarás, had a shop full of light metal objects, most of which he fashioned himself, cutting, rolling, folding, and soldering sheets of tinned steel to make baking pans, scoops for flour and feed, buckets (adapted from twenty-liter oil or petrol cans), and fanária – tin and screen cages which, hung from a ceiling, protected food and drying cheeses from mice and flies. From brass or tin he made bríkia for boiling up "Byzantine" coffee and compartmented boxes to hold the coffee and sugar. Here too beekeepers could find necessary implements: a tin and leather smoker (which burned cow pies) and long wire hooks for removing honeycombs from the terra cotta hives. No less useful were the leaded glass sconces for vigil lights and the ingenious little lanterns, *fanarákia*, whose small oil cans slid so securely into a clasp that you could swing them jauntily from a finger as you wended your way home along a dark country path. If he liked you, Yiórgos would make you candlesticks or mirror frames decorated with tin flowers bobbing on wires. By profession a tinsmith, by hobby he was a dancer, having in his youth danced on his small delicate feet in several national folk dance companies. When Yiórgos danced a *hasápiko* with the young men, his restraint and wit would put them to shame; he said more with a single small step than they with all their high kicks.

The *yíftos*, the "gypsy" or blacksmith, was another metalworker, who at his forge made tools for farm and fishing boat, plain or fancy gates for courtyards, hinges for doors, bars and locks for securing them, and shelf supports to pound into stone and plaster walls. The *yíftos*, with his need for massive, immobile equipment like a forge and anvils, is unlikely to have been an actual gypsy; Greek gypsies are still largely nomadic, coming and going among islands and mainland to make baskets, sharpen knives, sell cheap blankets and pirated music tapes, and, yes, beg and tell fortunes. I remember once seeing their black, probably goat-hair tents along the highway near the Corinth canal. But though they came regularly to the village, they were not welcome, and none would find there a permanent home. Possibly it was the heat of the forge and the iron oxide blackening the ironworker's face that gave rise to the nickname, since it is the gray-ish-tan skin that physically distinguishes the gypsies from the general run of Greeks.

Of the workers in metal, my favorite was Kýrios Yiánnis, the eighty-three-year-old goldsmith. Not for him the propane or acetylene torches, though they were available; he soldered necklaces and earrings with a small blowpipe and an alcohol lamp, sitting at his semi-circular antique jeweler's bench with its hand-turned railing. Wedding rings he made or remade by pressing an original into cuttlefish bone, melting the gold in a tiny crucible, pouring it into the mold attached to a harness, and swinging the whole vigorously around his balding head. In the back of his shop he had a bench for drawing wire, which he taught me to use. Silver and gold sheet he rolled from ingots of reclaimed metal using a small, hand-operated rolling machine. From the sheet he made *támata*, votive offerings with images of eyes and hearts; arms, legs, and ears; men, women, children, and cows. He allowed me to have his chasing and repoussé tools copied at the machine shop, though he gently informed me that part of his own training, seventy years before, had been to file his own tools by hand.

To my mind the most amazing artisans on the island – after all, even in America there are tailors and seamstresses, goldsmiths and the occasional blacksmith – were the shoemakers, shoemakers who actually made shoes. From the ceilings of their usually tiny shops hung cascades of lasts – toeless wooden feet – on which they would make to order the farmer's sturdy, rough suede T-strap sandals or boots or, astonishingly, dress shoes – shiny black lace-ups with pointed toes for men and the traditional Cuban-heeled Mary Janes for women. Around one such shop in the *hóra*, situated on a sort of plinth at a Y in the main street, a fringe of dozens of gleaming black shoes along the curb gave the shop the look of a prosperous mosque! Bárba Nikolís made me a pair of farmer's sandals, pointing out their virtue of being too tough for vipers to bite through. I wore them winter and summer for years; they were not even worn when I abandoned them in some transoceanic move, thinking that I would get another pair when I returned to the island in a year or so. But by the time I did get back, the shoemakers had vanished, even the ones who could, with awl and knife, bring back to life a frail but beloved pair of manufactured pumps. The shoemakers had disappeared, the shops were full of cheap factory-made shoes, and the farmers were having to make do with plastic imitations of the T-straps, which cracked their heels and split, becoming useless trash in a year.

In those days, not only could someone make for you almost anything you needed (excepting underwear, but even furniture, traditional or modern), but almost anything you had could be repaired. The shoemakers resoled shoes; Kýrio Yiánnis recast worn-through wedding rings; certain ladies mended nylon stockings; tailors and seamstresses took in, let out, and patched; welders mended iron bedsteads and plows; coopers repaired barrels; builders replaced roofs; boat builders replanked and caulked *kaíkis*. Even mechanics did not depend on "Athens" for simple parts for tractors and cars, but often machined their own. Filling in the gaps, certain specialists in repairs debarked from the ferry from time to time: the knife sharpener with his wheel on his shoulder and the *psathás* with a bundle of straw on his would call through the streets, looking for blades to hone and straw-bottomed chairs to mend. Once I met a man sitting at a café table who was holding a strange instrument like a gigantic one-string harp; he turned out to be Bárba Thomás, the mattress re-fluffer!

Shopping in the *agorá* I would touch a hundred people – touch and greet. It is a custom to speak to everyone every time you see them. *"Káliméra!" "Kalóstin-e!" "Hiérete!"* Even if you pass Eléni three times in your rounds from bakery to *bakáliko*, you are expected to greet her; otherwise, she will think you are mad at her or snobbish. Less brief meetings were always accompanied with an exchange. As I inspected the pomegranates, I would inquire after Pípis' mother and send greetings. As I paid for my crackers and cheese and pickles, the grocer and I would discuss his son's progress in learning English. At the bakery, I would learn who had just had a baby or announced a pregnancy, and sometimes who had died, for whom the *kambána*, the death knell, had rung that morning. While cutting my pork chops, the butcher might ask me to translate a letter from Social Security for an elderly relative. Somewhere along the way I would collect a recipe for spinach rice or, in grape harvest time, be offered a spoonful of *moustalevriá*, grape must pudding, to share in the harvest. So ingrained became this habit of greeting, that when I returned to the United States after five years on the island and went to do a course in a small college, I felt hurt and uncared for when my classmates saw me and didn't greet me or inquire after my welfare every time they saw me. I missed my "strokes" – the *Ti kaneis? Hiérete! Pos eisai?* – that said I mattered.

The *agorás* are not the same now. Tourists flood the narrow streets, so that one cannot see or call to friends or acquaintances. Tourist businesses have pre-empted most of the *apothíkis*, the stores, and the street-level homes of the *agorá*, displacing small merchants like greengrocers who can't afford the high rents. The *kafeneíos* have been so taken over by loud, half-naked foreigners that the elderly men have had to make a "club" in the back streets just to have a quiet place to read the newspaper and play *távli*. Probably three-quarters of the shops in the market streets are now restaurants, boutiques, travel agencies, and art galleries, and they all close from October to May. Then, although the (many fewer) neighbors become visible, the streets feel blind, with so many windows shuttered and doors locked.

Perhaps the *agorá* of the village was not so august as the one in Athens, with its marble stoa where Socrates paced about, quizzing his students on rhetoric and metaphysics (and possibly helping himself to an occasional apple from the greengrocer's). But with its oranges and peppers brilliant against sun-drenched white walls, its arbors of purple bougainvillea spanning the narrow streets, its aromas of baking bread mixed with the incense emanating from an open chapel, and most important, its human contact, the village *agorá* was not simply a place to buy things, but a place where every simple human need – for food, for wine, for friendliness – was met, day after day, year after year

III

Autumn

Autumn is an end and a beginning.

The land is as summer left it, summer with its sun white as molten platinum and relentless, glaucous sky devoid of even the memory of clouds. All summer, Dímitra, the goddess of growing things, has wandered the rocky paths of grief, searching for her lost Perséphone. Distraught, she cares not whether her plants live or die. Her tears salt them and they wither.

Autumn inherits this death from summer. The pale ochre hills are made paler by their cover of blond scrub: thyme naked of leaves or flowers, dried thistles sharp as paper, Queen Anne's lace bleached and spectral, wild sesame blowing with every breeze and loosing the last of its seeds. The oregano has flowered and dried, the sage also, its honeycomb seedpods shaken empty. All is tan, ecru, cream, bone.

The sun has leached from the land every color but a pallid reflection of its own – almost every color. The dark yellow sandstone, country rock and scree, of the hills is striped and shadowed by the gray of rock walls, stairstepping down from the summits. Here and there on the terraces, a few olive trees shimmer silver-green. The only strong color on this paleness is the dark green lacquer of *skinári*, low doming evergreen shrubs, and the occasional brighter green of caper bushes springing from the walls, their flowering done, their buds and seeds safely gathered and pickled. Sparsely scattered over the fallow hillside fields, the tall white plumes of sea squills spring from leafless bulbs, seemingly the only surviving flower in the landscape. And yet, hidden in the semi-shade of the *skinári*, clumps of delicate pink and magenta cyclamen rise from the stony earth. We have survived the blast of summer, they seem to say, and so shall all.

In this landscape of few trees, and most of those not deciduous – cypresses, cedars, citrus – autumn is not called fall, but *phthinóporo*, the waning of the fruit. Gone with the summer days are the peaches – the sensual, dripping, orange-fleshed *yiarmádes*, the delicate white *rhodákina*; gone the liquescent apricots; long gone the strawberries, almost gone the melons, the cool green ones, the golden, the peach-colored. Tucked away here and there in a north room, saved for a hot day in November or February, is a watermelon or two. They do keep, but they are not the same, never the same as the fresh, sweet ones still warm from the sun, split with a sharp crack in a July field, offered like a sweet translucent shish kabob on the end of a knife. This is not good apple or pear country, lacking the frost necessary for sweetness and bite, though here and there in an orchard stands a banana apple, grown for its curious taste. Of the orchard fruits, all that are left are the quinces, the late figs, and the pomegranates – a fruit which rarely falls from the tree, but in its rosy ripeness clings to leafless black branches, splits open to provide a feast of sweet garnet seeds for birds.

Despite the aridity of the landscape, however, life for land and people is beginning again. The year, the agricultural year, begins in September. According to the old folk calendar, New Year's Day is September first. No matter that emperors and politicians have proclaimed the New Year to be in January, the farmers know the old year ends with the wheat safely reaped, threshed, and stored, and the new one begins with the *trígos*, the harvesting of the grapes and pressing of the new wine. Some old-timers call the months by their old names: September is *Trigítis*, the Harvester, October *Spárto*, the Sowing.

While the hills and fields surrounding the village are still summer-struck and lifeless, in the village itself autumn is a brilliant time. As the cooler night air no longer draws up mist from the sea, the clearer light brings out colors bright and clear as flags. The sky is Greek-flag blue, clouds Greek-flag and whitewash white, sun yellow as marigolds that from their streetside gardens return the compliment. The sea outfits itself in sailor's navy, with here and there the white trim of foam on the wavelets. In the bright but not blinding light, shutters and doors flash intense blues and greens and occasional reds against the sparkling whiteness of walls.

Autumn is the time the village turns in upon itself again, becomes family, claims its own after the distractions of summer: the hordes of tourists clotting the *tavernas* and *kafeneios*; the housefuls of relatives sleeping in every conceivable corner. With the visitors embarked (the brother's family back to Australia, the students to Athens and Berkeley, the foreign tourists to the four corners of the world), the village begins a whirlwind of activity, like a hostess whose guests, though beloved, have stayed a little too long, keeping her from her cleaning and other chores. In a great Monday-morning bustle, out come the mattresses and blankets to be draped over the balconies, out come the buckets of whitewash to brighten the summer-worn streets, into the river go the sheets and rugs to be scrubbed and dried in the still hot but no longer searing sun. The autumn winds cooperate in the cleaning, blowing fresh but not-yet-chilly gusts through the narrow streets, flapping the sheets on the lines, fluffing the newly washed pillows and fleecy *flokátis* until every trace of suntan oil, siesta sweat, and the greasy smokes of spitted lamb and grilled fish are blown up the mountain or out to sea.

Houses and streets, no longer thronged with people and masked with signboards, revert to their natural shapes and uses: *pensión* and boutique are once again Anna's house and Manólis the grocer's storeroom. The village wakes and stretches itself. The walls of houses grow taller; streets curl and meander. Churches reappear, are opened; frankincense drifts out the unlocked doors. Unshuttered windows pour out the voices of housewives at their work calling to each other: "Asími, come help me turn these mattresses!"

The villagers walk the streets, greeting each other like long-lost cousins: "Myrtó, *yia sou!* How was your godmother? The children? Good, good." "My poor brother-in-law! The life he lives in New Jersey! He told me. . ." "Thanks be to God, it's not like that with us, e?" With the clearing of the sky, the neighboring islands, in summer obscured by mists and involved with their own visitors, wake up, appear, move in, beckon: "Winter's coming. Come closer and keep us warm!"

Down at the harbor, those fishermen who've spent the summer ferrying tourists to the beaches unbolt the benches from their *kaíkis,* dip them in the sea (sighing over a whiff of Bain du Soleil), shove them into the recesses of their *apothikis* and take up their abandoned nets. Even the cats, after miaouling pitifully around the shuttered *tavernas* for a few days, give up and slink back to the *apothikis* to crouch behind sacks of still-warm wheat and get on with mousing.

On such a day in October, when the air was clear as glass and the wind sharp, after shopping in the *hóra,* I boarded a bus and greeted the driver, Pétros, a villager. I was surprised that there were so few passengers and among them none I knew. When the bus turned off the main road and followed a steep winding road, I realized I had taken the wrong bus.

"No matter," said Pétros, "after I deliver some packages at the end of the line, I'm going home." We climbed and climbed, zigzagging up the mountain, losing passengers all the way, until we reached the end of the road high up on the north face of the mountain. On the veranda of a house above the road, a woman waited. Pétros took her packages – meat, by the look of them – and climbed the stairs. In a minute he called down, "Come up! You have to see this!" When I, panting, reached the veranda, the woman took me silently by the shoulders and turned me northward. From this near-summit, the mountain fell away steeply. Below us, in an arc from west to east, encompassing six or eight square miles, was spread out the entire *koinótita*, community, of Náousa. To the west stretched out the peninsula of Kolymbíthres with its strangely contorted rock formations, which sheltered a three-mile-long bay. Immediately below us was the village, its three hills of miniature white boxes and blue domes, its *platía* and harbor, situated at the center of a gigantic bay scalloped by smaller bays. From the village the clusters of houses thinned out on all sides to become scattered farmhouses with their orchards and vineyards, their fields and threshing circles.

"Look," said Pétros, gesturing left then right, "there's Kamáres, then Ksifára where my family farm is."

"And there's Lággeri, where I lived on Panayiótis' farm two years ago." The tiny island of Oikonómos seemed tucked into the crab-claws of two peninsulas which nearly closed the larger bay. Due east lay the strait between this island and Náxos. In the crystalline air, I could not only see the clusters of farm buildings, some resting on small crescents of terrace, but tiny people going to and from farmhouse and storehouse, plowing a field with a mule and a cow, hauling brush in a little red tractor. A green three-wheeler truck buzzed along the inland road from Ambelás, carrying a single steer to the slaughterhouse in the village. The air was so clear one could almost hear the music from the truck's cassette player, almost imagine the driver beating time on the steering wheel. But dominating the view was the sea, sapphire today with wisps of whitecaps. Seven islands I counted: Tínos, Mýkonos, tiny Dílos, large and mountainous Náxos, then in the distance but still visible, Skinoússa and Donoússa off the north end of Amorgós.

For a minute or two, we stood, still, gazing in silence at the serene world spread out beyond us. It didn't matter to the others that this view was always in their eyes. They knew it for what it was. Then Petros motioned toward the bus. I took leave of the woman who had given me this gift, and descended.

Corn, Wine, and Oil

Autumn is weather for work – in the fields, on the sea, the beach – when little breezes slightly cool but never stiffen working muscles. And there is work to do: the fields must be plowed and wheat sown, grapes harvested and crushed, olives gathered and pressed. The three crops are the Biblical corn (that is, wheat), wine, and oil, the solid base of Mediterranean life. Were times to get tough (and they have often been so), a person could live healthily on bread, wine, and oil. Of course, a few olives, some cheese, onions (who could live without onions?), a tomato here and there, honey, lamb, fish – these are not frills exactly, but without the Three, life, the mysterious unity of body and spirit, cannot be long sustained.

Corn, wine, and oil are not only food for the body, but for the spirit. Bread and wine are central to most Mediterranean religions. The communal consumption of bread and wine found in the Christian Eucharist derives from a practice of Judaism before the temple was destroyed by the Romans, now observed at home in the family *seder*. Because it grows stale as time passes, bread, a Jewish scholar told me, represents temporality, the sweet life we have now, vulnerable, waning, and, therefore to be cherished day by day. Wine, because with time it increases in beauty and power, represents eternity, the invisible and incomprehensible that we must always keep our eyes and mind on. At his last seder with his friends, Jesus took the same humble materials and reinterpreted them in personal terms: the bread his temporary body from which he would soon pass, the wine his blood which he would shed in a willing sacrifice to ensure eternity for all.

Bread and wine are especially symbolic in the Orthodox church because each is created by a metamorphosis. To be changed into bread and wine, wheat and grapes must undergo death and decay. Just as the original substances achieve a new physical form, a heightened existence through the natural processes of mortality, so when Jesus, who also experienced metamorphosis, comes to earth again, human beings, after their own deaths and dissolution, will all be transformed, will live a new life in new bodies in a world itself transfigured. It is for this reason that Orthodox Christians bury their dead without embalming, so the body can undergo the same natural processes that result in bread and wine, and so be recreated in a higher form.

Bread is not only consumed in the Eucharist, but offered as a sacrifice. On holy days special to them, villagers order a round loaf from the bakery.

It is the same bread baked and eaten every day, only the baker, saying a prayer, marks it with a special wooden stamp. The villager then takes it to church, where with other loaves it is piled on a table by the altar and blessed by the priest. With this blessing, the bread undergoes a symbolic transformation, changing its name from the demotic *psomí* to the ancient *ártos*. Cut up with a curved knife they say is the same as those used in ancient animal sacrifices, the bread is first offered in the Eucharist; later, at the church door, it is distributed to the churchgoers, who may eat it on the way home or take it to someone unable to attend Communion. On Áyios Modéstos' day, this bread is taken back to the farms and fed to the animals, blessing them as well as humans.

Oil has a different function in religion, but an equally long history. Mixed with myrrh, aloes, and other spices (and blessed by the Patriarch), it becomes *mýron* or *chrísma*, the substance used for anointing a sick person, a child at baptism, or a priest or bishop at his ordination. Each anointment signifies sanctification of the anointee's life. This use of oil is another inheritance from the Judaism of Jesus' time, and he himself is called the Christ, the Anointed One.

Oil as well as bread is a sacrifice. Bottles, green glass or plastic, of the best oil are brought to church by the villagers on their special festivals; the oil is used to fill the *kandília*, the hanging lamps that illuminate the ikons. If the gods have gifted us with bread and wine, they themselves have always preferred smoke, the least material substance. Homer tells us that when animals were sacrificed to the gods, only the fat parts were burned, the fragrant smoke ascending to Olympus. The flesh was roasted and eaten by humans. Since Christianity, animals have been replaced as burnt offerings by oil lamps and candles. Every little country chapel has a cupboard containing a bottle of oil, floating corks with wicks, and incense (another favorite of gods past and present). Often when I would walk out into the country with the *mamí*, after visiting a patient of hers, we would end up at a little church, unlocked in those innocent days. We would open door and windows to air it out, sweep the floor, fill and light the *kandília*, burn some incense, kiss the ikons, and make some coffee; there was almost always an alcohol burner and a couple of cups in a country chapel. We would then walk home, having done a good deed, gotten some fresh air and exercise, and made some contact with the Eternal.

Every grave also has at its head a little glass cupboard, containing the same things – oil, lamps, incense and a burner, along with a photograph of the *makarítis*, the dear departed. When Thanásis took me to clean his mother's grave the day before Good Friday, we scrubbed the marble tomb, rinsed it, filled and lit the little lamps, censed the Ajax-scented air, then sat casually on the tombs and smoked, speaking of our dead. A few yards away, his young niece was doing the same for her grandfather.

Oil is also used in healing. When a villager is ill, the priest goes along to the house, and, praying with the invalid all the while, rubs the *mýron* into the ailing body. This is not extreme unction, reserved for the dying, but a healing one, partly because the oil is blessed and partly because even unblessed oil is a folk remedy equal to none: To remove sea urchin spines from the feet, to ease the ache of sore muscles or the stretched feeling of a pregnant belly, massage the affected parts with olive oil. To counteract scorpion bites, rub the wound with oil in which a scorpion has been preserved. To treat an earache, warm oil and bathe the ear, then heat salt in a pan, pour into a clean cloth or sock and tie it around the head.

Among the words that have positive meanings in Greek and negative in other languages is *latherós*, oily. Many Greek vegetable dishes are cooked (not fried) in oil, a method that retains nutrients that would be lost in water cooking. The oiliness of Greek food gives rise to piteous complaints from most foreigners, who shake their forks over their plates like a kitten stepping in a puddle. That's because they don't understand the relation between oil and bread. More than half of one's meal should be fresh, crusty bread made from unbleached flour sopped into the delicious oily sauce of, say, eggplant Imam, redolent with garlic, onions, and fresh tomatoes. A village table of the recent past probably boasted of meat not more than once a week, fish and shellfish more often, with the predominant nourishment being bread and well-spiced vegetarian dishes and salads, all cooked in or dressed with rich, fruity olive oil.

Wine as well as oil is food. Wine as blood is not empty symbolism. Here the soil has little iron, and the grapes, particularly the dark ones that make *mávro*, the sweet black wine (white wine is a drink; *mávro* is Wine), concentrate iron. To build up the blood, drink *mávro*. Mersiniá pulls down her daughter Anna's eyelids: "Your lids are pale. You're anemic. Drink more *mávro*." Old people are also exhorted to drink *mávro*, but have no doubt, it is no soft drink, although its strength varies with its age and the taste of its maker. Aristotle said that a man cannot get drunk on *mávro* – not because it's not strong enough, I think he means, but because it creates the best *kéfi*, gaiety or high spirits, the classical *enthousiasmós* – the "being filled with god" – that Greeks since Dionysos have been famous for. *Mávro's* sweetness feeds sugar into the muscles so thoroughly exercised in dancing; its strength lifts the spirit, as the body lifts its arms and legs and voice, leaping and crying (still) "*Évghe!*" or more likely "*Opa!*"

Bread is the earthly body, wine the blood – the animator, like the blood which Odysseus offered to the dead that they might speak. Wine releases the spirit. Every day at dinner after hard labor, it releases communion with companions, including children, and then allows the tired body to rest, releasing the spirit to the privacy of dreams. This is the moderate use of wine. The occasional immoderate use of wine is for *panigýria*, celebrations.

Trígos

Before there can be celebrating, however, the wine must made – the grapes must be picked and crushed, the must barreled and "worked." In September, the entire village is caught up in the *trígos*, the grape harvest. Every day the vineyard owners go out and check the grapes and exchange news at the *kafeneío*:

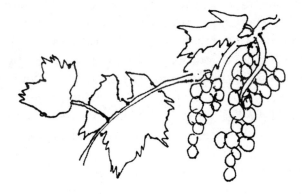

"Ready?"
"Not yet? Yours?"
"Another few days . . ."
"Will it rain?"
"Maybe." And the men shift in their chairs, pull at their mustaches. Hardly a soul exists who does not own some part of a vineyard or share with a sibling. The inheritance laws, under which children must inherit equally from their parents, have left an agricultural landscape cut up into small fields, orchards, and vineyards, and most who inherit vineyards tend them. Grapes are not a great deal of trouble, requiring only pruning once a

year, occasional hoeing or plowing, and picking. Those without a piece of land will trade labor, usually picking, for a share in the crop.

This labor, though brief, is painful. Throughout the village, people walk with their hands clapped to their aching backs, looking like divers with the bends. The old men sitting in the *platía*, exempt by age from this chore, call out, "*Trigoússes, e?*" "Been picking, huh?" And knock their canes on the flagstones, chuckling. After the treading, when the first of the *moústos*, must, has been made into *moustalevriá*, a sort of pudding, shopkeepers and housewives lean out their doors, offering spoonfuls of it to symbolically share the harvest with as many people as possible.

For several weeks in September, gentle donkeys with their backs heavy-laden by two or even four tall baskets of grapes will plod slowly along the roads, while trucks heaped with grapes careen madly through the *platía*, as though fueled by the not-yet-made wine. The donkeys are headed for *patitíria*, the small stone tanks for crushing found in many fields and vineyards, while the trucks are usually on their way to the farmers' co-op or the commercial press in the *hóra*, where Greek grapes are crushed, sucked through huge hoses into tankers standing in the harbor, and sailed off to become French wine. This trend has been reduced in recent years, since the new owner of an old local winery has begun to produce and export excellent native-style wines. The growers used to say, "The crop this year is poor. Let's sell it to Moraítis." Now they say, "Is this crop good enough for Moraítis?"

It's a return to tradition, this making of good wine for export. Páros has been famous for wine since before Classical times, but the culture of vines has waxed and waned with the availability of hands to tend them. When pirates ranged the Aegean, the low-lying settlements may have been abandoned. But in the twelfth century, the well-armed Venetians, conquerors of many of the Aegean islands and archtraders of the Mediterranean, occupied the island; they planted extensive vineyards and commercialized the trade in wine. How long this prosperity lasted into the era of Ottoman rule is unknown. But there have always been ups and downs. Stávros, the vice president of the village, remembers that in his childhood, in the nineteen twenties and thirties, the terraces on all faces of the mountains seemed one great vineyard rising to the sky, but the Second World War and the Civil War that followed caused many villagers to emigrate, and the vines (and the olives as well) died, fell prey to disease, and were cut up for firewood.

In the bay of Lággeri, there is a little cove whose beach and bottom are covered with terra cotta shards: rims of jars, handles, pieces of oil lamps that once looked like miniature teapots, fragments of the conical bottoms of amphóras. The shards are a jumbled timeline of Páros' wine trade: one fragment may be Early Cycladic – three to five thousand years old – the next Hellenistic, yet another, as Dimítris the archaeologist said, "only Roman."

How much wine was actually produced at any one time is hard to estimate now, but the terracing with stone walls of what seems every available inch of land in the hills suggests that at one time or another the trade was extensive.

"How old are the terraces?" I asked Dimítris.

Old, he said. Thousands of years. "There are pre-Cycladic stones in some of the walls." Like the shards in the bay, over three thousand years before Christ.

It would be nice to think that the Parian wine of today is the same enjoyed by the Ancient Greeks, who so admired and respected their wine that while drinking it, they wore wreaths of fragrant flowers on their heads, specific flowers to complement specific wines. But this is unlikely. In the first century A.D., the Roman conquerors of the island needed to supply wine and other comestibles to the soldiers and administrators of the Empire. The more soldiers Rome kept in Greece or Africa, the fewer farmers remained in Italy to supply their needs. What vines they planted (or forced the islanders to plant and tend) are unknown, but some of the shards of amphóras were "only Roman."

More than a thousand years later, came the Venetians, who took their wine seriously, sending to Venice for their favorite vines. They may have replaced native vines with the commercially viable *mandilariá*, a red or "black" grape. The climate is not really suited to the *mandilariá*; it is at once too dry and too humid – but in the last seven or eight hundred years, the islanders have adapted to the *mandilariá* and made it the base of their famous *mávro*, mixing it with the must of another Venetian introduction, *monemvasiá*. A white grape, *savatianó*, was not widely planted until after World War II, when the islanders began making *retsína*. And other varieties most probably have been imported and planted by curious and creative vintners. Still, even the Venetians couldn't check every vineyard, and somewhere high on a mountainside terrace, there may grow the great-great-grandclone of the vine that grew the grape that made the wine that caused the sculptor Skopas (a frequent visitor to the marble side of the island) to tip his wreath and sigh.

Before tourism claimed every spare space for restaurants and boutiques, before the little stretch of sand on the other side of the harbor was transformed into a proper marina for large fishing boats and yachts, the community *káva*, where much of the population kept its wine, occupied a large storehouse on the quay between the harbor and the beach. Early in September, the owners of the barrels stored in the *káva* – some tiny, some as large as rooms – would empty the remains of last year's wine into demijohns, then roll the barrels out onto the beach, scrub them inside and out with seawater and sand, and leave them to dry in the sun. If a barrel needed a new top or hoop, it would get rolled over to the nearby shop of the coffin-maker, who doubled as cooper. The barrels lying on the sand were very attractive to children, but the cooper/coffin-maker, old and grumpy, kept an eye on the beach, and though his threats and curses added to the fun of hiding in the great barrels and rolling the small ones, he and the fishermen mending their nets on the quay usually managed to protect the precious barrels. Fortunately, the kids were in school most of the time and most of the barrels survived their games. Any kid actually fouling or damaging a barrel would have "eaten wood" from his father, as the oaken barrels were, on this timberless island, hard to get and expensive, imported from Crete or France. The crowd of barrels on the beach, more than the brightness of the sky, more than the departure of the swallows, announced the end of the year, of last year's vintage, and the advent of the new.

Trígos takes place generally around Tou Stavroú, the festival of the Holy Cross in the middle of September, the time of the grapes' readiness depending on whether the vineyard is high or low, west- or north-facing. It's a nervous and exhilarating time. Rain must not fall on the ripe grapes or the sugar will not rise and the yeasts will wash off. But it is always almost time for the rains to come. Labor too is a balancing act: when the grapes are ripe, the farmer must have a crew ready to pick at a day's, even a few hours' notice. For that reason, few hire pickers; instead, to augment the crews of immediate family and neighbors, relatives from Athens and Piraeús take a few days vacation from their regular jobs to pick and crush the grapes. They can wait out a slow sugaring and work from dawn to dark if need be. Their reward will be a share in the wine, the *spitikó*, or homemade, wine so much more prized than any commercially bottled variety.

Picking grapes is backbreaking work. Here the vines aren't usually trellised, because the strong winds would parch the tender shoots; instead they are pruned to grow very low to the ground. I went to pick black grapes one day. It wasn't my first *trígos*: I had picked "blond" grapes a few days before in a vineyard that was in fact trellised because it was ringed round with a windbreak of cypress trees. In spite of that, I'd had the "bends" for a day or two but was assured that the best remedy was to keep at it. So I'd volunteered to pick for a family who had a low-lying field along the road to the main town next to the church of the Holy Apostles. The days were short but still hot, so Anárghiros the farmer knocked on my door well before dawn. I grabbed my new sharp folding knife and a wide straw hat and jumped on the tractor. As we chugged out of the village, Anárghiros stopped for another woman, also straw-hatted. "*Pas yia trígo, Annió?*" he called, "Going to cut grapes?" The merry woman with a golden smile hopped on the opposite fender of the blue tractor. She'd come from the town just to pick, not for the money, which is little, but for the holiday in the sun! "Like a tourist," she laughs. "E! I have three children, so my summers are no holiday! Now I'll sleep at my cousin's, and then on Ayíou Andréa, when they open the barrels, I'll take my pay in wine. Pray it doesn't rain," she said seriously, for if it were to, all our work, all the farmer's work, would be in vain.

A holiday? If I'd known! The dawn hours were cool and sweet. About ten people were in the field, Annió and I the only women. To cut these ground-hugging black grapes, we had to bend low, catch the bunch in one hand and cut the stem with the other. The grapes were hot to the touch, sticky with sugar, and the smell was rich. As I went to taste one, however, Annió giggled: "Stop! They're still dusted with sulphur! You'll fart like a sow!" She also warned me to rustle the bush with a bit of cane, lest a snake be coiled *kouloúra-kouloúra*, round and round the vine, seeking shade.

Bend and cut. Bend and cut. We laid the bunches on scraps of plastic, tarpaulins, newspapers. "The grapes must lie so for a few days," she said, "and look at the sun, which draws out the sugar."

Bend and cut. Bend and cut. I felt muscles in my back and legs I never knew existed. Some of the workers were singing, but gradually they stopped. Soon the singing was that of wasps, who had scented the sugary grapes and were fighting us for them. The leaves gave off a prickly dust, maybe the velvet fuzz on the leaves that was so soft in the spring. With a scarf, I wrapped my hair and face against sun, dust, wasps, and sweat.

By half past nine, we'd only been working three hours but Annió saw I was flagging. "*Ela!*" she said. "Let's go light candles at Ayíon Apóstolon, for the *trígos*! We can make coffee there."

The cool dark of the little church rested the eyes, but suddenly I was drenched in sweat; though it was blazingly hot outside, the breeze had dried the sweat on our bodies, a kind of natural air conditioning. Annió, who had already lit her candle and crossed herself, found an alcohol burner and made us two little glasses of sweet coffee. Back in the vineyard, she turned anxiously and said, "You did pray for it not to rain?"

"I forgot but I promise I'll go tonight in the village and light a candle at Ai Yiánni."

Bend and cut. We worked for another two hours. About noon, up rode Anárghiros' uncle on a donkey with its panniers stuffed with our lunch. From the small house in the vineyard where we had dumped our things, he brought out boards and trestles and chairs, setting them up under a tree. Then he covered the table with a cloth and set it with plates, glasses, and cutlery. Out of the panniers came pots and pots of food: turkey roasted with potatoes, tomato salad, olives, cheese, even white grapes (washed), bread. And wine, *mávro* of course, and cool water he drew from the well. After such a meal, though I ate a third of what the others did, I felt pole-axed. Fortunately, the little house contained a number of cots and mattresses, even sheets. Annió and I took pallets out under a mulberry tree, leaving the house to the men, who would assuredly snore. I slept like the dead for two hours, until a booted foot, Anárghiros', prodded me awake. Then it was back to bend and cut, bend and cut until nearly dark.

By early evening, the vineyard was completely harvested. The grapes lay in dark, shiny heaps between the rows, framed by the vines with the beautiful green palmate leaves like open hands. A field, in the golden evening light, of a myriad hands offering fruit – to us or the sky?

The sky it seems. Dropping with fatigue that evening, I forgot my promise to light a candle. During the night of the second day, it rained, rained on the piles of grapes, dark as blueberries, lying on the pale hard earth, only hours to go before being crushed. The short hard rain washed the sugar and yeast from the grape skins. One day of rain, and a whole year's vintage weakened, wasted – the *moústos* thick with earth, the sugaring aborted. There would be wine, but it would be weak in taste and strength. Poor wine, poor Anárghiros, poor Annió! I felt like a jinx. Ironically, it was the only rain of a long, dry September.

Neither of the vineyards I had picked had offered the opportunity to tread. The white grapes had gone to the co-op to be sold to a factory, and I was too heartbroken about the fate of the black ones to go back for the treading. However, soon I heard that Panayiótis, my former farm neighbor and the maker of the most famous wine in the area, was about to crush. So I hitched a ride out to Lággeri where he had his seaside vineyard.

I'd seen the treading at other vineyards. The grapes, usually in the tall cane baskets called *kofínia*, are dumped into a *patitíri*. Often built into a *mándra*, a rock wall, in a corner of the vineyard, the *patitíri* is a square, white-washed stone box, usually measuring about a meter deep and two to three meters to a side. On one side a pit allows a barrel to be placed just beneath a lipped opening at floor level. The grapes are tipped in from *kofínia* and weighted with stones. Then, a few days later, in go the treaders.

Some tread barefoot, washing their feet carefully; some go booted, because of the twigs, the greedy wasps, and other dangers. Then they tread, tread, tread, walking around and around. The odor rises, mixing with the autumn air. The mash smells not like wine, yet stronger than grapes – raisiny.

Tread, tread, tread. The level of the grapes drops, the farmer keeps pushing them around with a clean broom, tipping in more baskets. The dark red liquid, the *moústos*, flows slowly through its escape hole into one plastic barrel after another. These lightweight barrels have been a godsend; formerly, the *moústos* was transported to its fermenting place, either storehouse or cool room, either in wooden barrels, impossibly heavy for man and mule, or in cleaned goat or lamb skins, which were light and portable but left an odor in the wine if the journey was long. The barrels when full are hoisted up onto mule or truck, and taken to a storehouse where the *moústos* is poured into clean oak barrels, to bubble and sigh until judged to have "become." To make *mávro*, the vintner puts back some of the grape skins for a few days.

"How do you know when the wine is ready?" I asked my friend Thanásis.

"You can hear it working in the barrels. When we were kids, we used to go into the *káva* and listen to the knocking. We'd scare the little ones, saying there were devils in the barrels. But anyway, forty days. We draw off a taste of the new wine and close the barrel at forty days."

"In Tínos, they float an egg in the barrel before they close it. When the egg shows the size of a *táliro*, for red wine, or a *dífranco* for white, then it's ready." *Táliro* and *dífranco* are five- and two-drachma coins.

"Too complicated, " said Thanásis. "Forty days." Some people have thermometers, he said, but rarely use them.

At forty days then, the barrels are tapped and the new wine sampled. And the vintner knows whether a year's work of plowing, pruning, picking, treading, and barreling has yielded a year's pleasure or disappointment.

I never got to tread at Panayiótis'. Arriving at the house, I inquired of his wife, old Styllianí, where the *patitíri* was.

"Why?" she asked suspiciously.

"I'd like to help tread."

She regarded me sourly. "Women," she stated flatly, "do not tread grapes." She looked back to the melon rinds she was cutting up for chicken food. "And anyway, they've finished." Disconsolate, I started home by the sea path and ran into Panayiótis' son-in-law, Aristídis. Sure enough, he and his daughters were washing out the grape baskets in the sea. Out in the bay in his skiff, Panayiótis was rowing the barrels back across to their landing.

I accepted Aristídis' consolatory offer of a cigarette and sat on the edge of the *patitíri*. The grape residue was loaded down with large slabs of slate. This had only one meaning. "So you're going to make *soúma?*" *Soúma*, elsewhere called *tsípouro* or *tsipoúra*, is an ouzo-like liquor distilled from the skins and stalks remaining after the must has been pressed out. Aristídis smiled. Yes, he was going to distill for the first time in several years. Home distilling had been outlawed by the Junta, the military government which had just fallen. For a bunch of village boys, the Juntists had made some inexplicable political errors, unifying their own Resistance by outlawing both home-ground flour and home-distilled liquor along with the poetry of Ritsos and the music of Theodorakis. The farmers, who might have been indifferent to a censored press and muffled intellectuals, were enraged at the abrogation of their traditional rights. Most probably, they never thought of these natural practices as rights until they were outlawed. The Junta fell in summer of 1974, a result of its attempt to assassinate Archbishop Makarios, president of Cyprus, an act that invited the Turkish invasion of Cyprus.

The fall-out was bittersweet: Cyprus was invaded and occupied; Greece was free. And Aristídis and others would be dragging their copper kettles and tubing out from behind the splintered wooden plows, broken demijohns, unraveled baskets, and rotting sacks in their *apothíkis*. And the rivalry would begin: "Yéro Nikólas makes a decent *soúma*."

"Too sweet."

"Too dry."

"His *soúma*'s all right but he puts chemicals in his wine." A defamatory statement. A man who would put chemical preservatives in wine couldn't be trusted with your wallet or your daughter for a minute.

Whether pine resin, *retsína*, is a preservative or not, and how, when, and why it came to be added to Greek wine is a matter of disputation among oinologists, archaeologists, and folklorists. Locally, it's a matter of taste; some do, some don't. Purists think it's citified, not native. Resin is only added to white, rose, and light red wines, never to *mávro*. My own feeling is that pine resin is a flavor that Greeks (generally and historically) like, just as they like the flavors of mastic (a sap from a bush grown on Chíos), fennel (a taste they share with the Italians), and rose (a favorite with Turks and other Middle Easterners) and don't like the flavor of violet (French). Basil, manna to Italians, is not considered edible in Greece.

"What are you doing with all that basil you tease out of me," said Bárba Minás, "eating it?"

"Of course," I answered, puzzled.

"*Vre paidí mou!*" he expostulated. "Basil is a flower!"

On getting back to the village after my fiasco with Panayiótis' grapes, I tackled Stávros, a progressive politician and farmer as well as grocer. "What is this about women not treading grapes?"

"Superstition."

"Why?"

"E," he said, trying not to look embarrassed, his blue eyes round as drachmas under their white brows. "They say that, well, a woman might be, hmm, 'unclean,' you know? And then the wine would sour."

"Do you believe that?"

"Oh, no! Once I was crushing in my *patitíri* and two Swedish girls came by, and I let them tread."

"And?"

"As a matter of fact, the wine went sour, but I'm sure it wasn't the girls' fault."

Wine making is both a traditional art and a creative one; specific recipes – blends of types of grapes and their proportions – are jealously guarded secrets, which cry out to be discovered. "Hmm," said a particular connoisseur, staring after an old man riding a mule down the main road, "That's Bárba Yiánnis coming down from Lefkes with a goatskin full of must. I wonder . . ." However, my friend Tásos, a gentle and pious man, used no art. His small vineyard was planted with several varieties and all the grapes went into the wine. One year one kind of vine would yield more or sweeter grapes, the next year another fared better. Of his wine, he would say, "God blends it." His new wine that year was delicious: rosy-colored, light as new wine is, neither sweet nor dry, like the juice of a fruit you couldn't put a name to.

The usual practice on the island is to make a year's worth of wine. Only in exceptional circumstances is wine aged. Panayiótis' stomach trouble was such a reason. Sadly, everyone but he benefitted. I remember that wine, an unresinated white wine, copper in color, with the strength and sharpness of the old farmer himself. Beneath the surface lightness was something like the memory of brandy. I try now twenty-some years later to recapture the taste, the aroma of that extraordinary vintage, and all I come up with is the effects – the brilliance of the stars at night; the amazing bonhomie among strangers sitting quietly on the pier beside the lovely little family chapel with its buttresses rooted in the sea, the water of the cove gently lapping . . .

The Olive Harvest

The second great harvest of autumn, that of the olives, usually begins in October. The weather's still wonderful, bright blue and gold, cold in the shadows but warm in the sun. And the sudden squalls of rain are no threat to the oily little fruit that transforms itself into a multiplicity of delicious foods: olives themselves, green and black in brine (some use sea water); *throúmbes*, partly-dried ripe olives; and the miraculous oil.

The olive must be the most beautiful tree in the world. Other trees – the almond, the apricot – have a flash of beauty in the spring with their maidenly blossoming of pinks and whites. The pomegranate boasts a spectacular flower, a "skirt" of orange chiffon and long anthers of bright red, but its black trunk is rough and spindly. The olive conserves its beauty – the flowers are tiny and nearly invisible – and expresses itself quietly in subdued color and shape. It becomes more beautiful with age. The ages of trees are legendary – three, four hundred years? More! Impossible to tell until the tree finally dies and the rings can be counted.

The color of the long, slim, delicate leaves, which seem never to dry or fall, to be torn by winds, is almost indescribable. There is, in Greek, a color called glaucous, a gray-blue so pale as to be nearly transparent, the color of sea mist, of the sky in summer, of Athena's eyes. Change blue to green, and this is the color of the leaves you see while standing under the tree. Look down on a tree from above, and the color is greener but still silver. The crown is always in motion, shimmering against hill or sky. Watching an orchard from a hilltop is like watching the zephyr-ruffled sea from a cliff, all but mesmerizing.

The olives themselves grow along the length of the branches, interspersed with leaves. Not every branch bears fruit – maybe one in three. As the olives mature, they change from green to mauve to deep purple. As though the color were not enough, the shape of the olive tree is also amazing. Each trunk is a uniquely beautiful work of art: as the tree ages, it shapes its trunk into a sculpture. Wind, moisture, and terrain seem not to affect the way each tree divides itself, knots and twists, leans or reaches: trees identical at planting within fifteen or twenty years will be as different as a Brancusi from a Praxiteles. Most put me in mind of Michelangelo's half-finished slaves – the visible struggle of the material to achieve a shape, the design of the artist slowly manifesting.

No other tree in the world is so useful in so many ways to mankind. The olive was Athena's gift to the Athenians (whether she created it or borrowed it is uncertain), who built her the Parthenon in gratitude. But gratitude is offered every day in smaller ways by humbler folk, perhaps only a murmured prayer before eating. If the fruit is nutritious, the oil is more so, life-saving in some circumstances. The German Occupation caught Níkos and Eléni Kazantzakis while they were on a visit to the island of Aegina; put under house arrest, they would live there for four years. Food became extremely scarce. For the duration, there was no meat, no cheese, no milk, and at last no bread. Eléni found in the storeroom of the old house they were renting a huge *pithári* of olive oil. She spread the word quietly and, one by one, the children, the elderly, and the starving (more day by day) came to her door and were given a spoonful of oil. It lasted, I remember her saying, until almost the end of the war.

Like the grape harvest, the olive harvest is a time for hard but joyous work. Since October can still be hot, it is best to start at dawn or before, with the orchard lit by tractor lights. The first job is to spread out cloths under the trees to catch the little olives. In some parts of Greece, these olive cloths are a folk art, woven from goat hair for endurance, striped black and red, and bound in braid. But here a canvas – an old sail perhaps, or an awning – is sufficient. If the trees are old, the technique is to beat the branches with long poles, but when I picked for a young farmer, his trees, also young, were small enough that he and another worker could climb the trees and pick the top two-thirds while I sat in a chair and stripped the lower branches with a motion like milking a cow. Nikítas, the husband of the *mamí*, the midwife, was an accomplished singer and player of the *baglamá*; as he worked he sang, and the patter of the olives on the cloth mixed with the songs. One song spoke admiringly of the *eliá*, "olive," on the beloved's cheek, a dark mole considered a mark of beauty.

Nikítas and I picked all day, running from a brief rain and sheltering near the pigsty. "Fragrant, e?"

"More fragrant when cooked!"

As we filled the *kofínia*, the farmer took them to his mother, who dumped them into a wide shallow basket and carefully removed leaves and twigs. She separated the olives that would be pressed for oil from those that would be preserved for eating by soaking in barrels of brine. The brine for olives as well as for vegetables, peppers, and capers must be the exact saltiness of sea water, tested by floating an egg in it.

Next morning, the farmer hitched the wagon, crammed with *kofínia* filled with olives, to his tractor, and we drove the back way (longer but less steep) to the community press in Léfkes, a mountain village. Chugging uphill, we passed ancient terraces of vines and huge gnarled olive trees overhanging vertiginous abysses ("Like to pick those?"). For eons the only place on the island to grow olives commercially, Lefkes has the only steam-powered press, an enormous two-story affair that would make short work of a mere pickup load of olives. After weighing in, we walked around the uphill-downhill village, drank a coffee, went back in time to see his olives being layered up between huge rope mats, and, to deafening noise, pressed, the oil running out a gutter at the bottom. In the *hóra*, there remained for a while an ancient stone press, two huge wheel-shaped marble stones; the olives were spread on the mats in the same way, then the top stone was lowered, and a mule harnessed to it turned it round and round.

The farmer collected his oil and shoveled the residue into the wagon. This oily mash called *pyrína* used to be burned in braziers and bakery ovens, or boiled in caldrons to make the marvelous green soap. Now lucky cows and chickens fatten on it. Home-pressed oil is not much strained; the first, transparent pressing is kept for salads, and the subsequent ones, cloudy and darker in color and tasting of peanuts, are used for frying. "The first pressing is 'virgin?'"

"*Málista.*"

"What I buy in the States is called 'extra virgin.'"

"Where's it from?"

"Italy."

"*E lipon!* In Greece, *korítsi mou*, a virgin is a virgin. No degrees."

Panigýria

If Autumn is a time of hard work – harvesting, plowing, cutting brush for country hearths and ovens – it is also a time of many celebrations. In addition to national holidays, there are two types of traditional celebration – *yiortí* and *panigýri*. A *yiortí* is a holy day, commemorating either a saint or an event in the life of Christ, his mother the Panagía, or Áyios Ioánnis, St. John. The Greek Orthodox calendar is so crowded with saints and holy events that many days are three or four deep! With the exception of an occasional Achilléas or Aphrodíti, Greeks are mostly named for saints. Everyone who is named for a saint celebrates on that day instead of his or her birthday, so it seems that, almost every day, somewhere in the village – home, café, or *taverna* – sounds of music and laughter float out into the streets. These individual celebrations are different from the American-European birthday party in that the guests are not invited; rather one goes to the celebrator's house or favorite café to honor him or her, taking not material presents but sweets, snacks, and liqueurs to extend the hospitality.

In contrast, a *panigýri* is a festival for all: *pan* and *gyr* are old words, possibly Doric, *pan* meaning "all" and *gyr*, an old root for *agorá*, not "market" as now but "a public place." Ideally, all the people in the village celebrate together in one place, either the *platía* or the church courtyard. Alkis Raftis, a sociologist who studies dance, says, "The *panigýri* is a general mustering of the vital forces of the village." In the old days, every man, woman, and child had a place, based on age and gender, in the line of the dance that followed liturgy and feasting. This place was his or hers for ever (*older than Marigoúla, younger than Artémi*) and each dancer over a lifetime gradually worked his or her way to the front of the line and then – stepped into the boat of Háros, Charon the ferryman, to join, perhaps in dance, those who had gone before. The *panigýri* – the worshiping, feasting, and dancing together – defines the village. "Without it," Raftis says, "a village is no more than a cluster of houses."

Some holy days are so special that they are cosmic *yiortés*, celebrated everywhere in the Eastern churches on the same day. These are Christmas, *Pásca* or Easter, and the Dormition, "going to sleep," of the Panagía in August. Local *panigýria* honor a saint to whom a church in the village is dedicated. Náousa holds two official local *panigýria*: the Enniámera, nine days after the Dormition of the Panagía, and the day dedicated to the Beheading of St John, both in the late summer. However, two other celebrations meet the requirements for *panigýria* by tradition: *Ayíou Andréa* in the fall and the *Zoodóhos Pigi* just after *Pásca*. The celebrating churches are family ones, but all are welcome (and hundreds come) and in the old spirit, many families contribute to the feasts.

Whether *panigýri* or mere *yiortí*, the special day begins in the church dedicated to the saint (or holy event) with a service, called liturgy. Some saints celebrate in the morning and some in the evening, so some liturgies are sunlit and others conducted in darkness, with the gold and carmine of ikons winking and glowing in the lights from candles and oil lamps. The saint on his or her day is host or hostess to friends and family, who pitch in to make the day glorious. The day before, women decorate the church, wreathing the ikons with *stephánia*, garlands of leaves and flowers, strewing the floor with myrtle, and placing baskets of basil in the embrasures of windows. On the day, the celebrations inside and outside the church are complementary. Bells ring to announce the hour of liturgy, which is sung by the priest and several *psáltes*, cantors. In and out of the church the worshipers pass, lighting candles, kneeling and kissing the flower-bedecked ikons, crossing themselves – but dashing out from time to time to turn down the potatoes, run to the baker's for the *pastítsio*, see what those kids are up to.

After the liturgy, the ikon of the saint is sometimes disframed and carried on procession or litany, around the village, church to harbor to *platía* and back to church. The procession works in several ways, keeping the saint in the minds of the people and the people in the care of the saint. As well, it defines the village, like a ribbon or a belt drawing the people together. As the litany progresses, it may gather up those who have not made it to the service, bringing them along. After the ikon is returned to the church, attendance inside dwindles, though the chanters and the very old keep the priest company to the end. In the afternoon, after the end of the service, feasting begins.

What defines a *panigýri* is the inclusion of the entire village. Some major celebrations are sponsored by the *koinótita*, the community or township, who may hire a band and stake out the *platía* or the harbor or the largest *taverna* or hotel for a venue, as there is no longer a building that will hold the whole village. In the old days, however, after the liturgy, the entire community – men, women, children, and priest – assembled in the church courtyard. Tables would have been trundled up from the houses on handcarts, and loaded with a feast prepared by the villagers: pans of *moussaká* and *spanakópita*, gourds and green glass bottles of wine, baskets of fruit. There would be platters of stuffed grape leaves and salads of cucumber and tomatoes, and bowls of wild greens. Someone would have set up a charcoal grill and the oregano-scented smoke of *souvlákia* would be drifting into the noses of hungry people, already tearing into crusty loaves still warm from the oven, spearing juicy black and green olives, slicing cheeses – *féta*, *graviéra*, and *mizíthra*. The winemakers would be sampling each other's wine and toasting, "Eis *ygeía* " and "Hrónia *pollá*!" and always, "To next year, may we all be together!"

When the flesh was fortified, the dancing would begin. With a word to the musicians, if there were any – perhaps only a bagpipe, maybe a violin or even a lute – everyone would take his or her place in line: the men first from oldest to youngest, then the priest, then the women again from oldest to youngest. And thus united, having broken bread and sipped wine together in an earthly communion, they would dance.

Elsewhere, religion has set itself against the dance. Not here – at least, not successfully. One patriarch even encouraged dancing in the church itself. Religion and dance were one before Christ came to earth, before St. John created a theology out of a few words and a great silence. The pantheon, the habits of worship were in place: the *stephánia*, the litany, the *panigýri* are sculpted – in marble from this island – on the Parthenon and other ancient temples. The sequence remains: first, liturgy and litany, then, sensibly, food and drink, the consuming of sacrifices: bread and wine (and on Easter, the Paschal lamb). And to balance the lift of worship, to dedicate consumption of earth's gifts to another ascension of spirit, dancing.

Dancing

The first dance of a *panigýri* is always the *syrtós*. The most common and ancient, it is pictured in a frieze on the temple at Eleusis. The dancers, holding hands, dance in a line which progresses counterclockwise in an incomplete circle. A leader sets the pace, laying down the plain but not

simple steps (the beat is 4/4, but some steps are shorter than others). Then he or she plays with the line, perhaps leaping high or dropping down, twirling a handkerchief or pairing up with the next in line. The leader changes often, so everyone who wishes has a chance to show off a little. The *panigýri* is danced with reverence (but also with gaiety) for its ancient and present ability to join people together in a joy, a physical harmony. They dance, they say, when this harmony is reached, *"me to ídio pnévma,"* with the same breath.

Pnévma is also "spirit." A single spirit emanates from many bodies, ascending as far to Heaven as is possible in this life. In the *panigýri*, there is no separation of spirit from body. The liturgy, the ritual, the holy stories, the Eucharist elevate mind and heart; the sharing of food and wine brings this spirit down to earth. Wine elevates, food stabilizes, and dance makes use of both. In the integrated acts of celebration, the individual spirit rises to meet the community – the friends, relatives, neighbors, seen every day in circumstances of work, problems, disputes – in an intimacy that transcends the small and necessary barriers of everyday life. In wine, music and dancing, we share moments of communion with people with whom we do not, perhaps, share opinions or interests. We can eat and drink and dance and laugh with them and find in them something we can, somewhere inside, love.

The *syrtós* moves in circles, always in circles, but a circle never complete, because each round lifts the cycle of life into another dimension. The seasons go round and round: summer, fall, winter, spring, the same but never the same; the work goes round and round every day, the same yet never the same; the people go around the village every day, every month, every year – the same faces, and yet they too change: appear, bloom, shrivel, disappear.

We are bound to the turning earth, to the cycle of life, to birth and inevitable death; we are bound to these people around us – lovable, irritating, pleasant, hateful – bound by accident of birth, by obligation, by custom, by love. And there is no escape (unless you want really to escape; then you shatter the illusion and emigrate), no escape but in the dance. Round and round you go, moving with the clever and exquisite music. As you and your fellow dancers lift and contract the same muscles, you begin to breathe the same breath, become one body, as in those moments with a lover. And yet, suddenly you yourself, alone, are free, the leader of the line, and all are yours to tease, to challenge with your rhythm and your changes, until – having led and controlled, having created an artifact in time, unique and evanescent – you retire, satisfied, to submerge yourself into the line, the common body, to follow another leader, build another unity.

The islanders dance many dances beside the *syrtós*. *Kalamatianós* and *hasápiko sérviko* are line dances from other areas. *Bállos*, elsewhere danced in a line, is in Páros a couples dance. While *syrtós* is both restrained and social, *bállos* is as light and frothy as the waves on the summer sea, and open to individual style – whether restrained, lively, bold, or even wild. It is a dance of courtship: Both man and woman dance a simple box step, back and forth, back and forth, trying to match their strides. The man dances with his arms outstretched, as though wishing to encircle the woman. He may add a few twirls and kicks to the basic step to impress her. She dances demurely, eyes cast down and hands behind her back. They dance in a circle, not quite facing each other, the woman keeping the man just over her left shoulder, eluding him. They are feeling each other out: trying to match their rhythms, the length of their steps, their styles. And all the while she is not looking at him, concentrating on her turns and twirls, her eyes on the ground. And then – her eyes lift to his for an electric moment, the man explodes in a peacock display of leaping, and they are dancing side by side, in unison, achieving a harmony.

The lyrics of the music reflect the flirtatiousness: "I love a fisherman. . ."opens one traditional song; another wonders, "Which woman will he marry?" while a more modern one asks, "Maria in the yellow dress/ who do you love better – your husband or your neighbor?"

Styles of *bállos* on Páros were many. Both men and women in the mountain villages danced with large awkward strides, somewhat bent; they never seemed to co-ordinate. Men and women in the *hóra* often danced with an abstraction and demeanor of infinite boredom, perhaps to show that they were not peasants, since one of the characteristics of becoming middle class seems to be not dancing. But women in Náousa danced with delicacy and wit, twirling and lifting an arm or two, challenging the men, while men often incorporated high kicks and a sort of windmilling whirl, meeting the women's challenges.

Men also dance the *bállos* together, and then the flirtation is replaced by a dynamic of friendship with an element of competition. The partners find their rhythm, then they try to throw each other off, leaping and displaying. But before the end of the music they return to that harmonious unity, that *ídio pnévma*, which, whether of men and men or men and women, celebrates and strengthens the community.

Since *bállos* is a flirtation dance, you would think that lovers would dance with each other, but I discovered after a few seasons that the opposite was true; if we wanted to know who was "seeing" whom, we looked for people who were no longer dancing with each other. "Aha!" Alíki might say, "Tákis and Marína are not dancing with each other tonight. Do you suppose they are…?"

Music

Nisiótika, island music, is a distinct genre in Greece. It is like country music in the United States, which arose from English and Scottish ballads but continues today as composed music, picking up some new instruments (electric guitar) and themes (trucking) but always sticking to characteristic elements of its roots. The origins of Greek folk music are, Alkis Raftis says, most probably in ancient Greece, more surely in Byzantium, with influences from the conquering Venetians and later from Turkish music – although *its* roots are in Byzantine, Persian, and Arabic musical forms. The themes of modern *nisiótika* are the islands themselves, nostalgia for the village left behind, boats and fishing, and of course love – requited and unrequited. A typical *taverna* jukebox will offer a range of danceable *nisiótika* songs from traditional to modern. In one song, a wife asks her faithless husband, "Who's going to wash your *vraka*?" the long full britches worn many years ago, while in a newer song, the singer offers to get his lady "anything you want/ including a television."

The strong influence of Byzantine chant on Greek folk music was evident to me when I attended an all-night service in a small convent outside of the village. The liturgy, as sung by two nuns, sounded so much like island dance music I could hardly keep my feet still.

As the dances have specific steps on which the dancer may improvise, so island music generally has a stable melody from which the singer and/or players take off, very much like Western jazz. Unlike Western music, however, island music may make use of several modes or scales in one song. All the traditional instruments are tuneable, allowing for a wide choice of scales from European to Eastern. When Eastern elements show up in dance music, even if the rhythm says "*bállos*," dancers respond with "belly dance" gestures, resulting in a form of dance locally called *tsiftetélli-bállos*. Although most songs for both *syrtos* and *bállos* are in 2/4 or 4/4 time, some are 7/8, reflecting (or demanding) a sort of half-skip in the dance sequence. This was very hard to learn; I found the best way was to partake generously of the fruit of the vine and just give myself up to the common rhythm.

Violiá

Ah the *violiá*! the "violins," as the musicians are called. While some celebrations may depend upon a cassette player, a PA system, or a juke box, an official *panigýri* will most likely boast a group of musicians special to the islands. "Strangely enough," Alkis Raftis said, as we sipped wine in the harbor of Chíos one August evening, "the 'island' musicians are likely to be gypsies. It used to be that no ordinary Greek family wanted a child to be a musician. Parents were afraid he would never learn a respectable trade or earn a living, would just go from *panigýri* to *panigýri*, drinking and carousing. But if a child showed a consistent interest in music, they would give in and apprentice him to a craftsman, for instance, a blacksmith who also played an instrument. The blacksmith would teach the child smithery, but not music. That the child had to learn, without help, by copying his mentor's instrument and eavesdropping on him when he played. Gypsies have no such prejudice." The exception has been the Konitópoulos family of island musicians from Náxos. The father Yiórgos was a famous *nisiótika* composer and violinist, his sister Eléni Legaki an equally famous singer. Children and other relatives are also musicians.

Nisiótika music, like the dances, is light and quick in contrast to the heavy and deliberate music of the mountain areas, where the dances are often based on martial exercises. Island orchestras include at least one violin, a guitar or two, maybe a *bouzoúki* or a lute, maybe a *doubéki* or drum. The band makes its money from the dancers, who in their exuberance throw money at the feet of the musicians. The greater the *kéfi*, high spirits, the more money the musicians make.

The *violiá*, players and singers, are not so much performers as priests of a second liturgy. Once they begin playing, they will not stop for breath or food or drink (well, drink, yes) until, with the faint light of dawn, the last dancer drops with fatigue – all his money tossed in pride and gratitude to these creators of ecstasy, these Orpheuses – and the last tractor or motorcycle coughs or sputters and moves off slowly, carrying beings as exhausted and empty, as light and full of bliss as brides and bridegrooms, carrying them off to begin – without sleep – a workday driving buses, hauling nets, slaughtering and butchering beeves, baking bread, picking olives, boiling cheese milk, minding children, cooking dinner. At midday, yes, the weary celebrators will sink into oblivion, and in the evening, refreshed, will relive the happiness: "Po, po, po! What I drank!" "How Lámbis was danc- ing!" "Did you see Tína in her new green dress?"

Perhaps something has been lost now that the village has grown so much. The church courtyard can no longer hold the entire population of the village, and official *panigýria* – for which bands are hired – are usually held in the *platía* or the largest *tavérna*. But neither of these spaces can hold the multitude, so celebrations are scattered all over the village – in this *tavérna*, that hotel, the central *platía* or the harbor. Only a few *yiortés* are celebrated in the old way, with everyone contributing: the Zoodóhos Pigi in Lággeri and Ayíou Andréa in the mountains west of the village are celebrations of family churches, but Ayíou Ioánnou, in late August, is a real, old-fashioned *panigýri*. On this day, people, tables, chairs, food, and wine are loaded onto the *kaíkis* of the fishermen and sailed across the bay to the abandoned monastery dedicated to the poor beheaded Baptist. There in the waning summer night, the village enjoys its old-style *panigýri*. People bring and share the good things of summer – the last fruits, the last wine, on perhaps the last warm night of summer. And under the stars or by the light of the moon, they dance this year's last *syrtos*, hand holding hand, stepping together, breathing the same breath.

Tou Stavroú

Autumn's first important holy day is *Tou Stavroú*, the festival of the Holy Cross. This festival is special to country people because it has al- ways been this time of the year when annual contracts for shepherds, sharecroppers, and other laborers were renewed. Odd that it should be so, because the *yiortí* itself is associated with Ayía Eléni, Saint Helena, the mother of Constantine, the Roman Emperor whom she converted to Christianity and who, by moving the seat of the Roman Empire to Byzantium – Constantinople – effectively established what is now the Eastern Orthodox church. The day celebrates Ayía Eléni's finding the re- mains of the True Cross. The pious Eléni traveled extensively in her search for the Cross, stopping by this island, where she decreed the building of a church in the *hóra*. It was not actually built until some time later, by a student of the master architect of the Ayía Sophía. The master, it is said, was so jealous of the student's work that he pushed him off the roof! But there are many legends of builders contributing their blood to the fabric of their churches, and we can believe them or not as we choose. This church, dedicated to the Panagía, the Mother of God, though damaged and restored, still stands, the oldest church in Christendom in which the liturgy is still sung. Like its greater sister, Ayía Sophía, the jewel of Byzantium, it is large and elaborate with marble columns, carved and gilded wood screens, and glowing ancient ikons.

In contrast, the local church of Tou Stavroú, the Holy Cross, is as plain and simple as a loaf of bread. It stands far up a terraced mountainside some miles outside the village. A small chapel, it can hold perhaps twenty people. Most of the ikons are faded paper images cut from magazines and framed. The little building, however, is lovingly whitewashed inside and out, and its barrel roof washed sky blue. Although its owners, a farm family, are not well-to-do, their piety and love for this little church shows in the immaculate upkeep and the forethought and labor involved in its decoration today. Outside in large tubs are immense, thriving basil plants – the small-leaf type which makes a perfect green dome. Inside are baskets heaped with cut basil, some on the floor and others all but filling the embrasures of the open windows. Bouquets of basil in jars stand under the ikonostasis. The ikons are ringed with garlands of the herb. The spicy fragrance censes the air, both inside the church and outside in the stony open space that acts as a churchyard. Basil is special to this celebration because it is said that where the cross of Jesus fell, basil sprang up and, four hundred years later, it was basil that led Ayía Eléni to the site where the Cross was buried. So, although on all other *yiortés*, in all other churches, the wreaths surrounding the ikons would be flowers – roses, carnations, stock, dahlias, marigolds – here, on this day, plain green basil is the only decoration.

There is no formal courtyard; the bare country rock here is too uneven and too steep, but there are stone walls, and people are perching on them, exchanging news, waiting for the priest. Donkeys are tethered to olive trees in the adjacent orchard, their wooden saddles underlaid with colorful rag blankets, and a couple of tractors are parked down below on a piece of level ground. The people are dressed simply but formally, the men in the dark suits they put on only for church and, occasionally, for sitting in the *platía* on Sunday mornings. The women are still wearing their summer prints, though many of the older ones are in black, for the older one gets, the more often one is in mourning. People are going into the church, paying reverence to the ikon, lighting candles and saying prayers, and returning to converse with friends and neighbors,

Suddenly, all the heads turn and some people stand up: a loud grinding of gears is heard, and the noise of tires ineffectually grabbing at the scree of the steep driveway. It is the taxi bearing the old priest. A tiny, almost doll-like man with a beard white as dove's feathers, he is helped out by Chrýsanthos, the driver, who delivers him into the hands of several younger men and women who have come running to kiss his hand. The taxi backs down the track to make way for a shiny red Volkswagen minibus, packed with children and a few elders, and driven by the young, newly ordained deacon. He too grinds his gears and spins his tires but it is no go. He backs up, the doors open and the children pile out, and he tries again, gaining a few meters. Eventually he stops, gets out, chinks the wheels and helps out an elderly lady, his mother, and an old man, his father. He waves to the people above and pretty soon, red-gold beard flying, black *ráso* already whitened with road dust, his arm around his mother, he arrives, crying, "Hrónia pollá!" The old priest, after shaking hands with the owners of the church and their relatives, goes in to the church to dress. Robed, he comes to the church door and says quietly, "Ready! Let's begin!"

The tiny church holds so few people that most remain outside, helping to keep the children from yelling too loudly or climbing olive trees. The liturgy, chanted in a soft voice by the old priest and a stronger, more musical one by the deacon, drifts out the door of the chapel, along with the fragrances of frankincense and basil. When it is over, the family distributes the *prósforo*, or communion bread, and branches of basil. A relative who owns a sweet shop offers *loukoúmi*, Turkish delight, and butterless cookies, because, although Tou Stavroú is an important γiortí , it is also a strict fast day. When the celebrators descend the mountain and go to various "tables" at the surrounding farms, they will eat neither meat nor fish nor dairy, but snails perhaps (it rained a few days ago and the snails "walked" in legions) or squid, stewed or grilled without oil, and salads with only lemon or vinegar, although the wine will flow, and, if someone has brought a phonograph, there may be dancing to scratchy old records. Later, in the village, all the Stávroses and Stavroúlas will be holding court at home or in their favorite hangouts. The ouzo and wine will also flow and even though there will be no charcoal-grilled *goúna* fresh from the sea, no bites of *féta or graviéra*, no *souvlákia* of lamb or pork to fuel the dancing, and only green olives, what is allowed will suffice, and everyone will have enjoyed a wonderful celebration.

Áyíou Dimitríou

The next great *yiortí* of Autumn is that of Áyios Dimítrios. Dimítrios is one of the aristocratic warrior saints martyred in early Christian times. An officer in the Roman army, he was put to death by his superiors for not renouncing his faith. Like Áyios Yiórgios and Áyios Minás, he is depicted wearing a Roman soldier's garb and riding a horse, in his case, a spirited red one. Equestrian saints have a reputation for riding out of their churches to accomplish miracles. Dimítrios is known as the "Myrrh-streaming," because of the beautiful fragrance which emanates from his tomb and marks his passage through the streets. Áyios Dimítrios is interred in a church in Thessaloníki, whose patron saint he is. It is not thought to be a coincidence that the city was liberated from the Turks on Dimítrios' name day, October 26, 1912, nor that in 1939, two days after the name day of the defiant martyr and the day after that of Dimítrios' friend and fellow martyr, Néstoras, both of whom stood up to oppressive authority, the dictator General Metaxás was emboldened to refuse passage through Greece to the Italian Fascist army, thus precipitating Greece's entry into the Second World War. This event is celebrated as *Ohi*, or "No," Day with patriotic panoply, and the proximity of the two holidays leads to three days of celebrating.

Usually, October has been rainy – at least, the farmers hope so: the newly sown seed needs rain to germinate and the olives don't at all mind a little plumping before harvest. But around Áyíou Dimitríou, the villagers expect a week or so of warm, bright weather, called the "Little Summer of Áyios Dimítrios." It is the last good weather before winter sets in and the north wind howls down from the Caucasus, bringing with it the glacial cold of the snow-capped mountains.

The village church of Áyios Dimítrios stands in a little secondary bay of the village and turns its long side to the biting north wind, which dashes sand against the seaward wall. On that side the building is gray and pitted – it cannot hold a coat of whitewash. But on its other sides it is snowy white, lovingly and freshly whitened for its special day. I am not sure how old it is, but most churches within the walls of the village date in their present condition to the seventeenth century, though they may have fallen and been rebuilt a dozen times before that. Inside the church is lovely, and typical of the village churches of the period. A black-and-white tile floor frames a large white marble slab before the altar, graven with the double eagle of the Holy Roman church. The *ikonostasis*, which stands in the apse before the altar, is of carved wood, vines and flowers polychromed and gilded. It holds the main ikons of the church: to the right of the double half-doors to the altar is Christ; to the left the Panagía with the Infant; and to the far right the ikon particular to the church, here that of Áyios Dimítrios, mounted on his red horse and spearing another Roman soldier. The small double doors in front of the altar are painted with a scene from the Garden of Eden, and another door to the far left with the image of Michael the Archangel, also dressed as a Roman soldier. In his role as the Angel of Death, in one hand he holds a sword, giving the *coup de grace* to a corpse at his feet, while in the other he lifts up the tiny released soul. Unique to this church are a pair of slender white marble columns, about chest high, candlesticks for beeswax candles three or four inches in diameter and a meter high. The columns are carved with the image of eternal life, a cypress tree with a dove flying over its top.

Today, dressed for its festival, the church is brilliant with marigolds – about all that is blooming now. The thick orange and yellow garlands, interlaced with myrtle and other greens, ring the ikons and the sanctuary doors. Vases of marigolds of all shades stand on the floor and swags of them radiate from the chandelier. Women in the village have spent the previous day raiding every garden and stringing the garlands, and this morning hanging them. They are now sweeping up the fallen leaves and petals and bundling up the newspapers in which they brought the garlands. They have filled and lit the brass lamps hanging in front of the ikons, and the dark little church glows with flames and color. The women leave now but will return at sunset for vespers and tomorrow for matins, then the procession when the saint is removed from his frame and carried around the village.

Dimítrios, or Dimítris in Demotic or spoken Greek, and its feminine form, Dímitra, are very common names in Greece, both deriving from the name of the ancient goddess of vegetation and agriculture, Dímitra or Demeter. The Thesmofória was an autumn festival which honored this goddess, credited with having introduced the Greeks to agriculture. Autumn is a proper time to celebrate Dímitra, to both praise and importune her, since the newly sown seed for next summer's wheat lies in the ground, unseen. Is it germinating or not? No one knows or will know until it sprouts in December or January. The wheat is associated with Dímitra's daughter, Persephone, who is yearly "reaped" from the fields in the late spring by Hades, the king of the underworld, and taken down to his subterranean domain, where she remains until winter, when the wheat sprouts and she rises from the ground to rejoin her mother.

Because the name is so common, after the liturgy there will be great rejoicing as each Dimítris or Dímitra celebrates his or her name day. Since Áyios Dimítris is not the patron saint of this village, there will be no public party, but the *tavernas* will be full of eating, drinking, and dancing villagers, and there will be much traffic to and from the houses, with guests carrying boxes of cakes and sweets, bottles of ouzo and liqueurs. The etiquette of Greek name days is confusing to foreigners, especially those who have been indoctrinated not to crash parties they're not invited to! It took me years to accept the fact that it is the opposite here: on people's name days, they are the hosts of the party to which anyone who wants to greet and honor them comes without invitation. The guests bring not material presents but snacks or drinks to expand the hospitality. As well, there is no need to try to remember people's birthdays, because their celebrations are linked to the calendar!

Taxiarchón

The next to last *yiortí* of Autumn is *Taxiarchón* – in English, St. Michael and Archangels. The local church of Taxiarchón stands high on a hill four or five miles south of the village and, although no longer in use, it is in the care of the famous nearby monastery, Longovárdas. Every November eighth, the monks gather in the empty chapel to sing the liturgy. It is the only time women can hear them chant, as the monastery itself is closed to them. The church was once part of a smaller monastery, now abandoned, and so it is not much decorated. The plain whitewashed walls form a fittingly stark background for the ascetic monks, robed in black *rásos* and *kalimáfkis*, cylindrical hats. The cool November sun streaming in through windows below the dome illuminates their pale bearded faces, as they lift their disciplined and melodious voices in the ancient Byzantine psalmody.

Michael and his fellow archangels, among them Gabriel and Raphael, are not saints in the usual sense, but original supernatural beings. However, they are the messengers of God to humankind, the only ones of the heavenly host (comprised of seraphim, cherubim, princes, thrones, dominions, and powers) who interact with mortals. Michael, although he drove Adam and Eve from Eden with his flaming sword, once interceded with Satan on behalf of Moses, saving from damnation the prophet who would otherwise have been lost because he had killed an Egyptian before leading the Jews to the Promised Land. Michael and Gabriel both are considered angels of death, who take human souls to heaven, and Gabriel will someday announce the end of the world with his trumpet.

On his *yiortí*, the Archangel is said to write in his notebook the names of those souls he will take in the coming year; to avoid his notice, on this day one should do no work, not even chores. Few now truly believe this, but a spirit of holiday pervades the village. Buses take the villagers most of the five kilometers to the church, though many walk, the weather being mild, and there is a steady stream up the hill. As usual, few lay people stay for the complete service but, instead, wander in, kiss the ikon and pray, light a candle, listen to the chanting for a while, and wander out again to gossip and socialize, perhaps walking down the hill in the crisp air with seldom-seen friends or relatives. Tonight the Michálises and Gavrílises will celebrate in much the same way as the Dimítrises did a week or so ago.

Ayíou Andréa

Autumn ends exactly three months after the agricultural New Year, on November thirtieth, the feast of Ayios Andréas, St. Andrew. There is an old saying, "Áyios Andréas comes, and the cold gets stronger," a play on the sounds of Andréas and *andriéve*, to strengthen. This *yiortí* is traditionally the time of the opening of the wine barrels. In a way, the opening symbolizes the seasonal metamorphosis: as from grapes to wine, so from autumn to winter. In this area, the *yiortí* of Áyios Andréas is particularly well-celebrated because the church dedicated to him belongs to a well-to-do farm family who inhabit a seventeenth-century monastery high on a hill overlooking both sea and fields. The church, with its barely visible frescoes and once-beautiful, now worm-eaten, carved and gilded ikonostasis, can hold over a hundred worshipers. There is a large interior courtyard as well as a little-used refectory and wide covered balconies, so the family can and does entertain hundreds of guests, all day and all night. Relatives contribute to the general feast both in goods and labor, serving up *souvlákia*, roasts, fish fried and grilled, pies, salads, cheeses, and fruit. Not a few barrels of wine are tapped and carafes are constantly being filled. To fuel appetites for dancing, tape recorders are turned up ear-splittingly high. The island music fills the courtyard and spills out onto the mountain, shaking the almond trees, disturbing the grazing cows, audible almost to the village, miles away. The high walls shield celebrators from the already nippy wind, while eating, drinking, and dancing warm their bodies. They will go home happy and replete, to days as cool as nights have been. Autumn is over.

But, with the fields plowed and sown, the grapes and olives harvested, the tomatoes mashed into puree, the quinces and sour oranges preserved in sugar and the olives in brine, the chickpeas and squash seeds dried, wheat in the shed, wine in the barrel, olives in crocks, oil in green glass bottles, cheeses drying in their screened cages, brush cut and heaped in the country courtyards for hearth and oven, and wood stacked in the village street for the bakery, the villagers are at last ready to face the winter.

Plowing

The earth is plowed three times a year: orchards and vegetable gardens in spring, fields for winter wheat in autumn, and vineyards in late winter when the ground is covered with silene, a small flower the color of a wine stain.

The plow goes round and round – a man, a pair of oxen – furrowing the earth, following the lines of loose stone walls. The man, the animals, the wooden plow are the colors of the stones – cream, tan, gray, ochre – and of each other and the hills beyond. Round and round they go, plowing the earth, turning up stones – after seven thousand years still turning up stones. The stones are picked up and tossed onto the walls, where they settle, fall, and are picked up again and taken away, perhaps to a farther corner of the field, to be piled up into another wall, a stable, a house, a church. The stones are mortared with earth; the floors of the buildings are earth or stones over earth, the roofs earth over cane, and the whole structure – loose, tentative, shifting – filmed with a skin of whitewash, which, when renewed year after year for decades, for centuries, for millennia, holds the shape, gives it solidity, light, and presence. When the whitewashing is neglected, the film splits, flakes, dissolves. Then the earth dries and crumbles, the stones fall. Abandoned for decades, the house, stable, chapel becomes a ruin, for centuries a rocky hill, for millennia a field again, a stony field shadowed with lines and corners. And then in some time comes a plow – a man, a pair of mules – each the colors of each other and the earth and the stones, to dig again into the earth, going round and round, furrowing, following the lines of walls, turning up stones. And the stones are picked up and piled onto the walls and round it goes.

The plow turns up many things. Stones. Shards of terra cotta – handles, spouts, and rims of pots, casts of the thumbs and knuckles of potters (millennia broken, millennia dead, millennia forgotten). Stones. Fragments of marble hands and feet, grooved by the chisels of sculptors (millennia broken, millennia eroded, almost forgotten). Stones. Jugs of gold coins (centuries buried, still uncorrupted, still remembered). Stones.

The mountains are bare stone, stone over stone. The stone is ochre sandstone, white marble stained with rust, granite gray with stripes of white and flecks of mica. The gray mountains turn violet in some lights. One hill is pure marble, white, unfractured, smooth as a god's skin. On a cliff, among marble boulders, purple thyme pushing between, open crystal caves of rust quartz lie exposed. And all – sandstone, marble, granite, quartz – from wind, from rain, from the ceaseless restlessness of the earth, fissure, fracture, split, slide, crumble.

From cracks where there is no soil springs *spárto*, broom. Where enough of the rock has crumbled to hold a root the size of a currant, anemones. Where stones the size of hands overlap, thyme. Where water may rest for an indrawn breath, asphodel. Where runoff is checked by a wall or boulder, wild fig and caper. Where winter streams have cut a bed, sage and oregano. Where stones break down to gravel, to soil: mallow, gladiolus. Where fields are plowed, poppies, *mandílithes*, and vetch. Along walls and roads, fennel, acanthus, lupine, cistus, *mandragóra*, chicory, thistle. Where soil meets sand, beach poppy, statice. Thrusting through the sand, sea lilies. Where sea washes the rocks, a tiny fuchsia rock flower. Plants live as men live, as stones, water, and wind allow them, briefly – briefly flowering, quickly forming seed, scattering it, drying, crumbling, becoming dust.

Man lives among stones, plowing them, turning them up, gathering them, piling them into walls, into pens, stables, houses, churches. The stones are always moving. The mountains shift, fracture. Boulders split from the country rock, slide, settle. Rocks fall from walls; the rest adjust to the absence.

On an autumn day, lucid and cold, the wind dies. Standing far up the side of a mountain I see, count, seven islands. The sea surrounding them is like green glass. Nothing moves. All is silent. For minutes, the scene is as still and glazed as an ikon. Then the silence is broken by the chinks of stones dislodged by goats, their bells sounding like *kambánas* from the distant islands. A stone falls from a rock wall with a small hollow sound. With an almost inaudible groan, the wall resettles. Stillness again, for a day, a century, a millennium.

A lizard sits on a wall and I the same, and we breathe together, until, with a flick of tail, he disappears. These moments last in the mind, last forever, even as the mind moves away, itself shifting, fracturing, scattering thoughts like seeds.

In a serene moment, we wish for stillness, for nothing to move, to change. But the real stillness is in the cycles, round and round the year, around and around the field, around and around the threshing circle (a man and a mule). All these are the same, have been the same for thousands of years. But the years are never the same, as the field is never the same: never the same stones, the same seed, the same plants, the same men. Only Earth herself is unchanging. And so of her vines, her wheat and poppies, we weave a wreath, *stepháni*, to crown our eternal Mother (her forehead marble, her shoulders gray granite, her feet yellow sandstone standing in red clay). But just as the wreath is finished, she is off on her restless journeying. She leaves the point of stillness. A stone falls out of the wall, the lizard slides away.

Noikokyrió

Only thirty years ago, when I first lived there, the island of Páros was almost an ecologist's utopia. Island life was not simple; it was complex in its own way, but in its great respect for and harmony with nature, the polished results of thousands of years of living and learning, it exemplified the environmentalist's dream.

Island life was neither primitive nor austere: All the villages and the *hóra* had running water and some, if not very dependable, electricity, though people in the country drew their water from wells and lit their homes with oil lamps. The villagers used the electricity sparingly, getting up with the dawn and making sure to do tasks that needed light before sunset. Work done, darkness was nothing to be feared or banished: on a summer's evening, the unlit streets would be lined with neighbors sitting outside on chairs, in their courtyards or on the street itself, gossiping and greeting strollers in the blue velvet dark: "*Yiá sas! Yiá sas! Kalispéra! Hiérete!*" The greetings flowed like a warm breeze.

Telephones there were also, though lines were few. In the country, public telephones were installed in houses central to each area. In the village, the few householders or shop owners with phones also took messages as a matter of course, but off-island communications depended largely on the lone operator in the small telephone company office, Kýrios Themistoklís, who would take messages and yell them out the door to the coffee-drinkers in the *platía*, at least one of whom would haul himself to his feet or snag a passing child to deliver the news or call someone to the phone. Themistoklís, as intermediary, was always the first to hear of births, deaths, engagements, operations, and other juicy items, and he enjoyed much attention and prestige by spreading the word. When he was replaced by an automatic system, he grieved his loss of status more than any deposed monarch.

The most usual form of transportation was walking. Children walked a mile or two to school (beyond that, they might ride a donkey and leave it to graze in a field next to the school). To shop and work and visit, villagers walked everywhere, even miles into the country. There was bus service between *hóra* and villages, but it was limited to the morning hours; the last bus left the *hóra* at one, taking the high school students home to dinner in the villages. If you needed to go to or from the *hóra* or another village after bus hours, perhaps to catch a boat to Piraeús, you took one of the three or four taxis, and you were not surprised or put out if the driver took on other passengers or even stopped at a house along the way to deliver a package, perhaps a prescription from the pharmacy or a kilo of lamb chops. If you had a lot of stuff to haul, if for instance you were moving out to your summer place – beds, chairs, tables, kids, and all – you contracted with one of the small, green "taxi" trucks, generally three-wheelers with motorcycle engines, which were for hire to anyone. These little trucks kept busy delivering goods off the ships to shops and homes as well as lumber and bricks to building sites. Where streets in village and *hóra* were too narrow and winding even for the small trucks, goods for shops and homes were trundled in by handcart. Both trucks and carts, however, needed paving; most farms and country homes were connected by *monopátia*, narrow, rocky paths that ran alongside stone walls or dry river beds. Here the strong and dainty donkeys and mules were the most practical way to haul both people and goods; in every village and town they had their own shady parking lots. The only two private cars on the island, one in the *hóra* and one in the village, belonged to doctors.

Despite these modern conveniences, there was a strong tradition of what is called *noikokyrió*, which translates as husbandry, good housekeeping, economy, and providence that reach beyond one's own house to become, in Gary Snyder's words, "earth housekeeping." One of the most complimentary epithets for someone in island society is that he is a *noikokýris*, she a *noikokyrá*. No adjective is necessary. This principle of caring and sparing use was reflected in every aspect of life: the things people used, the way they used them, the work they did, the food they ate, and their relations with their families and neighbors.

Although manufactured goods, especially plastic ones, had already by the early seventies made an appearance in the stores, the great majority of objects found in the *agorá* and in homes were simple and useful. They were made by hand of natural if not native materials that, like the islanders themselves, endured hard and long use. Although changing functions as they aged, they were just as useful in decrepitude as in youth. When finally outworn, they decomposed gracefully in the earth or (objects only) the sea. Everyday objects – brooms and mops, baskets and roofs, washtubs and boards, jugs and casseroles, blankets and rugs, saddles and plows, to name but a few – were made from materials found in the environment: straw, cane, grapevine, agave, olive wood, stone, clay, sheep's fleece, and seaweed.

Cane, *kalámi*, a grass similar to bamboo, is commonly planted on the edges of orchards and fields; its flexible stems and blonde-tasseled heads break the crippling and parching force of winter and summer winds, yet allow enough air to pass over the crops to prevent mold from forming. Like its oriental cousin, *kalámi* must be annually cut back and ditched to keep it from taking over, so there is always a lot of it but always a use for it too: tied into rafts, it makes strong but flexible roofs for verandas, ceilings for traditional houses, and supports for mattresses.

Grapevines are planted for the table fruit and wine, of course, but shoots from the vines – pruned every spring – are plaited into basket handles and burnt in the fireplace or a *fou-fou*, a small terra-cotta brazier, to grill meat and fish. Onto twisted grapevine, flowers and leaves are tucked and tied to make *stephánia*, the wreaths and garlands that decorate the churches on their holy days, and the *mai*, the wreath of flowers people make on May Day and hang on their house doors.

Olive trees are valuable for fruit and oil (oil has a myriad uses: for food, medicine, light and sacrifice), but no part of the tree or the olives themselves is wasted. After the olives are pressed (the first pressing is for salads, the second for cooking), the rich oily residue, called *pyrína* – once burned in copper braziers to heat homes – is now fed to poultry and cattle. When, after centuries of life, an olive tree finally dies, every bit of it is used to make tool handles, butchers' blocks, mortars and pestles, and beams for houses. So vital is this wood that even after being cut down, sawn up, and built into a house, it often sprouts new growth. A country house I lived in had an L-shaped olive limb, bark and all, that formed both lintel and joist; the house, the owner said, was at least three hundred years old. The limb was without a spot of rot. Olive wood is blond and fine grained, a carver's delight, allowing for delicate detail – a whisper of a halo round the head of a Panagía, the nails of a baby's hand.

Agave, a huge, spiky-leaved succulent, shoots up a candelabra-shaped flower whose stem may reach five meters in a season. A New World desert plant, agave demands no water, and its fearsome spines make it a good cattle fence. The stalks of the flowers, when dried, become a spongy, wood-like timber useful as beams for veranda roofs or small animal sheds; the wood doesn't last many years, but it saves the farmer from buying and wasting real, always imported, pine or oak.

One plant no farm is without is bottle gourd, a quick-growing annual vine. Its large leaves create a cooling shade for summer verandas, but die back in the winter when sun is welcome. It sprouts a great variety of shapes and sizes of gourds which, when dried, make excellent bird feeders, containers for next year's seeds, or a way to carry a gift of wine or milk to a neighbor. These gourds were once widely used as fishermen's floats. The fishermen would choose the most spherical gourds, paint them distinctive colors, and tie their baited lines or nets to the curly stems. When lines or nets sank beneath the surface of the sea, the floats held them up and marked the fisherman's territory. On calm days, one could look out beyond the harbor and see lines of yellow, red, or white gourd floats bobbing in the sea.

The sea plant *phíkia*, ribbon weed, is heaped up on the beaches by every storm that blows; when harvested, it finds use as animal bedding, mulch on fields, and, packed on top of rafts of cane, insulation for ceilings in traditional houses.

Native stone, from limestone to marble to gneiss to slate, is the basis for all traditional building. Stones picked up from the surface of the land or cleared from plowed fields have more uses than Odysseus had stratagems. Piled expertly, these stones make dry stone walls that divide fields and hold up terraces, many incalculably old; some roughly shaped boulders from the time of Homer's hero still form the bases of not a few of them. Until recently, all houses and churches, stables and warehouses, shops and civic buildings were built with found stones mortared with clay. This method of building is very ancient, going back to the Bronze Age, and possibly beyond.

In the buildings, simple boxes of found stone, the stones were not only mortared with clay but the walls, inside and out, were plastered with it (a well-to-do householder might spring for *porseláni*, a finer clay for the interior walls). Roofs were rafts of cane heaped with ribbon weed and topped with, again, more clay. The same clay, pounded to terra cotta hardness, made warm, rust-colored floors, though floors were also laid with slate. Buildings were then completely whitewashed inside and out. For at least three thousand years, the islanders built in the same way. Only since the late sixties have they begun to build with "modern" materials – concrete block, brick, and concrete.

The clay, used also for pottery, is still found in the marble quarries, layered between the veins of *lychnítis*, the famous translucent white marble used by Phidias and Skopas. The marble itself, though it is no longer brought out in sculpture-sized pieces, is now used in large slabs for tombs, in smaller ones for window sills, in fragments for terrazzo floors, and as dust in whitewash. More opaque marble and slate, quarried in only slightly more recent times (twelfth to seventeenth centuries), still pave streets and floor houses and churches.

Whitewash itself is a kind of miracle. Limestone (the most common stone on the island) is crushed, heated, and then soaked in water. The result is the highly caustic lime. Whitewash is diluted lime thickened with plaster and sometimes, for brilliance, marble dust. It is brushed onto walls and roofs and over mortared joints in streets and floors. The tissue-thin skin both seals the wall against moisture and kills insect eggs and bacteria (a can of whitewash used to stand in every toilet). Thousands of structures all over the island, all over Greece, the Mediterranean – even the world – are literally held up by layers of whitewash no thicker than a sheet of newspaper – although, where it has never been stripped, centuries of whitewash may build up to the thickness of a slim volume of poetry! But if the seal is cracked, water may get in and eventually the building will collapse; to prevent this, whitewash must be frequently applied. On this island, the custom is to whitewash everything – streets and *platías*, houses and churches and shops – inside and out during the week before *Pásca*, Easter, so that the village, like the celebrators, wears new, clean clothes for the holy day.

The beauty of the traditional Cycladic houses, apart from the dramatically simple structure which inspired so many modern architects, is that almost every bit can be found and gathered free from the mountains, the fields, and the seashore. Any ruined building can also be a source of materials; many buildings in both village and *hóra* boast inscribed or sculpted classical or Byzantine lintels, floors, or columns. All a householder has to pay for is windows and doors. In the old days, one could begin with a single room and over time add on others as materials were collected, as children were born and, eventually, married. All the buildings were constructed in the same way, so a stable could become a house, or conversely, a house a stable. A builder was desirable, but a householder with average skills could certainly construct his own. The tragedy is that the architecture which inspired Corbusier has come back, like a prodigal son, in an impoverished form; now pale imitations are built of concrete block finished with cement. The uninspired buildings may have the plain, block shape of the originals, but the beautiful uneven texture created by the irregular stones, which softened the austere lines, is missing.

Kalámi, besides roofing houses and protecting tender fields from the wind, finds another use in the making of baskets, the most popular and useful containers in village and countryside. While a few farmers or farm wives on the island wove baskets, most of the baskets were, and may still be, woven by gypsies. About once a year, to the uneasiness of the villagers and farmers, rattly trucks driven by dark-skinned men and crowded with brightly dressed women and children would debark from the ferry. After making a deal with a farmer or landowner, the gypsies would set up their tents and pick-ups in a field, bargain for *kalámi* and grapevine, and, sitting in companionable circles behind a canebrake, proceed to turn out baskets.

The barrel-shaped basket, woven of cane with a grapevine handle, was used in every household for shopping and, by means of a hook attached to ceiling beams, for storage of everything from extra clothes to potatoes and seed onions. A cloth stitched over the opening turns it into the most popular suitcase, seen by the hundreds on any ferry boat to or from Piraeús.

In the method of fishing called *paragádi*, fishermen use a wide, shallow cane and grapevine basket into which they carefully wind multiple hooked lines, snagging the hooks on a rim of cork attached to the braided edge. The ends of the lines are tied onto floats; when the float is tossed out onto the sea, the line with its baited hooks unreels neatly and safely from the basket.

Besides the common barrel-shaped and flat *paragádi* baskets, another highly useful basket is the *kofíni*. Tall and cylindrical with handles, it is used in the harvests. Grape pickers gently gather the clusters in smaller, leaf-lined baskets and, when these are full, empty them into *kofínia*, which are then roped to donkeys' saddles or slid onto trucks and taken to the *patitíri*, the stone vat where grapes are trampled, or to the farmers' co-op. Olives are gathered differently, being shaken down or stripped from the tree onto a canvas or wool blanket, but these are emptied into the same *kofínia* to be taken to the press. Baskets, like their engendering plant, allow the passage of air around the harvested fruit and do not bruise it. As well, they are lightweight and easy to clean – by rinsing in the sea. When a basket is finally through – its bottom rotted out – it often finds its way to the sea as a fish or octopus trap. On her truck farm, my flower-loving neighbor Anna used spent baskets to start seeds of flowers and vegetables.

Another basket, woven from grasses, is used in cheese-making. Hot curds are ladled into the baskets, then set on plates to drip; when reasonably whey-free, the cheeses are removed from the baskets and hung outside in a *fanári*, a screened cage, to dry in the wind. The imprint of the woven grass remains on the cheese. The cheeses, especially *mezíthra*, are either eaten or sold as fresh cheese or placed into barrels of brine or oil to cure.

Farmers whose major form of transport is donkeys or mules use another sort of basket to take fruits and vegetables to market: these are oval-shaped and made of thick slatted wood, possibly oak, and bound with osier. Roped on each side of a wooden saddle, they carry the precious cargo safely. A small truck farmer, rather than take his produce to the shops, may roam the streets of the village in the early morning with his donkey, calling in a melodic voice to housewives to come out and inspect his wares: "*Domátes ého, angoúria ého, maítano, sélino frésco! Fáte to ároma!*" "I have tomatoes! I have cucumbers, parsley, fresh celery. Eat the aroma!" In the spring, he may have bunches of wild narcissus and wood hyacinths tucked among the spinach and peas.

Other sturdy and useful materials come from animals, especially sheep and goats. Along with meat and milk, animals provide hides for many purposes. *Touloúmia* are inside-out hide sacks for curing cheese and hauling wine. From a whole sheep or goat skin (plus a cow horn and a leg-bone "flute"), a shepherd-musician who used to play in the village had fashioned his own bagpipe. And of course, the animals give their fleece, which almost every village woman used to spin with a simple drop-spindle. The spun wool was woven into blankets or knitted into socks and sweaters, especially the typical *fanélla*, an underwear sweater. Sadly, while knitting is popular, little weaving is still done. "The loom is torment," an elderly woman told the poet Eléni Fortoúni. She was glad to be free of the necessity of weaving all her family's clothing, bed coverings, and rugs. "Knitting and crochet," said Moursiniá, "let you have company. The loom makes a lot of noise; you can't talk and weave." Nor keep an eye on a grandchild or two. She spins her fleece by hand but sends the thread away to be woven into blankets.

Páros in the 1970s was by no means self-sufficient; however, many goods came from other areas of Greece where there was an abundance of specific natural resources: pottery from Siphnos, wood from Crete and Thessaly, bricks from Chíos. The best *kofínia* came from neighboring Náxos. These goods were often brought on the inter-island cargo *kaíkis* which took local products to sell, especially the excellent black wine. Even among the goods that arrived on the ferry boats from Piraeús, however, a preponderance were of natural materials: wood; steel, tin, and brass; cotton and wool – all long-lasting and, as we who have had to create a word to retrieve an idea would say, "biodegradable."

"Recycling" in those days did not consist of throwing away once-used objects to be manufactured into new ones. The life of every object was carefully prolonged: clothes and sheets were mended, collars and cuffs turned, trousers patched; when mending was no longer useful, the cloth was stripped and woven into rag rugs and saddle blankets. These rugs were woven in two-foot widths and never joined, so they were easy to whip out into the sun to dry out the winter damp. When the rugs were too faded for respectability, they were placed under mattresses to deter mildew. But that was not the end: everywhere one could see the remains of rag rugs in use, here to scrub a boat deck, there to cushion a chair seat, elsewhere to block wind or water from seeping under a door or window. As well as being flat-woven, rags were knotted onto an old piece of canvas or burlap to make a thick pile rug generally used as a saddle blanket.

Long before they became rags, however, clothes were carefully hand washed and dried in the sun and wind. Before Tide, they were washed with *prássino sapoúni*, that gentle but efficient green soap, in sun-warmed water, either at home or in the little river that had flowed through this village without cessation since pre-Classical times. The nutritious suds (lacking phosphates) either flowed down to the sea or were emptied into potted plants. The traditional washtub, the *skáfi*, made of wood, metal, or stone, has sides that slant at an angle that uses the leverage of arms but spares the back of the launderer. So easy to use is this tub that my friend Stella, who received a washing machine as part of her dowry, goes to wash in her mother's *skáfi*. Sadly if understandably, however, like most new mothers today, Stella has abandoned cloth diapers for the nondegradable "disposables."

The unique short-handled but long-strawed broom is another traditional tool with a long useful life. One needs a while to get the hang of it (the motion is indeed all in the wrist) but, once mastered, this broom is amazingly quick and efficient, faster and less clumsy than the electric "Hoover," and much longer lived. When new it sweeps floors, catching even sand and whitewash dust in its long, tapered fibers; when less new, it washes the same floors; when eroded to half its length, it sweeps and scrubs the stone-flagged streets; when smaller still, it white-washes them; and when reduced to a hand-sized nub, the broom fans the coals of a brazier sitting on a doorstep to grill a fish. The beautiful, rust-velvet earth floors, even in the seventies all but vanished, were maintained to terra-cotta hardness by being daily swept and sprinkled with water by these little brooms.

In the halcyon days of *noikokyrió*, everything possible was used and re-used until it could be used no more. Bottles – wine, beer, and soda – went back to the factories on the mainland not to be crushed and recast but simply to be refilled. One summer sunrise, while I was drinking coffee in the harbor of Ios, a neighboring island whose mountain-top *hóra* is connected to its seafront by a mile of steep, winding, stone-flagged stairs, I began to hear a faint but exquisite music, like the jingling of a thousand silver bells, but with some sort of percussion. As I strained to listen, it became louder. The music filled the bright morning air like a celestial symphony – but of what instruments? Celeste? Too strong. Xylophone? Too high. Santoúri? But there would have to be a hundred of them! As the music came closer, suddenly into the harbor trotted about twenty donkeys. Strapped to their saddles were dozens of wooden crates of pop and beer bottles, and from the shaking and clinking of thousands of bottles on their way to the waiting ferry came the heavenly music.

Food was another thing that never went to waste. Few villagers owned refrigerators so they bought perishables every day in small quantities – just as much butter, say two hundred grams, as was needed for a New Year's cake; just as much tomato paste, olives, vegetables, fruit, meat, or fish as were to be eaten that day. Few foods were sold in predetermined quantities. Most cooked foods, often containing acids such as lemon, vinegar, or tomato, needed no refrigeration to last a day or two. In the country, houses made use of nature to keep things cool. Milk might be placed in a terra cotta jug in an open north window, meat hung in a dark cool *apothíki* or storeroom, eggs slid under a bed on a stone floor. A house I lived in had a bed built like a stone vat, with a raft of cane over it to hold a mattress. Into the cavity, said my landlord, who had slept on it as a child, his father would pour the newly threshed wheat; the stone kept the wheat at a safe temperature, while the wheat warmed the mattress and the backs of the children.

Food scraps and the few leftovers were fed to chickens. My neighbor Asími shyly asked me if I would keep my vegetable scraps for her chicks, and then showed me exactly how to cut up melon rinds for them. "Bring it fresh, understand? If the food rots, the chickens get gas." My reward for this service was a warm egg or two every once in a while. When I lived in the country, I would walk over the mountain to Stylliani's farm. Seeing me toiling up the hill, she would have ready a cool slice of melon or a peeled cucumber. After I refreshed myself, she would hand me a knife and a bowl full of scraps for me to cut up for her chickens.

In the bare rocky islands, wood is very precious. Foreigners with little historical knowledge commonly blame the deforestation of Greece on goats – another example of blaming the "little guy" for the depredations of international business. This island's cedar forests, probably small in any case, given the terrain, went to plank and keel the navies of the conquering and occupying Romans, beginning in the first century B.C., and from the twelfth to sixteenth centuries A.D., the conquering and colonizing Venetians. Some woods may have been uprooted to provide more land for vineyards, as wine was a major export of Venice. If there was a tree left standing, it went to the Ottoman conquerors, who also maintained an extensive navy. Whatever the practices may be in other parts of Greece, here goats are few, used one or two to a flock as "sheepdogs" to control the skittish ovines, and depredations from them are correspondingly insignificant.

In any case, the islanders I knew had great respect for wood and took good care of wooden objects. Oak barrels, wooden washtubs, as well as roughly adzed saplings for roof beams and hafts for mattocks and axes are imported from Crete and are expensive. Pine for furniture, windows, and doors comes from even farther away, the forests of Sweden or Oregon. In all my years of visiting farms, I never saw a wooden object left out in the elements. Barrels were re-hooped and mended time and again; leaky wash tubs found new uses as bread troughs or mangers.

In the days before Greece entered the European Community, even paper was precious, and was reused in many ways: when you bought butter or olives, squid or *marídes*, sardines, the grocer or fishmonger twisted a cone of thin, clean oiled paper, dumped in your purchase, then wrapped the whole in newspaper. A newspaper might have been, metaphorically speaking, "fish wrap" before it found its way to the fish store, but it had been read by several people, most likely in a cafe. Needles, sold one by one, might be wrapped in a tiny twist of the storekeeper's child's homework. One bakery in the *hóra* collected waste paper from the schools and government offices and fired its three-hundred-year-old beehive oven with a mix of spelling tests, tax forms, and aromatic brush. The brush – thyme, oregano, sage – gathered annually from the mountain fields in the fall, heated all the farm ovens as well as this village one. How crusty and delicious, how fragrant were the loaves! When eventually the baker acquired electric ovens, the bread – from the same flour and starter – was pallid and crustless. The waste paper did double duty; with one firing of the oven, after the bread was baked, the residual heat roasted the islanders' midday meal.

These native goods with the economy of their reiterated shapes (the washtub, the manger, the bread trough: all rectangular with the same slant to the sides), the multiplicity of their uses, their ultimate ability to decompose, and the thrifty and conservative practices – all embodied the belief in and practice of *noikokyrió*.

Strangely, English doesn't really reflect this concept. "Husbandry" is almost archaic. There are "thrift" and "frugality," but these imply a dourness and lack of generosity that ill accord with Greek concepts of virtue, among which are those of hospitality and open-handedness, *philoksenía*. In fact, *noikokyrió* makes *philoksenía* possible; the intent is not to have more for yourself but to have enough to share. When an islander celebrates his or her name day, or the name day of a family church, it is the celebrator who is the host, dispensing hospitality to all who come to pay their respects.

136

Material gifts are not customary. It is more blessed and practical to entertain one's friends than to receive a lot of knicknacks and dustcatchers.

Noikokyrió as concept and practice is, or rather was, an assumption of most villagers. But their understanding of it would equal that of any academic ecologist

"They're tarmacking the road out to your place," I said to my farmer neighbor, Yéro Dimítris; he had just split a watermelon for us to share as we sat on the well head in his field.

"Yes," he sighed, "and now the boys" – his thirty- and forty-year-old sons – "will make me buy a tractor and I'll have to give up the donkeys and mules."

"Why is that?" I asked, carefully hoarding at his request the seeds of the "best yet" melon.

"Moré," he said pityingly, "donkeys' and mules' legs are strong. Loaded, unloaded, they can manage any surface on the island – dry stream beds, soft earth, stone-flagged streets – but the macadam ruins their knees. And if I can't use them to go to market every day, I can't afford to keep them just for plowing. And tractors!" Here he spat his contempt. "They leave a swathe of weeds around the field, they compact the earth they plow, you have to pay money for their feed, and they shit poison. The animals plow every mite of ground clean, they leave their droppings, they grow their own food, they produce their own successors. And when you're drunk, which" – he arched his shaggy gray brows – "I am from time to time, they take you home safely." I'd seen, or rather heard, in the wee hours, Dimítris coming home, singing, after a celebration, his large intelligent mule pacing carefully so as not to dump him in the road.

Begin anywhere, with any traditional Greek object or practice, and you'll discover noikokyrió. The famous dolmádes use leaves that must be thinned to allow sun to fall on the grapes. Fasts in the Orthodox calendar, over a hundred days a year, seem to coincide with seasons of spawning of fish and birthing and nursing of animals, or of scarcity, as in August when the hens lay few eggs. Foods are seasoned chiefly with native herbs – oregano, rosemary, bay – that grow wild on the hills. Ouzo is flavored with wild fennel. Regularly gathered and eaten are dozens of wild greens, hórta, such as dandelion, rocket, and wild asparagus; vlíta, the leaves of a shrub; the buds and seed pods of capers; and even wild lily bulbs, volví. Kalliópi, who lives in the U.S., is deeply shocked that people poison dandelions in their lawns. "Why don't they gather them and eat them?" she mourns. "They're delicious."

The teas many prefer to coffee are brewed from sage, oregano, chamomile, mint. These and almost all the abundant wild herbs and flowers carpeting the meadows and dotting the hills have been discovered over the millennia to have myriad uses, not only as flavorings but also as medicines, preservatives, cosmetics, dyes, moth repellents, and even rat poisons. In flower they give nectar to honeybees, and when their season is over, the dry branches are stuffed into ovens to bake and flavor bread.

And yet, even the least of these generous gifts of the Earth are endangered. As the tourist economy swelled in the eighties, the land – at first the rocky, non-arable land where the sheep grazed and the herbs grew in abundance, and later the farmland itself – suddenly became "real estate," absurdly valuable sites for building hotels and villas. As the limestone scrabble was dynamited for foundations, bulldozed for driveways, and covered with concrete slabs, the thyme and sage which fed the bees, the thorny peterium which sweetened the air of summer nights, and all the other shy and useful herbs gave way to "low maintenance" plantings of the ubiquitous, non-native ice plant, the showy geranium. Gone the glossy mastic bush and the cyclamen hiding in its shade. Goodbye to *hórta, volví,* and capers, to mint and chamomile and sage, the food and medicines of the poor – and the knowledgeable.

Since the "modernization" of the village, there has been virtually no recycling. Beverage bottles and fast-food containers are routinely thrown into the trash (previously, if you wanted to take food out from a restaurant, you brought your own plate or pan). The thousands of summer visitors now contribute hundreds of thousands of plastic bags and plastic pop and water bottles to the metastasizing garbage dumps, and the noxious smoke of their burning taints the once-pristine air.

Another casualty of modernization has been the rapid loss of traditional skills, some inherited from generations millennia gone, and the self-sufficiency and creativity they entailed. Even in the early seventies, wooden plows were still in use on many farms. Many farmers preferred them, as they were more sensitive and economical than tractors, but if one broke, it was hard to find anyone to repair it. The *hóra* boasted a saddle maker, but as saddles began to outnumber donkeys, he must have experienced more and more unemployment. So did shoemakers and tailors, blacksmiths and tinsmiths. Manufactured goods and clothing replaced the hand-made products. The loss here was double: as craftsmen disappeared, the possibility of having things repaired disappeared with them. As well, when goods and clothing were handmade to order, the process demanded knowledge not only from the craftsman but from the buyer. With no way to participate in the design of, say, a new suit or a front door, buyers become passive consumers rather than connoisseurs of the everyday.

Perhaps the greatest loss of skills has been in the building trade. Even thirty years ago, builders who could or would build or even repair a foundstone, clay-mortared house were few and aging. Most new buildings were being made of cement block and brick. Unlike the traditional houses, they were hot in summer and ice-cold in winter. When remodeling, the "modern" builders preferred to cement over the age-old stone walls and earth floors and the clay and cane roofs; this made them "permanently" waterproof, but when both renovated and new houses cracked and leaked (inevitably in earthquake country), the house owner needed a builder to make repairs. In contrast, the traditional island houses, built in the same way for over five thousand years could be maintained by almost any householder, using inexpensive or found materials. The new cement was usually unable to hold whitewash, necessitating the use of chemical paint, which has neither the smoothness and brilliance nor the sanitizing effect of whitewash. Whitewash itself began to disappear.

For a while, even as the natural and sometimes native materials began to be replaced with synthetics, some islanders continued to practice *noiko-kyrió*: fishermen replaced bottle gourd floats with empty bleach bottles; housewives stripped colorful plastic shopping bags and crocheted the strips into doormats. I remember seeing a plastic garbage can, cracked and split, carefully mended with nearly surgical sutures. But the truth about synthetic materials soon became obvious: despite their lightness and cheapness, their useful lives are short, and when they break, crack, and split, even the deftest hands cannot repair them, and neither the sea nor the earth can decompose them What the skilled islanders could not begin to repair were the appliances that came with prosperity, with entrance into the European Economic Community: the electric ovens, refrigerators, dishwashers, televisions, tape recorders, and automobiles, and the washing machines for which village housewives abandoned the little river, which itself soon became polluted by seepage from new hotels and, losing its usefulness, was concreted over for a parking lot. Most of these goods, cheap ones at first, came from Germany or other Common Market countries, often without manuals in Greek. When they broke down, despite efforts to prolong their usefulness, there was nothing to do with them but abandon them at the now overflowing dumps from which stinking smoke issues constantly.

The beautiful, pristine bays also suffered from the tourist boom. Previously, seaside houses channeled household waste directly into the sea. In fact, many homes did not have toilets; people took their chamber pots to the sea or used the public ones in the harbor. These opened so directly into the sea that on a stormy day, a person using the privy risked being splashed by waves! The sea easily accepted and processed the human waste of the small population, along with its food scraps, old baskets and brooms, broken chairs, and chicken feathers. But with the new hotels and *pensions* along the bays, the sea reached its limit. For years, sea water you could once have used to pickle olives was too polluted to swim in or, worse, take fish from. However, by the time I visited in 1995, the community had realized that the old way of waste disposal was not working. A sewer system was being laid down and a treatment plant built. Of course, this had to be done; the population of the village in the season is a hundred times greater than that of the small village I knew in the seventies. But, as with the importation of Israeli tomatoes, it meant another industrial process interrupted the natural reciprocity between people and nature.

Decomposition is central to Orthodox Greek belief. The Orthodox do not embalm nor cremate their dead, but allow them to decompose in the earth. The bread and wine of the Eucharist are substances that have decomposed, fermented, and undergone metamorphosis, symbolizing the transformation that human beings will undergo when, at the Second Coming of Christ, all the decomposed bodies of the world will be reassembled, molecule by molecule, and bone by bone, from the earth of their graves, and the dead will live again in new bodies in a world transformed. How lamentable that the Earth herself, our mother, long the very embodiment of this cycle of death and transformation, will, at the End, be buried beneath a crust of plastic, glass, and enameled steel, which feed neither worms nor fishes but hang on for a sterile eternity.

And yet, what is most lamentable is not the pollution of land and water by nondegradable and even toxic materials; not just the replacement of fresh locally (and mostly organically) raised foods with frozen meat from New Zealand, two-week-old tomatoes from Israel, yoghurt with "expiration dates" from factories in Athens, and irradiated milk from Germany; not the overfishing of the once-bountiful Aegean Sea, made profitable by the tourist trade and the European Market; not the disappearance of time-honored skills – skills that enabled a large part of the living population to recently survive seven years of enemy occupation and previously decades of poverty – but the death of *noikokyrió* itself, an idea, an ethos, a way of life that for over five thousand years sustained life on this small rocky island, and now is but a memory.

It is of course hopeless to even think of turning back. The modernization that has resulted in such pollution and loss of skills has benefited many. Rural electrification, despite the ugliness of the poles and wires and the noise of the electric factory, means that elderly Anna and her husband Pantelís can live comfortably on their farm all through the year, with an electric heater to warm the house in winter, an electric pump to water the vegetables in summer. Perhaps the most valuable innovation for the general populace is the up-to-date medical clinic in the *hóra*; no longer must an appendicitis sufferer or accident victim lie and hope that sea or sky is calm enough for the boat to Sýros or the helicopter from Athens to arrive in time.

With the advent of modern conveniences and outlooks and the jobs they have created, many emigrants have returned to their families from America and Australia, and nothing means more to Greeks than family. To serve the tripled population of the village, both a *lyceé* and a *gymnásio* – high and middle schools – and even a kindergarten have been built. Village students can now more easily go on to university and, on graduating, find teaching and professional jobs at home. But the returning emigrants and the new groups of resident foreigners have brought with them a mixed blessing: a strange, or stranger's, view of traditional customs, putting them in a sort of archive, removing them from ordinary people. The houses being built of stone rather than concrete block are the villas of the wealthy, mostly foreigners.

A bittersweet fruit of the sophistication of the island is the revival of traditional music. In the past, there were on the whole island only three musicians (two clarinets and a bagpipe), and musicians for a wedding or a festival had to be imported from Athens, and these, with their electric instruments and trap drums, were fast drifting away from tradition. Now there are two large orchestras of perhaps thirty players of traditional instruments, who play for dance performances by several folklore groups. The performances, mostly by schoolchildren, while both masterful and authentic, are nevertheless performance. For millennia, dance was a joyous activity involving the entire community – grandmothers and grandfathers, aunts and uncles, mothers and fathers, young men and women, youths, and even toddlers – but the attempt to preserve tradition, laudable though it is, has transformed dancing into a spectacle in which few, and those only the young, participate. The dances and music will not be lost, which is a good thing because they are beautiful, but they have been set at a distance, as though in a museum, and will no longer serve the community in the same way they did in the past. What is wasted is the union of body and spirit, exuberance and artistry, community and individual consummated in the dance.

Why mourn? Why even indulge in nostalgia for what has passed as irrevocably as last year's winds? Fazil Iskander, who wrote of the past of his native Abkhasia, says, " In idealizing a vanishing way of life we are presenting a bill to the future. We are saying, 'Here is what we are losing; what are you going to give us in exchange?'"

The Poloneza

When the *kambána*, the death knell, tolled one chill autumn day, I was huddled next to the stove in Thanásis' carpentry shop, watching him work out a design for a wardrobe. Thanásis was one of the *paréa*, the circle of seven or eight friends, who had adopted me when I moved into the village. A knowledgeable traditionalist, he had become in a sense my guide to the village and never tired of answering questions.

"Who's died, I wonder?" I asked.

Hanging up a steel ruler, he answered, "The Polonéza."

"Oh no! The poor thing!" Tears filled my eyes. The *mamí*, the midwife, had recently told me that the Polonéza, the "Polish woman," whose real name none of us knew, had gone for the second time in a year to hospital in Athens, this time to be treated for a septic womb.

Thanásis' news was, as it happened, a *koroídema*, a put-on, one of the games of wits in Greek culture I had not gotten used to in the almost three years I had been living on this island, and never saw coming. As a *koroídema*, it was uncharacteristically sick but, as it happened, also prophetic.

A week or so later, I saw the Polonéza getting off the bus, carrying a basket with a cloth sewn over the top. Furious, I stormed over to Thanásis' shop and chewed him out, but he was imperturbable; in fact, he gloated over my credulity. He knew I felt pity for the Polonéza and her three children, whom I had known while living on a farm near their isolated seaside home. He had rejoiced (having put one over on me) to see me burst into tears and run to the *mamí*, who had also cried (score twice for Thanásis) to discuss what would happen to the family. I was worried not so much about the boy Dimítris, who at twelve was old enough to work and could be taken on by a farm family, but about the two thin, ragged little girls, six and four. Their white-blond hair, tangled and dry, was always dark at the scalp with nits; their pale skin, sun-reddened, was shadowed with grime. They never spoke when they met me. But often during the summer when I had lived on Panayiótis' farm, they would come and stand silently outside the door of my house, their deep blue eyes seeming to plead for something I was helpless to define or remedy.

If any other village woman had died, the fate of her children would not have involved me. The machinery of kinship would go into motion and this aunt or that cousin would emerge to adopt one child or the other. But both the Polonéza and Evstrátios, her husband, were foreigners to the island and, as far as anyone knew, had no kin at all. Where Evstrátios had come from, nobody knew. Yes, he was Greek, had shown up shortly after the war, looking for work. He had been taken on for a while by a well-to-do farmer in Kamares, who did not pay him but allowed him to trade labor for an unused stable and a certain amount of the less profitable produce. The farmer demanded labor from the young Polonéza as well, the moment she could get up from the flea-ridden mattress on which she had borne the first child.

The farmer had in-laws with more conscience than he. They discovered that before the war, before Evstrátios had been taken prisoner and sent to a forced-labor factory in Poland, he had been a shepherd. They gathered together a small flock of sheep and goats, the scanty remnant of those not slaughtered for food by the occupying Italian and German soldiers, and hired Evstrátios to build up the flocks.

Hired? They had no money, or if they had, it was needed to restock, to buy unbelievably expensive tractors and threshers to replace the hands that had left holding rifles and never returned. They arranged for the shepherd and his wife to occupy an old, long-abandoned house on the bay of Lággeri – needing repairs, of course, but near grazing land, and with outbuildings that would shelter a good-sized flock. It was not an unfair arrangement: the shepherd family was to have the ewes' and goats' milk which they could either sell in the village or to the island co-op, or boil up themselves to make *mitzíthra*, curd cheese, which they could sell or trade. They would also get a certain percentage of newborns, and with *noikokyrió* – good housekeeping and husbandry – they could expect in a few years to be in comfortable circumstances.

They were, in the beginning, not much worse off than their neighbors, who were suffering from the effects of the war; not only had men been killed, but families had been decimated by hunger, plow animals had starved or been slaughtered, and, at the end, even the seed wheat had been eaten. What made the difference between the neighbors and the shepherd couple was the possession of land. Most of the neighbors had, despite terrible hunger, resisted the temptation to trade land for food on the black market. Carefully hoarded gold *líras* had gone first, then jewelry: earrings, baptismal crosses, wedding rings. But, one heard, rather than trade a *strémma* – about a quarter of an acre – of land for a few kilos of lentils, grandparents had willingly starved. Even when land had been sold, shortly after the war a law was passed that voided all sales of land during the occupation. The law was proposed by an Athenian who had sold his neoclassical mansion for gold, first to the Italians, then when the Italians left, to the Germans, and ultimately to the British. He'd had to call in a few debts among the parliamentarians to extend coverage to the British period, but he managed it, and his self-serving craftiness had hastened the reconstruction of rural Greece. What this meant to the shepherd, however, was that soon his neighbors were harvesting potatoes, fruit, wheat, chick peas, olives, and animal feed, and were once again raising chickens and doves, pigs and cows, while he had only his share of kids and lambs – most of which he wound up eating, so his own flock did not grow fast. His personal quiver was full, however, and the Ponéza was birthing with the lambs most every year, though few of the babes survived.

The greatest disadvantage was that Evstrátios and the Ponéza were foreigners. To prosper in the country, both husband and wife must be adept at *noikokyrió*, the wreath-like intertwining of habits and practices which results in high productivity and negligible waste. The foods the local people consume the most – vegetables, fruit, grains, oil, wine – not only nourish them but produce edible scraps for hens and pigs. The animals help grow their own feed with labor and manure, contribute milk and young, and, in time, are themselves consumed. Bees feed themselves from orchard and scrub and give precious honey; doves, kept for their rich manure, glean the wheat fields. The hundred and twenty fast days in the church year also inhibit the consumption of foods that are expensive in terms of labor, feed, and time: meat, milk, cheese, eggs, fish and oil. Fasts give animals, fish, and the earth time to breed, nurture, and rest. In hard times, farm people fall back on the most economical foods – beans, bread, wild greens, and, for beverages and medicine, teas from wild sage, oregano, chamomile.

The shepherd family, having no fields or orchards, ate milk, butter, and meat, the foods of the bourgeoisie, from whose scraps only dogs can be fed. Dogs, of which they had one or two, produce nothing, not even usable manure. Wherever Evstrátios had come from – some thought Macedonia – he had no knowledge of the sea, so although his family lived on the edge of it, he knew no way to avail himself of its charity. He didn't fish, didn't gather shellfish, and, said the neighbors when the tch-tching began, didn't even know to gather salt from the rocks. Because his knowledge of the land extended only to the rocky plateau where few edible plants grow (and those – thyme, sage – useful only for teas), he didn't know where to gather the wild field greens that had sustained life among the natives during the famine of the war. The greatest affront to the neighboring *noikokyrés* was that the shepherd's family "bought bread in the village."

If they had known there was something to learn, the shepherd's family might have learned it, but the lessons of *noikokyrió* take years. To identify and gather wild plants, for instance, a child goes out with its mother or father season after season, learns when and where to cut the tiny leaves of dandelion or tips of wild asparagus, where to dig the roots of orchids to boil into *salep*, a nutritious drink. The neighbors would say to the shepherd's family, at first compassionately, "Here, go look for this behind Ai Yiórgi, or next to Battísta's well," but when the family went, if they went, the leaves would not look the same; they would be confused, and come home empty-handed.

If Evstrátios, a Greek, was a "foreigner," the Polonéza was foreign beyond the village's horizons of foreignness. For all practical purposes, she might have been a millionaire's daughter or an aristocrat. She was beautiful enough, even at forty-some. I was startled by her beauty when I first met her, standing alone, staff in hand, on a wide plain of rocky land, the grazing sheep bleating softly around her. Hearing me approach, she had turned, and, seeing another woman, had dropped the fold of thick white scarf with which she had quickly covered her face. From beneath the scarf, silver blond hair, only slightly dulled, escaped in long, floating strands. Pale blue eyes leapt out from a tanned but unlined face. Her bones, like the bones of the hands holding the crude staff, were long and delicate, those of a princess in a fairy story. Only when she spoke, and I saw the gaps in her teeth (the remaining ones miraculously straight and white), did I accept the poverty announced by her ragged clothes, her broken men's shoes and filthy sweater.

She looked like a princess cursed by a witch or exiled by a revolution. In fact, as she told me in very broken Greek, she had been a city girl, a factory worker born of factory workers; it was at the factory, commandeered by the Germans, that she and Evstrátios had first seen each other. After the liberation, awaiting transportation home, he had gotten himself billeted at her family's flat. They had fallen in love, two young people released from slavery, the dark young Greek and the Nordic "princess," and he had painted for her such a picture of Greece, of his family, his house, the lands he owned, the abundance of food, the scents of thyme and jasmine, lemon blossoms by moonlight – had painted this over the gray devastation of freezing rubble, the certainty of continued starvation, the fear of the Russian takeover, the dearth of young men – that with the blessing of her family, they had married. When the spaces were allocated, she had climbed onto the train a bride, glowing with hope, headed for a new life with a husband, himself still a boy.

What happened to the house and the lands? Was it a *koroídema* ? Lies? Extravagant dreams? Or did the young man arrive to find the house in ruins, bombed, the family dead, perhaps killed by Germans, poisoned by spoiled wheat? Or were the lands real, but in an area where the andartes, now split into warring factions, had started to slaughter each other and terrorize villages? If his home had indeed been in Macedonia, it might have been reapportioned to Yugoslavia or Bulgaria. Whatever the truth, the young couple found nowhere to settle. They wandered like gypsies. Finally, they were rescued by a displaced persons agency who found them the job on the island.

She was no more suited to the work than a princess would be. She had never ground wheat for bread, nor baked it in a beehive oven, nor killed an animal and butchered it, using every scrap, making soap of the fat, and so forth. Before the war, she had taken her little pay packet, stopped at the baker's for fresh black bread, at the butcher's for sausage, at the greengrocer's for apples, and gone home to her family. A late child and spoiled, she was never asked to do more than peel potatoes, dry dishes, sew buttons on a baby niece's dress. She could knit but not spin, and there had not even been a garden behind their big, plain flat in the workingmen's section of her city.

She looked back on this life as paradise. Going out to work every day, riding a tram there and back, coming home to a dozen people, all of whom spoke her language, words flying out of mouths like butterflies, circling the crowded dining room with its smells of pickles and coffee – this was her fading memory of Eden. Though she had never learned to speak Greek, except to communicate simply with her children and her husband, she had almost forgotten her native Polish.

A Catholic, she might have found friends through the church on another island such as Náxos or Sýros, but on this island there was not one other Catholic, the descendants of the Venetians having centuries ago been assimilated into Orthodoxy. So while her religion brought her no company, no solace, it did bring child after child – twelve, of which eight were born alive and four survived. It was the thirteenth, in her forty-fifth year, dead three months in the womb, that forced her to walk the three miles into the village, where she had been only twice in nearly thirty years. Because Evstrátios had to stay to tend the flocks and the children, she took a boat to hospital in Athens alone, with a note from the doctor pinned to her dress like a child.

The summer I lived on the farm on the bay of Lággeri I first met the children while walking homeward along the sea path. I was eating candies from a cellophane bag, to which their three pairs of blue eyes became instantly riveted. I offered them some, and they helped themselves but never spoke. Soon afterwards, the boy Dimítris and occasionally the little girls took to coming to my cabin and standing outside the door, silently. The candies were soon exhausted, and I thought I had nothing else to offer. But still they hung about. One day, while I was away, some of my things – a camping knife, a fountain pen, water colors – disappeared. So ashamed was Panayiótis that someone would steal from his guest, that he went himself to pull Dimítris' ear and get the things back. He returned, with a ruined pen and no watercolors or knife, indignant and worried.

"The Polonéza's in hospital in Athens – pregnant again, and the *mamí* thinks something's wrong: another stillbirth, maybe." Panayiótis looked very angry, twisting his gray mustache. "There's no food in the house of any kind, except spoiled milk and moldy bread." I offered money, but money was not the answer, he said. They had to get food, cooked food, *faí*. I felt helpless; I lived myself on salads of his tomatoes and cucumbers, and his wife's bread and cheese, and ate *faí* only when I went into the village. In any case, Panayiótis had already shouldered the burden, and was just practicing on me his announcement to his wife and daughter. "The children will take their meals with us, every day," he said and strode up the hill.

Shortly I heard, borne by the wind, scraps of the shrill protests of old Styllianí, who objected to the filthy, lice-ridden children sitting down next to her grandchildren. Panayiótis insisted, and finally they compromised: she would prepare a good noon meal every day, which could be picked up by one of the children. This worked for a while: sometimes, the six-year-old picked it up; sometimes the tiny, fragile four-year-old would struggle down the hill with a basket nearly dragging the ground.

Once Dimítris came. The next morning, Panayiótis awoke to find his tomato field stripped. The farmer, wild, saddled his donkey and rode into town. Following half-eaten discarded tomatoes all the way, he tracked the thief around the village and found him sitting in the sweet shop eating his second pastry and drinking orangeade. Panayiótis retrieved the proceeds from the tomatoes (pitifully little, the boy having been cheated by his buyers) and hauled him off by the scruff of his filthy shirt, turning over in his mind what to do about him.

Panayiótis was fond of children, had raised three adopted ones, and was for all his gruffness a doting grandfather. What was in the old man's heart as he roughly pulled Dimítris along the dusty road home? For the first mile, perhaps anger that the fruit of his labor had been ripped from him.

For the second, disgust with a thief (and an incompetent one). But coming in sight of his own fields and orchards, tucked beneath the dry and rocky hills, he was moved to pity for a boy whose only work was standing and counting sheep on lonely hills. With a kind of trust in the moral power of his own happy environment, Panayiótis decided to threaten Dimítris with the police and settle for his working off the value of the tomatoes, thus learning some decent farming. The boy's presence would be an incentive for all the children to come and eat.

Panayiótis reckoned without the boy's attachment to his parents and to their own way of life. Farmers' hours are long; they rise before dawn to harvest and irrigate in the summer twilight. And the work – hoeing, reaping, threshing – is backbreaking, nothing like the dreamy, lonely hours walking the hills with a grazing herd. And, of course, the food. Dimítris had been, in some fashion, to school, so he must have known that while most children, including Panayiótis' granddaughters, ate beans and zucchini, his family fed on lamb and ewe's butter.

Panayiótis also reckoned without his wife, who saw bad influences – lice and fleas and pellagra – and potential sons-in-law everywhere. Dimítris and the elder granddaughter were the same age, and she was not about to risk that. She gave Panayiótis an earful I could hear two fields down. Nevertheless, he yelled louder, and the younger couple agreed with him, so Styllianí threw up her hands.

The plan worked for a day or two. Then Dimítris disappeared, and when Panayiótis went to look for him every day for a week, the Polonéza, who had returned from hospital, cried and said she hadn't seen him. However, a set of marking pens and more bread and cheese disappeared from my place. Then the little girls also stopped coming. Perhaps Styllianí had not completely restrained herself on the subject of cleanliness. On the other hand, perhaps they preferred being with their mother to eating *fai*.

I moved into the village in the fall and lost sight of them, except for seeing the six-year-old girl and Dimítris walking home from school once in a while. "Once in a while" was the word for it, Pantelís the teacher said. Neither of them really spoke Greek, and they showed up too infrequently to stitch together the few commands and common words they knew into a language they could learn in.

"Now their sister . . ." said Pantelís.

"What sister?"

"Iríni. She spoke Greek pretty well . . ."

"Where is this sister?"

"How should I know? She left school after the sixth grade, as you could then. . ."

"When?"

"Ten, maybe twelve years ago."

Yes, said the *mamí*, to get the girl out of the way of a local married man who had tried to molest her, the priest had gotten her a job as a maid on Sýros. "She never comes back; the man was insane about her, and she only thirteen."

The Polonéza was not the only member of the family in ill health. Evstrátios was said to be suffering from his *stomáchi*, which probably meant ulcers. Some months after Thanásis had prompted my tearful consultation with the *mamí* (and after I had learned that, as a single alien, there was no way on earth I could adopt a Greek child, even with parental consent), a helicopter came one day and took Evstrátios to the hospital in Athens. This left the Polonéza with three children and perhaps thirty sheep and goats to care for.

Fortunately, most of the spring birthing was over. Probably the shepherd had held on, getting sicker and sicker, until then. Dimítris resurfaced and was seen on the hills with the animals, but the Polonéza still had to milk the nannies and ewes, and try to sell the milk. She came to Panayiótis, who agreed to buy all the milk for his own cheese-making. He again offered produce in exchange, but the Polonéza needed every drachma to send to Evstrátios in Athens. At that time, farmers and shepherds had no medical insurance; presumably, some of the hospital costs were being borne by the priest, as such exigencies are part of a priest's responsibilities. But it was doubtful that he was able to raise or contribute all that was required. Besides, Evstrátios needed small things – cigarettes, soap, extra or special food.

About Easter time, a blow fell from which the family was not to recover. They had been living rent free in the old house on the sea for nearly twenty years; rents on such half-ruined places were so low, even to foreigners, as to be almost not worth collecting. The house belonged to an invisible rich man – invisible because, for much of that time, he had been living abroad as a sort of political exile, since he was a passionate monarchist for a monarchy that had ceased to be tolerated by either left or right. He was also a wealthy bachelor, so politics was not the only reason he was living in Paris, Vienna, and Monaco. However, with the fall of the Junta, the whitening of his hair, and perhaps a decline in his bank account, he had felt the umbilical pull, hired himself a yacht, invited a small group to join him, and sailed off, perhaps to get in touch with his roots.

One fine spring day, he sailed into the bay of Lággeri, several hundred acres of whose sandy, rocky, juniper-covered shores made up part of his patrimony. The day was not only fine, it was the festival of Zoodóhos Pigí, the *yiortí* of the little church on Panayiótis' land, built centuries ago to celebrate the beautiful spring, issuing from a cliff face into a dell green with ferns and wild fig, which had made this rocky peninsula habitable and cultivable for millennia.

On this day that celebrates the simple charity of the Mother of God, the exile sailed into the exquisite harbor among a flotilla of gaily painted *kaíkis* from the village. Anchoring, he rowed his sophisticated guests to the small dock, where they admired the gleaming white church strung with blue and white paper flags and decked with myrtle. Did he detach himself for a moment to kiss the unremarkable ikon? Did he dare? With other celebrants, the rich man and his guests ascended the hill to where Styllianí and her family were bustling around a number of trestle tables in front of the house, setting out Panayiótis' famous wine, the women's famous bread (dark and thick), lamb, pigeons, potatoes, lettuces, peas, cheese, eggs, oil, olives – all their own simple and abundant produce. When greeted, Styllianí only nodded and extended a greasy finger, but Panayiótis solemnly poured each of the foreigners a small glass of his four-year-old wine. Did the visitors politely hide their grimaces, or was one of them pleasantly surprised with this light golden liquid? They didn't stay to dine with the villagers but returned to the yacht, to nibble canned European delicacies and listen from afar to the whine of Bárba Iosíf 's bagpipe and the "Opas!" of dancing peasants. One of them, surveying the beauty of the jade and sapphire bay, the cluster of half-ruined farmhouses, the green and mauve hills, likely had a vision: a colony of villas, gleaming in the sun, a yacht harbor, a simple but elegant hotel? Someone certainly said, "Leónidas" (or probably "Leon"), "you're sitting on a gold mine."

A few weeks later, the village policeman rode out to the Polonéza 's house on his motorbike. She saw him coming and screamed, thinking he bore bad news of Evstrátios. But he bore, in fact, a registered letter. The young man had offered to take it out; no one in the family had ever received a letter, so the postman had hesitated to leave it in the tobacco shop which served as the village post office. Since none of the children could read the formal language, the policeman read the letter to her, and tried to explain what it meant. Eviction. They would have to leave the house in a month. It seemed she could not understand. The policeman, desperate, took her to Panayiótis, where everyone in turn repeated the policeman's pantomimic explanation.

Finally, she understood. At least they thought she understood, because a change had come over her pale blue eyes. She neither ranted, as a Greek woman would have done, nor wailed, nor wept. She simply looked from her children to the horizon, and when she looked back at her children, the eyes were still focused beyond them, far beyond this shocked and angered group of Greeks. She refused tea or ouzo, allowed the two pale, begrimed, beautifully-boned children to eat the sweet *mastíka* Lélla offered them, and then, grasping each one by the hand, walked home, the letter folded into her apron.

The next week, the policeman came again, and this time it was Evstrátios. The priest was too old and too ill himself to come so far to see her. Again, the policeman took her to Panayiótis. She showed no interest in the question of burial. All she could say was, "No money, no money." This time, Lélla put her to bed – lice be damned – in her children's bed, sent her eldest to collect the small ones, and then Dimítris.

They stayed for three days, the Polonéza apparently prostrated with grief, and then one day she simply died. As it turned out, she had been dying for months. Her womb (a fetus dead in it three months) had been gangrenous. From before the time Thanásis said the *kambána* tolled for the Polonéza, she had not had a hope. Most probably, she had not known. I never heard that there was a funeral, but there would have been a burial. Father Kosmás was not one to worry about whether Catholics or foreigners should be buried in sacred ground with Orthodox rites. He would just have done it, quietly. There is no marker in the cemetery, not even a wooden one.

With both their parents dead, the little children, shocked and silent, found themselves back under Panayiótis' conscientious roof and Styllianí's jealous gaze. The old farmer had been half-ready to take on the wild boy, but now there were three small feral creatures. And after six years, Lélla was expecting again. The *mamí*, who was always right, predicted a boy.

For a week, the Polonéza's children simply had no fate, no future. A blank. And then, one day, getting off the bus, came a girl who could only have been the Polonéza's child: she had her aristocratic bones, her tow hair, but eyes of a darker blue. Although poorly dressed, and with work-roughened hands, she shed a clear light. The priest had found her, tracking her through the lawyer in Sýros to Astypalaiá, where she had married a young fisherman. She walked out to Panayiótis' farm, collected the children, and took them home. The landlord had agreed to let them stay outside, and to use the brackish well, for a month, until work on the villas was begun. So there they lived, on the shore of the sea, with a tree for shelter; sun, moon, and stars for light. One by one the owners of the sheep came and took them away, hustling the bleating animals into trucks, paying outstanding bills, buying Evstrátios' remaining ewes and goats. Seeing the poverty – the rusty beds and rotting mattresses, the fish boxes, broken tables, gray sheets laid out in the open – some were touched and were generous, some were crafty.

Finally, one day, a green and yellow *kaíki* sailed into the bay. A dinghy beached: the young girl's husband. The rusty beds were stashed in a stable, the few possessions loaded into the *kaíki*, and then Iríni, wading in to her waist, carried the little girls on her shoulders. Dimítris jumped in last. Lélla and Styllianí heard the engine, and getting up from their veranda, saw the little group of orphans, white gold hair shining in the sun, sailing out of the bay. No one in the village, not even the *mamí*, who knew everything, ever heard another word about the children of the Polonéza.

Some years later, Thanásis and I are sitting at ease under his chinaberry tree. I have just translated the story for him. "So, what do you think?" I ask.

"It's a nice story," he says, tapping a cigarette on its box. "But it's a *koroídema* not as good as mine – maybe just *psemáta*."

"What lies?" I challenged, indignant. "It's all the truth."

"Lies. I rang the *kambána* for the Polonéza , but you killed off old Evstrátios. And he's not dead. You ought to be ashamed."

I let that pass. "What do you mean, not dead?"

"He stayed in hospital a long time, but he got better. He's living in Tsipídos – all of them are. I saw them a few weeks ago. Dimítris is a waiter. The middle girl – what's her name? She's engaged to a fisherman. Irini's got two babies: you can tell them easy, hair like white silk."

"I don't believe you. You Greeks are so sentimental: you just want a happy ending. This is another *koroídema*."

"If it is," Thanásis said, pouring us each an ouzo, "you'll never know, will you? And so it's a better one than the first."

Laundry

On a brilliant morning in autumn, the sky is as blue as the Greek flag. Against the blue drift flocks of white doves, settling like a soft blanket onto the golden stubble of the reaped wheat fields, then rising suddenly as though blown away by a brisk wind. A train of wheezing and snorting donkeys, carrying a group of eight or ten tourists, clatters up a dry river bed winding up from the seaside *hóra* to a convent near the summit. Like the others, I am seated sidesaddle on a donkey. We pass a rock-walled field in the corner of which is a *stérna*, a square white-washed stone reservoir. Its still water reflects a windbreak of black-green cypresses. On the gray rock wall, laundry is drying: blazing white triangles and squares: dowry sheets and pillowcases, faggotted and lace-edged; a *hrámi*, bed cover, cream wool lightly striped with white cotton and deeply bordered by fine white crochet; flat curtains with cut-work patterns – birds, flowers, ribbons – showing dark against the stone. As I pass, the laundress, dressed all in black, looks up from spreading another sheet over a dark green myrtle bush. She pauses, unties and lifts her black scarf, revealing hair as white as sheets, as doves, then resettles the scarf.

Any windy October morning in the village is a feast day of laundry. Striped blankets, fleecy *flokátis*, and multi-colored rag rugs, draped from sunny balconies and weighted down with stones, struggle like dancers in winter clothes to free themselves from gravity. Flying from roof-high lines like flags on a holiday is a brilliant spectrum of red towels, yellow T-shirts, black slips, white diapers, green pajamas, blue and yellow striped sheets – all fluttering wildly, revealing and concealing, like an irregular strobe, flashes of the Bristol blue of a church dome. Here and there on a line is a drying octopus, its tentacles stretched out in a broken star, or a dozen little fishes, salt-and-oregano cured, pegged by their tails, looking like a line of exclamation marks.

Doing laundry in a Greek village is less a chore than a celebration. Early on a blue and white morning, Kyría Kassianí emerges into her high-walled, stone-flagged courtyard, bringing her canary in its cage and hanging it on a vine; she feeds the bird and whistles to it. Then she brings out a short table and a wooden *skáfi* – a shallow, rectangular, slant-sided wash tub. She fills the *skáfi* with water from a hose and leaves it to warm in the sun, disappearing back into her house to make her morning coffee. An hour later, she reappears and places a long rope of rag along the flags of the courtyard out under the gate to the gutter in the street. Then into the *skáfi* go the clothes. Quickly, she draws each shirt or dish towel up on the slanted washboard, rubs it briskly with a large cake of green soap, rubs the cloth against itself, flips it and repeats, wrings, tosses it into a bucket. When everything is washed, she tips the sudsy water out into another bucket, which she empties onto the roots of the grape and bougainvillea vines climbing the walls of her house. The clothes go back into clean water, are soaped and rinsed once more, and, after they are pinned up, she again doles out the rinse water among her many pots of flowers and herbs. When she's finished, she spills the remaining suds onto the flags and gives them a good scrubbing with a broom. When she rinses, the water obediently runs along the rag out to the street, Kyría Kassianí following to use it up in a brisk rinse of the street itself.

All the while, the canary and she are trilling to each other, the sun is pouring into her garden, the roses are soaking up the nourishing suds, the bougainvillea is bursting with shoots, and the clean, fragrant laundry is flapping in the sun and wind.

Skáfi, Prássino Sapoúni, and Louláki

Laundry as done in the village or countryside is a perfect example of *noikokyrió*. The concept is evident in the shape of the *skáfi*, the qualities and manufacture of *prássino sapoúni*, green soap, the use of water and sun, and the attitude towards labor. All of these are vastly different from prevailing American equivalents, emblematized by the typically solitary (and mentally abstracted) use of the washer and dryer with their greedy demands for energy, water, and polluting detergents.

The *skáfi* is a miracle of simple physics. Whether made of stone, wood, metal, or plastic, it is a longish rectangle with inward slanting sides. The slant (about forty-five degrees) and the height (about navel level) use the leverage of arms and wrists and eliminate bending. Far from being backbreaking labor, washing in a *skáfi* is a gentle workout. The shape of the *skáfi* is repeated in other containers seen around farms and villages: kitchen sinks, mangers, and water troughs, but the prototype is the *skáfi* itself. In contrast, the prototype of the Western laundry tub is the round barrel – beer or whiskey – an awkward and back-breaking shape to wash in. Barrels in Greece are used for fermenting wine, salting cheese or olives, and never for washing. In Greece, equal respect – in the form of engineering – seems to have been accorded women's labor and men's.

There are wooden *skafis*, sheet metal ones, and now gaudy blue or orange plastic ones, all of which are portable and require a table or trestles cut to the proper height. But the best are the fixed stone ones with slate or stippled marble washboards, found in every farmyard, some courtyards, and many community laundry centers. On the farms, the stone *skáfi* is usually built beside the well or a *stérna*, a reservoir, the greater width and depth of which adds to the ease of rinsing and washing large things like sheets and rugs. The used wash water drains directly into shallow ditches that irrigate vegetables or trees. The edges of the *stérna* are almost always crowded with pots of carnations, sweet balsam, basil, and other tender flowers, and covered by a shady vine, passiflora or jasmine. For each new *noikokyrá*, the stone *skáfi* is adjusted to a comfortable height by adding a slab of stone, or digging out a little earth, beneath the feet.

After washing for years in *skáfis* both permanent and portable, I was puzzled, when living in an old house on another island, to experience backaches while washing in the built-in *skáfi*. The sink in the kitchen (a shallow marble slab that drained directly into the orchard below) was so perfect for my height that I felt myself the physical double of the seventeenth-century woman for whom it was built. But the *skáfi* built into a small room beneath the front staircase was about four inches too short and made my back and arms ache. Then I noticed that the floor had been freshly cemented, and measured the thickness at the doorsill: four inches.

I was taught to do laundry in a *skáfi* by my first farm neighbor, eleven-year-old Eléni. One day she came into my house – uninvited as usual – and found me trying method number ten of washing sheets: treading them like grapes in an oversized dishpan. After laughing until she cried, she took me by the hand and led me to her house, got the metal *skáfi* down from the wall, and filled it about half way. Had it been earlier in the day, she, like Kyría Kassianí, would have left the water to warm in the sun. She began by dousing a single sheet, then folding it into panels small enough to fit the washboard. Drawing the sheet onto the washboard, she showed me how to rub it vigorously with a cake of green soap – turning, unfolding and re-soaping it. When all the sides were done, she drubbed the whole briskly on the board, anchoring the cloth with one hand while rubbing with the other. This one-handed method she also used to wring out excess water; it uses the weight of the body and, as opposed to two-handed drubbing and wringing, does not strain wrist joints.

Eléni dumped the soapy sheet into a basin and doused another in the same tub. "You use the same water to wash the rest?" I asked, vaguely shocked. "Of course," Eléni said scathingly, "water is precious." I was reminded of something the Bauhaus potter Marguerite Wildenheim used to tell her students: "Learn to wash your hands clean in dirty water." I had not understood it was possible.

It was afternoon when I had my laundry lesson, and Eléni was caustic about that: "You have to hang the clothes out to dry early in the morning. And never let them hang out all night."

"Why?"

Eléni was evasive, but later I heard that bad spirits can inhabit clothes left out at night and cause sickness. The superstition may have a basis in fact: Stanford Cook, a biologist, told me years ago that morning sunshine has a sterilizing effect. He had stopped a pinworm infestation cycling through his children by having them launder and hang their bedclothes out in the early morning sun every day for a week.

Although never previously an enthusiastic housewife, after mastering the craft of laundry I found that I enjoyed it tremendously. The process was quick, free of drudgery and pain, and gave me a kind of intimacy with my clothes, such as potters have with clay. I could be gentle with a lace-trimmed blouse or rough with jeans, and could see when a button or armhole was about to go. Although I never had a canary, I made sure that my wash place was pleasant, perhaps with a sea view to soothe my eyes or pots of basil to fill my nose.

Often, walking in a village street, I would feel some small drops of what seemed like rain, only to look up and see, spanning two balconies, poles of cane on which freshly washed snow-white sweaters were threaded by their sleeves. These were the *fanéllas*, the fine, hand-spun, hand-knit undershirts of the farmers and fishermen. *Fanéllas* are decorated with delicate intricate patterns at the chest where they show through an open shirt, and sometimes at the edges of the three-quarter-length sleeves. The hand-spun wool is a little scratchy on first wearing, but after several washings it becomes as soft as a down quilt. I was amazed to see men engaged in dirty jobs – hosing out fishing boats, mixing concrete, spreading manure – wearing these white *fanéllas* and white wool socks, the older men also wearing yards of fine white wool wound into cummerbunds to keep the cold from their sacra and kidneys. I pitied whoever – women, I was sure – had to scrub and scrub all this white wool – until I learned how easy it was to keep it dove-white by washing (in a *skáfi*) with *prássino sapoúni*, green soap.

Even in the seventies, no one I knew was making *prássino sapoúni*, but everyone knew how to. All year long, the housewives would save their cooking fats (largely olive oil). Then, when the olives were pressed, they would take the coarse final pressing and add this to the used fat, and boil it all in large caldrons with burned seaweed – the omni-useful ribbon weed. The weed has the same effect as lye and also colors the soap. This brew smelled so awful, I am told, that the whole community would make soap on the same day to get it over with for the year. The soap itself, however, smells quite nice, rather like ripe olives. The hot soap was poured into marble molds and when gelled, sliced into kilo-size cakes. The soap is now made in factories, but it is the same soap: green to ochre in color, and often molded with a cameo, perhaps of Athena, the goddess who won the worship of the Athenians with her gift of that tree of infinite uses.

Green soap not only gets clothes "cleaner than clean," it does not pollute ground water, streams, or sea like the detergents even now being touted to the conscientious but ecologically naive housewives of Greece and other cultures still using earth-sensitive traditional practices. One characteristic of a traditional practice is that few people rationalize it – they just learn it and do it. They are therefore vulnerable to sophisticated marketing, which implies to them that their soap is inefficient and old-fashioned, and that they are remiss in their duties to their families if they don't buy, at greater cost, detergents "scientifically" created to get their clothes cleaner. The back of the box, however, doesn't tell them what detergent use is doing to their own food of choice, fish, to that food's habitat, and to their husbands' livelihoods, not to mention their clothes.

Despite the onslaught of Tide and its cohorts, green soap is holding its own – it is still widely available and is even being exported as a luxury item, a matter of some amusement to the villagers. Another traditional miracle, however, is fast disappearing: *louláki*. *Louláki* is woad, a wild plant that makes a beautiful blue dye. It comes in a small cake of pressed powder and is used as bluing in the final rinse water of laundry. Does it color the wash blue? No, the blue is an optical trick; without it the wash would look slightly yellow or gray. Sadly, the majority of launderers in my village have fallen for the claims of chlorine bleach, rather than the organic and benign *louláki*.

Louláki is the secret of that blinding brilliance called *kátaspro*, intensely white, of Greek villages; it is crumbled in small amounts into whitewash – a cake of a couple of tablespoons to a five-gallon can. Another cake or two makes a delicate autumn-sky blue used to wash the surrounds of windows and doorways, and even more results in the brilliant cobalt that protects the domes of churches from the dangerous eye of the sun.

Water

Skáfi, sapoúni, loulάki – all homely miracles. But nothing is more miraculous in this dry land than water itself. Here water is precious, is holy, its mere manifestation a miracle, its origins obscure and surrounded by myths and rumors. These small rocky islands own no alps, no cloud-capped sierra whose snow melt descends annually in frothing streams. Nor does the thin topsoil trap enough moisture to fill wells by seepage. Where does the water come from? Alkis the hydrologist told me that some of it, rising in springs and wells here, may have originated as snow melt from the Caucasus, a thousand miles away. Rivers of fresh water, it is said, flow uncontaminated through the salt sea to surface in underground caves. Another view is that the water here was, millennia and millennia ago, precipitated by the metamorphosis of limestone into *lychnítis*, the pure white crystalline marble the island is famous for. In its transformation, the rock shrinks, creating aquifers which hold the fossil water until a quake, a settling, or a geological sigh rives the country rock, opening a channel, and water as clear as diamonds bursts up to the thirsting world as artesian springs.

Good water is treasured, walked miles for, tasted, judged, savored like wine.

"I brought you some water," a neighbor said one day, returning from a walk.

"Is the town water not drinkable?" I asked, alarmed.

"It's all right," she said, sniffing a bit, "but this water is delicious."

The *vrísi* – a spring, tap, or fountain – from which she had drawn the water was near the ruins of a classical *Asklepeíon*, a hospital and shrine, and its water may once have been considered curative. So precious is sweet water, and so important to the community are the springs, that in many towns or villages, benefactors have had them enclosed in carved marble, adding perhaps a drinking trough for animals. There are none in this village, but in the more elegant port town there are three eighteenth-century fountains, made of marble beautifully carved with vases of flowers and birds. As well, they commemorate the donor, Prince Mavroyénis. A verse engraved on one fountain invites people to drink but to be sparing of the precious water.

Water is also celebrated in song and dance. In a delightful *kalamatianós*, a traditional line dance, the singer begs a drink of cool water from "my praiseworthy Vangelió," who is watering her orchard:

A little water, Kyrá Vangelió
A little cool water, please
Drawn from where it falls,
Blessed Vangelió!

Women and Water

It is natural for Kyrá Vangelió to be called upon for a drink of water because, traditionally, women have a special relationship to water – the fresh, sweet water of wells and springs. In archaic times, the spirits of all sweet water (except large and raging rivers, perceived as muscular males with flowing beards) were female, nymphs called nereids, from *neró*, water. The ancients honored these spirits by building little shrines near the stream or spring. The loveliest remaining of the Classical shrines is the delicate white marble shelter for the Castalian spring in Delphi, but there must have been thousands of simple ones, perhaps just a special stone on which to leave flowers.

Since the advent of Christianity, gratitude for a remarkable spring has been is often expressed by erecting a chapel dedicated to the Zoodóhos Pigí, the Panagía or Mother of God as the Life-giving Spring. The small chapel on Panayiótis and Stylliani's farm in Lággeri, dedicated to her, celebrates the ancient and generous well. The ikons which hang in the chapel shows the Mother with Babe, sitting in a chalice or fountain. Mary is identified as the source of water and so of life.

The first Life-giving Spring welled up in a shady wood outside Constantinople, where a kind worker named León was trying to find water for a dying blind man. The Panagía spoke to León, calling his attention to the spring and then prophesying that he would shortly become Autocrat of Byzantium. When León bathed the blind eyes, the man's vision returned. And he, in fact, against all probability, became Autocrat. Multitudes, including generations of Byzantine autocrats – León's successors – were subsequently cured of illnesses as severe as leprosy by the waters of the Zoodóhos Pigí.

Tínos, slightly north of Páros, is called the "holy island." There, in about 1823, the existence of a long-buried ikon of the Panagía was revealed in a dream to a nun called Pelagía. After some months of excavation, the ikon was found, and on the site a spring arose. Today people go to Tínos to pray to the Panagía, kiss the dark and now bejeweled ikon, and leave gifts – golden legs or arms, emerald rings, silver ferry boats – in gratitude for small or not-so-small miracles. The pilgrims drink from the spring and take away bottles of the holy water. The water is holy not because it is blessed by pope or bishop, but because it is the simple expression of the Mother's love. The bottles are set carefully among the family ikons, and the water is used to bless animals, ensure a successful journey, or cure headaches or other misfortunes brought about by the Eye, the folk version of Nemesis.

In antiquity, springs and fountains were guarded by nereids, female divinities, though the rougher rivers were considered the province of male ones. To the ancients, who did not believe in an afterlife, the greatest misfortune was death itself, and so a constant quest was for the *athánato neró*, the water of immortality, usually thought of as the black water of the river Styx, into which the water nymph Thetis dipped (but, sadly, not completely immersed) her son Achilles. Alexander the Great, having braved the Clashing Rocks to retrieve some of this water, left it sitting in a glass on his bedside table, where his thirsty sister found and drank it. Alexander died, but his sister lives on as an immortal mermaid, consumed forever by guilt, rising up in the sea to demand of sailors, "Does Alexander yet live?" A truthful answer brings on a storm, so wise sailors answer, "He lives and reigns," and the mermaid subsides, for a while, in peace.

The Christian version of *athánato neró* is the water of baptism. On Theophánia , called Epiphany in the West, the priest re-enacts the baptism of Christ by submerging a gold cross in water. This water is distributed to the congregation who, like the people in the ikon, bring jars to the service, and take water home to be used for minor miracles. In this case, the power of the water derives from the divinity of the immersed – divinity publicly acknowledged at the moment of Jesus' baptism by his father in the form of a dove. Styx and Jordan: two rivers, two versions of *athánato neró*, but in the classical, the power derived from natural sources is associated with a woman, and in the Christian the water itself has no power, needing to be blessed by an anointed one, a man.

Ordinary water may be used for blessing, but if a church has a well or spring on the grounds, that water is preferred. The ancient church in the *hóra*, dedicated to the Panagía, has such a spring beneath the altar. The church is founded on the site of the death of Theoktísti, a saintly young woman who escaped from pirates and lived as a hermit on the island when it was deserted. Whether the spring is blessed by saint or Panagía is uncertain, but its water is considered helpful if not quite as miraculous as Tínos'.

Woman as source of water and thus of life, an idea older than Christianity, conflicts with the Christian idea of baptism, performed by a man. I wonder if that's why, in Orthodox tradition, the poor mother is banished from the ceremony (or was – things are loosening up) until after the baby is safely reborn, washed clean of her own suspect waters which nurtured the child physically but tainted it with original sin. We tend to forget how hard the early church fought classical (and pre-Classical) religion, dismantling temples, scattering and dismembering legends. It couldn't beat them in the beginning – the chthonic, nature religions – so it joined them, annexing attributes of Dímitra and Ártemis and Apóllo for its own deities. But, for a millennium and a half, it has continued to chip away at this and that pagan concept, especially the powers of women, who in ancient times were priests and prophets but to whom the Christian church, once established, refused any active religious role except that of cloistered nun. It seems possible that the ambivalence of the church derives from its Judaic tradition, where women are considered to be contaminants. In Exodus, God says to Moses, "Go to the people and sanctify them today, and tomorrow let them wash their garments, and let them be ready against the third day, for the Lord will come down in the sight of all the people upon Mount Sinai." After the laundry was done (and it was almost certainly women who scrubbed those dusty caftans, beating them with rocks and sticks), Moses added, "And come not near your wives."

In the classical Hellenic religion, which wove itself into early Judaic Christianity, the spirits of water were women, and so unto the present are the bringers and users of it. What this meant, of course, was hard labor: going to the community well, drawing and carrying water to the house, terra cotta *stamní* balanced on shoulder, and doing the laundry. However, since hauling water from a distant well or *vrísi*, spring, or doing laundry at a river was, in the old days, about the only way a girl could get out of the house by herself, these jobs have romantic associations, especially for the peeping Actaeons of these folk songs:

> *My golden vrísi, how do you hold cool water?*
> *Poor me, how do I bear the pains of love?*
> *I wish I were a vrísi or a stérna or bubbling stream*
> *So I could wash your little hands and your white throat.*

Down by the white river, angels are playing in the water.
Partridges are roosting in the plane trees,
And a blonde girl is bleaching her dowry.

Girl, when you go to the river to wash, take my clothes too.
Don't wash them with water, but with your tears
And the fragrant soap you wash your hair with.
Spread them on the bitter almond tree that blooms in January
So the leaves and blossoms will fall into your apron,
the bitter almonds into your embrace.

Love and laundry are so strongly associated that in an Epirote song, a man named Menoússis kills his wife (mistakenly as it turns out) for washing another man's handkerchief. In another song, an "old husband" not only beats his poor young wife – a "*panagía*" – but sends her to the well "*m'ena vari stamní kai kondó skiní*," with a heavy jug and a short rope!

But while the women's work was hard, it was lightened by *paréa*, company, which lightens all labor. Working alone is unthinkable in Greece, and communal laundry is institutionalized, carved, you might say, in stone. Every village has its communal washing places, whether simple or ornate. In Kardianí, a village on Tínos, the cluster of communal *skáfís* are elaborately carved from white marble. Venetian lions roar forth the water into the tubs, while all around grow ferns, mint, and naturalized snapdragons.

In Náousa, communal washing took place at the "river." This narrow little stream of sweet water is a blessing in a place too near sea level for wells to be anything but brackish. Although less than a meter deep and two across, it is said to have been running continuously without a dry period since pre-Classical times, defying earthquakes and the slow heaving and fracturing of country rock. Some say the village is named for it, "Náousa" in the archaic tongue meaning, perhaps, "flowing water." The river descends in a shallow rocky bed from artesian springs in the mountains. It flows to the eastern edge of the village, where some of the water is diverted to an enclosed reservoir above Bárba Minás' house. There the water flows not only into his garden, freshening his lemon trees, beans and okra but also through pipes into the houses on his side of town. In the time before it was piped, the water used to flow in stone channels through the streets. Perhaps fifty years ago, the community modernized the system, piping water to various locations around the village. Before piping was extended into individual houses, the women would come to the nearest *vrísi* to draw water and wash vegetables and exchange news. Surprisingly, when the community was able to pipe water into the houses, some women scorned it: "I didn't let them put water in my house," says quiet, frail Marigoúla, who draws water and washes her vegetables at the public tap by Chrístos' restaurant, "because it brings bugs!"

From the diversion point, the rest of the stream runs outside the village walls and eventually to the sea through a narrow canal bordered with eucalyptus to deter mosquitoes. Here in a sun trap formed by high, white-washed stone walls, the flow was dammed for a space of five or six meters. Slate washboards were built into the sides of the trough. This washing place reminds me of the river in the *Odyssey*, where, at Athena's behest, Nausicaa goes to wash:

> By the lower river...
> were washing pools, with water all year flowing
> in limpid spillways that no grime withstood.

At the river village women gathered to do their wash. Even those with *skáfis* in their own courtyards (or now, machines) would come to the river to wash heavy woolen blankets and rugs, partly for the ease of handling them, partly for *paréa*.

Water in the houses is an undisputable convenience. It means that housewives no longer have to haul heavy jugs from the neighborhood *vrísi* to their houses – often up steep hills – or lug their washing to the river. But even when the women accept the convenience of piped-in water and machines, they are aware of the loss of *paréa*, company. Stella kept her dowry washing machine covered with an embroidered cloth and went to wash in the *skáfi* at her mother's or in the river, so as not to be closed in the house all day with only machines and babies for company.

When my neighbor suggested I wash my blankets at the river ("You need *paréa* for such work!" she said), I approached the washing place with trepidation, half-expecting Nausicaa and her maids, half-expecting also a critical chorus of older Elénis who would laugh at my clumsiness and igno-rance. I was appalled to find eight or ten women kneeling on the ground next to the built-in washboards of a little reservoir. Kneeling to me meant servility and, more important, pain. As well, it was not summer but nippy late autumn. I anticipated chilblains as well as stiffness, and started figur-ing out how to escape. But every one of the women had turned her head to watch the foreigner coming to do her laundry. Among them was Tzanétta, the bubbling and gossipy daughter of Kapetan Linárdos, the *árchon* of the harbor. If I chickened out, I knew, I would be the butt of scornful jokes all over the village. I took a deep breath and reminded myself of all the brave things I had ever done that turned out well – roller-skating, trying out for valedictorian, eating octopus, to name a few – and advanced.

Tzanétta called me to a place beside her and began to show me how to wash in the river. Immediately I was surprised to find that the clear water was not freezing but pleasantly lukewarm; it had been flowing for miles over sun-warmed limestone. As I worked, dunking my sheets and blankets, I realized also that the place was a sun trap, blocked against the wind by high walls on one side and a thick break of *kalámia* on the other. The sun shone gently on my back and shoulders, and I felt quite relaxed. All the women helped each other, and me. One lent me her *kópano*, a wooden beater carved from a log, to whack the soap into the heavy fibers of my blankets. And when I needed to lift or wring the sodden blankets, or drape them onto the stone walls to dry under the eucalyptus trees, one or another of the women jumped up without offering or being asked. So when Itho's mother's old-fashioned, peach-colored bloomers escaped over the dam and headed toward the little estuary the fishermen used for cleaning their boats, I leapt up, grabbed a stick, and chased along the opposite side of the canal from Ítho, both of us convulsed with laughter, trying to capture the drawers before they caused a scandal. Despite being twenty years older than I, Ítho snagged the pantaloons first. Years of kneeling at the washboards, it seems, had kept her legs limber. I left the river with blue and white sheets scented with the myrtle they had been dried on, blankets white and soft as dove feathers, and only a little stiffness in the knees.

The Slaughter

One afternoon in November, I braved the knife-sharp wind off the sea and climbed the marble road to the house of the *mamí*, the midwife. For over thirty years, the *mamí* had walked the village, uphill and down, going into every house. In all the village and even the outlying farms, there was scarcely a woman whose belly  she had not palpated with her slender red hands, a child or an adult from whom she had not once washed away the afterbirth with chamomile tea, nor a bottom she hadn't bared for a shot – even the old priest's, for he was diabetic. And so, though she kept many secrets, neither was there a story she didn't know. When she had poured out foamy coffee into her best tiny cups and set out a plate of honey cakes, I brought up something that had been puzzling me. "Mamí," I said, "yesterday in the *hóra*..."

"In the *hóra*?" she said. "Twice in one week? Ah, *yirístra!*" To most villagers, my visiting the *hóra* so often would qualify me as "gadabout," but the *mamí* was teasing. "Go on," she said.

"I saw – a butcher." He had been standing in the blue-painted doorway of a butcher shop, a tall gray-haired man with blue eyes, wearing a long red butcher's apron. He had nodded at me gravely as I passed, and I'd returned the nod, with some surprise. "But I think he's from this village." Indeed I had often seen him sitting in the eucalyptus-shaded *platía* with other old men, their canes between their knees, taking coffee from small glasses and talking almost not at all, a word every few minutes, as though everything they had to say, even about the government or their grandchildren, had already been said, many times over.

Seeing him there, in the doorway of his own shop, surprised me because, except for a civil servant or two and a bank clerk, village men did not as a rule work outside the village. The villagers' loyalty to their own made it possible for any artisan or shopkeeper to make a living. And not only was this man not a civil servant, he was a butcher, a *hasápis*, something the village had sorely lacked for nearly a year. Since the last *hasápis* had closed his shop to open a gas station, the villagers had been hard put to it to find meat. In the *hóra* there were half a dozen good butcher shops, but getting there and back on the bus ate up the precious morning hours the housewives needed to cook the noonday meal. Taxi and bus drivers would occasionally fetch back dripping packages of chops or *kimá*, ground meat, but there were only four of these "deliverers" for a village of eight hundred hungry souls.

The less fastidious patronized one Evphímis, a farmer who slaughtered once or twice a week. But the risks were great. He was a scandal – often drunk, always dirty. Just the sight of him, laughing and cursing, dragging screaming animals through the streets toward the *sphageío*, the slaughterhouse, was enough to cause pious housewives to cross themselves, while the stench of his blood-stained, offal-strewn shop polluted the usually bread-fragrant air of the *agorá*.

In contrast to the vile, puny Evphímis, the man I had seen was clean and handsome, big-boned and strong-looking, though he must have been well over sixty. The *hasápiko* behind him was immaculate, even the sawdust on the floor unstained, although it was nearly closing time on a holiday eve.

"Oh, that man!" the *mamí* exclaimed, twirling her hand in a circle. "Yes, he is from this village. But – he keeps a shop in the *hóra* because the people of this village would not buy from him even a half-kilo of suet."

"Why? He seems clean and strong. Not like Evphímis..."

"Oh, that little man! *Káko hróno na'hei!*" Here she crossed herself because she had cursed. "He's not a real *hasápis*. A real *hasápis* not only slaughters and butchers, but goes to the farms to watch over the animals – in the old days he knew more about animals than any of these young vets! And clean? Cleaner than a priest's wife! Has to be: our health is in his hands." She glanced at her own hands, reddened with scrubbing and swollen with chillblains. "But that Evphímis! They say he buys diseased animals." The *mamí*'s husband was a farmer, so the news was from the horse's mouth. "And the shop! I've seen dung on the floor and... Oof! But the man you saw, though he was a real *hasápis*, is dirtier than Evphímis, for he killed a young woman, though not with his knife but with his. . ." She motioned towards her lap and blushed.

"Long before the war, even before I came here, he had a *hasápiko* here in our own *agorá*. He was a young man and, they say, handsome. You can see that still – eyes like the sea, hasn't he? And then he had dark brown curls and a great *moustáki* like a Cretan! What a *pallikári* he must have been! You can bet the girls made ox-eyes at him and that their fathers bought all the meat! Where was the shop? In the *agorá*, of course, next to the little church of Ayía Ekateríni, you know, where the vine makes an arbor over the street?"

Yes, I knew this place, though it wasn't any longer a shop but a store-room, the ground floor of a row house, overarched by a double flight of stone stairs, ending in a balcony. The walls were, like all walls, plastered stone, thickly whitewashed inside and out. Here and there, the dull green paint on the woodwork had flaked away, revealing an old coat of sky blue enamel, traditional butcher's paint. The panes in the double door were opaque with dust. The front had been altered – where the wall had been built up, cemented, the whitewash was crumbling. Probably once there was no wall at all, just an opening the full width of the space, closed at night by a series of panels but in market hours wide open to the street, the sun, the wind, the housewives' critical eyes. Clean, spare, the shop would have had few furnishings: the block, a massive trunk of an old olive tree, sanded and golden; above it, a rack of shining knives and cleavers; a marble counter; sheets of rose-pink paper skewered to the wall. Across the width would have run rods of black steel from which dangled hooks, empty, waiting for the carcasses.

"Across the street," the *mamí* continued, "upstairs, was the house of – well, I don't know if he was a captain, as they say, but anyway he was on the ships. He had married on Ai Yiánni a beautiful but poor young girl from the countryside and moved her into that house – a nice house with long windows that catch the morning sun. If I lived in that house, I'd have carnations, pink carnations, in pots all up and down the stairs." The *mamí* was famous for her flowers, which fell in cascades from her balcony and scented her neighborhood. "Maybe she did. I think she would have started plants. She had little else to do. The groom had completely decorated and furnished the house; nothing but a little embroidery did she bring to it, and probably she didn't dare change anything. Very soon after the wedding – oh, a month or two – the groom went back to sea, leaving her, as the song says, 'waving her scarf from the shore.'

"Why did he go away so soon? E! captain or not, he was a mariner. They live two lives, those men, and none. They're away on their voyages two years, maybe three, sometimes more, and then when they come home, they expect to find everything unchanged. And of course – ! You see them even now, wandering around the village, not recognizing children who've grown, expecting to see people who've died. But then, the sea's the only way a man from here could ever make real money. And this one had made a lot of it. Probably he was not so young and really a captain.

"Anyway, the butcher always stood in his doorway when the shop was open – they weren't open every day then. No, on certain days, a farmer would bring in an animal, or the butcher would walk out and fetch it in himself, and he would take it to the *sphageío* and slaughter it. You know the *sphageío*? Just a little stone building on the edge of the sea close to the windmill. They slaughtered the old way then. First the slaughterer prayed for forgiveness and made the sign of the cross (something we forget to do these days). Then he caressed and soothed the beast, and when it was quiet, shoved in his knife and cut its throat. He gutted and flayed the carcass immediately. Although the *sphageío* faced north and was cool, the meat couldn't hang long. We didn't have refrigerators then; the *psaropoúla*, the boat that took the fish to Piraeús, would leave ice for the fishermen, but there wasn't always extra for the houses. So tough or not, we mostly bought our meat freshly killed and cooked it the same day. About every other day, then, except during fasts, the butcher would slaughter."

His naked arms and chest drenched in hot blood from the spouting carotid of ox or pig, his black rubber boots sliding in blood on the floor, the tall young *hasápis* leans down to hook the stiffening fetlocks of the animal. He raises it with a rope or chain, or wraps his sinewy arms around the still-hot carcass and lifts it with his great strength to the hook, where it hangs head down to drain. On the marble floor, garnet blood is already jelling, while from the urine and excrement of the animal's last release, steam rises. With one swift motion of a great knife, he guts the carcass. The white, slimy entrails fall to the floor, unwinding like dull snakes. Of the organs, he cuts what he needs – kidneys, lungs, the liver of anything but pig, and the intestines if he will make sausage – then throws them into one bucket, the offal into another, and descends over stepped and tilted rocks to the sea. In the sea, he washes the blood and muck from his boots and hands, cleans the organs swiftly, strips the long tubes of guts, and tosses the waste far out into the waves. He returns with a bucket of water and sloshes the floor; he does this half a dozen times, purifying room and animal. He beheads the beast, flays it (laying the hide aside for the tanner), then strips the thick congealing suet. Another few trips to the sea. Soon nothing remains but the carcass, no longer an animal but a rough pointed ellipse of rose–red and white marble, chilling, hardening fast. The knives, the bloody apron, and the boots go into the sea and maybe he himself strips and plunges into the cold brine.

"Did I say that before the *hasápis* cuts the animal's throat, he makes the sign of the cross?" continued the *mamí*. "Because we cannot take life lightly, but only to survive. *Sphaghí* in our old tongue is 'sacrifice' as well as 'slaughter.' So he must ask God's blessing, and keep away the Eye as well.

It's the Eye, you know, that we attract when we think we can do whatever we want, despite God or man. Perhaps one day he forgot, or perhaps. . . who knows? We are all animals, and blood runs hot in youth. In any case, that summer, he stood in the shade of his *hasápiko* and watched the young wife, alone except for visits from her mother, go up and down her sunny stairs.

"I wonder why she was so alone. Maybe the captain had no family to keep her company, or maybe . . . It was a mistake for the captain to marry without a dowry. I know what they say now, but then it was different. You see, the husband, for all his charity in the beginning, well . . . You know how men are once they get what they want. They forget how badly they wanted it, how mad they were to sacrifice anything to have it. Maybe they start, a little, to add up the cost. More than the groom himself, his mother and sister also might have counted up the price of a dowerless wife – so much off a sister's dowry, a mother's security in old age. Other young women in the village might have resented a poor stranger, a farm girl, catching such a groom. For whatever reason, she was alone: no one to talk to, no one to watch her.

"Except the *hasápis*. When he didn't have lamb chops to cut or *kimá* to grind, he stood in his doorway, watching for her to come down the stairs to shop. Perhaps having little to do, she went out often: down early for a loaf of bread and up, down later for a bucket of water and up, then down for a slice of butter, a half-kilo of oil, a twist of embroidery floss. His eyes dwelt upon her slight calves, her tender haunches. She'd buy very little meat; alone as she was, she'd eat mostly fish, easier to grill.

"One day he called to her, 'Despinís Matína!' He shouldn't have called her *despinís* but *kyría*, for she was a married woman, though so young... How young? E! In those days? She could even have been fifteen. Anyway, he called to her and offered her a slice of fresh liver. Maybe he saw her looking pale, or said so. And how could she resist? You know what one has to do to get liver! When we had a decent *hasápis* here, my husband would go round with a bottle of wine or a basket of new beets to get us a half-kilo of fresh liver. Of course it's illegal, but . . .. *ti na kánoume?* So the poor young girl must have been flattered. I don't know if that's the way it started, but I imagine so.

"They do say she began to dress, that is, to wear her good dress. You know, every village woman wears just a cotton *róba* and slippers at her work, even shopping. A *foustáni*, a dress, and shoes, she wears only to church or on a holiday. The bride wouldn't have had many clothes, only what her husband had bought her or what she'd made herself. And no jewelry, save her baptismal cross and a pair of earrings, maybe a wedding bangle. But the poor young girl began to wear what she had: dress, jewelry, silk stockings. The women of the village might have thought that, having married her rich husband, she'd begun to give herself airs, style herself an *archóndissa*, and so they drew back, no doubt, farther than before. 'Kaliméra sas,' they'd greet her (using the polite form) as she neared them hanging out their wash, 'Kaliméra, kyría,' so polite, but 'Anathemáse!' – a curse on her they'd cluck when she'd passed, perhaps swaying a little as her high heels rocked on the paving stones.

"Summer became fall, then winter. The *hasápis* bided his time, or didn't know what he was starting, or did and, young himself, couldn't see the end. One or two have said that he had a grudge against the captain. I do believe he was a captain, because the house is so big, five rooms with tall ceilings and wooden floors. Well then, liver by liver, you might say, or it might be brains or sweetbreads, the *hasápis* wooed the captain's bride.

"I wonder how he had the nerve. If you live in the *agorá*, your life is an open book. There are a thousand eyes to watch your every move, day and night. No night is so black that someone doesn't have an errand to do, a wine cask to turn, nets to mend, salt to borrow, oil to dip from a jar in a storeroom. Or just a bottle of *soúma* to share with friends in the warmth of a café."

A winter night without stars. Nothing is visible. The white walls of the houses do not give back even the faintest silver sheen, nor the shuttered windows betray the finest golden thread of light. On the little beach behind the *agorá*, the sea grinds pebbles like teeth; the sand-filled wind erodes the year's whitewash from the seaward wall of the church of Áyios Dimítrios. A lone fisherman, reeling home through the cold with a skinful of *soúma*, starts at a shadow under the captain's stairs. "Who is it?" he whispers. When no answer comes, he hurries on by, crossing himself, for it is after Christmas, when the wicked *kallikántzari* play tricks on mortals. And up the dark stairs, where the carnations are stiff and brown, moves a shadow. A dark door opens – no flickering yellow lamp throws a rectangle of light against the opposite wall – and they are in each other's arms and soon, between chill sheets, hot flesh seizes hot flesh, organs steam, slide against saliva, sweat and sperm. She arches her throat to cry but he stifles her."

But in the daylight, the man who was afraid recovers his courage: "That was no *kallikántzaros*," he chides himself, "but a man. What man? What man would not answer me?"

"More people knew than saw shadows slinking up stairs. The women knew, the older women, you can bet that. Mating is their specialty. They can tell by the way a girl carries a basket of grapes whether she's a virgin or panting not to be one, by how a young wife bends to scrub a pan with sand whether she's pregnant and how far gone. They look at the lines or lack of them around the eyes of a woman whose husband is in America and know whether she's consoled or faithful. They would know from how often and with what zeal the captain's bride whitewashed her steps and the stones in the street (her feet in rubber boots, her skirt pinned up). They would know, most of all, because she wouldn't dare to take her sheets to the river, where all the women washed, without washing them first at home.

"Did someone write to the captain? It's possible; people in this village can be cruel, and there are always a thousand scores to settle, a thousand jealousies and spites. But perhaps no one wrote and the captain said to himself one day, steaming into a foreign harbor, 'Why have I furnished a house and married a young and beautiful wife and locked myself up on this ship like a monk? Haven't I hidden safely in my house a great *stamní* full of gold líras?' This was what we did before banks: kept our savings in gold coins in a terra cotta jar and hid it. They still turn up, those old *stamnía*, buried in earth floors or plastered up in wells. 'That's a fortune,' he must have thought,' enough to last my little wife a lifetime of widowhood if the ship went down tomorrow. Why wait for shipwreck? It's time I got back to my village and started a family.'

"Anyway, one day shortly after Easter, the young bride – still a bride, not married even a year – received the letter, and nearly died of shock. The mail was very slow then, we had no telephones or telegraph, so the letter arrived only days before the husband himself was due. Did the letter bring her to her senses?

"You know," sighed the *mamí*, "when the farmer leads the cow or goat or lamb down the road from the farm, it is frisky. Out of the pen or stable or pasture, down that road that's been beckoning all its life, it trots. It kicks up its heels; it ambles to the verges to taste unfamiliar plants, drinks from the marble trough at the spring on the edge of town. But when it comes within sight or scent of the *sphageío*, I give you my word, it knows. Its eyes start white from their sockets; it pulls against the rope, bucking and leaping sideways, bleating or bellowing. The last half-mile is a struggle: the farmer pulling and cursing, the *hasápis* coming to his help, grabbing horns or tail, beating the animal with a stick. Those who witness turn away and cross themselves.

"The young bride must have felt that way. Free she had been, for a little while, free for the first time from the strict watch of her family – because then, well, a young girl who strayed did not get married, but became, you know, a woman for all men, like that Roúla out beyond Ambelás – three children with every color of hair and eyes! Shame! Maybe she felt free of her husband too, if he were older and had taken her for his own pleasure, without thinking. And now . . . You see, because she had no dowry, she was entirely dependent upon her husband for food and shelter. A woman with a dowry, a house that is, could have said to this captain if he started to roar, 'This is my house. Go sleep at your mother's.' He wouldn't have done that, you understand, because of the gossip. He'd have put a face on it. He'd have simply turned a deaf ear, inner and outer. Nothing would have happened. They'd have made it up. We're islanders, you know, not Maniates; we don't murder for pride. Of course, there would always have been the muzz-muzz and the sly words: 'Lovely loin the hasápis has today,' a neighbor might say to another in her hearing, or worse; there were a dozen puns with which to prick her skin, or pierce the captain's hide. He might have been offered too often a dish of bull's amílites. But if he'd any pride, he would have stood the test – after all, he wouldn't have been the first or last seafarer to wear the horns. And sooner or later, she'd have birthed a child and sealed the marriage, and they would have grown old and even longed for the days of tears and passion.

"But for this to happen, there had to be no evidence. Of the usual," and here she patted her belly with her clean blunt hand, "there was none. They had been careful, or she was really too young, or for all his brawn, perhaps . . .? Certainly he's had no children since, that I know of, and I would know. So that was all right. But the hasápis in his madness – for one must believe him mad; there is no other explanation – had left undeniable evidence of his presence in the bride's house. He had stolen the captain's golden fortune.

"No one ever learned how he discovered it. Had he found it himself or had she betrayed the hiding place, maybe a niche behind the plate rack or the bottom of a wardrobe? No one knew, no one knows, except the hasápis."

One night he comes, long after midnight, long before dawn. The door is unbarred. Yellow lights flicker from the bedroom. He creeps in on shoeless feet, unbuttoning as he goes. On the great brass bed (glowing gold), under the wall of ikons (winking gold), she lies, illuminated by a dozen lamps. She has oiled her dusky skin and bedecked her naked body with hundreds of the small gold coins, arranged them like the jewelry the women wore long ago: in her dark hair over her brow sparkle golden disks; on her smooth young breasts gleam crisscrossed lines of gold; loops of golden dots dance on her belly. As he enters the room, she raises her arms, hums a tune, carefully rotates her gold-hung shoulders in a soft sketch of a sensual dance. He stops, stunned, ox-eyed. She laughs and sits up. The coins fall to the bed; four or five stick to her damp breasts. She picks them off, scoops the others into the jar carelessly, upsetting it. It gushes gold like an opened vein. She spreads her arms. But as he peels back the trousers from his hot and tumid flesh, even as he falls upon her, panting and salivating, his eyes stray to the golden pool.

"So. The letter arrived. Could they have met once more? One night of panic, anger, tears? Who knows? The next day she rushes to the cache, to take money to fill her cupboards, to buy oil for the lamps, pirína for the brazier to welcome this husband even now sailing home, even now upon the sea between Piraeús and the island. But the hiding place is empty, as empty as a water jar left in the courtyard that howls as the wind passes over it, that howls for what had filled it and is gone. In the cache – no stamní, and not a single golden coin sparkling in the winter sun."

Early morning, cool and bright. The unkempt young bride in her róba and slippers rushes down the stairs to the street. At the bottom of the stairs, on the white-flagged road between the captain's house and the hasápiko, lies the broken stamní. She stoops, picks up the shards, turns them in her hands, fitting them together. Then she looks across the street. The hasápis stands in the doorway, smoking, his body wrapped in a clean red apron. She moves across the street, step by step, as though dragged. She confronts him, whispering anxiously. He replies not at all but, smoothing his mustache with his knuckle, regards the sunlight on the opposite wall, his blue eyes cold as winter sky. She whispers more loudly. A customer approaches, and he smiles and greets her: "Kaliméra, kaliméra!" But the bride is wild; her hair unravels from its plait, flies in her eyes. "Where is my gold?" she bellows. The customer starts, draws back and crosses herself. The hasápis calls to her: "Look, auntie, I have such nice lamb today!" He reaches down a bony haunch from a hook, lays it on his block, where all his knives lie gleaming, newly sharpened on his white marble slab. The bride's eyes show white with terror. She rushes in, grabs a knife longer than her arm. "Where is my gold?"

The butcher drops back to the street. "She's mad!" he cries. "Get out! She's mad! Call the priest!" Neighbors pour from houses and shops, herding together in the narrow street. The bride, knife in hand, faces them all, faces ruin, faces emptiness. She shifts the knife to her left hand, crosses herself three times slowly and, shifting again, with a single motion passes the knife over her throat.

"And so," sighed the *mamí*, "the captain came home to a funeral. He sold the house and went to live, alone for the rest of his life, on a farm high up the mountain near the monastery. He never again came to the village. As for the *hasápis*, he went to sea for a while but then he came back. There was nothing anyone could do, you see. They couldn't prove he'd seduced the bride nor stolen the gold, since it was found months later in a sack in the captain's storeroom. But from that time – why, it must be nearly fifty years – everyone in this village would rather fast all year long than buy a single chop from that butcher. And so, while he continues to live here, and he has family, of course, and some old men for company, from that time he has worked in exile, as you might say, in his *hasápiko* in the *hóra*.

"And until a few months ago, when, I hear, some foreigners rented it for a boutique, that shop has stayed closed all these years. They – his family – whitewashed it, as is proper after a death, and they had the priest in, *vévaia!* Two or three different priests – one all the way from Athens! But no amount of censing or chanting or sprinkling with basil and holy water would induce any villager to enter that shop, much less rent it. We're not fanciful here, but they say, *sto theó!*" – here she crossed herself – "where the walls were splashed with the bride's bright blood, even now, as the whitewash is brushed on, stains seep through, pale rose like the flesh of a slaughtered lamb."

Late on a warm July night, the narrow dark street is lit only by a dim street lamp and, as I approach, the faint flickers of vigil lamps in the little church of Ayía Ekateríni. Twining up from a hole in the flagstones is a flowering vine, a "tree of midnight," which censes the air with a deep sweetness. In front of a new, large, well-lit show window, three young village girls stand whispering. Their moving shadows play over a square of pale light on the white wall opposite, like shadow puppets on a Karaghiozi screen. It isn't foreigners after all who have rented the old *hasápiko*, abandoned before these girls' mothers were born, but my friend Katína. She has bravely painted the woodwork heart's-blood red and stocked her little boutique with clothes which appeal not to foreign but to village taste. In the window, puffed out with tissue paper is a small-waisted, tight-bodiced dress of snow-white cotton splashed with full-blown roses, pink and red.

The girls' eyes are dark; their hands stray into the light, touching waists, breasts. They whisper rapidly, and sigh. Each in her dream is whirling in the dance: from beneath the flowery skirt, her thighs flash brown and smooth; from the low bodice, her breasts, shining with sweat and gleaming with the gold of a cross and chain, lift high and round. The young men, the *pallikária*, stumble in the dance, stand stock-still, stunned, wiping their palms on their tightening trousers. The warm animal bodies, garlanded with roses, loose upon the summer night a fearful fragrance.

The Schoolteacher

Through the yellow-painted windows of the schoolroom, she looks into a back garden, now in November deserted, overgrown. Unpruned and rotting fruit trees, rusted tins, and decaying fish boxes lie among scattered clumps of calla leaves – glossy, dark green, shaped like stretched-out hearts. At the back, screening the garden from the road, is a break of *kalámi*. The canes, long-dried and splitting, rattle in the wind. The rose which bloomed all summer, lush with buds, with deep pink blooms, is now a tangle of thin wires, thorns, and shriveled orange hips.

She looks out her window past the lone pomegranate tree, naked now, stripped of the small, fine leaves, its branches black, broken, gnarled like arthritic claws. Hanging among them are the fruits, split and dried, dull rust color like old leather pouches, all the garnet seeds spilled out months ago.

Rhódi, rhódo, rhodokókino. Pomegranate, rose, rose red – the blush of rose over tan. "Your rose-red cheeks," said the island love song they danced to in the summer. Rose-red cheeks, tan skin, black lashes like feathers fluttering over his strong, smooth face, black-brown hair, a shadow of beard like smoke over the blush – all bathed in the sun, sweat standing in the dark hairline, running down his neck but never over the skin of his face, dry and smooth as fine leather.

She looks through the garden, past the canebrake, waving like wheat in the fierce wind, to the wall, beyond which is a road where a red tractor might pass.

Behind her she hears small, soft noises. The pupils, given a task, are yet aware of her abstraction. They have begun to giggle, the girls to drop their pencils, the boys to slyly kick the ones in front. She turns and chides them. The small disturbances still for a short time and she returns to the window.

She is remembering that day, only a year ago, harvesting olives on his farm, she in a faded red *róba* that became her, hair tied up in an old scarf, her bare, tan feet resting on the worn white canvas cloth under the tree. They had begun in the dark, before dawn, the orchard lit by the headlights of his tractor. He climbed the young trees and shook down the olives while she sat in a chair and with brown hands stripped the lower branches, looking carefully under the silver-green leaves to find the hidden olives. The bitter little fruit – blue-purple, green, gray-blue – pattering down on the canvas made a sound like soft, slow rain. They worked, laughing and singing – all love songs. "*I mána sou i poniri*," he sang, "Your mother, that wise old bird." And, "*Dío prássina mátia*," "Two green eyes have made me crazy," his tribute to her hazel eyes. His own amber eyes shone. She worked, stripping, stripping. The lap of the *róba* was covered with leaves. The tall cane *kofíni* filled with olives – once, twice, three times.

The warm *sirókos* stirred the leaves, and the sun as it grew higher flashed through the moving branches, dazzling her. Laughing and singing and sometimes, on his way to empty a *kofíni* into the truck, stopping to kiss, to fondle, they worked through the morning. It grew warmer; sweat began to dampen her hair. She removed her scarf and shook it out, running her hands, slightly oily from the olives, through the length of it, then retied the scarf. She was growing weary with happiness. Finishing his song, he climbed down from the tree, erect, strong, taking her onto him there in the open grove – hot skin, black lashes lying on red-bronze cheeks. She stretched her body to meet him. The light, the leaves. Ecstasy.

As they lay among the olives, his mother called them to dinner, a meager meal in a dirty kitchen. The woman was a well-known miser and slattern. The wine was watered and bitter. The younger woman could eat almost nothing, and exhausted, she collapsed onto the old white bed in the *salóni* and slept like the dead. When, a few hours later, they woke and went out to the grove, "Would you marry me," he said, "and sleep in that bed?" And she, dazed with the afternoon light and sleep, could say nothing, but looked and looked at him, breathing in warm air.

She had loved him since they were schoolchildren, tiny tots in blue smocks, he the older, a protector. Then she had gone on to high school in the *hóra* and he had gone to sea to make money for a tractor. She went to teachers' college and he came back to run the farm, his father aging fast. In her schools there had been friends, boyfriends even, but never lovers. She knew in her heart he would be her first and only lover, and now here they were, back, together, working together, lovers from the first night she returned to the village.

The next day, he'd hired a worker, the *mamí*'s husband Nikólas. The work went more quickly and gaily; the older man, seeing they were lovers, teased them, singing love songs:

> Your eyelashes shine
> Like the flowers of the field
>
> You lower your eyelashes
> And take my mind and reason away.

She left for a few minutes to fetch water for them. When she returned, Nikólas was subdued. A sudden shower sent them to take refuge in the pig house. To avoid the stink, she stayed outside under a large tree and so overheard them talking quietly.

"You are a fool," she heard Nikólas say. "You could have a wife who knows letters, who would improve you."

"My mother is getting old," her love replied. "She needs a *nífi* to clean and bake and wash for her. No educated woman can keep house, not on a farm."

When they returned to the trees, her lover began to sing, "*Mávra mátia, mávra fridía, mávra katsará malliá.*" "Black eyes, black eyebrows, black curly hair." He sang loudly, somewhat off-key, not looking at her. "It's only a song," she thought. "Only another song."

But *mávra mátia* she had, the awkward young woman from another island he married not two months later, this *nífi* who would clean and bake and wash.

And now the schoolteacher stands, looking out the schoolroom window at the abandoned garden, looking beyond it to the road where a red tractor might pass. Among the random clumps of calla leaves are chicken coops made from a discarded *kaíki* cabin, a decaying pastry case. The chickens peck freely among the trash. The hens are pure white, speckled, and black. The one rooster is a deep glossy rust, brilliant and oriental, his tail feathers long and stirring in the wind. He is standing among the lily leaves. Without moving his body, he turns his head, his scarlet comb waving. He calls the white hen. She comes, stepping delicately through the mud. They stand for a moment immobile, despite the strong wind, making a still picture – white, dark green, rust – clear and glazed as enamel. Then he moves, mounts her in the quick irritable way of roosters. She squawks in the indignant way of hens. And it is over.

The children are restless behind her. She turns, asks them to pass up their notebooks. From the principal's room, the bell sounds. She dismisses them and for once they leave quietly. She does not return to the window but sits at her desk, her head in her hands. She remembers another song Nikólas sang that day in the olives:

> *Youth only comes once…*
> *When it goes it doesn't come back,*
> *However much you ask it to . . .*

The years fly away like birds
and you can't take them back . . .
From hour to hour the storm approaches.
The first wind takes them and they fly away.

IV

Winter
Paréa
Taken by Haros
The Eye
The Deluge
The Ikon Carver
Priests
Pápa Ilías

Winter

"*Krío! Himónas!*" the bundled-up, rosy-nosed villagers call to each other. "Cold! Winter!" Voriás, the North Wind, whips down from the frozen Caucasus. His bright blue eyes are like lapis flecked with gold, his cheeks like two red balloons. "Here I am!" he says, roaring with laughter. "Phhhhhoooooooo!" The wind rushes upon the village like a Vandal horde. Doors slam, shutters bang. People dash to find large stones to prop them open or closed. Chairs left out in streets and harbor from the sociable summer are tumbled legs over backs, and the wind careers away to freeze begonias and blacken basil.

The housewife hanging out the icy, wet, flapping laundry wrings her poor hands, red and swelling with chilblains. Fishermen gather their saffron nets and shuttles and retreat to the *apothíkis*, storerooms in the harbor and *agorá*. They sit on low stools, one leg outstretched to anchor the net, and weave all day, mending the hundreds of meters of nets torn in the summer by dolphins. Every hour or so, someone gets up in turn to go to the *kafeneío* for coffee or sage tea. They mend and talk, mend and drink coffee, mend and complain about the fragility of nets, the deviousness of fish brokers, the elusiveness of fish.

Housewives dive into trunks, removing underwear of fine, white, generally homespun wool. For farmers and fishermen, there are finely knit, white wool socks and *fanéllas*, undersweaters knit in lacy patterns at cuff and throat; long johns, and, rarer these days, cummerbunds to keep working backs from stiffening. The women pull out for themselves full slips of the creamy, fine-spun wool. The children all get caps and vests, sweaters and jackets, with wool pants for the boys and skirts for the girls to wear under their cotton school uniforms. For the babies, out come full suits of hand-knit wool, caps with pompoms in pink and yellow. The knits are washed again, to get out the smell of mothballs, and are hung on the line. The *fanéllas*, knit with dolman sleeves, are dried by running a length of cane through the sleeves and resting the ends on two balconies. Over every balcony rail hang the winter rugs and blankets, airing in the still-dry wind. Long-fleeced white and red *flokátis* share the railings with hand-woven blankets with stripes of black, white, and rust. Soaking in the cool sun are the pure, white-on-white homespun wool *hrámis*, bedcovers deeply edged with fine white crocheted lace. On every sunny, blowy day, the white village will be draped with these flags and banners, fluttering like gossip from balcony to balcony. The wind is dry now, but once the rains start in earnest, the moan of every housewife will be "*Igrasía!*" "Damp!" *Krío* and *Igrasía*, Cold and Damp, work together to make life miserable for the villagers: knees stiffen, hands gnarl, ears blaze, noses drip. Only the aging sun, so cruel in its summer prime, affords relief, passing through open windows to dry damp walls, gathering itself in walled gardens to warm old backs and wrap orange trees in its paternal embrace.

The harbor *kafeneío* has two doors, one on the harbor, one at the back. It is very bad luck to enter by one door and leave by another, but anyway no one uses the front door in winter; it would slam into the room and the cold would grab the sitters and frost them blue. Whoever enters from the back door shuts it immediately or else hears a polyphony of "Close the door! Close it! Don't you have doors in your house?" from the backgammon players, clacking their dice and disks down in the wooden boxes. The tobacco smoke gathers and makes a fog inside the room. The crowded little shop smells of stale tobacco, damp wool, old newspapers, coffee.

In the winter, when the North Wind is blowing, people avoid the main streets and open spaces like the *platía* and the harbor, but go about their shopping and other chores by means of the *stenákis*, narrow winding streets sheltered from the bulldozer wind by the two-storied houses. Still, sometimes it's necessary to come out from a *stenáki* into a more open street or the *platía* and then, if the wind is fierce, you must lean into it, head down, and clutch very tightly your jacket or coat, for this is not the weak wind who lost to the sun in the folk story, but a wind that can knock you down and tear the boots off your feet, strip the whitewash off a house, freeze the leaves of almond trees, and, with a handful of sand, etch marble.

The gulls love it. They sail and play in the wind like children in the waves of the sea. The anemones, named for it (*ánemos* is wind) love it too. But human beings only endure it, muttering, calling to each other, "*Krío! Himonas! Ánemos!*"

Winter's colors run the spectrum: there are days when the sun is lemon yellow, the sky bright blue, the sea navy, the white caps frosty white. And then there are the gray days when the lines of rain end in tiny splashes on a sea like slate. To dispel the gray-day blues, get out in the country, perhaps to a citrus grove. There, hanging among the glossy, dark-green leaves, the globes of brilliant oranges, mandarins, and lemons light up the world like lanterns at a gala party.

As the days draw in, so do the people. "*Ela!*" they call to each other, "Come close and keep warm!" This is a greeting and an invitation. With the short days, the shops in the evening send their lights out into the dark streets like beacons; people crowd into these oases of light and warmth, prolong shopping for a good gossip and a bit of warmth before braving the arctic wind of the streets.

Winter is a time of retreat. The harbor, north-facing, is all but deserted. Most of the chairs and tables that blanket the pavement in summer have been stacked and stored. Only the boldest among the fishermen may sit and sip a coffee in a patch of sunlight. Traditionally, the boats would not put out to sea again until the first week in January. A proverb says, "From the Cross, tie up. From the Cross, cast off." From *Tou Stavroú*, the feast of the Holy Cross in the middle of September, to *Theophánia* (Epiphany), the sixth of January, when the priest throws a cross into the sea, the fishermen should stay in harbor, careening their boats, scrubbing and painting them, mending their nets. In reality, whether they go out or not depends on weather and prices.

Before television, gossip was the main winter activity, at least for the women, who would gather in each other's houses in late afternoon to knit, embroider (the girls and their mothers working on their *prikas*, dowries), and "turn the coffee cups" to read their fortunes. Village women, except perhaps at New Year's, do not play cards, although at one time urban women were so addicted to playing a card game called *Koún-kán* that the Junta outlawed it to improve their morals. For men, cards and *távli*, backgammon, are the winter standbys. When they are not working (early morning for farmers bringing eggs, cheeses, and other goods to market; mid-morning for fishermen out before dawn setting their nets; mid-afternoon for village shopkeepers), they gather in the cafés to play, listen to the radio, and argue about what it is the government is not saying.

This winter cold is something you cannot outwit, cannot make sport of. You can't ski in it, skate on it, sled down it. Sport is a life activity divorced from original necessity: in years past, Norwegians would ski and Hollanders skate to get from one place to another in the winter, but now sports skiers and skaters expend quantities of fuel in cars, trains, and even planes to get to where they can ski from nowhere to nowhere or skate in circles. On Páros no activity had yet been divorced from the environment. Imagine this: a winter pentathlon of Grumbling, Shivering, Shopping Fast, Hunting for the Electrician, Hovering over the Heater. Perhaps the most gymnastic thing my friends and I used to do on winter days was walk out to certain stony fields, a mile up a dry riverbed, fighting the brilliant chill of late January to find the anemones – the windflowers, with their delicate flat faces of white, mauve, pink, and an occasional brilliant magenta; their smudgy, soot-black eyes; their lacy leaves like green fichus – to whom this freezing, tossing wind is *Zoí*! Life! The anemones draw their plasma from tiny pockets of not-quite-soil (not a Turkish coffee-cupful each) in fields of exposed marble, limestone, and granite that break down an ounce in a century, if that. Cruel that we dug them out, roots and all, took them home to set in a bowl of moss. They would bloom for weeks, hardy, delicate, winning, in houses barely heated, where we sat, embroidering, gossiping (*"That Zambétta!"*), turning the coffee cups (*Will he? Will I?*). When the anemones faded and the petals dropped, brushed with black powder, I would take the roots out and plant them in a field, on the chance that a spark of life remained.

Two Divinities

Almost unnoticed in this cold, birth is taking place. In the ashes of the summer, fertilized by gentle rains, Persephone is rising green and sweet in the fields, and Jesus is growing in his Mother's belly. The wheat is as delicate and soft as a boy's beard, green as a parrot's wing. Green again veils the naked earth, the rocks, the shards.

As the Child grows in the Panagía's womb, slowly, so slowly, the new wheat sown in the autumn germinates, puts down roots, nurtured by the Mother. Slowly, slowly, it greens and grows, weathering and being strengthened by the cold, bending to the wind. In late winter or early spring, it flowers, a hardly noticeable stage. At the same time of life, the boy Jesus confounds the scholars in the temple. But then the quiet years pass. His thought matures while the child Persephone grows slowly into the tender transparency of a nine-year-old girl. Slowly, slowly. The field flowers know they are coming, both of them. They have seen these litanies; they join, one by one, the procession. They too germinate, form roots, buds. As the Child grows, the Mother recedes. What begins beating through each stalk, each maturing being, is the necessity to separate, to leave the self of the child; to cease taking, begin giving; to expand, become more, become universal; to multiply – if not in body then in influence – and, having spent life and burnt energy, become spirit.

What matter if the individual dies if his spirit lives on, if her seeds find fertile ground? As each moves toward his or her end, the brilliant poppies like prophetesses begin to sigh, to sing of blood. There is no achieving spirit without blood. "This is my body: take, eat." Persephone gathering flowers. Betrayal, rape, the spear in the heart. To achieve resurrection, the individual must die, but must he be cut down violently, must she be raped?

It seems so. The sacrificed one gives up life in the world for an existence in another dimension, an eternity of influence for myriad generations who follow. So Jesus, simple Jesus the villager who spoke of bread and wine and fish, sharing and forgiving, becomes total and eternal spirit, and Persephone marries her rapist and spends half her time in Hell, her childhood left behind, gone to nourish those who, no longer believing in myth, no longer remembering, take the sacrifice for granted.

Panigýria

Winter is as wrapped up in holidays as children in sweaters. Celebrating helps people keep warm, especially during the *Dodecámeron* or twelve days of Christmas, when five especially holy days and several popular name days – Christos, Manólis, Maria, and others – mean that almost every day the people are drinking wine and ouzo, eating sweet *kourabiédes* and *melomakárona*, not to mention winter-defeating dishes such as fried *bakaliáros*, salt cod, with garlic sauce, pork with celery, or lamb fricassee with spinach – all of which fuel dancing, whether at home, in the *taverna*, or at the *ouzerí*.

The *Dodecámeron* begins on December 25 with the *yiortí* or celebration of the birth of Christ, continues on through the *yiortí* of Ayios Vasílis (also New Year's), and finishes on January sixth with the triple celebration of the baptism of Jesus, the miracle at Cana, and the coming of the Magi. But even then all is not over! The very next day is the well-celebrated *yiortí* of the Baptist himself, Áyios Ioannis, for whom so many Yiánnis and Yiannoúlas are named. The sweet bakers are kept busy turning out *galaktoboúrekos* and *koulourákia*. The grocers are hard put to keep supplies of ouzo and cognac on the shelves, and the *taverna* owners are anxiously knocking on their barrels, hoping there will be enough wine to see them through the season. And everywhere, the streets are full of the cheerful sounds of "Hrónia pollá!" as villagers wish the celebrators, "Many years!"

The extended holiday season, however welcome, is the result of massive confusion in the ancient world about calendars, combined with canny opportunism on the part of early Christians. Celebrating the birth of Christ was not common until about the fourth century, when Christians in the Roman Empire, newly recognized and encouraged by the emperor Constantine, rededicated the week-long Roman winter solstice holiday, Saturnalia, to the celebration of the Nativity of Jesus. Saturnalia had been a kind of "free week" which made up for the extra days not accounted for in the old lunar calendar. When the considerably (but not entirely) more accurate Julian calendar replaced it, the solstice tended to fall on December 25. The popular Persian cult of Mithra observed the "return of the invincible sun" on that day, so the Roman Christians were able to celebrate their holy events without depriving themselves and others of merrymaking. Egyptian Christians did the same, coordinating (or co-opting) the January sixth celebration of an Egyptian god, Aiona. Later this date would be assigned to the baptism of Christ.

As all the calendars had faults, dates for fixed feasts tended to vary wildly from region to region. Attempts by the early church (or churches) to link seasonal observances such as solstices with specific calendar dates actually resulted in a wide range of days according to an assortment of calendars. While the majority of European and Eastern Christian churches are now on the almost faultless Gregorian, quite a few Orthodox denominations, such as Russian, remain loyal to the Julian. Greece officially adopted the Gregorian in 1923, but the transition was not smooth. Even in this tiny village, a couple of dozen people refuse to acknowledge what they consider a heretical calendar, continuing to celebrate all fixed feasts almost two weeks after the common holidays have passed. My landlord Yiánnis, not himself an Old Calendarist, was married to beautiful and pious Iríni, a member of that sect, and I was always trying to figure out when I could wish him or her "*Hrónia pollá*" without upsetting one or the other.

It seems no accident that winter boasts so many holidays, so many occasions for feasting. The north wind blasts the houses stair-stepped up the faces of three hills and howls through the narrow lanes. Neither houses nor shops are much heated; even the *taverna* and the sweet shops depend for warmth on the mass of human bodies. The bodies keep warm by eating and moving, and the preferred movement not connected to work is dancing.

Winter Sea

Winter holidays have a lot to do with winter weather, particularly the winter sea. Despite the annual blessing of the waters for the last two thousand years, the sea remains, for the seafarer, a wild and untamable force – in the words of the liturgy, the "lair of dragons."

Certainly the sea in winter is something to be reckoned with. When the north wind blows steadily, it is safe for the fishermen to go out, though

the question is passed around the *kafeneío*, "How many Beaufort?" referring
to the measurement of wind force. When winds blow from other directions, the seafarers walk up and down the moles, counting white caps,
trying to estimate the danger. Science inevitably bows to experience, as
a young fisherman consults an elder: "*Bárba*, what do you say? Can we go
out?"

"Your wife have a black dress?"

"Yes."

"Then go out. She'll make a pretty widow."

Storms endanger not only the *kaíkis*. The large, clumsy ferries from
Piraeús are often stuck in harbor for days, waiting out a *fortoúna*, storm.
If the storm arises or worsens while at sea, the captains on this route will
try to make it to this village's mile-long deep water inlet, protected by
high hills on three sides, rather than the *hóra's* wide, shallow harbor open
to gusty crosswinds. It is not unusual to see in the inlet, perhaps while
shaking out a blanket from a balcony, two or three large ships riding out a
storm, noses to the wind. If, like ships of old, they had female figureheads,
their long hair would be streaming back over the decks.

Ayíou Nikólaou

The earliest winter holiday, on December 6, is the festival of Áyios
Nikólaos, patron saint of seafarers. Before becoming a saint, Nikólaos was
a fourth-century bishop in Myra, an inland area of Asia Minor. While he
was on the sea leg of a pilgrimage to Jerusalem, a gigantic storm arose and
the rudder of the ship was broken. Nikólaos prayed to God to calm the
waters; the storm ceased, and left bobbing in the gentle waves was a large
piece of wood which the sailors were able to fashion into a rudder. The
pilgrims reached port safely. Nikólaos' view of the matter was that Satan
had caused the storm, reminding us of Homer's "angry Poseidon."

For this and subsequent marine miracles, Nikólaos is considered the
protector of the seafarer. Many boats are named for him, and every one
carries his ikon. It's a rare harbor that doesn't have a church dedicated to
him. In this village, his chapel sits at the very end of one of the moles in
the harbor. From the sea, it is the first thing you make out as you sail in,
nearing home – almost a beacon with its blindingly white walls and cross-
surmounted roof.

On the morning of Ayíou Nikólaou, following the liturgy, the priest
leads the villagers in a procession from the church down to the harbor,

where all the *kaḯkis*, gaily decorated with flags and pennants, crowded gunwale to gunwale, are bobbing up and down in a slight breeze. There he asks God's mercy on the seafarers and their craft, sprinkling holy water on the boats. Níkos is a very popular name, so many shops are closed as their owners sit at the cafes and treat their friends to drinks. In the evening there will be "tables," dinner parties in the houses as well as the *tavernas*. Nikoléttas entertain at home; their friends come, bringing boxes of sweets and pastries and bottles of *kítro* and other liqueurs.

A parallel event is the *yiortí* of Áyios Modéstos, some days later, when shepherds and farmers feed their animals *prosforá*, the bread of the Eucharist they have brought home from the church. Both boats and animals, vital to the survival of the humans, are thus folded into God's grace and human embrace.

Christmas

Between Ayíou Nikólaou and Theophánia falls the celebration of the Nativity. Northern European and North American winter visitors to Greece may be surprised to find how little hoopla surrounds this day which, in their climes, is perhaps the most important holiday in the year. But if we remember that Christmas was meant to be celebrated on the solstice (the old Roman one), we may understand that, although the days are short in December and long in June, nothing so dramatic (and fear-inspiring to the primitive mind) as the days with no sunrise or sunset happens in Greece. Nor is the island winter a barren waste of ice and snow. In fact, at Christmas the fields are newly greening with the delicate, fall-sown wheat, a sign of renewal more meaningful than an evergreen tree, because it says not that life continues despite apparent death but that we will eat again next year, God willing – and if it rains enough in the months ahead.

No tradition of gift-giving exists. No Santa Claus, no presents under the tree for Yiannákis and Yiannoúla, no crass commercialism. Children do get special attention on New Year's Day, which is the *yiortí* of Ayios Vasílis, called "the Lettered." Ayios Vasílis is dear to children because he teaches them their *alphavíta*, counting the letters off on his staff: *álpha, víta, gámma, délta*. He rewards the children for learning; these rewards are small but meaningful, mostly candies.

However, in recent times Santa's appeal (to whom, children or merchants?) has co-opted Vasílis' privilege. Even though the ascetic saint is called "the father of Orthodox monasticism" and in his ikons in no way resembles a jolly old elf, one New Year's Day in the *hóra* he circulated the town in full Santa Claus outfit with a sackful of sweets for children. So foreign did that seem to the dog of Phíllipas, a café owner, that the dog bit the saint in the seat of his crimson pants.

Christmas is celebrated first on the Eve, the fortieth day of Advent, with a supper of *nistísimo*, fasting food, perhaps a hearty bean soup or vegetable stew, and then on Christmas Day, after the liturgy, with a traditional dinner of pork – although in recent years turkey has crept onto the menu. However, each house must have a loaf of *Christópsomo*, an egg-rich bread redolent with orange peel and anise seed. I watched my neighbor Marió make a very large one for her very large family. After shaping the round, she topped it with a cross whose even arms she split and curled at the edges. Glazing it with egg yolk, and covering it with a clean cloth, she took it proudly to the bakery, giving peeks of it to whomever greeted her on her way.

As Santa Claus and turkey have sneaked into the culture, so has the northern druidical Christmas tree. Athens erects a huge, brilliantly lit evergreen tree in Syntagma, the central *platía*, but such a custom had not yet penetrated the island when I lived there, where the traditional symbol of Christmas was a boat – a wooden model of a *kaíki* about four feet long. It was displayed in the *platía* during the Twelve Days, and on one evening during that time a *paréa* of young men carried it through the village, going from house to house, singing the *kálanda* and collecting money (and drinks, of course). The money would be distributed to a needy person, perhaps someone who had been injured or suffered damage to vital equipment such as a *kaíki* or tractor.

The *kálanda* is the only Christmas "carol" in Greece. There are two versions: one for Christmas and one for New Year's. Usually it is sung by children who race around the streets from house to house, ting-a-linging on a triangle, banging on the doors. "*Na ta poúme?*" they cry, when you open your door, and if you agree, they sing a breathless four or five verses (out of probably twenty) while waiting impatiently for you to pony up with a few drachmas and some hard candies. Then, pocketing the money and unwrapping the sweets, they call "*Hrónia pollá!*" and race off to knock on your neighbor's door. You hear them up and down the street: "*Na ta poúme?*" the ting-a-ling-a-ling of the triangle, and the echoes of the old familiar words in an unfamiliar language: "Christ is born today . . . Hosts of angels singing . . . All nature rejoices." *Hrónia pollá!*

Kallikántzari

"The twelve days of Christmas are a dangerous time," said my friend Thanásis the carpenter, who kept me informed on traditions, teaching me to greet people with "*Kálomína*" and "*Kalí evdomáda*" on the first days of the month and week.

"How so?" I asked. A few days before Christmas, we were sitting in Spiros' bar and everyone seemed pretty merry to me.

"*E lipón*, there are bad little demons called *kallikántzari*, who live in the underworld. They're called the 'enemies of the sun.' Most of the year they stay put, gnawing on the tree that holds up the world. They're always about to gnaw through the trunk, when the twelve days roll around. Then, once a year, a split opens up between the two worlds and the demons can rise up and make mischief among people."

"What do they do?" I asked.

Thanásis was vague. "Oh, sour the milk . . . stop up the chimneys."

"They don't steal babies?"

"Never heard of that. *E*, Spiros, ever hear of *kallikántzari* stealing babies?" Spiros lifted his chin to say no. "To protect the people from these demons," Thanásis continued, "the priest sprinkles the houses with holy water on the eve of *Theophánia*. And the world is saved for another year."

"Why does he wait eleven days?" I asked. Spiros looked blank.

"You need to protect yourself," he said, pouring us another ouzo . The discussion had by this time become general. "Keep a log burning in your fireplace all twelve days," called a farmer from across the room.

"Log? Where can I find a log?" The only firewood in the village belonged to the bakery.

" Leave a saucer of meat on your hearth at night. They like meat."

"And if I don't?" Everyone looked very glum but no one mentioned specific threats.

In any case, the priest takes care of the *kallikántzari*. Several days later, on the morning of *Theophánia*, a windy morning, brilliant and freezing, I heard shouting and laughter in the street. Sticking my head out the front door, I saw – swooping through the narrow street like a great, wind-maddened raven, black sleeves and skirts of the *ráso* flying, stovepipe cap falling off at every corner – the new young priest, Pápa Ilías. Dashing ahead of a band of shrieking, panting boys and girls, he leapt into doorway after doorway, sprinkling holy water inside the houses with an aspergill, a sprig of basil saved from the freezing wind in a sheltered garden. The boy swinging the smoking censer was so small he could scarcely keep it above the street. He was helped up a doorstep by a hand suddenly still and patient.

In a folk poem, the *kallikántzari* are calling to each other:

Go! Let's get going!
Mad priest is coming!
With his aspergill
Wetting the evil things on the head!

And, continues the poem, the little demons "vanished like smoke." The world was safe for another year.

New Year's

New Year's Eve and even New Year's Day are celebrated with feasts and gambling. All the New Years I lived in or visited in the village I celebrated with the Maroulídis family: Maria and Iordánis, their daughter Alíki and son Háris. They had befriended me my first summer, when Alíki had folded me into her *paréa*. Owners of the best, for a long time the only real, hotel in the village, the Maroulídis lived in the winter in Athens but always came to the village for the holidays and opened the hotel just to entertain their friends. Not only were they hospitable, the whole family were superb cooks, so when they mounted a feast, whether New Year's or name day, it was a feast indeed.

Maria celebrated on December 26, Iordánis (Jordan) on *Theophánia*, and Alíki in late August, always the end-of-season blowout for the *paréa* and the family. The family hosted so many feasts that I cannot now distinguish one from another. The table was always covered with *mezédes*: rich *moussaká* with bechamel light as sea foam, meat-filled grape leaves in egg-lemon sauce, crisp fried *kalamarákia*, zingy *tzatzíki*, smoky eggplant salad made with tahini, maybe steak or liver grilled and cut up, and of course bitter black olives and creamy féta. Winter salads might be boiled beets with garlic sauce, romaine with fresh fennel fronds, or lacy, tissue-thin, lemon-dressed cabbage. And for entree, perhaps beef in a red sauce, or pork stewed with celery. Fried potatoes always.

At New Year's there would be no dessert, because we would all be waiting for the *vasilópita*, the moist yellow Vasílis' cake that contained a lucky coin. This cake would be cut by the hostess at midnight. The first slice was for the Christ Child, the second for the Panagía, the next "the house," then the master of the house and the mistress, then everyone present by age from oldest to youngest. My first New Year's in the village, I found the coin in my slice, which should have meant prosperity for me in the coming year. Did it? Prosperity comes in many forms. I remember that year was particularly rich in experience and learning.

While eating and drinking, we danced – what a luxury to have an entire hotel dining room to dance in! Here we could make a line of a dozen or so to dance syrtos or *kalamatianós*. At this *gléndi*, Yiánnis (a cousin of Thanásis who lived in Athens) and I first danced *tsiftelli bállos*, which combines belly dance with *bállos*. We did it not too badly, and in after years it became a sort of tradition. But dancing soon gave way to serious card playing (although for very low stakes), because how one wins or loses at New Year's predicts one's prosperity or lack of it in the year to come. "Everybody gambles," says Kalliópi, "even Grandma. We do it to tempt our luck. 'For the good, for the luck,' we say."

New Year's Day is a very quiet time. Most stores remain closed. Custom is slow in any case, as many people are suffering from overindulgence and lack of sleep. Groceries open for an hour or two, but the owners, red-eyed and grumpy, lock the doors as soon as possible. The smoggy cafés are filled with dedicated card players attempting to beat the odds and gain the promised good fortune. No talk of politics today, no discussion of the weather. It could be minus ten degrees or as warm and bright as August, and no one would notice. Cards are slapped on the tables with an aggressive "*Na!*" Those not playing stand around and watch, playing vicariously, not risking any money but generous with their advice: "Play that one! No, that one! Ach! Tch." The watchers dispute with each other about what the players should have done.

On New Year's Day, Alíki and I went to visit Anna, to play cards. Earlier, she and her mother Mersiniá had walked out to the country to dig sea squill, a large bulb with straplike leaves like a giant hyacinth, and nailed it to the front door jamb. "For good luck in the New Year," Mersiniá said. I guessed, from the shape, it was a forgotten fertility symbol.

Theophánia

Theophánia or Epiphany, which celebrates Christ's baptism on January sixth, is as concerned with sweet water as Ayíou Nikólaou is with salt. Such water, in the form of winter rains, is vital to the growth of wheat, the renewal of the vines and fruit trees, even the filling of summer-depleted wells. Although baptism is an important Christian practice, it seems to have derived from a Jewish ritual bath requiring complete immersion called *mikveh*. In Jesus' time it was required for women after menses and childbirth, priests at ordination and before services, and adult males once in their lifetimes. The immersion was to take place preferably in a stream or river, or, if none were available, a large tub filled with rainwater. The *mikveh* was administered by a priest. Christ's cousin, Áyios Ioánnis, is said to have been from a priestly family, so it seems that Jesus' baptism, far from being unique, may have been the *mikveh* prescribed for all Jewish males. However, in ordinary baths of purification, the bather is cleansed by the water. Jesus had no need of purification but humbled himself to undergo the ritual. At the moment of Jesus' rising from immersion, God showed Himself in the form of a dove, and all there heard His voice, saying, "Thou art my beloved son in whom I am well pleased." Jesus' divinity then flowed into the waters of Jordan, and thence into all sweet waters – rivers, creeks, and springs – purifying them, it might be, of all the influences of the classical Greek nereids and river deities, and any other surviving nature spirits.

On the morning of Theophánia, perhaps the second loveliest of the Orthodox liturgies is sung, the most stirring being the midnight service at *Pásca*, Easter, with its flood of candlelight and explosive climax of pyrotechnics and rockets. Theophánia , "the manifestation of God," celebrates God's announcement of his fatherhood of Jesus. In the service, two blessings of the waters take place. In the first, a quantity of water from the church well is blessed. With this water, the priest sprinkles the villagers with a sprig of basil, blessing them. They also take this water – called *ayíasmos* – home in jars, to be kept on the shelf with the family ikons and used to cure ailments, secure a safe journey, or exorcize the Eye.

After the water is blessed, the priest reads Ayios Márkos' account of Jesus' baptism: "And straightway coming up out of the water, He saw the Heavens opened, and the Spirit like a dove descending upon him." At this moment, a white dove is released from behind the altar and flies upward, over the congregation, circling the dome of the church. Even though whirling white clouds of the birds against the blue sky are a common sight, at that moment this particular dove seems indeed the Holy Spirit, fluttering above the worshipers to both acknowledge and commend the Son and bless all of those assembled.

To witness the second blessing of the waters, the villagers follow the priest down to the harbor, where he again attempts to bring the wild sea into Christ's embrace. Three times he dips a golden cross into it, then finally throws it – not too far – into the icy sea. Retrieving the cross is a sort of contest, reserved for boys. Six or eight brave (or intending to be brave) ones stand at the edge of the mole, shivering in their bathing suits, hopping up and down, impatient for the prayers to be over. When the cross splashes into the harbor, the boys leap or dive into the freezing water, ducking up and down like otters, searching the silty bottom for the glint of gold. After a few minutes, a streaming head shoots up; a hand clutches the golden prize. All the divers are quickly wrapped in towels and hurried home, leaving the chattering winner to accept applause and congratulations. He will be a hero for a year and the trophy is his to keep and wear on a golden chain.

Theophánia commemorates another event in Christ's life concerning water. Some days after his baptism, he was attending a wedding at Cana with his mother. Perhaps because he had brought along his disciples, the wine ran out, and Mary urged Jesus to do something about it. He demurred at first, saying his "time was not yet come," but eventually, like a good son, he gave in and instructed the servants to pour water into several stone vessels, "after the manner of the purifying of the Jews," and from the water he created wine. The giver of the feast praised him, as the wine was better than that which he himself had originally offered the guests.

The Magi

The third event that is celebrated on January sixth is the visit of the Magi to the infant Jesus. Again, the timing of this event was the subject of dispute for centuries. Western artists usually show the Wise Men kneeling in the straw of the stable on the night Jesus was born, but others believe it was not until many weeks, months, or even years after the birth that they arrived to pay homage to the Babe.

Who were these Magi? Where did they come from? How did they get to Jerusalem? Although they are often called kings, the best guess seems to be that they were Zoroastrian priests from Persia or Babylon, skilled astrologers and scholars who had studied prophecies and anticipated the arrival of a messiah. Their journey to discover him is reminiscent of the Tibetan priests' search for the Dalai Lama, except that the Magi's journey was over a thousand miles each way.

Like many scholars, the Magi were not wise in the ways of the world. When they reached Jerusalem, they went straight to King Herod, thinking that he would be overjoyed at the news that a messiah was born in his kingdom. Fortunately, after finding the Babe, they decided not to go back to Herod and tell him where the child was to be found, and so saved Jesus from the slaughter of the first-borns. It is not clear where the holy family was when the Magi arrived – they may have lived quietly for some time in Bethlehem or elsewhere until the Wise Men unwittingly drew Herod's attention to them. Then, warned by an angel, the family fled into Egypt where they remained for some years, safe from the infanticide of the jealous king.

The oddest thing about the Magi is that they appear on the scene, seeming with their gifts of gold and incense to validate the prophecies of the coming of a messiah, and then they disappear, back to Persia perhaps, where nothing more is heard from them. Nor does their discovery seem to have had any lasting effect in their homeland. And yet, two thousand years later, in every church in Christendom, small boys in their bathrobes, caped and turbaned with the family towels, kneel at straw-filled cribs to commemorate the visit of the wonderful, elusive, mysterious Magi.

Another name for *Theophánia* is *Ta Phóta*, the lights. Religion says this is because Christ is so identified with light: he is "Light of Light," "the Light of the World," is "clothed in light" – by all of which is meant that his words and deeds save mankind from ignorance and despair. However, because again these celebrations take place around the solstice, it seems probable that somewhere, sometime, there was a festival of lights on that day, perhaps not unlike that in India. But if there ever was such a custom in Greece, it has not survived.

Ayíou Ioánnou

The day after *Theophánia* is Áyios Ioannis' *yiorti*. Yiánnis, the demotic name for Ioánnis or John, is such a popular name that there is a saying, "Without Yiánnis or Yiórgos, the house is empty." So many Yiánnises and Yiannoúlas will be celebrating today that it might as well be a national holiday. If your plumber or electrician is a Yiánnis, you will just have to put up with a dripping faucet or a blown fuse until the next day. Ayios

Ioannis is called "Pródromos" or the Forerunner, because he denied his own importance and told followers that a greater than he was soon to appear. So important to Orthodox Christianity is John's role in Jesus' life – they were first cousins through their mothers – that the ecclesiastical calendar accords him almost as many holy days as the Panagía, celebrating his meeting with Jesus on January sixth, his nativity on June twenty-fourth, and, alas, his beheading, brought about by the infamous Salome, on August twenty-ninth.

Winter Activities

After twelve, or actually thirteen, days of feasting, the villagers are generally glad to get back to work. The fishermen's mended nets lie in neat, yellow coils on the moles, waiting to be loaded onto the decks of the sea-hungry *kaíkis*. The housewives' kitchens are undergoing a thorough cleaning. The shopkeepers are taking inventory, counting cans of tomatoes, cases of biscuits, and barrels of wine, all preparatory to making out their tax forms. If there is a winter sport, it is a kind of fencing between the tax assessors and the business owners, the former trying to discover cheating and the latter trying to get away with it. Such maneuvering was a lot easier when all transactions were in cash; computers with point-of-sale programs are taking the joy out of it. "But fear not," says Manólis. "Cheating is our national pastime. You know how creative Greeks are! Besides, the word for legal is *nomimon*, a word you can read forwards or backwards. So what is legal is a matter of interpretation!"

Women in the winter spend their free time (after a long morning of cleaning, shopping, and cooking the midday dinner) embroidering, spinning, knitting, or crocheting. Embroidery is the traditional woman's art; museums all over Europe attest to the beauty, complication, and creativity of Greek traditional embroidery. In the Benaki Museum in Athens there is a shift from this island, white cotton with long, wide sleeves and a hem thickly embroidered with brilliant flowers, meant to show under a high-waisted jumper. The brilliant embroidery recalls spring meadows rich with poppies, vetch, and daisies. Traditionally, every woman was expected to take to her marriage a chest full of elaborately embroidered clothing, covers for mantelpiece and tables, and linen towels called *tsevrédes*, said to be gifts exchanged between bride and groom. In addition, she was expected to have a lifetime supply of faggoted and hem-stitched sheets, cut-work curtains, and hand-woven wool bedcovers dripping with crocheted lace. Despite modern ideas about dowries (they are now illegal), most of the young women and their mothers I knew kept busy all winter embroidering, although they generally worked cross-stitch patterns from women's magazines or needlepoint designs (such as the "Last Supper") preprinted on canvas. Some women's magazines occasionally publish a traditional design but mostly they are lost, gone to museums in Europe and Athens.

Aside from cheating, embroidery, and gossip, life is dull. Winter weather rules all. Shopping is a necessity, not a social occasion. Quickly passing shoppers call, "Kaliméra" through a scarf over the nose and do not stop to exchange news. Anyone who has relatives in Athens, home of movie theaters, central heating, and department stores, finds reason to go there. The twice-yearly sales are a powerful attraction, drawing crowds even when the seas are black and treacherous and the ships' decks slippery with seasickness. Occasionally a storm will arise so severe that travelers for this island must be offloaded on Sýros to wait for a break in the weather. Despite anxiety to get home to the kids or back to the store, few are much put out. Sýros is a beautiful small island with hotels with radiators and an all-weather movie theater, and the ones left at home can be comforted with gifts of Sýros' famous nougat. Otherwise, January and February, as over most of the Northern hemisphere, are dark, damp, and dull.

The tedium is broken during this time by name days. Those named for any of several dozen saints or holy events offer hospitality to all their well-wishers at home or in their shops. Wherever you go in the agorá, if you run into a Haralámbis or an Ipapandí, you are apt to be offered an ouzo, a spoon sweet, or a cookie by the celebrating shop owner. Red-haired Grigóris, the popular sweet baker, was even more popular on January twenty-fifth, because whoever went in to wish him "Hrónia pollá!" would receive thanks and a chunk of syrupy, nutty baklava or a millefeuille to accompany a coffee.

The only reasons a Greek man or woman does not celebrate a name day are illness or death in the family. My friend Thanásis, whose yiortí is on January eighteenth, did not celebrate for two years after I first knew him. The first year his mother was very ill and the next he was in mourning for her. Because I was then away from the island over several winters, it was not until many years later that I was able to show up at his door with a bottle of ouzo and wish him good health and many years.

Apókries

The next period of celebration – *Apókries* or Carnival – is, rather than a *panigýri*, a three-week long *gléndi*, or party. Although it is tied to the dates of Lent, *Apókries* is a purely secular occasion. It stretches for three weeks before *Sarakostí*, or Lent, the date of which is determined in Orthodoxy using the Julian calendar. Although Greece and the Greek church adopted the Gregorian in 1923, it was thought fitting to celebrate *Pásca*, the major Orthodox holy day, with the other Eastern churches, who refused to change calendars. (There were riots in Russia when the government tried to impose the Gregorian.) So *Pásca*, Easter, is a moveable feast, dated according to a complex formula incorporating the equinox, the full moon, and several algorithms. The resulting date can fall anywhere from the last week in March to the first week in May, so *Apókries* may begin as early as the first week of February or as late as the first week in March.

Whenever it takes place, *Apókries* is a welcome distraction from the tedium of winter life. The *tavernas* may hire a band from Athens for a public dance, people host parties in their houses, the bars and *ouzerís* are full. The character of *Apókries* echoes that of the Roman Saturnalia: an upside-down world. Of course, there are no slaves to act as masters and vice-versa, but gender switching is rampant. I remember, in Spiros' bar, a brawny fisherman in a wedding dress lifting it up above his hairy knees as he danced, and at a dance in a *taverna*, Takis the baker showing off very pretty legs in green nylons and a red velvet mini-dress.

And man-to-woman is not the rule. My first *Apókries*, at ten o'clock one night, I and another American woman, Alexis, were scooped up out of a café by a middle-aged couple we knew, Aspasía and Yiórgos, and their friend Danílos, and stuffed into a taxi. "We are going out to the country to wake up my cousin," Aspasía said, giggling. We drove miles out into farm country; then, hauling snacks, wine, and a phonograph, we climbed a mostly but not entirely dry stream bed two miles up a mountain. Half an hour later, we arrived at a completely dark house. Aspasía began yelling, "Wake up! Wake up!" *Oh*, I panicked, *they're going to shoot us*. But no, suddenly heads poked out of windows and laughter poured out into the night. In a minute the doors opened, and the cousin's husband, still in his long johns, began lighting all the kerosene lamps. Soon we were ensconced in the *salóni*, wine glasses in hand. Aspasía was a tall, very quiet woman; her cousin was possibly not quite five feet tall. While just as shy and demure as Aspasía, she was prettier, with a long braid of red-gold hair. After drinking a glass or two and setting out the *mezédes*, the two cousins went off to grill some sausages on the outdoor hearth, while the men stayed behind and cranked the portable phonograph. Pretty soon we were dancing *bállos* to the old scratchy 45s, the usually somber Danílos calling *"Opa!"* as Yiórgos danced with Alexis.

Suddenly there came a banging on the door, and in burst two men wearing raggedy suits, rubber boots, and old felt hats with stockings over their faces. The men leapt in and started dancing roughly with the other men, grabbing their arms and throwing them around. One had a cane with which he was beating the men about the heads. Yiórgos and Alexis were yelling, "Ow! Ow!" and hunching their shoulders. I was terrified, looking for an exit, until I saw, first, that the host and the other men were half-yelling and half-laughing, and then that a red-gold braid was escaping from under the shabby fedora. Although they pulled off the stocking masks, the two women didn't put on their own clothes for quite a while, and while dancing and eating happily, they would occasionally jump up and "beat" one of the men with the cane.

A couple of hours later, replete with wine and merriment, we five visitors headed for home, walking of course, probably five miles. The stars were so thick in the winter sky they looked like silver sprats in a fish hatchery. As though, if you only had a net, you could catch enough stars to light all the dark nights of your life.

Cross-dressing and rude behavior enable people to crash parties they aren't invited to, where for a little while they abuse the guests physically and verbally until given a drink or two and then it is *"Hrónia pollá!"* and on to the next party. To do this successfully, you have to dress so as to be unrecognizable. I blew it for my *paréa*, because for me dressing up meant assuming a character, so although I managed to squeeze into Thanásis' sailor suit, I made the mistake of painting my face white á la Marcel Marceau. At our first house, Marió said to me, "You're quite wonderful, but I know who you are, so the others must be Thanásis," pointing at the six-foot tall lady in a long dress and picture hat, "Katína, Alíki," and so forth. No treats for us! So we just went to Alíki's hotel where her parents and friends dutifully admired our get-ups and we were offered drinks all around.

Dancing in *Apókries*, whether at private parties or public dances, tends to be wilder, more individualistic, and showoff-y than at other times of the year. Men display their skill with dances from other parts of Greece: the acrobatic *tsámikos* from Epiros with its dramatic crouches and leaps; the tough and contemplative *zembékiko* of the Asia Minor refugees; the

203

popular *hasápiko*, with its clever footwork danced by two or three in perfect unison. The women respond with more and wider twirls in the *bállos* and, occasionally, a daring *tsiftetélli* or belly-dance. The sensual *tsiftetélli*, oddly, is the province of adolescent girls, who may grind and roll, sway and shimmy, until they are perhaps fifteen. Then custom (or an outraged father) drags them from the floor, and they must desist until they are safely married, when they seem to forget about it – until, perhaps, age frees them: I remember well a witty *tsiftetélli* danced on a table during *Apókries* by a sixty-year-old woman in a sparkly dress. "Old," she seemed to say with every roll of the belly, every teasing pass across the eyes with beringed fingers, every suggestive hitch of the hip, "old, but not dead!"

At an *Apókries* party in the home of Víron (Byron) and Kassianí, guests danced a dance they claimed was unique to the village, and which, in fact, I never encountered elsewhere, called *ayéranos*. It was done with a shuffling step, in a tight line, each dancer facing the back of the one in front. The "music" was an *a cappella* song, with a chorus of "*mahéria, psalídia,*" "knives and scissors," which, I deduced from the giggles and guffaws, had obscene if humorous significance. Víron claimed that the dance came from ancient Crete and represented Theseus leading the youths out from the labyrinth. The sexy atmosphere of this party of middle-aged married couples was emphasized by the ordinarily strait-laced hostess passing around a covered dish which, when opened, revealed a large – a very large – wooden phallus.

After the last wild Saturday night of *Apókries* comes "Cheese-eating Sunday," a fast from flesh with dairy allowed, a transition to the strict fast of *Sarakostí*. For many, the fasting is not unwelcome: indulgence turns into surfeit and then to desire for lightness of body and soul, so the arrival of Clean Monday, the first day of *Sarakostí*, is greeted with relief. Unlike the sad and gloomy Ash Wednesday, Clean Monday is a joyful occasion. Whoever can do so shuts up shop and heads for the country, carrying a picnic out to a favorite farm or a summer house opened up for the day. The weather on Clean Monday is likely to be clear if windy, a plus because the traditional occupation of children and helpful adults on this holiday is the flying of kites. The kites are red and yellow or green and blue hexagons, homemade of cane and tissue paper. Out in the windy open fields or on the seashore, the kites soar into the clouds, no trees to entangle them. The children run across beach or field, screaming with laughter. One little boy stumbles and his kite flies off to the mountains. His father is there to wipe his tears. "There, there," the father says to a five-year-old named for a great hero, "an Achilléas doesn't cry." Brave Achilles rubs his eyes and straightens up, while his father reflects on the relativity of tragedies.

Clean Monday is a fast, so the picnic is free from animal products, fish with scales, and oil. There are liable to be raw shellfish – winkles and *pína*, an oyster-like mollusk – boiled or grilled *kalamarákia* and octopus, *taramasaláta* made with salted fish roe and bread, leaves of lettuce and green beans, bread, green olives, and oranges, and such dietetic sweets as *loukoúmi*, Turkish delight. *Lágana*, a flat loaf of unleavened bread, is baked for this day only. Of course, there is wine and ouzo , and for the children lemonade and sour cherry drink. The main activities besides eating, drinking, and disentangling kite strings are walking in the fields and hills, napping in the open air, and always, dancing. Thus is the long Lent, fifty days as opposed to the Western forty, opened with rest and cleansing of the body and soul.

And so begins *Sarakostí*, a long, solemn Lent with no *panigýris*. *Sarakostí* of course commemorates Christ's forty-day fast in the wilderness. But again, there is a practical side to the custom: ewes and cows are birthing, so the babies need the mothers' milk, fish may be spawning, and the fruits of last year's harvest are definitely low. Time to hold back a little, in order to have plenty in the year to come.

For the faithful who fast, the food is repetitive: lentil soup, bean soup, white bean salad, stewed *kalamári*, octopus casserole, vegetables in oil. Every Friday, chickpeas with herbs, tomatoes, and onion go into a special pot sealed with dough and spend the night in the baker's oven. It's good the first time, and the second; after that . . .

As though to add variety to the diet, some foods are reserved for *Sarakostí* alone, not available at other times: sesame tahini, which makes a creamy soup, and its sweet version, *halvás*, are only sold during Lent. Pickled vegetables – onions, carrots, peppers, and cauliflower – make their appearance now. For two days in the fifty the ban on fish is lifted. Some people choose not to fast, but only children, travelers, and the sick are truly exempt. Some cheat. A middle-aged woman in my street, hearing that there was fresh liver at the butcher's, sent me to buy some. "And tell him, be *sure* to tell him," she said, passing her hand over her clearly unfeverish brow and closing her eyes, "that I am ill."

This fast cleanses but depletes the body. It is as though something were growing inside, using up energy – an immaterial fetus, nourished on hunger. I fasted one year, gaining some respect from the villagers, not all of whom were observant. At the *taverna* where I took most of my meals, as I came in Liggéris would hail me: "*Nistísima?*" and reel off what "fasting foods" were in the kitchen. It might be octopus in casserole with orzo, or *kalamári krassáto*, squid stewed in red wine. Spring is a good time for *hórta*, wild greens, boiled and served with lemon and oil. As he was dishing up my supper, Liggéris would inform all the customers that the foreigner was fasting. "*Nistévi*," he would say proudly, mildly admonishing the non-fasters with a glance. Still, he cooked veal stews, pork steaks, and fish soup thickened with rice and egg for anyone who wished it.

Liggéris and his wife Zambétta kept the only *taverna* that was open in the winter as well as the tourist season. What a lifesaver that was for me! With no refrigerator, cooking for myself was wasteful as well as lonely, and drachma for drachma the cost was about the same. Unusually for a village *taverna*, the food at Liggéris' was carefully prepared and the kitchen was clean as an operating room. There were no better cooks in the village until the season opened and the Maroulídis family opened the hotel. And though Liggéris and Zambétta then would slip to second place on my personal Blue Guide, they were definitely three-star even then. Not only did they feed me, but they educated me as well. "Not that fish," Liggéris would say quietly as I looked over the assortment in the refrigerated drawer. "Look for the ones with shiny skin and bright eyes. When the eyes go dull, the taste is gone." For whom he was saving that dull gray fish, I never asked.

The food was not the only attraction for me at Liggéris'. There was what a friend called *piatikí paréa*, "plate company." I could go there noon or evening and find company. They might be some of the few single people in the village – Stávros, the sixty-year old vice-president of the village; Pantelís, the young teacher from Crete; or Náousans who lived in Athens or Piraeús, back to attend to village business.

I remember one couple, perhaps in their seventies. The old man had the very high coloring of a heart case. They came to Liggéris' every day for a month, and gradually we began to be friendly. Every day the woman would go to the juke box and play the one waltz, among the dozens of *bállos* and *hasápikos*. Then one day, she came up to me and invited me to dance with her. I was a little taken aback but did not wish to be ungracious, and so we waltzed, there in the *taverna* at one thirty in the afternoon, through two playings of the waltz. When we finished, she thanked me with tears in her eyes. "My husband can't dance," she said, "because of his heart. And I do love to waltz." I dropped a dancing-school curtsey, and all the customers and cooks applauded.

An occasional diner was Vangélis, the pious son of the elderly priest and a clerk in the bank in the *hóra* – a branch of a huge private bank owned by a very wealthy man named Andriádis. Although well educated – he had been to a monk-run prep school in Corinth – Vangélis was a humorless and rather snobby young man. Early in my residence, he had offered to give me Greek lessons, an offer I accepted but regretted when I discovered that he was teaching me not demotic or modern spoken Greek but the old-fashioned Puristic used only by bureaucrats, lawyers, and the military juntists. As well, Vangélis had a cleft palate. My strange out-of-date nouns and verbs, spoken, in spite of myself, in imitation of the poor man's crippled voice, clued Stávros into what was going on. He suggested I ask Pantelís, the new schoolteacher. As Pantelís spoke good English and wanted to improve, we were able to trade lessons, and became friends.

It may have been hunger that prompted me to bedevil poor Chrístos. One afternoon in the *taverna*, Pantelís and I were *piatiki paréa* with him and Stávros. Vangélis was high-hatting us a bit as usual, implying that we were uneducated dolts and un-Christian besides (despite the fact that I was fasting). Conferring only with our eyes, Pantelís and I began to put together a *koroídema*, a leg pull. Carefully I described a situation I had heard about from a banker friend. "Two men, a teacher and a bank manager, and a foreign woman pulled a scam on a number of branch banks." I described how they did it, the hole in the system they exploited (subsequently plugged, but I didn't reveal that). "They got away with many thousands, and wouldn't have been caught except the woman fell in love with a policeman and told all. Now I," I emphasized, "have no love for policemen. And here we are, a foreign woman, a teacher" – nodding to Pantelís – "and a bank manager. What would you say to relieving our bank of a little cash?"

Vangélis was horrified. "That would be stealing!" he exclaimed.

"Well, I don't know," said I. "Are you not a good Christian?"

"Of course," he replied stuffily.

"Well," chimed in Pantelís, reading my mind, "do you think it's Christian to store up wealth? What does the Bible say: 'Lay not up for yourselves treasures upon earth'"?

"It's not my money," Vangélis said doggedly.

"But," said I, "is it not true that it is harder for a rich man to enter the kingdom of heaven than for a camel to pass through the eye of the needle?"

"Yes," said Vangélis, puzzled, "but..."

"And is it not," intoned Pantelís, "the duty of all Christians to bring their fellows into the right way of life, so that they may be saved and go to heaven?"

"*Ma-ma-málista*," stuttered Vangélis. By this time, Stávros' very round blue eyes were brimming with tears as he attempted not to laugh out loud. Quite a few of the other diners were also avidly following the conversation.

"Then," I pursued, "can't you see that it is our Christian duty to help poor Mr. Andriádis get to heaven by relieving him of some of the impediment, that is to say, his money?"

Vangélis, suddenly realizing that he was being tempted by devils, got up with a certain composure, paid for his dinner, and departed. It was some weeks before he would sit down with us again. I do hope that "angels ministered unto him," as they had his Lord in a similar situation.

During *Sarakostí*, everyone was a little hungry, busy with tedious, repetitive jobs, mostly inside. We didn't get out much. *Sarakostí* was like a gray tunnel, a dark wood, which it was necessary to pass through to get to the paradise of spring. Used to winter, to avoiding the cold, the wind, and the rain, we were too inwardly focused to notice when the equinox came and went, hardly noticed the landscape waking up. Only from the bus one day I would see pink almond blossoms covering the mountain behind the Monastery, rosy silene blanketing the vineyards, or wild gladiolas pushing up in a fallow field. Time seemed hardly to pass, yet one day wheat was just pushing up, and only a few days (or was it weeks?) later, suddenly the grass-like stalks were knee-high. Tired old Winter, having done his work, retires to snooze away the next nine months, while sprout by sprout, bud by bud, blossom by blossom, busy, lively Spring is opening up the world.

Paréa

Noikokyrió is a traditional concept that binds people and land. *Paréa* is one that binds people with people, at once a circle of friends and a code of behavior towards those friends. Greek friendships are based on family, childhood, neighborhood, and work relationships. Social and economic status, education, and "lifestyle" are rarely factors. In the village, *paréas* begin early and are almost always for life. They are exclusive: one "makes *paréa*" or keeps company with one group; one may have individual friends outside the *paréa* but will socialize mostly with its members. In a village, if someone doesn't have a *paréa*, he or she has no social life beyond the immediate family. And since in a village there are no clubs or organizations, and the church is not a social center, a person without *paréa* is a pariah indeed.

Paréas begin early and may last a lifetime. Zélos, an Athenian friend said, "For over thirty years, until I moved to the island, my *paréa* met at the same *taverna* every Friday night to eat and drink, argue and sing." The *taverna* was a traditional neighborhood one where regulars brought their own *tapsía*, pans of food, to be cooked in the *taverna* ovens. The *taverna* made its money on the home-brewed wine, barrels of which lined the walls. Since *paréas* are usually formed in childhood, they are not based on shared political views. "In our *paréa*," continued Zélos, "there were royalists, socialists, and two kinds of communists. You can imagine the conversations." The diversity of opinion among members of a *paréa* can lead to shouting, but never to abandonment by or of the *paréa*.

A *paréa* of single people in the village would meet every evening after work and decide what to do: play cards, drink *soúma* in the *ouzerí* in the harbor or coffee in the sweet shop in the *platía*, walk out to another village to eat and dance – or nothing. In a city, there might be more alternatives – movies, concerts, football games. But whatever the amusement, the decision is taken democratically. Also democratic is the paying of the bill. Whatever the *kéntro* – *taverna*, bar, or disco – there is some agreement about choice of foods and wine, all served family style, but any member who feels the need for another bottle or another plate of steak or salad, simply orders it. When the bill comes, everyone pays an equal share. The old way was for the bill to be divided among the men, but with a rise in the status of women, they now pay their share as well. If your share comes to more than you have, someone else will make it up – "lending" is not involved.

Vital to a *paréa* is the *stékki*, or meeting place. The *stékki* may be someone's house or shop or a particular *taverna*, *kafeneío*, or *óuzeri*. The members of the *paréa* simply drift in, hang around until everyone has assembled – probably downing an ouzo or beer to pass the time – and then go together to the agreed-upon entertainment. I remember, while living in the *hóra*, passing down the dark streets at night and seeing, in a lighted window of a plumbing shop, a group of young men, nicely dressed, sitting on the edges of tubs and seats of toilets, smoking and talking. When I expressed curiosity, I was told, "Oh, that's their *stékki*. They meet there every night." The advent of the telephone has somewhat eroded the concept of *stékki*, since arrangements can be made without first gathering, but the tradition of the workplace as *stékki* remains. Employees of businesses, especially small shops, may consider their workplace appropriate for meeting friends and socializing, but even government offices and banks may be *stékkis*.

Paréa is a concept that defines the roles and responsibilities of the members, mainly to conserve the unity of the group. For instance, if the group decides to go to a disco, even if one member is not enthusiastic, he or she should not "break the *paréa*," but go along and, instead of sulking, work at building *kéfi* or high spirits. To create *kéfi*, the friends toast each other and the group, "*Stin uyeía mas!*" "To our health!" They also bestow compliments on each other: "To you in your lovely red dress!" "*Yia sou, levéndi mou!*" *Levendiá* is a quality – of men or women – that is only roughly defined as courage, generósity, "dash," and the ability to create *kéfi*.

I haven't forgotten how hard it was for an individualistic American to understand *paréa*. Early in my stay in the *hóra*, I was once part of a party. Reaching my limit of both wine and fatigue, I decided to leave and go home. I made what I thought were polite apologies and was surprised by the look of shock on the faces of the members of the party – and by the criticism that came my way the next day. "You broke the *paréa*," said the only member who would speak to me. "You ruined the *kéfi*. We all left." By the time I went to live in Náousa, I had had sufficient education in *paréa* not to make such egregious mistakes, but I was not always successful.

Although *paréas* in the "real time," September to May, are exclusive, in the summer they are more elastic. Relatives come from Australia or Chicago, students come home from university, and they are gathered into the *paréas* which they belong to or are adopted into by a cousin or sister-in-law. In Náousa, usually the natives kept to themselves and the tourists found company with other tourists, though there were exceptions for long-time visitors. And once in a while, Alíki, who worked in her parents' hotel and spoke English, would take a liking to a young guest and bring him or her along on expeditions with her *paréa*. It was Alíki who gathered me in during my first summer and left me as a legacy for the winter *paréa*, years before other foreigners came to live in the village year round; for this gift I would be grateful the rest of my life. Since I was adopted by Alíki's and Thanásis' *paréa*, and ultimately by their mothers, sisters, and brothers, I was able to engage in the everyday life of the villagers before that life was so radically altered.

Alíki was an Athenian, but she had spent every holiday of her life in the village and grown up with the village kids. Although more educated and worldly than the others in her *paréa*, she was no snob; she worked twelve hours a day at the hotel, cleaning and cooking, but was always ready to play in the evenings. Vibrant and fun-loving, she was the very spirit of the *paréa*, the one who organized outings and kept everyone's spirits up with her jokes and witty gossip. Her *paréa* consisted of Thanásis, a young carpenter, four or five single young women – mostly neighbors of Thanásis, including the "two Katínas" – and about the same number of young single men, many of whom were brothers and cousins of the women. These "chaperones" were necessary to the women's ability to go to festivals or even *tavernas* and discos, but the brothers and cousins were freer than the girls, and not always happy to be ordered to accompany them (having perhaps other fish to fry). All the parents, however, trusted Thanásis to keep their daughters out of trouble and so he played a vital part in the *paréa*.

A "holiday" member, although a native, was Yiánnis, nicknamed "Truman." His *paratsoúkli* or nickname reflected his adoration of the American president who had had school supplies – including pencils, crayons, and paper – distributed to Greek children after the war. This generosity encouraged Truman to pursue a career in art. Truman was somewhat peripheral to the *paréa*, partly because he had lived many years in Athens and partly because he was a flagrant *poústis*, "queer" or "queen" – an attribute distasteful to many Greeks, who judge a man against an ideal of masculinity without caring much to what uses it is put. *Paréa*, however, supercedes human flaws: once you're in, you're in, unless you commit unspeakable crimes such as leaving a party early or going to a *panigýri* with another *paréa*.

Paréas are not unalterable. Marriage may cause realignment. As everywhere, having children crimps one's style for a while as baby-tending supercedes *panigýria*. One by one the girls married and although they never emotionally withdrew from the *paréa*, they no longer participated in evening activities. They would, however, put the babies in a stroller and take them to Thanásis' house or the hotel for coffee and conversation. As Náousa grew, Alíki and Thanásis slowly opened their *paréa* to new restaurant and shop owners and to returned emigrés. Thus their *paréa* expanded and contracted, like a collective noun or a giant amoeba, in a tradition that changed and yet kept itself authentic and alive.

Taken By Háros

The *kambána* sounds.

Dong . . .

Dong . . .

Dong . . .

More slowly than that. Once a minute. Sometimes the clapper hits the bell on the way up: Clang-dong . . . Clang-dong . . .

For a drawn breath, everyone in the village is silent, stands where he is lifting a crate of canned milk from the back of a green truck; where she is pinning sheets to a line stretched across an alley; where he or she, white-haired, dark-clothed, sits with back to the sun. Gnarled hands knitting or netting stop, still. For a minute. Then movement begins, but in silence. The carton is slid into the doorway of the grocery shop; the sheet is pinned to its mate. Less quickly, needles add another row to a white sweater, a shuttle closes a gap in a yellow net.

From windows, from doors of shops and houses, heads emerge, and the quiet question is asked – asked usually of the neighbor nearer to the big church, the Panagía, which stands up a long slope of flagged, white-washed street, a wide flight of stairs from the center of the village. There, now, the sexton is pulling on the bell rope. Already the nearest neighbor, wiping her hands on her apron, is walking toward the church. She walks through the courtyard, past the great pine with its limbs supported by stone crutches, and climbs the stairs. The pale yellow church with twin bell towers is backed by blue sky into which rise cypresses – slender black-green arrows on whose tops will once in a while perch, briefly and insecurely, a white dove.

The woman questions the tolling man, returns down the stairs, speaks to the next nearest neighbor, she to the next, and as the question flowed uphill the answer flows down, down, zigzag down like the runoff of a gentle rain, until it reaches sea level and spreads like a pool.

So whole is life in this village of Náousa that seldom is the news received with shock – sorrow, yes, almost always, for everyone has been born and grown up and lived side by side, one with another: kinship, nearness, love, friendship, enmity, charity, jealousy, admiration, desire, trust, profit, betrayal, loss – all are netted, knitted, intertwined like hair on a pillow. Here people don't need to be told that no man is an island. They are all an island – is not Greece a world of islands? And are there not islands of Greeks everywhere in the world and in time, time an archipelago greater even than the world? Nor need anyone be reminded that the bell tolls for his own body, her own soul. Death is too frequent, too familiar, too open for any child to avoid seeing its pale face, paler today than yesterday. No, here one needs only to know which part of the island has given way, broken off, sunk into the sea – which familar rock, which favorite face, has split, showered down, crumbled into fine, shifting sand beneath the blue-green sea.

There is no hiding death here. Someone dies: Katína's grandmother. This morning she was well. She ate something, Katína said, expressed pleasure, pressed Katína's hand. In the afternoon, Katína and I drank coffee at Thanásis' place. They were catching me up on the gossip – the love affairs, marriages, and births that had occurred during my three-year absence from this village where I had lived for many years and to which I kept returning, an immigrant in reverse. Katína left, passed by the grandmother's again, and she was gone. She had been alone only briefly. Perhaps she had waited to be alone.

Katína runs to tell her mother; a neighbor comes as witness. Yes, she says, she is dead, the face is cool, the hands are limp.

Now begins the busyness, the urgent errands of arranging for the kydía, the funeral. Crisscrossing the village, Katína goes to the priest's house to tell him, to her own to put on black clothes, to the village office to register the death, to the carpenter to order a casket, to the store to buy five meters of common white cloth for winding clothes. The sexton comes to prepare the body, to tie the hands before they stiffen. But Anna, Katína's mother, is strong; she wishes herself to undress her mother, wash her for the last time, dress her in clean clothes, lay her on a clean sheet on her bed.

Women are coming, bringing and lighting candles. One brings coffee, sugar, and paximádia. Another opens the glass-fronted cupboard and takes out the grandmother's best coffee cups. "She would fuss at me lately," sighs Anna, "if I served her coffee in one of these. 'There must be enough for the mourners,' she'd say."

Her work done, Anna sits down, suddenly tired. Mariánthi makes her a coffee; it's foamy, so she says automatically, "There – wealth!" then bites her lip, but it's nothing. The grandmother had only her pensión and the little house, which she had long ago deeded to Katína, the granddaughter named for her. The dead woman lies on the bed; the neighbors sit around it, drinking coffee, crying, speaking of her, of other dead, of death.

Katína is crying the most; the shock is greatest for her – the coldness of the skin, the sudden absence. At the police station, she had watched her grandmother's name being erased from the village roll. "Nothing," she says. "We are nothing! We are here and then, suddenly, not here! And where does it go, whatever it is we are?"

At sunset, they cover the grandmother's face with a scarf, and her body with a sheet. Friends and neighbors come in, cross themselves, weep a little, embrace Anna and Katína, return to work or duties. Everyone is wearing black. There are sobs, but these are soft; the grandmother was old, had had two strokes, was bedridden a long time.

All night the women sit among the smoky beeswax candles, crying, drinking coffee, and talking. No one says, "Don't cry. Get some sleep." Tonight is for crying because they must, because life will go on regardless and one must not feel betrayed or a betrayer. Grief is for the one who is no longer, as we shall all be no longer some time, some other day like today.

An old man comes and touches the dead woman's hand. He wipes a tear away with a swollen knuckle. "We went to school together the first day," he says, "and then she grew up and married my cousin, had babies, grew old, and now . . . *Tin píre o Háros . . .*"

They say this still: Háros, Charon the ferryman, has taken her in his boat to the place of the dead. Háros, he who ferried Orpheus and Hercules to the land of shadows, he who fought the great Dighenis on the marble threshing floor, has handed the frail old woman into his bark and pushed off from the land. Háros, not the Taxiárchis, Michael the Archangel, the golden-winged, armor-clad warrior of death. Not Michael, though his ikon reigns in every one of the dozen or so churches in the village, in the hundreds on the island, in hundreds of thousands all over the Greece that is and the Greece that was in the millennium and a half since Christ replaced Apollo. Not Michael, but Háros. Perhaps if one lives on the edges of the sea, a port from which so many depart, it is natural to think of leaving over water.

In the morning, the carpenter brings the coffin: plain unvarnished pine with a bottom of open slats. The tired-eyed women go and find men to lift her into it. Even dead, even so old, so long ill, she is heavy. The open coffin goes on the kitchen table, where so many thousands of times they have sat eating, drinking, talking, quarrelling, laughing. The lid remains outside the doorway as a token.

The *kambána* tolls every two hours.

After a while, the priest comes, subdued. Two little boys in robes struggle with thurible and censer. The house is censed. Into her mother's hands, Anna places an ikon and a bouquet, white stock and a few pink roses, cut from the little public garden by the statue of an illustrious superintendent of schools. Then the grandmother is lifted up on the shoulders of her son, her son-in-law, her nephew, a neighbor, others, and takes her last walk around the village. As the coffin leaves the house, someone breaks a plate on the threshold. No one knows why: it is done this way. The shards will remain in the courtyard for three days.

As she is carried through the narrow streets, uncovered face to the sky, she passes the same houses that she passed first as a newborn baby (carried in her mother's arms to be presented to the priest), later as a bride (walking arm-in-arm with her mother, the violins and the clarinet leading). She is on the way to the same church in which she was baptized and married, where she baptized her children and stood godmother to a half-dozen others, where she attended funerals, first of her elders and then, gradually, of her own – a brother in the war, a child, her husband. She passes the houses she visited every day as long as she could rise from her bed, those of her siblings, her schoolmates, her children, her godchildren, her gossips. And from each house someone joins the throng, just as though she were a bride again, and they her guests. The *kambána* sounds as she approaches, borne forward and upward by a dark tide of mourners, their murmurs and quiet footsteps sounding like the slow shuffle of small waves on a dark beach.

Her grandson carries a wreath of green bay, bound with black ribbon. He isn't wearing a black suit because he hasn't got one, hasn't needed one until now. He has borrowed a black sweater. Sooner or later he will buy a black suit, as the occasions for its use increase. Perhaps he will buy it for his wedding, and then one day, when it is old and shabby, he will be carried to the church in it as his grandmother is now being carried in her own black clothes of mourning for others.

In the church, over the pale uncovered face of the old woman, the priest speaks of the Life after Death, the Resurrection, the Second Coming when all the bones shall be joined again – sprout cartilage and tendons, grow flesh – and though he promises that we all shall then be whole and live in the presence of God, few truly believe in either the Christian or the archaic life after death, the one a brilliant paradise, the other a shadowy cave. No one wants to have seen the last of this loved one, this familiar one. And yet . . . If you ask (not on a day of grief), "Is there an afterlife?" the affirmative answers are few, the negatives many, and the balance expressed by the equivocal "E!" which says, "Rationally speaking, no, but allow us a little respite from reason, a little doubt to mitigate this terrible certainty."

Following the coffin, finally closed, the mourners have moved out to the little graveyard beside the church. Walled and lined with cypresses,

scented by a jasmine here, a thorny rose there, the graveyard could be
– except for the irregular rows of tombs – any village or farm orchard.
One tomb is open; its marble slab, newly washed and dripping, leans on
the whitewashed wall. With his last pull on the *kambána*, the sexton had
coiled the rope and stuck it high on a shelf (out of the way of children),
gone to the graveyard, and, with crowbar and wedges, pried off the lid of
the grandmother's family tomb.

Most tombs here are sarcophagi, plain slabs of white marble with, at
one end, a small, windowed black marble box like a little shrine, containing photographs of the deceased, an oil lamp, a small censer, and, tucked
not quite out of sight, a bottle of corn oil, a tin of incense, a can of Ajax.
What wealth there is in the village is fairly recent, so most of the sarcophagi are new. There is only one late-nineteenth-century obelisk with
a carved wreath of roses and ribbons. In the cemetery in the *hóra* are a
few statues of angels, a marble memorial to an admiral (a ship in relief, of
course, framed by ropes), but here the graveyard is not a museum. It is a
field where we plant our bodies, all that remains of who we were, for the
earth to do its work, relieving our survivors of the problem.

We are only a problem for three years. After that, the living open the
tomb, remove our bones, and take them home to wash them with wine,
anoint them with oil (our last sip of our grapes, our olives), put our bones
in a box, and stash the box in the family storehouse among the wine barrels, the oil barrels, the cane *kofínia* still smelling of grapes, the drying
cheeses, the perpetually useful burlap sacks. Later, someone who doesn't
remember us will take the bones to a field and dig them in. Then the plow
will pass over.

So the coffin is finally closed and lowered into the stone-lined cavity, the marble slab levered into place, the wreath laid upon it. Prayers
are said, and the priest, on Anna's behalf, invites everyone to gather at
the *kafeneío*. As the mourners leave, snuffling and red-eyed, Katína and
her brother offer to each a fresh white roll and a little bag of *kólyva*, a dry,
crumbly sweet made of grains of wheat, almonds, sugar, and cinnamon.
These mourners, quiet for once, drift downhill to the *kafeneío* (no clack of
távli today, no news from the radio, no heated political arguments) to sit
stiffly in their black clothes, drink coffee, break bread, and eat a spoonful
of *kólyva* in memory of the long life, joys and sorrows, virtues and short-
comings, successes and humanity of the woman who yesterday at this hour
had herself drunk with pleasure her own little cup of sweet black coffee.

For three days, a dish of *kólyva* will be taken to the tomb. Do they
expect her to eat it? No. Who will? No one. There are not even any squir-

rels, but perhaps pigeons or crows will find it, or a mouse will brave the graveyard cats. After three days, then nine, other plates are broken in the house, and candles are kept lighted for forty days. To light her return? No. Why three days? No one knows. Some say it takes the soul that long to get where it is going. Others scoff, since there is nowhere to go. But after three days Christ ascended, and after three days the body of the Panagía joined her soul.

Other important events – Christ's wildering, Lent, and Advent – also take forty days. After forty days, then, there is a memorial service. Anna has ordered notices from Sýros, chosen a plain one, with borders of black myrtle leaves, a gold cross at the top, the name in its old form, Ekateríni, followed by "Beloved mother, grandmother, aunt." These Katína has affixed to corners of buildings, telephone poles, lamp posts. The service is shorter than the funeral, less well attended. There is kólyva again, coffee-drinking again, but tears have mostly given way to sighs, reminiscences.

The next day, Katína and Anna clean the house, give away or discard all the grandmother's things: her ikons, the stephanothíki that held her wedding wreaths; her dowry embroideries, lace tablecloths, pillowslips; her remaining china, glasses, cups. Neighbors come and ask for plants, a table or stool, a sepia photograph of a common ancestor. There is not much to give. The house is whitewashed, inside and out.

And it is over. Born, named, lived, died, buried, dissolved, erased.

As beliefs change, rituals change – or most rituals, but not these. Here death is faced squarely, and nothing but ritual can impel the muscles, bear the numb mind through the washing and carrying, the breaking of habits and loosening of love, through shock and denial to acceptance.

For those first forty days, Katína wears mourning – black, dead black, no relieving white collar, no pearls. She wears it as a bride wears white, possessing it, being expressed by it. This is not constrained behavior; it is voluntary, but it serves a function. The black reminds us that Katína, who loves bright, light colors even in winter, is slowed down, hushed by sorrow. We are careful to respect her grief, to keep our paréa, our socializing, intimate, at home, away from the grating revelry of bars where others are drinking, singing, and dancing in forgetfulness of the quiet, the long still quiet that awaits us all.

Katína is young, though, and shortly she will open her ice cream shop, which she is now cleaning and whitewashing, and the yellows and blues she is painting her chairs will slowly draw her to their present. As winter passes into spring, she will find her joy again, laughing as usual as she dips us cones of pistachio and apricot.

Wearing mourning is not an obligation; here tradition is always tempered with sense. Ipapandí's mother-in-law, before she died, had made her life miserable for ten years. "Mourning?" she said. "Forty days – for my husband's sorrow – and that's it." Or the village, knowing all histories always, would cry "hypocrite," and not behind her back.

But Anna, the daughter, will wear black for a year, or two, or three, mourning not merely the absence of the frail, old woman but that of the bride whose breast she nestled into, the impatient plaiter of morning pigtails, the vigilant guardian of nymphal virtue, the glowing *koumbára* at Anna's own wedding, the devoted dandler of toddling Katína. All these have passed too suddenly, and with them, Anna's own life. "Now," she sighs, "I am alone." She has siblings, relatives, friends, husband, children, but . . . "Now I am alone. And," she says, "now I am next."

On a day of cool sunshine before Good Friday, when the priest will come out and bless all the tombs in the graveyard, Thanásis and I are washing his mother's tomb. After we've scrubbed and rinsed the white marble, filled and lit a *kandíli*, and censed the tomb, we sit and smoke. He introduces me to some of the dead, telling their stories – unremarkable lives, like most. Some of my dearest acquaintances are there: Bárba Minás – my first landlord – and his brother Panayiótis lie head to feet in shiny, cold modern tombs, which seem so at odds with their characters. Both were farmers and traditionalists, reaping and sowing by hand, threshing with mule and ox. Minás was a keeper of bees and Panayiótis the supreme wine-maker of the community. Somehow I would have expected them to be buried on their land, among the vines and hives.

I have lost my mother since I was here last, and only to Thanásis can I speak of her. His mother, like mine, and his father too were ill for years. The difference was that he was with his parents, caring for them day by day, easing them into death, and I was not. There is only sorrow here; we need make no excuses for guilts and regrets and tedium and resentment. Only, I know that, as his graves are fuller and nearer, his life is deeper and stronger.

After a year, there is a second memorial service; after three years, the disinterment.

"I thought," said Andónis, "it would be dreadful washing my father's bones. I went out in the barn to do it by myself, not to upset my mother.

But it was . . . I never felt so close to him. He always complained about his left hip, how it hurt him. The doctor never found anything wrong. And there I am washing the thigh bone, with his own wine I saved, and it is bent: thickened up near the joint. I turned it in my hands and looked: regular bone, and then this smoother material. Probably he broke it sometime, not a heavy break, maybe during the war, and it calcified.

"And another thing: we put off opening the tomb for five years because we were all away – Athens, Australia. Fortunately, we didn't need it, but anyway everything was dissolved, even the cartilage, so his hands were just two piles of little bones like pebbles. I held them, and I thought how those hands used to beat the tar out of me – I was a wild one – and how they grabbed me firmly when I came back from Australia, how they trembled and begged for support at the end. I wasn't afraid, or disgusted, or even sad. I guess I thought most, I'm forty myself and have no son to wash my bones, and I was glad my father had known I would do it."

The Eye

To Máti, the Eye, is a belief
Greeks share with other Eastern
Mediterranean peoples. It is not really
a superstition, although it is inter-
woven with many strands of magical
practices. The idea behind the Eye is
that excessive admiration, or perhaps
lack of humility, attracts retribution.
Excessive admiration (as we can see
by the behavior of so many film and
sports stars) turns people's heads, so
they forget they are subject to the
rules of society and of nature. In the
admirer, admiration easily turns to
envy, and envy is the cause of theft, adultery, and murder, even genocide.
So the Eye is not an empty superstition but a strategy to prevent social
disharmony.

This demotic belief and the ancient one of Nemesis are very similar.
Nemesis is a formless force that seeks to re-balance the world when an act
of man has upset it. Man most upsets the balance when he forgets that
he is not God and commits acts of *ívris*, hubris, usually called "overween-
ing pride." Agamemnon, making a triumphant return to Argos after the
Trojan War, glorying in his hero status and forgetful of the fact that he had
slain his own daughter Iphigenia to call up a good wind to Troy, is invited
by his wife to step onto a red carpet, the red dye being so precious it was
reserved for kings. "Such as this is for the gods," he says, but overcoming
his reluctance, he steps on it anyway, and so commits *ívris*. In his case, it is
Clytemnestra who is the instrument of Nemesis. But the crime that aveng-
es his is not the end. His actions in going to war affected all the Argives,
and it takes another generation – his remaining son and daughter suffering
madness and oppression, and another parricide – for the world to return to
balance.

The Eye is not the evil eye of Irish belief, for the evil visited upon the
victim here is not intentional. Many practices are intended to ward off the
Eye. Young children are especially vulnerable to it, and young women are
most likely to have it. If you enthuse too much over an infant, the mother
will not only cross herself but also spit three times (usually but not always

to the side), and declare, "He's a stupid baby" or "She doesn't eat." Pinned to the baby's sweater will be a little blue bead, blue being the protective color.

Mules and donkeys have blue beads worked into their tack, because young animals are also targets for the Eye. Once, when I was visiting a farm with a friend, she asked to see the newborn lamb that was being saved for Pásca. As we neared the stall, the farm wife, seated at some distance from us, suddenly showed great agitation. "Stand back," my friend whispered. "Don't look."

"What was that about?" I asked as we wended our way out of the farm-yard.

"She was afraid you have the Eye," she said. "She knows I don't."

"Do you believe this?" I asked. My friend was an architect from a prominent academic family and had been educated in an American college.

"I am not religious, and about most things I am a strict rationalist," she said, "but I do believe in the Eye."

So accepted is belief in the Eye, a marine lawyer told me, that when one of his clients, an international shipping firm, had lost three vessels in as many months, the owners called in a bishop to exorcize the headquarters.

In modern Greece, deflecting the Eye is ingrained in everyday practices. Much of the onus is on the potential target, which could of course be anyone. Routinely then, one must avoid ostentatious display and neutralize any compliment with a denial. If little Yiánnis got 100 in arithmetic, his mother must quickly point out that he only got 70 in reading, or some such. But people must also protect others from the Eye. The ability "to Eye" is not a permanent characteristic, but a situational one. All people must be on the alert to protect others from their own possible envy or excessive admiration. If Frangíska has a new dress, or Vasílis a new motor-cycle, or Panayiótis a new tractor, you must say, "Me yeiá!" meaning wear it, or ride it, or use it "in health." To a newly married couple, you say "Na zísete!" "May you live!" and for a new baby, "Na sas zísi!" "May it live for you!" Every day you must wish everyone you meet "Kaliméra," good day, or "Kalispéra," good evening, and every Monday you must wish them a "good week" and every first of every month a "good month." As well, whenever you know someone is about to eat or is eating, you wish them "Kali órexi," good appetite, and when you are drinking together, again you toast them with "Eis ygeía!" – to your health! – so that food and drink may make them healthy and happy. On their name days you wish them "Hrónia pollá!" (many years!) and on their birthdays wish that they live a hundred years.

Still, despite all these precautions, *mátiasma*, "Eying," will happen. The symptoms of it are many and varied. One indication can be simply, as for the shipping company, a run of bad luck, a cluster of minor or even major accidents. The most usual symptoms are illness or just a feeling of malaise, especially headache. Suspecting one has been Eyed, one finds a person who is skilled in *ksemátiasma*, or removal of the Eye. This is almost always a woman, as the knowledge is handed down from woman to woman, usually from mother to daughter, and is a closely guarded secret. Some say that if the words to the ritual were disclosed to someone not in the family, they would no longer be efficacious. The usual ritual consists of the exorcizer dropping oil into a glass of water while reciting a chant which, as I heard it, consists of a prayer to the Panagía, said in triplets. The exorcism is successful if the oil does not rise to the top of the water but bonds with it.

I have heard somewhere that one of the ways to avoid the Eye is to deflect it back to the giver, so that the Eyer suffers the evil effects of his or her own Eying. I think this is what happened to me the day I visited Margaríta, who lived in a small monastery that had been built in the seventeenth century by a rich man for his monastic son. The son died before the monastery was finished; it was never consecrated but passed down in the family as a private house, locally called the Monastery of Ayios Andréas. The present owner's family had purchased it sometime in the nineteenth century when they re-emigrated from Russia. The house, completely walled and buttressed, sat high on a mountain, surrounded by fields and orchards. From a distance it looked like a small castle. I knew Margaríta, the fifty-year-old widowed mother of the owner, from the village, where she lived with two daughters and two sons in a small crowded house. The family had had to move into the village when the youngest daughter suffered an accident that confined her to a wheelchair. Margaríta had bowed to the necessity but had never given up life in the Monastery, where she kept her animals and where she spent as much time as possible. "Come up and spend a day with me," she invited shyly, "and you will see the way we really live." So one summer morning I rose as early as possible and set out to walk a mile along the road and then a mile or more straight up the mountain on a donkey path.

From the moment I pushed open the gigantic three-ply wooden doors, revealing the courtyard of the magnificent building, I was dazzled by its stark beauty. The Monastery was a two-storied hollow square. Low arches supported a balcony that ran along two sides of the square; on the balcony Byzantine half-columns of white marble with more arches held up the roof.

The great wooden door and a stairway leading to a dove cote occupied the third side, and a church the fourth. The courtyard was blazing with flowers: green-domed basil in pots, pink and white roses and carnations in cans, fuchsia bougainvillea and purple passionflower climbing the columns. The white-gold sun beat down on the white walls and the white marble flags of the courtyard, sending my eyes to seek the deep shadows beneath the arches.

As I stood at the open door, panting, sweating, and amazed, Margaríta, in widow's black, her black and silver hair all but covered by a black silk scarf, was sitting on the steps down to the courtyard, sifting wheat in a great wooden-and-wire sieve. Around her feet white doves fluttered, pecking at the small handfuls of grain she threw them. She welcomed me with a smile. "*Kalós órasis!* Let me finish and we'll have some coffee," she said, scattering a bit more grain on the paving.

In search of shade, I wandered into the church. There in the dimness, I found the ghosts of beauty. Two stories tall, domed, and definitely not the small family chapel common to country houses, the Monastery's church was almost empty – no pews, no altar except a blue-painted wooden table. One wall was occupied by a fresco so pale and flaking that its subject could not be made out – just a hand here, a fold of cloth there. Only one face (whose?) almost whole but pale, as though seen through a veil, stared out with aching dark eyes. The worm-eaten remains of a carved and gilded *témplo* stretched across the apse, and hanging on a column was an ikon of the saint, Andréas, to whom the church was dedicated. It too was eroded and tattered, the paint granulated. "It was painted on canvas in Constantinople," Margaríta said, behind me, "in the seventeenth century, and sent here. There were two, one of the Panagía, but that one . . ." She looked very sad, and I remembered a story about a (possibly) thieving "art expert" who had taken an ikon away to be restored and was never seen again.

From the dimness of the church we emerged into blinding sunshine. "Let's make coffee," she said, and motioned me up the stairs. One side of the balcony held a series of small rooms that must have been intended for monks' cells. One of these had been converted to a kitchen with a table, a two-burner gas stove, and a dish rack. Nothing else. "The oven is at the end of the passage," she said. "I bake every week." I had also noticed a large loom farther down the open corridor.

"Do you weave, too?" I asked. I had done some weaving in college and loved it.

"No longer. I used to weave all our blankets and rugs, spin and dye the wool. But all my children now have wedding blankets, in use or waiting for them."

When we finished our coffees, she said, "Come. I'll show you some of my weaving." The corner room was her own. Such a beautiful room I had never seen, neither in books nor in the real world, and I was almost breathless. The floor was earth, a terra cotta clay tamped down to the hardness and soft glow of tile. The walls were of course stark white, and large wooden pegs held a few black dresses and scarves. The large brass bed was covered by a *hrámi*, a black, rust, and white striped blanket. "This is from my dowry," she aid proudly. "I spun, dyed, and wove this myself, while still a girl. Forty years old and not a thread worn or raveled." The rust was the exact color of the earth floor.

In the outside wall was a long slit window with a marble block beneath. Margaríta motioned me to climb up and look out, and when I did, I saw terraces of golden reaped fields sloping down to a sea as blue and sparkling as a star sapphire. So high and far away were we that buses and cars passing on the road below were like toys.

"Look," she said, "there's the bus from the *hóra*, and across the road, my brother Stávros is walking through his vineyard, checking his grapes. And in the bay, there are one, two, five little *kaíkis* braving the *meltémi*." This view of the ordinary life of the villagers made me feel like one of the Olympian gods or Christian angels, looking down with serene compassion on humankind. I imagined the builder had hoped to achieve just that combination of detachment and involvement for the monks.

I could have gazed forever, but Margaríta was anxious to show me the other rooms, especially the refectory, which boasted another pale and flaking fresco. It seemed the subject was Jesus at table with his disciples, perhaps a "Last Supper."

The rest of the day we spent talking about her life, what she did every day. It seemed to me quite beautiful. A strong traditionalist, she had refused her son's offer to electrify, resisted unsuccessfully his cementing the other floors, and had finally accepted his running a water pipe to the stables when their well developed a crack But she was adamant that water be kept outside the house. "As long as I can carry it, I will." I was amazed, because, when I helped her water her flowers and vines, we each made ten trips outside to the standpipe with five-gallon buckets.

In the afternoon, because it lacked only a few days to the celebration of the Dormition of the Panagía, we ate a fasting meal of yellow lentils, bread, and tomatoes without oil. Just as we were gathering up the plates, we heard terrible squealing and snorting. Margaríta rushed down the stairs and out the door, down a path to the pigsty where one sow was farrowing and another, wild and angry, her piggy eyes red, was killing the shoats. I grabbed a large log and tried to keep the murderous sow away from the others while Margaríta took loose stones and quickly built a wall between the two animals. The dead little piglets she tossed into a field, but I could see she was grieving for them and for the mother sow.

Margaríta left to do chores in the storerooms under the arches. So I sat silently on the stairs, gazing around me and dreaming about what it would be like to live in this beautiful, austere, remote, and lively environment, weaving and baking and planting flowers.

Soon she called me back from my dream. "Do you want to milk the cow?" I was thrilled. We went out to the barn where I met the cows, very large beige animals with horns. Laughing at my sudden desire to flee down the mountain, she drew me over to the cow and showed me how to gentle it, stroking its head and talking to it. Then she taught me how to grasp the tough muscle of the teats, one in each hand, and strip them alternately. Except for a little fear that the huge animal would step on me with all its one-ton weight, I did pretty well; Margaríta could only squeeze a few more squirts from the udders I had worked on. "Will you take the milk down to the village?" she asked. "I would like to sleep here tonight. There will be a full moon." Only imagining what the courtyard would be like bathed in the mercury of a full moon, I waited for her to put up the milk in several large thermoses and pack them in a tote bag.

I am not sure when I began to feel ill. I remember only thinking that, though I suddenly felt headachy and nauseous, carrying the milk to the village was the least I could do in thanks for this marvelous day. I took the bag and set out down the mountain. I was still within sight of the monastery when suddenly, without notice, I vomited. Now I should say that only once since I was a child had I done this – never with the flu, nor even with appendicitis, only once with mushroom poisoning. So it was quite a surprise. More surprising was that I continued to vomit – twice more on the path, once again from a tractor driven by a friendly farmer who picked me up, and once again from the village bus which I caught on the road. By the time I got to Margaríta's village house with the milk, I was drained and had a sore stomach and a violent headache.

"You don't look well," Margaríta's daughter Nina said. "Come in and have a cup of tea." I told her what had happened and how I would be unable to go dancing that evening as we'd planned. "I think," she said, "you are *matiasméni*. Come, I'll fix you up." I lay down on a cot in the kitchen and sipped a little chamomile tea while Nina readied her equipment – a glass of water and a cruet of oil. Then standing above me, she began to chant softly. The only word I could make out was the name of the Panagía. Slowly she dropped oil into the water, repeating the words, and then the chanting.

"There," she said after a while. "The oil is finally rising. The Eye is gone from you." She closed the door and I slept in the dark kitchen for several hours. When I woke up, I was perfectly well, rushed home and put on my party dress, raced off to the *taverna*, and danced all night with not even a memory of the headache and nausea.

If I was not Eyed, why was I so uncharacteristically ill? I had eaten nothing that could have been spoiled, drank only tea that had been boiled. If I was Eyed, who did it? Clearly Margaríta had nothing to envy me for – me a single woman without home or children. Quite the opposite. I admired and to a certain extent envied her the extraordinarily beautiful home, her austere lifestyle, even the terra cotta floor and the view from her window. Only many years later, when I learned that some think the Eye can be deflected back to the Eyer did I come up with an answer.

The daughter of a prominent family, Margaríta had married a well-to-do farmer and gone to create what must have seemed a perfect life in the Monastery. Yet suddenly her life fell apart; for two years, tragedy followed upon tragedy. First, her eighteen-year-old daughter fell from an olive tree and broke her spine, leaving her paraplegic. Some months later, her last child was born prematurely and feeble-minded. Soon afterward, her husband died of colon cancer. As though all these devastating events were not enough, before two years were up, her beloved older brother died when his tractor rolled on him. This series of accidents would most likely have been attributed to the Eye, and Margaríta not only would have had her house exorcized, possibly even by a priest, but would in the future take every precaution to deflect or neutralize the Eye. Quite possibly, overcoming such a series of blows had strengthened her spirit so that her resistance to the Eye was enough to turn it from its course and back onto the giver. And so it seems possible that it was I who indeed had the Eye at this time. I am only glad that Margaríta was strong enough to divert it so that I did not, in my ignorance, cause her any more sorrow.

Later, when I told Thanásis about my experience and my thoughts concerning the Eye, he laughed. "Nonsense!" he said. "Everybody knows that Margaríta wants a *nífi*, a daughter-in-law. Her son is wasting all his inheritance, whooping it up in the *panigýria*. And last I heard, he wanted to turn the Monastery into a disco. But he is such an idiot no local girl would marry him. So here you are, milking cows and saving pigs, and saying how lovely the house is, and how you'd love to bake bread in her oven, *kai ta lipá, kai ta lipá*. The perfect *nífi*! Yes, she Eyed you all right."

"Hmm," I replied, unsatisfied. "Can pigs have the Eye?"

The Deluge

One bright, wind-swept winter day, my second winter in the village, I
was hurrying along the *agorá* – all doors shut and no one in view – when
Dimítris the barber rapped hard on his window and motioned to me to
stop. Dimítris with his crisp gray curls and lean, well-shaven features was a
handsome and pleasant man. I stopped and he came out of his shop waving a magazine. *"Kíta autó!"* "Look at this!"

"This" was a copy of *Stern*, a German magazine much like the
American *Life*. Dimítris spoke and read German and was often seen in
the summer with a pair of middle-aged German ladies, who must have
sent him the magazine. As I stood in the chill and empty *agorá*, Dimítris
opened the magazine, showing me six pages of exquisite color photographs
of the village – or rather, of the rural areas, as though there were no village. All the people in the photographs were clearly models, presumably
German with the exception of one Greek, the handsomest of the young
fishermen. Most of the models were blonde and nude: nude blonde women
sunbathing on the contorted rocks of Kolymbíthres, nude blondes playing chess on the beach at Santa Maria, and nude blond men and women
swimming off a yacht in the aquamarine sea of the bay of Lággeri.

"Isn't it wonderful?" Dimítris said. "We're famous."

I was speechless. How had the photographer managed to sneak in a
yacht and, clearly, a helicopter (something whose presence, for the villagers, meant a life-and-death medical emergency), and then find all those
popular places empty? No one in the village had reported seeing such a
party – not in the harbor, the *kafeneío*, the *taverna*. Probably they had
come in early October and stuck to their yacht. I hoped those models had
turned blue, swimming in the icy sea.

Although I didn't read German, I recognized the name of the writer.
He was the ex-husband of a woman who for years had been bringing her
two young daughters to the village for the summer. Justine was one of a
small group of foreigners who lived in Rome and came to the village every year, renting the fishermen's winter homes, valuing the village for its
quiet beauty and hospitable people, never complaining about the primitive plumbing or the lumpy beds. For two weeks she would go to Cairo and
visit her elderly parents, and the ex-husband would come and stay with
the girls. The last time he had come, he had brought hashish and offered it
not only to his subteen daughters but to the village kids as well. When the
girls' mother found out what he had done, she forbade him to ever come

again to the village, or else she would turn him in to the police. And here, flapping in my frozen hands, was his revenge. He was turning loose on the until-now-obscure village the vandal horde of international tourism.

Dimítris was thrilled.

I was devastated. But I thanked him for showing the magazine to me, oohing and aahing over each transcendently beautiful photograph. And I went off to dinner afraid and down-hearted, haunted by a vision of the future. The barren, rocky land where sheep grazed and gulls nested would become real estate where hotels and villas would be built. The scree, with its occasional crystal caves of rust-colored quartz, its fragrant herbs – purple thyme and modest peterium, oregano, and sage – would be scraped clean by bulldozers. The pristine sea water, so clear that, floating on the surface, one could watch the slow movements of an octopus twenty feet down, would become polluted with waste and choked with algae. Even worse, the villagers would become the servants of the tourists, catering to their needs while giving up privacy, autonomy, and limited resources to the demands of a tourist-centered economy. But perhaps the greatest damage would be done to the beautiful, sensible customs. In the bitter Voriás, I leaned on the bridge across the little river, staring down at the small *kaíkis* hauled up on the sand, until Pantelís the schoolteacher shook my shoulder. "What are you doing here? You'll freeze. Come along to the *taverna*." I sheltered under his arm and went along, comforted only by his presence and the warmth of the *taverna*.

The consequences were not long in showing up. Mere weeks later, as I entered the *taverna*, Liggéris came and sat down at my table after bringing me my order. "What is this?" he asked, handing me a letter. It was from a German travel company – fortunately written in English – and listed eight dates over the late spring and the summer.

I said, "They're planning walking tours and they want prices for meals for their clients. Look here: one appetizer, one meat or fish, one vegetable, one salad, one sweet, one coffee. Twenty tourists for each tour."

"That's not the way we work," said Liggéris, puzzled and irritated. "You know, people share things – salads, *yemistés*, *kalamarákia*."

"Family style, we call it."

"And sweets – I don't make sweets, or coffee." Liggéris' brow was furrowed with frustration. "How do I know in February what the prices will be in June? The market police in Athens won't set the summer prices until May, at least."

"You could guess, couldn't you?"

"If I guessed too much and the market police found out, they'd close me down."

"And if you guessed too little, you'd lose a lot of money." I thought for a minute. "Look, Liggéris, this has happened to some other *taverna* somewhere, maybe Mykonos. Somebody has to know how to do this."

"I'll talk to the tourist police in the *hóra*," he said, getting up, "but I don't see why they can't just come and eat what they want and pay for it." He sighed. "And another thing: twenty people. We're always packed in the summer. Where can I seat twenty people?"

"They'll probably eat earlier than Greeks, maybe six-thirty or seven. That should help." I promised to write any letters he needed when he discovered what to do. Eventually he did.

This scene was repeated time and time again over the next two years, in Liggéris' and other *tavernas*, the sweet shops, the *pensións*, and hotels. I was kept busy translating and writing. The first wave showed up the first summer; it was but lightly felt, and even welcome, but it was not a one-time event. Next winter, the *Stern* article was reproduced as a flyer for European tourist agencies. The invasion had begun.

Most of the villagers were pleased, at first. Katína's mother Anna was happy to make some money renting out Katína's dowry apartment, since there was no groom in the offing. Marió and Adrianí opened a little shop selling crocheted and embroidered clothing. One or two warehouses on the harbor opened as *óuzeris*. But these small-scale endeavors were soon eclipsed. By the second summer after the *Stern* article, existing facilities were stretched to the limit and construction, especially of hotels and "bungalows" – studio apartments – hastily begun. With the tourists came entrepreneurs. Soon there was a German, a French, and a Swiss restaurant. Boutiques, most opened by foreigners, replaced groceries and produce shops. Driven from the harbor *kafeneío* by the presence of drunken, bikini-clad foreigners, the old men retreated to the interior of the village, creating a "private club." The foreigners would follow with their own forms of exclusion.

Over the following years, grazing lands, orchards, and fields would become hotels, *pensións* and apartments, restaurants and discos. Storerooms under village houses would turn into boutiques and *souvláki* shops. From June to October, the streets would teem with torrents of people, and from November on, the village would look like a ghost town, the blue and green painted windows and doors shuttered, gaudy signs for empty restaurants and ticket offices splashed like graffiti across the plain whitewashed stone walls.

Even time was affected: no longer would the year be marked by saints' days and harvests; there would be only "the season" and "the off season."

The worst damage would be done to the wholeness of the community. Every public space and function would be devoted exclusively to the entertainment of foreigners; only after the "season" was over would the villagers be able to gather for saints' days and *panigýria*. Even then, the discos and bars would appropriate aspects of the celebration – the drinking and dancing – but reserve them for the young, and divorce them from the eating that had traditionally prevented wild drunkenness. Rarely would families gather as before, mothers and fathers, children, grandparents and grandchildren, all eating and drinking and dancing together. The lines of *syrtos* would be broken into by clumsy tourists stepping on people's feet, making fools of themselves for the amusement of their fellows, but never, never breathing the same breath.

The Ikon Carver

One day, while the wave of tourism was still a pleasant ripple on the sea of the island's serenity, the ferry debarked a certain foreigner, an Athenian, a carver of ikons. He had the name of an ancient king, which he cut into a wooden sign and hung outside the small shop that became gallery, work-shop, bedroom, and, every evening, *stékki*, a sort of salon, to all the friends he made so easily. King he wasn't, though he looked it, but noble he was. One morning, rummaging in a portfolio of sketches of ikons, he drew half out his patents of nobility, creased and yellowed parchments swirled with Ottoman calligraphy. "The fruits of collaboration," he laughed ironically, "two hundred years ago," and slid them back among the drawings.

A mystery man. The day he arrived, he rented the shop across from

Michális' dry goods emporium. He set up his bench at a right angle to the large casement window that opened directly onto the main street, really a footpath, used by handcarts and three-wheeled trucks only when a ferry came in bringing coffee, sheets, china, newspapers, underwear, and beer from Athens. He spent a few days honing his chisels and then began to carve ikons, something he did with exquisite respect for tradition. And to curse, something he did with great creativity. Roughing out, for instance, an arch of twin winged dragons to surmount a yet-to-be-painted image of Áyios Yiorgios, he would grumble his way through the ordinary blasphemies : "I fuck your Virgin! I fuck your Christ! I fuck your Cross!" move on to the folkloric versions: "I fuck your ikon lamp, and your mother's, and your grandmother's!" and finally, in an ecstasy of frustration (usually at the cheap, uncured wood he was forced to use), he would roar, "I fuck the slippers of St. Barbara when she was a bride!" In what became an antiphony, Michális, sitting at his cash desk at his window across the narrow street, would call, "But, moré, the saint, she never married!"

Alas, the carver began also to drink, most particularly and with increasing frequency the local ouzo, which he called, in another dialect, tsípouro. A stunningly handsome man, even at sixty, he had a long square face creased with deep, vertical lines, of suffering rather than ill temper, and across his wide forehead were etched horizontal lines of thought. The mouth was firm, the nose strong and straight. Noble.

From the beginning he was as poor as a church mouse, which, in a sense, he was, a mouse creeping into the church to pick up crumbs of ártos (holy bread), or wax, old stoles or sexton's shoes; a mouse so at home in the great cathedral of church history that he could tell you in a minute whether a particular ikon was indeed a fifteenth-century Ayía Ekaterini or a seventeenth-century copy of same, or whether the frame or a témplo was carved in Pilion or Kríti; but all the same a Communist mouse, railing at the church for its vanity, its cowardice, and its gluttony, for isolating itself on mountaintops, enclosing itself in stone and marble, blinding itself with gold and carmine, deafening itself with psalmody, stuffing its nose with incense (and its belly with lamb and its pockets with drachmas), so as not to see, hear, feel, or lift a hand to relieve the desperation of the hungry, the ignorant, the wretched, the dying, the oppressed.

Hungry he was himself. While painting or carving holy scenes, a proper ayiográphos, cleric or lay, lives only on bread and water, which may explain the relatively small size of Eastern ikons as opposed to, say, the enormity of the Sistine ceiling, whose painter was presumably dining like the Medicis. The carver, however, dined on patsás (tripe broth) and fakés (lentils) out of involuntary poverty, and on tsípouro out of hunger. His day and diet were all but invariable. Breakfast: tsípouro, to ignite the fires; a few hours carving; lunch: fakés, to stoke the furnace; a little sleep; then, in the evening, tsípouro, always with paréa, the company of friends, in the shop for music (classical or rembétika) and politics – and a little more carving; then supper: patsás to damp the flames, and a final tsípouro to induce sleep. Hungry, yes; ignorant, no. He had not always been a carver. No, he said, he had been a radio repairman. But that did not explain his fluency in six modern languages, though German and English he would not speak for political reasons, which did not apply to Turkish, which he spoke when the occasion presented itself for sentimental ones. He displayed, though modestly, a philologist's ease in all forms of Greek – Ancient, Koine, Puristic, and Demotic – and a connoisseur's knowledge of European and Greek music, art, architecture, literature, history, linguistics, politics, economics, theology, and so on and so on.

Sometimes the veil of mystery was lifted, if briefly. One evening in the shop, Molly the American violinist played him part of a concerto she was working on. The carver sighed with pleasure. "*Oraío!*" he said, "beautiful!" Then he began in an apologetic way to discuss a slight disappointment with Mozart's predictability.

"Where did you learn all this stuff?" asked Molly. "Did you go to university?"

"Me?" laughed the carver. "I went to the universities of Makrónissos and Yoúra," naming two of the most notorious political prisons. "Such a faculty: theologians and economists, even a musicologist! Nothing to do but read, when they let us have books, or talk when they didn't." In one prison, he had learned to carve from an old man who died and left him the tools.

"They let you have knives and chisels?"

"*Paidí mou*, they didn't care if we killed each other. They had machine guns."

Another time, Takis, who represented the literary left of the village, brought a new, covertly printed volume of poetry and began to read aloud. The carver joined in, tears in his eyes. Takis, stunned, exclaimed, "How could you . . .?"

The carver twirled his hand in a circle. "In prison. When the poet ran out of paper, we said, 'Recite to us and we'll memorize. Write it down when your wife brings the paper.' '*Ohi*,' he says, coughing his lungs out, 'I'll give you all TB.' '*Den pirázei*,' we said, 'The hell with the TB. Speak us the poetry!'" Here the carver recited a stirring strophe, blew his nose and said, "E! Enough of that! Time for *tsípouro*!"

These confessions seemed so to embarrass the carver that he never otherwise spoke of his life in prison. Takis, who had done a month in jail, speculated that the carver, like many others, had been on a list made up in the Metaxás dictatorship and kept in a folder in some police station, and, as regime gave way to regime, the designated subversive was taken, held and released on the whim of every new bureaucracy. "He probably never did anything," said Takis, who, it was rumored, had himself been only a bystander at a demonstration.

"What was it like, prison?" Molly asked once.

The carver did not look up from his work, rubbing beeswax into a mirror frame. "*Kápote Athos, kápote Adis.*" "Sometimes a monastery," he translated, "sometimes Hades. Like the army! Boredom, lice, and no *tsípouro.*"

The carver was an idealist in everything: every falling away from perfect Christianity, perfect Communism, perfect craftsmanship, or perfect human decency struck him a blow which only *tsípouro* could anesthetize. For a while, he struggled with some compromise in the area of craftsmanship. To enhance his livelihood (and augment his diet), the government (ironically, the Junta) had lent him the money to buy a pantograph for roughing out, at least, duplicate saints or mirror frames. He used it the way an aging demimonde would use an aphrodisiac – secretly and in great shame – and finally, unable to make the payments, saw it go out the door with enormous relief: "Hideous great soulless mass of metal and electric wires – a Juntist conspiracy! Good riddance!"

The ikon carver's idealism, or the *tsípouro*, had perhaps made him a less-than-perfect husband. Indeed, though he never said so himself, his friends maintained the situation was reversed; that is, never having once tasted the briefest moments of paradise with his wife Déspina (it was east of Eden from the beginning), he had no way of balancing the bitter with the sweet, and so he turned to *tsípouro* to deafen himself against the complaints and recriminations of his importunate *strígla*. After fifteen years of marriage relieved by frequent vacations in prison, the carver at last had fled to the island which he hoped would be a sort of Mt. Athos for him (his idea of chastity being limited to abstention from Déspina), where he could somehow reconcile all his angers into a kind of holy anticlerical simplicity of life among pleasant peasants and easygoing artisans (and the occasional easy *tourístria*), sustaining body and soul on fresh bread and cheap *tsípouro*, bathing in the immaculate sea, dancing in the *tavernas*, and so on.

However, Athos is entered only by basket and only at the will of the inhabitants, females of any species including hens being strictly excluded, while the island was penetrable three times a week by ferry. Déspina, needing no invitation nor giving any warning, would swoop down upon him at her whim like a *fortoúna*, a howling gale, scooping up available cash and salable items, destroying peace of mind, scattering the friends, and, in one ultimate, magnificent spasm of spite, confiscating a lifetime's collection of carving patterns for which she had no earthly use.

So utterly devastated was he financially and emotionally by Déspina's depredations, that the village, witnessing and sorrowing, constituted itself a resistance organization. Seconds after the great maw of the ferry had opened, revealing the plump middle-aged form of Ate the Destroyer, old Bárba Nikolákis, who unloaded and delivered small goods in his handcart, would rush away, trundling cartons of cigarettes and chocolates for the kiosks, and hiss to any of the loafers sitting at the harbor café, "Tell the carver his wife's coming!" The message would be instantly relayed, in the ancient manner by runner or in the modern by telephone, to Michális of the dry goods, who would then lean out his door, and call the alarm. The carver would quickly gather up whatever pitiful till there was, the better carvings and ikons (leaving certain plywood peacocks of the pantograph era as a sop to Cerberus), lock the shop, and flee. If the Fury's prey was, for instance, collecting a shave at the barber's against a promised ikon of Ayios Ioánnis, whichever of the friends was drinking coffee in the shop would dash to gather up the hounded artisan (lather and all) and hide him in someone's apartment, shop, or studio.

Déspina, arriving at a closed shop, would then canvass neighboring merchants. "Where is my husband?" she would demand, fists on hips. Alas, the resistance was never all that organized so the drama unleashed fictive talents; she would hear, within ten minutes, that he had gone to another village, left the country, gone to Náxos (unlikely, since that was where she herself kept a tourist shop), and fallen seriously ill and been taken to Sýros by helicopter. The last was especially clever, as there was a boat leaving in an hour and none returning for several days.

Déspina would then send for a locksmith (none would appear) or simply pick up a rock and smash a pane in the door. If anyone protested, for instance, the landlord's niece in the embroidery shop up the street she would announce in tongues of flame, "I am his WIFE!" and install herself and luggage in the shop. She would make a little sweet coffee, get out her crochet hook and thread, and, thus occupied, wait silently for the unfortunate to (as he always did) slink in.

He came not just for his *tsípouro* supply, nor for his underwear, toothbrush, and so forth – the friends were willing to provide – but from a kind of pride or courage, arguing (though his friends assured him that this was not a parallel situation) that a man who had been tortured by the Germans during the world war and by the rightists during the civil war and by the secret police after the war should not flee in terror before a woman whom he could, though with difficulty, remember as a flirty little seamstress he had managed to overwhelm with charm and passion one summer night in the National Garden, when he had just been released from prison and was in ecstasy to be alive and free.

Déspina's terrible bitterness was in part due to the fact that this charm and passion had not outlasted an honestly acknowledged paternity, a quick marriage, and endless years of bourgeois conversations: "What shall we eat at noon, tonight, tomorrow? If you would just work a little harder, and talk politics less . . . Why don't you . . . I can't understand what you see in that bolshevik/artist/bum/bitch/whore/scum . . . I don't understand . . ."

And indeed, poor Déspina, she didn't understand, and what she didn't understand she willed to destroy, and what she willed to destroy was destroyed, and the area surrounding the target laid waste to the horizon.

One time she came bearing gifts. It was the *yiortí* of all those with non-Christian names: of old deities like Artemis and Okeanís; of trees or flowers like Dáphne, Lemoniá, and Violétta; or of heroes like Jason and Byron. The wife of the ancient king got off the ferry in the late afternoon carrying boxes of treats. As the friends one by one sauntered into the shop, still yawning from their midday sleep, they were greeted by a grim carver and an effusive Déspina: "Sit down! Have a *báklavá* – I made it myself – or a chocolate, a liqueur."

"*Hrónia pollá*," they wished him and sat or stood silently, nibbling at unwanted sweets and eyeing each other covertly as their own plans for celebrating fell apart. Later, in the *taverna*, the guilty carver tried to simulate high spirits, snapping his fingers, calling "*Opa!*", and even dancing with his wife. The friends one by one responded to the plea in the humiliated carver's eyes, and got up, slowly and reluctantly, to dance. But this travesty of joy weighed so heavily on each one that the next day, one after the other, they girded their loins and tackled the source of their friend's misery – who, in apron and head scarf, was combining a thorough cleaning of the shop with an inventory.

First, Pávlos the painter, whose Alexandrian charm had never before fallen on stony ground: "You're a young woman still; he's nearly sixty. You can still have a full life."

"He's my husband, and I love him."

Next Molly the American: "If you love him, give him a divorce. He's a poor, sick man."

"I married him in church. If he's ill, it's my duty to care for him. But he wouldn't be ill if he would come home to our house."

Then Takis the educated peasant, smelling greed: "What can you want from him? He has nothing."

"He has a plot of land he owns with his brother. Let him get his brother to sign it over to me, and I'll think about a divorce." But the brother wasn't born yesterday, so the carver's credulous pleas went unheeded.

The fruit of this union was a reasonably good-looking teenager, who occasionally fled the maternal hearth himself; once he was found by the local police and put on the boat back to Déspina, who was waiting at the dock in Piraeús. He would come for a week or so, hang around the shop, share the *patsás* of an evening (although the carver would go secretly to the *taverna*, begging credit for meat and vegetables for the boy), but, sooner or later, despite his father's earnest if impractical invitations to stay ("We'll find a house somewhere in the country; we'll fish – would you like to fish?"), he would mooch onto the ferry and go home.

As the carver's destitution increased, his skill blossomed. From his chisels sprouted vines and dragons, ascended eagles and peacocks, emerged little flat cities and steep, riven mountains. He carved an altar door for a farmer's little chapel so pristinely rich with the plants and animals of Paradise that it was rumored never to admit a false-hearted priest. A dowry trunk he made for Michális' daughter was so sweet and smug with fruiting olives, smoking chimneys, and dove-topped cypresses that it seemed to guarantee an immortality of domestic bliss. But what he carved almost always went out the door the day he set down the chisel or the emery paper, went for barter or a few drachmas to the villagers. What would have saved him, commissions for or from the church, were not forthcoming. The donors of these – publicly pious petty bourgeois money-changing Philistines – hired carvers from Athens, who came with pantographed panels of yellow wood, flourished a chisel over the surfaces, sprayed them with dazzling varnish, and pocketed for a few days work what would have sustained the craftsman over an entire winter of his slow, meticulous carving, his monastic diet, his blasphemous dedication, his despairing and enraged adoration.

So exquisite was his work, so humble his demeanor, so strong, informed and brilliant his discourse, that he never lacked for friendship – true friendship which sought to bring him both temporary comfort and recognition of his art. Takis periodically announced *yiortés* – his own, his mother's and father's – which obliged him to treat to *souvlákia* and wine at the *taverna*. A charmed American widow bought, for a large family of children and grandchildren, as many carved and polychromed ikons, mirror frames, and boxes as her pension would allow. Pávlos the painter designed for carving a series of modern *kareklákia*, sconces, replacing the traditional double-headed eagles with sly but loving caricatures of local fishermen, priests, and donkeys. But he did not succeed in getting the carver to save the pieces for a show in Athens which might have brought him fame and orders. This a Dutch tourist almost accomplished, arranging an invitation to an international exhibition of religious art. All winter and summer, the carver held back from sale or barter his most beautiful pieces, even consenting to borrow money for better wood, a wool *fanélla* against the cold, a little *tsípouro*, the shipping charges. But for some undiscoverable reason, the carvings sat uncleared and uncollected in Dutch customs for the duration of the show. The carver's disappointment was bitter and his debts many, so that when the collection was returned, it was dispersed quickly to creditors. Many would have waited for the season, but the carver was proud in the way of a noble who has learnt the bite of hunger.

The day came (could it have been three years?) when the carver got on a boat, and never returned. Three months rent the landlord had forgiven him, but no more. To the dry goods merchant's assurance that this summer, within six months, the tourists would descend like a tidal wave (they did), he answered that even Christ hadn't fasted that long. To the friends' sincere offers of housing, food, even *tsípouro* (although they were divided about the advisability of the latter), he replied that charity is a leaking boat, and that he'd better push out for other shores before it, and he, went down. He cleaned up the shop, took down the signs, said goodbye to Michális, the barber, the *taverna* owner, Bárba Nikolákis, and the other friends, and boarded the ferry. He left behind him . . . an empty place. The friends after a while found they had less in common than they thought, and drifted apart. No one heard from him. The shop window became opaque with dust, the carver a memory.

But all over the village, in this house and that shop, traded for wood, underwear, haircuts, bread, *patsás*, and of course *tsípouro*, can be seen the carver's legacy – the ikons, exquisitely detailed on smooth, golden olive wood: noble, young, and proud Ayios Dimítrios; the dashing rescuer of ladies and slayer of serpents, Ayios Yiórgios; Ayios Stéphanos stoned and hounded; John the Evangelist, his ear cocked to the voice of God, his eyes on the Apocalypse; wild and straggly-haired John the Baptist, climbing shattered rocks, looking behind him (for Salome?); the Prophet Ilías fed by ravens in the wilderness.

And the one he never would sell, until the very last, when either it or the tools had to go to pay for a ticket to another fragile Athos: the serene, smooth, infinitely delicate Panagía, holding in the folds of her cloak the innocent, adoring babe with, faintly traced over each head, haloes scarcely more than a wish.

Priests

January, night – black night. All over the island, the power's out. Furious winds snap some electric lines from their poles. The remaining lines fizz and spark. Roaring down from the frozen Caucasus across the wild Aegean, the wind drives waves over the balconies of houses in the harbor. Icy rain slashes at windows and doors, forcing entry, pooling on sills and floors. Black water runs half a meter deep, turning hilly streets into roaring cataracts. Windows are shuttered, stores and houses dark and blank. Only from the rain-streaked windows of the *kafeneío* is light visible – the cold blue glow of a propane lamp. When the glass door of the cafe opens, it slams flat against a corner table, threatening to shatter. Two men manage to close it again.

The small, chilly room is packed with damp men, the gas lamp hisses overhead, and one of the oldest arguments in the history of religion rages and roars like the storm outside.

"Hold it, Stamáti," says Grigóris, the *kafetzís*, shoving a small cup of coffee across the counter, then leaning over it and raising his hand like an umpire. "Sit down and stop yelling. Now you're saying, 'If religion is any good . . .'"

"If there's a God!" yells Chrysóstomos, Stamátis' partner in the carpentry shop.

"Whatever. Then why are the priests – "

"And monks!"

" – who get the most of it, corrupt? Right?"

"*Málista!*" Stamátis, miffed at having his anger so coolly summarized, looks round him for support. "Greedy skinflints! Drunkards! Like old what's-his-name in Pródromos?"

"Pápa Vasílis."

"Vasílis. Have you ever seen him sober?"

Nikolákis, the builder's apprentice, sniggers. "I saw him baptizing a kid once. Dropped it in the font and nearly drowned it!"

"Shut up!" barks the *kafetzís*. "That poor bastard . . . the war . . . What do you know, little man?"

"There's a priest in the *hóra* as fat as a pregnant elephant," growls Thódoros the machinist.

"They're all fat," sniffs a lean, dark man with shadows under his eyes, "and rich! That faggot monk Theophilos talked my grandmother out of her big town house. Now he's renting it out, and us three generations in one country hovel. Bah!"

Vangélis, the son of the village *pápas* (priest) recently returned from a seminary high school, stands embattled in the small space before the counter, grasping at retorts. Although supported now by the *kafetzís*, he still feels deeply the collapse, with graduation, of his hopes to enter the priesthood, his hope that God, seeing his passionate devotion (in fifteen years he has never missed a liturgy, has gotten almost all 100s in psalmody and theology), would remove the one stumbling block to his eligibility: the hare lip and cleft palate. It is Vangélis' crucifixion that his voice, so fueled by love for God and the church, when raised in chant and magnified by loudspeaker, goes flapping around the village like a gull with a broken wing. Stammering, he falls back on his learning, counters Stamátis' anger with "Have you read this? Have you read that? No?" He shames himself with his useless arrogance, aware he is slashing at them with a flail they don't even feel, repaying their juvenile cruelties. "You can't say . . . my father . . ." His father is tiny, white-bearded, humble Pápa Kosmás. ". . . as innocent as a child."

But a voice growls, "Where's Venézis' ikon?" reviving a scandal. Old Pápa Kosmás had taken an "art expert" to see the Venezis family's seventeenth century ikon, to advise on its restoration. Ikon and expert had disappeared, and suspicion had fallen on the bewildered priest.

"Shut up!" warns the *kafetzís*. "This is a discussion, not – "

Whoosh! The door crashes open, the rain in an instant soaking the thighs of the men sitting next to the opening. In stumbles a tall, skinny, drenched young man whose slicker, already short at the wrists and knees, has been ripped from his shoulder by the wind. He's lost his hat as well, and his sparse red hair is plastered to his skull. This is Ilías, the would-be successor to Pápa Kosmás. Stamátis leaps to his feet and, strophe by strophe, repeats the argument and shoves it at the dripping man.

By the time Stamátis has had his say, Ilías is standing holding a pink pastry box while the *kafetzís* searches for a plastic bag.

"Well?" from pugnacious Stamátis.

"Friends," laughs Ilías, "Chrissoúla s going to give birth any day now. Chocolatinas she longs for, and for chocolatinas I've walked three kilometers in this storm, not to solve theological problems. Ask me after the baby's born!"

Surprisingly, it's Thódoros the agnostic who offers to drive Ilías home on his motorcycle. The remainers joke and grumble about Ilías. His going for the priesthood has unnerved the younger men. Once they were all boys together, robbing orchards, stoning cats, learning blasphemies, spying on girls, masturbating in the hen houses. Now Ilías, by a decision no one saw coming, is separated from them, elevated above them.

Barely visible through the window, Ilías struggles to hold on to his box and his slicker and straddle the motorcycle. A man in the corner muses, "I wonder what kind of a priest he will make, Ilías."

"Kind of priest?" roars Stamátis. "Any ordinary guy, dress him in a *ráso* and cap him with a *kalimáfki*, and Na! He'll be a *pápas* like all *papádes*. Bloodsucking hypocrites."

"One thing," says the *kafetzís*, "he'll never be fat!"

The priest in a village, the *pápas*, lives in a spotlight, suffers a scrutiny more constant and intense than that of politicians or film stars. Visually, he is the most conspicuous person in the village: among the mostly clean-shaven and close-shorn men, he alone wears his hair and beard uncut from the day of his ordination as deacon. His dress as well sets him off: every other man in the village is trouser-clad, but around the ankles of the priest swirl the skirts of his cassock, the *ráso* – black for good, blue or brown for everyday. And while the others wear caps, on the *pápas'* head balances the stiff cylindrical *kalimáfki*, occasionally replaced by a skullcap. However, even though symbolically set apart from ordinary men, in his other-than-ecclesiastical life he is as much like them as possible: married, part of a family (usually local), part of a community, often a farmer or fisherman. But he carries a great weight, for by the priest the village judges the Church itself.

I was in the *kafeneío* the night of the argument. Like the improvident virgins, I had forgotten to keep my lamps full of kerosene against the frequent power failures, and so had braved the near-hurricane to seek light and warmth. Finding the tiny cafe packed with so many men, I squeezed by a row of damp knees to sit on the zinc-covered counters in the kitchen, where Evangelía, the *kafetzís'* wife, was cooking syrup in a copper kettle. As the shouting declined to grumbling, I asked her why there was so much hostility on the subject of priests.

"What should I tell you?" she sighed. "Partly because they usually get rich. Also, they get out of going to the army; all the other men have to go, and they hate it. And then, you know, politics . . ."

"What kind of politics?"

"Here? Family rivalry, mostly. You remember Byron?"

"Who worked in the government office in the *hóra*?"

"Yes, him. He was also waiting to be a priest, waited eight years, but they say Pápa Kosmás hung on though he's old and sick with the diabetes hoping, year after year that his son . . . ah, poor Vangélis! You know a priest has to be perfect in his body? They say the doctors can fix that now, the cleft palate, but not when he was born. Nothing to do but pray for a miracle. Maybe five years in a row, Vangélis' mother, the *papadiá*, took him to Tínos." To Tínos, the famous thaumaturgical church of the Panagía, the Virgin, where invalids and their relatives walk, if they can, on barely wrapped knees over a mile of stone paving from the boat harbor to the church. Inside, strung on wires across the nave, thousands of silver and gold votive offerings in shapes from simple arms and legs and eyes to fully modeled cows and steamships jangle in the breeze, bearing witness to a multitude of miracles.

"But he wasn't cured."

"No, and Byron got tired of waiting and went to Athens to be a *psáltis*, a cantor. Now his relatives are jealous of Ilías. But it probably wasn't politics. Byron was too early, that's all."

"And what do you think of priests?"

"Me? I think that, as with everyone else, there are good ones and bad ones: gluttons, drunkards, lechers or misers, draft dodgers. This is only natural," she said, shrugging her shoulders as she ladled the syrup onto pans of *baklava*. "In a poor country, the money is too good to attract only the pure in heart." The word she used, *agathós*, I was to hear many times in reference to priests.

Here in the village, such virtue is the prime requisite. Education is not important. Some older priests are barely literate; old Pápa Kosmas' own sons, sent by him to prep schools and university, were ashamed of him because, though he lined with his finger the letters of his missal, he in fact sang his liturgy by heart, thousands of pages of it.

Mostly, the villagers say, the vice of priests is avarice. They take no vow of poverty. Considered civil servants, they receive small salaries from the community, but unlike, say, the village president or secretary, they are free to augment their stipends with fees for baptisms, weddings, funerals and memorials, blessings of homes and shops and fishing boats – always once a year, or when new. On occasion they will also perform a sort of exorcism, removal of the Eye, a service requested not only by villagers whose cows have mysteriously died but by such sophisticated folks as, a marine lawyer told me, an international firm of insurers who had paid out on three sunken ships in three months. Donations for such services are so easily raised by the lifting of an eyebrow; elderly widows are so easily led by the pressure of a hand, the deepness of an eye, to bypass nephews and nieces and deed this little orchard, that little house or a small bag of gold *líras* to the dear *pápas*, that for any priest, great or humble, accumulation of wealth is almost a certainty.

The money a priest earns beyond his stipend, however, is expected to form a resource to help him care for his flock. From the *perihélia*, the stole he wears during the liturgy, hang fringes of gold thread called *krósia*, which symbolize both the mercy of God and the responsibilities of the priest – not only to offer the sacraments, console in sorrow, and advise in dilemma, but also to alleviate pain and poverty. Like his Master, the priest must feed his sheep. He might, for instance, pay for a helicopter to fly an injured farmer to the hospital, or for uniforms, books, and bus fare so a bright, poor girl could go to high school. Again, he might advance a loan payment on a *kaíki* engine when a fisherman, caring for his children and wife after her heart operation, runs short. Or he might replace a dead goat for an elderly widow. This charity the unworldly old Pápa Kosmás was known for; his advice was worth little, but his heart and purse were open, and his prayers, they say, effective.

Alas, a little hardness of heart, a certain ennui with the ever-present poor, swells the coffers and the bellies of many *papádes*, hangs with gold the ample breasts of their wives, polishes the crystal and silver of their tables or the chrome of their Mercedes, while the *krósia* tarnish with neglect.

Still, in a small village like this, such abuses are rare. For one thing, a village priest is chosen by the parishioners. Just as this church believes the native herb has the greatest virtue to heal and grow, ideally a village priest is native too, known to the villagers since birth. The church has a few requirements, though traditionally no education is needed. Many older priests, like Pápa Kosmás, were unlettered; today, however, a candidate would be expected to have graduated from high school. If a young man decides he wants to be a priest, and it seems likely that the present priest will soon retire, he declares his intentions, perhaps to the retiring priest and the elders. He stays in the village, working at an ordinary job, chanting in the local church, and, most important, marrying and having (God willing) children. After some time, if he has the respect and support of the community, he may be ordained, first as deacon, later as priest.

The long years his fellow villagers watch the young man as he grows and matures ensure that they get the kind of priest they want. They know, for instance, whether as a youth he showed leadership, and what kind. Was he a charismatic football captain, able to organize for action but also maybe led astray by power and recognition? Was he a reclusive student, religious and otherworldly, likely to inspire piety but also to be at loose ends about economic or political issues? Is he a working man, a man of the people, in touch with everyday problems but also, maybe, too common to inspire respect for the church and her traditions? Whatever the community wants, the community gets, but it must think carefully, because it gets him for life.

Once a priest, the young man is also an *árchon*, an elder, and much like the village president, the vice president, the head teacher, the important businessmen, perhaps the doctor, is a shaper of the community's present and future life. But how much influence he has depends upon his own vision of his role, or perhaps upon his strength of character. Pápa Kosmás, long before age hunched his back, had recoiled from the eternal contention of village politics. Perhaps too often stunned by the quarreling of irreconcilable factions, he occupied himself with the cleaning and preservation of the dozens of village churches and their sacred artifacts and thus innocently had precipitated the scandal of Venezis' ikon.

The villagers have their priest for his lifetime, and, sadly in some cases, the priest has the village. Poor Pápa Vasílis, priest of a tiny village ten miles away, was indeed a drunk. One could see him there any day, reeling about the village in a ragged once-black *ráso*, or slumped over a table in the local *taverna*. But . .. "The war . . .," the *kafetzís* had said, and the next day, when I asked him, he told me the story.

When the island was occupied, first by Italians, then by Germans, Pápa Vasílis was a young man, with a young wife, one toddler and a baby on the way. A villager, he was most likely uneducated, chosen because he was *agathós*, innocent, even naive. But the pregnant girl was shot in an initial show of force by the local commandant. The child died too, whether from hunger – and there *was* starvation – or violence, no one remembers now.

A priest is married for life; if widowed, he can either stay to serve his parish alone or go to a monastery. Had the desolate man any choice? Could he, in those days of darkness and death, have left his villagers without the shadow of sustenance of the sacraments, without the breath of hope? Storehouses were emptied, animals slaughtered, and trees stripped to feed the enemy soldiers. Desperate parents fed their children with words, stories of meals they could barely remember. Perhaps Pápa Vasílis, with whispered words, helped them imagine the wine and bread of the Eucharist, the oil of unction, the golden flames of candles, the fragrance of myrrh.

246

At war's end, as life slowly returned the lambs to the fields, the fruits to the trees, Pápa Vasílis realized his loss. Natural to seek some comfort in the new wine, natural not to find it. He went, and would go on for years, from house to house, alone forever, enclosed forever in the village that had been his Bethlehem and would be his Calvary. And wherever he went, they gave him to drink and did not turn him away.

The fat priest in the *hóra*, Thódoros' anathema, was another kettle of fish. He was enormously fat. This weight, which he carried all in front, held his *ráso* out so far that it is doubtful that he could see his feet. Whether ascending or descending to his fine, renovated house on the Kástro, the Venetian acropolis which commanded the sea, he must always have been in danger of mis-stepping, plunging down the steep, twisting flights of broken slate and marble steps. Perhaps he always took the long way around, avoiding the stairs which led up from the sea front, coming in the back way from the market street, where there were fewer steps, feeling these with his feet like a blind man. Though young, only in his late thirties, he had in a very short time accumulated somehow (Stamátis would say by gluttony) kilos and kilos of flesh, heavy compact flesh. Looking at him, one thought of the red and white carcasses of beeves that hung on the hooks of the butchers in the early morning. And one night, while he slept on his back, they say, the weight of his fat pushed in his ribs and crushed his heart, and "*Na! Terma!*"

Pápa Apóstolos, who followed the deceased priest, was like neither his predecessor nor any of the other village priests on the island. He had not set out to be a priest, but had come as chief *psáltis*, cantor and teacher of psalmody, to the main church in the *hóra*. The Panagía, as the islanders call it, is the oldest church in Christendom in which the liturgy is still sung. Ayía Eléni, the mother of the Emperor Constantine, founded this church as she was returning from Jerusalem in her quest for the True Cross. The Ayía Sophía, the most famous church in Eastern Christendom, is older by a few years, but it stands dusty and empty with weeds in its churchyard, a museum for silent pilgrims in a hostile land.

Not an islander but a stranger, Pápa Apóstolos was something of a mystery, and his modesty exacerbated the situation. He had arrived quietly and taken up residence in a room that had once been a cell, in the once-monastery that surrounded the church and was now used as offices and a museum. His devotion to duty, study, and seclusion from most society showed clearly a vocation, though he himself was perhaps unclear from which direction the call was coming.

The man, at least forty, was unmarried – a fact that intrigued and frustrated the matrons of the *hóra*. Was he a solitary monk or what? He was handsome, in an Oriental sort of way: well-fleshed but not fat, smooth-skinned, dark, black-bearded with deeply black eyes like Kritian olives. From this darkness and a trace of accent, the gossips guessed origins in Asia Minor. Certainly, he was of an age to have been a child of catastrophe, genocide, expulsion, exile: People surmised flight from Ataturk's nationalist bloodbath, from Stalin's purge of Georgia, or from even more recent Turkish persecutions of Christians – the burning of homes, closing of churches, sequestering of property.

The tales spun in the churchyard and courtyards by reverent and even fervent attendees at liturgy would have astounded the shy man. Some were sure he was a *politis* from Constantinople, an aristocrat dispossessed and exiled. Others said, no, an Albanian fled from the Communists. Still others, inspired by his monk-like demeanor, believed that, orphaned and without relatives, he had been raised in a monastery. He was so foreign to these islanders that some questioned, in whispers, whether he was even Greek. Perhaps he was Armenian? Or Turkish?

The most inventive and anachronistic rumor made him the favored son of some polygamous Pontian aga, spirited away by his mother's rival (jealous, vengeful, but jibbing at poison), hung with a cross, and left outside the *giaour* church for the priest to find – a thin, dark-eyed, knock-kneed child of five, dumb with shock, devastated by death, by the loss of all, delivered finally to the grace and peace of a monastery, raised in the church by the church to be the church's own.

Wherever he came from, he must have been chosen to come to this church for the beauty of his voice – a voice that, born into another body in, say, Italy, would have found its way to La Scala – a deep, full voice which achieved a high range through the nose in the Byzantine mode, as though its lungs played both the bassoon or oboe of the West and the nose flute of the Middle East. To hear him singing the liturgy at Epiphany was to begin in the depths of flesh and rock, to be washed by clear waters, to be thrown aloft like a white dove, to circle in the dome of the church and fly out into the breathtaking blue ether of the spirit.

This voice that transcended and yet never left the heavy earth must have been called by the church itself, as a voice worthy to celebrate its own unique and sacred beauty. The interior of the Panagía has been so destroyed by iconoclasts, earthquakes, and restorers that, except for a sixth-century cruciform baptistery, it gives little hint of its history. This is revealed, but gently, in its courtyard littered with classical, Hellenistic, and Byzantine marble fragments nobody quite knows what to do with, censed by trees of roses and arbors of jasmine, and dominated by an immense pine tree in which the bells hang. Most important churches have bell towers or belfries; only tiny, rustic, mountainside chapels hang their bells in an adjacent tree. But the Panagía shelters an amazing huge and ancient pine, and from the pine hangs a clutch of green-bronze bells whose ropes drop to the marble pavement. Pápa Apóstolos would often go himself to ring the small bell on his way to dress for vespers.

Next to the church is a wood of smaller pines, surrounded by rock walls and, on one side, a row of white marble sarcophagi, classical, Hellenistic, all carved with similar scenes: the *makaríiis*, the blissful dead, lies on his or her bier, welcoming the funeral guests. There they sit – hosts, guests, and sarcophagi – by the roadside, sprinkled with pine needles, because again no one quite knows what to do with them. Nor does it bother anyone, particularly Pápa Apóstolos, who is not the sort of priest to worry about implications of paganism. Let the marble reliefs of garlanded bulls lean against the church walls; let the babies be named Okeanís or Achilléas. The soul, he knew, is wafted to God in little puffs: the clang of a bell drawing the ear from the daily spite of gossip, the sweetness of a star of jasmine held to the nose, the eyes of the Panagía flickering in the lamplight, the purity of a note echoing a syllable of the word of God through the centuries-old dome, the gasp of the crowd at the spreading ripple of hundreds of candle flames on the night of Resurrection.

By whatever road, Pápa Apóstolos had come into their midst a stranger, unmarried, middle-aged. This argues, perhaps, another road followed for a time before the call, like Paul's, had come. Was this road the slow pacing round and round the cloister, the tracing of lines of violet ink across ancient manuscripts, learning, contemplation, praise? Perhaps the old monks, watching the winnowing of their numbers, the crumbling of stone, the falling of the tiles of the monastery itself, had seen in him or hoped for him a genius, an energy, an intellectual quality beyond that necessary for quotidian work and prayer, and had bent him toward the episcopate. That road would take him through the seminary, perhaps beyond to a doctorate in theology or church music. Upon deciding, he would be ordained, take a vow of chastity, become attached to a cathedral or the patriarchate, and rise slowly through the ranks of ecclesiastical power.

But something deflected him from these paths: a light? a voice? Perhaps it was his own voice, his spirit, which like a dove circled and sought to fly up, out, over sea into sky. Watching it batter itself against the conspiracies, or grow weak from poverty and decay, some bishop or abbot opened a window.

And here he flew, here he roosted, and here, perhaps home at last, he touched ground. Day after day, walking about in the astounding hemisphere of blue and salty air, breathing the fragrances of the ancient but unexhausted earth, he experienced a freedom, a richness he had never known. And, looking into the (perhaps deceptive) brilliant innocence of island eyes, witnessing the simplicity – what he in his own innocence thought of as the nearly Judean simplicity of island souls – he discovered for them a compassion, a simple Christly compassion. And for his own life a Christly direction.

After he had made his decision, Apóstolos went to the *mamí* – the old one in the village, not the new gynecologist – and asked her to find a wife for him.

"He was so good," she said, and she was not an idolizer of priests, having birthed too many of their unwelcome girl babies and punched too many of their backsides with her syringes. "There was no question of dowry, nor beauty, nor youth. Were it allowed, which it isn't, I think he might even have taken a widow. Only the girl must understand how it is to be a *papadiá*, a priest's wife." For a shy woman, a humble woman, that life can be a torture. She is a focus of all eyes: she must be the cleanest, the most modest, the most pious. Her children must be the best scholars, must never get into fights, have tantrums, and so on. Or else. She has no off days. No outlets. There must be no slanging matches for the neighbors to overhear.

The list is endless. She must never complain, except perhaps to her godmother, so that there is never any gossip. "Well, if they succeed in that," said the *mamí*, "then they become as proud as queens. They always get rich, these priests and their wives!" She grimaced. "Most of them should go to hell for pride and coldness. But Papadiá Apóstolou! I found her at last in a tiny village, an orphan living with a poor aunt. As good as gold, this girl. Lame, a hip problem, easy to fix at birth now, but she was born during the war, when even I was in the military hospitals. Saying nothing, I took her to church."

But the young woman must have known the *mamí* was up to something, and Apóstolos did, of course, and when, after the service, there in the courtyard, in the magnificent litter of centuries, among marbles and mosaics, cats and winter roses, they looked at each other, it was as though into two deep dark wells the same sun began to shine.

The *mamí* knew this priest-to-be, and she had, she thought, more to explain to the girl, so she wrapped up one cold day a week or two later, and went to visit. She was going to say, "You will be very lonely." Hard to say this to an orphan, lonely for years, longing for a love to end all aloneness. The *mamí* was going to say, "This man is part saint, lifted up off his feet like saints in the ikons." But he had been there before her. He had said to the young woman, "This is what I will find difficult: the *krósia*." He had lived little in the world, he said, and less in this small scoop of earth, so that he had no judgment: whom should he help, and in what way? Would she work with him?

So this frail, sheltered, lame girl who had dreamed of being enclosed in his house, folded in his wings, sung to sleep by his voice, made whole by his touch, saw that instead she was being given the streets of the *hóra* to limp through, the pain of others to bear, injustice and grief and hate to listen to – and love to bear it with, to be transfigured by.

In the late afternoon, the sun streaming almost horizontally through the branches of the little pines, *Pápa* Apóstolos is walking, holding the hand of his small daughter. The long, deep-blue cassock concealing his feet, he seems to float slowly over the dusty ground, led by the tiny hand, held down by her frail weight. They move to where, in the sun-streaked shade, a white goat is tethered. Slowly he reaches out for the child's hand and with it strokes the goat – head, neck, back, belly. Taking a pail from the child, he begins first with his hands and then with hers in his to milk the goat.

From the church comes haltingly and sweetly the chanting of the learning boys:

Kai nin, kai aei . . . Kai nin . . . Kai nin kai aei . . .
eis tous . .. eis tous aiónas . . .
Kai nin, kai aei, eis tous aiónas ton aiónon…

Now and forever, and unto the Ages of Ages. Amen.

Pápa Ilías

The night of the storm and the argument, I had asked Evangelía not only about priests in general but about Ilías, the "priest-in-waiting," asking the same question asked in the *kafeneío*. "What kind of a priest will he make, do you think?"

"Ah," she had said, laughing. "I would be prejudiced. He's a third cousin of my husband; did you see they have the same red hair?" She thought a minute and then said, "He's a good guy. And – we'll see, won't we?" Over the next fifteen years, as I was in the village intermittently, I did see. These are the images I remember:

A new deacon, his beard a wispy sprout, hair not yet long enough to tie up. The long clumsy sleeves of his blue *ráso* flapping, he gallops across frosty fields, mattock on shoulder, boots muddy. Chrýsanthos, the taxi driver, coming from the *hóra* with a car stuffed with shoppers, workers at the new generating plant, and me, has stopped to call, "Want a ride?" Somewhat to my embarrassment, Ilías wedges all two scrawny meters of himself onto my knees, sighing, "When I get to be a priest, I won't be able to do this anymore. How about some music?" he asks the driver.

"What do you want?"

"*Ta varia!*" The "heavy stuff," *rembétika*: jazzy, bitter songs of exile, despair, love, and hashish. The workers, who had stiffened in fraudulent respect, now look at each other sideways.

Five years a priest. It's the fifth of January, eve of *Theophánia*, Epiphany. Earlier he has rushed wildly through the streets followed by racing children. Now he is soberly processing to the harbor, followed by adults. The day is cold, the sea slashed with tiny whitecaps, but the boys who are to dive stand nearly naked in the wind. Sympathizing, perhaps remembering his own shivering impatience years ago, he hurries through the interminable liturgy, tosses the gold cross into the sea three times, twice draws it back by a cord, and finally drops it into the black water.

Ten years. On a white-hot day, as I pass his godmother's house in the country, he calls out, offering me a glass of water. Resting in the dappled shade of a grape arbor, having just dug her tomato beds, he's sweating lightly, wearing just an undershirt and shorts. On top of the red-gold hair, glowing in the afternoon light, is a black silk skull cap, the only sign of priesthood. The radiant vitality is momentarily at rest. Daughter Angelikí, twelve years old, dark-haired, smiling, shy, stands behind him: an acolyte nymph. Energy, humor, curiosity.

Mersíni's baptism. As she, almost a year old, stripped of her clothes, is dipped into the font, she yells indignantly. He stops chanting to say to the embarrassed father, "Never mind. All my own howled like jackals." Earlier, the child's mother had been hovering in the shadows at the back of the church, but Ilías called to her, "Mother! Anna! *Ela!* Come close!"

Winter plowing. Beard and face caked with grime and black grease, with his left hand he steers the tractor over a tumbled wall onto the road by the church of Ayi Apóstoli, crossing himself with the right.

Holy Friday. Walking behind the garlanded coffin of Christ, followed by hundreds of mourning villagers, he spots a tourist in shorts, her legs splayed out over a cafe chair. He stops the procession, addresses her. Indignation like lightning flashes forth from him, his hair and beard blazing above the sun-gold cope: "If you have no respect for our God, or us, get out of our village!" The harangue falls on ears deaf to Greek. "What the hell was that?" she whines, as the procession picks up, taking Christ to the tomb.

"What made you want to become a priest?" I ask him one summer noontime in his office, the sun through the slats of shutters lighting his red-gold hair like a halo. Curious children run in and out, leaning on his knees. "Did you experience a vocation?"
"Nothing so dramatic!" he laughs. "After high school, I was restless." The farming his father urged upon him (which his elder brother had fled to become a maritime officer), while in his blood, was somehow at seventeen not enough. But when he followed his brother's path, after two months in the naval school, he decided, suddenly, that he wanted to be a priest. His confessor, the *igoúmenos*, abbot, of the local monastery, had asked him once or twice to think of it, but had not pushed. The decision, Ilías says, seemed to come from nowhere.
His member-of-parliament uncle arranged for him to enter late a preparatory school in Corinth. "It will be hard," the uncle said. "They live like

monks." But the politician, after decades of life in Athens, had forgotten what it was like to be a farmer. What to fellow students was at first torture – the rising to a bell at five – was no hardship to Ilías, who from boyhood had crawled out of bed before sunrise to harvest olives by tractor light, feed livestock, or walk an hour up a mountain to chant with the monks before catching the bus for school in the *hóra*. Here, the hours set aside for silent study were a luxury for one who had propped his Ancient Greek grammar on the dashboard of a noisy thresher. Only his muscles missed the familiar and exigent movements, an hour of football not enough. Also he missed the scents of animals, the sounds of bees and goat bells, the richer quiet. And the sea.

Still, he says, the school awakened the thinker in him. Here there were both ordained and lay teachers, both conservative and liberal: some consumed with the exquisite untangling of theological problems, others impatient of outworn traditions; socialists trying to turn the remote eyes of saintly faces to the modern world, near-fanatics fronting the same world with miraculous ikons and relics held high like flags. Naive at first, he was often baffled by conflicting accusations – of pragmatism, of reactionism, liberalism, other *isms* he hardly recognized. Confused, he couldn't always answer straight, would think later of the cogent point.

In Lent of his second year, the Athenian uncle showed up one weekend and took him out to dinner. Ilías stuck to his monastic lentils but accepted a glass of retsína. The uncle then sprang a surprise on his nephew: "What do you think of going to theological school?"

"What?" The young man nearly choked on his wine. "Four more years?" It had never entered his mind. Many of his fellow students were, as he'd planned, about to return to their villages to work, marry, and hope to be ordained. It was not thought necessary for a village priest to be highly educated; he should know liturgy, and yes, some church history, but beyond that? The Apostles themselves were working men, fishermen mostly. And Ilías was a farmer. "Four more years?" His thoughts flew to his father, elderly now, working the farm alone, expecting him back in July. Disappointed and gruff at his elder son's defection, he had been reconciled by Ilías' promise to return in two years, nursed a secret hope that the boy, like many others, would give up.

"Why, uncle?"

"Well," his uncle said, "the principal has high praise for your studies." Ilías, though pleased, concentrated on peeling an orange, sensing more to come. "Also, when I was last on the island, the *Igoúmenos* spoke to me." The *Igoúmenos*, Ilías' spiritual father, is himself the spiritual child of the not-long-deceased saint, Nektários of Aegina. His wish, while not a command, is not to be disposed of without thought, prayer.

"What a barrage! Are they trying to make a bishop of me?"

"No," said the uncle, "they respect your choice. But . . ."

"What do you think, uncle?"

The politician was thinking of social changes, sweeping modernization. The reactionary religious Junta had kept a cap on development in order to counter or reverse the "degenerate" morality of European culture. "Societies all over the world are changing, turning upside down. The day is coming when we'll be finally shed of all the leftovers of monarchy and fascism," meaning the present government, "and we'll see changes, seismic changes – industrialization, greater unity with Europe, tourism. Women's liberation – that can no longer be restrained. There'll be changes in property laws, civil marriage and divorce. And tourism – with development will come greed. Our village – we've been poor; with tourism, money will come like a tidal wave. Those who wouldn't cheat their neighbor of a hundred drachs will smother their grandmothers for a million. It's coming."

Ilías laughed. "Excuse me, uncle, but . . . aren't most of these changes what you have dreamed of and worked for all these years?"

"Of course, of course, I've dreamed of modernization, of economic parity, more education, but . . . now I fear, as you farmers say, that the green will be burned with the dry." He saw loss of values, erosion of the community, the family. "I think a priest in this world will need all the knowledge, all the authority he can find."

"Father . . . ?"

"I'll talk to him."

"No," Ilías said, "I'll talk to him. He'll decide." He had first to separate his duty to God from his yearning for his family, work, his friends, the village life. He was clear in his mind, though, when he talked to his father.

The old man, outflanked by his politician brothers, the *Igoúmenos*, and his wife, hardly spoke, tears tight in his throat. "First your brother goes to sea," he said. "Now you want to go . . . where?"

"Pátmos." A former fellow student, also an islander, had written to him from the famous theological school: "Why not come here? At least it's an island. From every window of every room, you can see the sea. We went night-fishing – *pyrofáni* – on Tuesday and caught four octopus."

So Ilías' nostalgia for the sea took him to the oldest, most famous, most rigorous nursery of priests in Greece. There, nine hundred years ago, one Christódoulos, self-exiled from the golden intrigues of Constantinople, with his bare hands built the monastery around the summit of the single mountain and endowed it with his own considerable antiquarian library. There also, a thousand years before that, the exiled Apostle John, after forty years of silence, was riven, like the rock of his cave, by the voice of God, and spoke: "*En arhí ein O Lógos . . .*" "In the beginning was the Word . . ."

Words? Sometimes there was nothing but words – read, written, spoken, chanted. It was his senses that really informed him. He compared sights and sounds: the stark, homogeneous elegance of swaying rows of black *rásos*, black beards, and lined black eyes with the ragged, faded heterogeneity of his villagers in their work clothes; the perfectly schooled intonations of psalmody swirling upward through the ancient dome with (in his village church, not so venerable) the rough chaos of faulty, disremembered chanting funneled through a devout *psáltis'* cleft palate, the liturgy underlaid by murmuring gossip, crying babies. He swam in the heady air, and, dizzy, sought clarity on the windy shore, in the muddy fields, the friendly fug of the local *kafeneío*. He began, almost without volition – partly through feeling, partly through thought, partly by disputation – to form a style, a stance, a point of view that wouldn't show itself for years.

One thing he did know: he was on the side of the beard shavers and hair cutters, those who wanted to modernize the church, lessen the separation between priest and people. No medievalism for him! He got away with a certain wildness of opinion (he didn't know this) because of his spiritual ancestry. Alone of all the young men, he was the spiritual grandson of a saint.

Graduated, he comes back to the village. All the schooling, the monastery life, is behind him. A farmer again, he picks up where he left off, in some ways. Hoeing around newly planted grapevines, unaccustomed muscles aching, he finds his recent past unreal: the black ranks of monks, the white austerity of the cloister; the overwhelming richness of ancient ikons his lips had kissed; vessels of pure gold his hands had held; the delicate manuscripts, rust ink on violet sheepskin, his eyes had traced, over which the eyes of saints Chrysóstomos, Makários had also moved; the silent suppers, the hours of solitude. He awakens in dark now not to join a file of sober monks to praise God but to warm up milk and make coffee for himself and his father. He does it quietly, not to wake his mother and sister, who jump to wait on him, proud and awed. The old man, left out of all this pride, still cherishes a hope Ilías won't make it, will settle down on the land. He grumbles constantly about what will happen to this field, these trees, these hives, and so on, when his son puts on the *ráso*.

But the old man worries needlessly: it is so much Ilías' dearest wish to stay here that he can almost utter his assurance that he will not leave. What if God wills otherwise? Or the bishop?

While away, he longed for home. Now back, he sees it with different eyes, sees differences in the way he is greeted, received, ponders on those differences. He is not a man without pedigree: in addition to his spiritual father, there are his uncles, two committed socialist politicians who, with the fall of the dictatorship, are finally coming into their own. The younger uncle, the member of parliament, has survived both the Junta and its fall. The elder, a farmer and grocer, is building a local party; he is the village's *antipróedros*, vice president. As Ilías walks with his friends – a baker, a sea captain – in the harbor, plays *távli* in the *kafeneío*, he finds himself a focus of expectations, assumptions, even – prematurely – demands. As a priest, he's expected to be conservative; as a member of his family, progressive. He spends time – when not plowing, hoeing, pruning, milking, mucking out – sorting conflicting reactions. And curbing his impatience, his good farmer's instinct to get on with the job. He watches his uncle the *antipróedros*, how he fields and balances, decides and temporizes, listens and speaks, and only to him and his confessor does he open his mind. And these, too, are two poles, and he spinning between.

And still Pápa Kosmás, the village priest, over seventy and diabetic, has not expressed his wish to retire. Ilías is chanting in the great church in the *hóra*, partly to learn from the golden-voiced Pápa Apóstolos, partly to avoid crowding the old priest who had baptized him now over twenty years ago.

Nor has he himself made any headway with his first requirement: marriage. It is not every young woman who, in any case, would want to be a *papadiá*, is prepared to be a paragon among women, raise little paragons. Previously, there have been great advantages: security if not wealth, position, and, if she earned it – or could avoid the opposite – the respect, even love, of the community. An educated husband. And more likely than not – the village having the eyes of Argus – a faithful one.

But he's been away six years, and things are changing: a democratic government, tourism, the EU. Young women have begun taking their dowries and opening shops and travel agencies, getting more education, going to discos without their brothers, and moving out from the family, marriage no longer their only destiny. In the village way, feelers are sent out: "What about your niece?" says his godmother to her cousin, and "What about

Ilías?" an aunt asks her niece. But round and round the circle, the answer is the same. "I? Marry a priest?" The worthy, the smart, the dependable ones do not consider it, foreseeing the loss of hard-won freedom. A priest is the epitome of male authority, something they're edging away from, too congruent with the passing (but not passed) patriarchal father, the moralistic dictatorship. The young women are too fresh from the battles (months and years of pleading, crying, yelling, plotting) for even the mildest forms of social and sexual freedom: to go to *gymnásio* or university, even to work outside the village. The men, the older men, haven't taken all this lying down: one fisherman hired a detective to shadow his daughter when she was in Athens studying for the exams to work for Olympic Airlines. The daily reports were telephoned to the harbor *kafeneío*: "She went to a movie with a boy, but her cousins were with them."

To add to his difficulties, there is the matter of Stavroúla, his sister, older than he by almost ten years, normal to look at and with the same red-gold hair, but who has the mind of a four-year-old. None of the mothers of daughters approached by his own mother and aunts speaks directly of the risk of idiocy in grandchildren, but, shying away from the subject, they cast their eyes down at whatever they hold in their hands – teacups, plates of sweets.

When Ilías thinks of marriage, he sees a woman he calls modern, not the traditional submissive maiden of downcast eyes but a woman to whom he can talk who'll talk back, make love, make deep and lusty love, a woman who won't let him slide, be seduced by the "Pápa this" and "Pápa that," the ring-kissing, the power. Yes, this wife should be bright and modern, and lusty, and he . . .

The beardlessness was a dream. The bishop, on a visit to the great church in the *hóra*, while speaking pointedly of his commitment to placing priests in their own villages, seemed not to hear the young man's stuttered manifesto, merely patted Ilías' large red hand with his tiny frail one, on which hung the massive ring, and murmured his respects to the aging village priest. And so Ilías goes back to grimace in the mirror, morosely comparing the eccentric figure he will make with the growing elegance and modernity of his rivals for the young women.

There is a woman he likes. In school they were always aware of each other, sometimes competitive – but while he's been climbing toward priesthood, she's been at university discovering another vocation. Now a teacher in the *lycée* in the *hóra*, she talks of the new cultural association, a planned film series, the possibility of a library, a bookstore. A strong feminist, she has started a women's group. When he teases about marriage, she says clearly, not for five years; she wants five years to give herself to this way of modifying the influences of the village's sudden wealth, of preserving – even restoring, it disappears so quickly – the spirit of community. She will counteract discos with books, loss of innocence with consciousness. It is all good, he agrees; he is glad she will be there. But he is still wifeless.

The solution, when it comes, is bittersweet: the modern man is mated through the oldest tradition, a go-between. A distant cousin of his mother, come for the summer, knows a girl from another island whose sister is married to a priest: "Good girls! Pure gold!" He prepares for the meeting with a sinking heart. Is she a born *papadiá*, proud and removed? A hopeful third daughter of a family of six girls? A not-quite nun? A model of cleanliness? A religious fanatic? Perhaps she is beautiful, tall and dark, an Eiríni Páppas with black eyebrows and the eyes of the Sorrowing Mother. This worries him; he is not handsome – tall, gangly, pale, freckled, and with thin reddish hair. (Who, certainly not he, would have thought that hair, grown long in obedience to his elderly and conservative bishop while his former fellow students and even older priests were cutting theirs, would, with the beard, also red – a scratchy nuisance – transform him into a kind of Apollo, haloed in red-gold, Apollo the bringer of light to fields, the lover of gentle kine?)

Then again, he's afraid, as any man would be, that she's ugly.

Suddenly, she's coming. It is the feast day of *Taxiarchón*, the Archangels, the name day of the monastery above his own lands, so he is up and away before dawn to chant, and doesn't see her arrive. It is hard to focus his thoughts on the psalmody, so he strains his ears to the meticulous enunciations of the leading *psáltis*. The go-between will be helping his mother and sister prepare the noon meal, which, the autumn weather being bright and warm, they have decided to serve on his land. There's only a small structure there, a storehouse, but the orchard and vineyard are at their best, the leaves golden and russet. Being there shields them, her and him, from the thousand-eyed village, gives them, if they wish, a place to walk apart from the countless relatives – mother, father, sister, godmother, uncles, aunts, cousins – and get out of the wind of their hopes and judgments.

His stint is over; he leaps down the hill, conscious he is causing himself to sweat, to be covered with dust. His mother has insisted that he wear a suit; it's hanging in the farmhouse. Yes, they aren't there yet, so he has time to wash. Then he remembers the chickens, so when the taxi pulls up, there he is, dressed to the nines, with a bucket of corn in his hand and muck on his shoes.

There is a lot of handing out of casseroles and pans, of bags of bread, and suddenly from the taxi she emerges, and his heart – crows, doves, hawks flapping and soaring in the same sky – comes gently to roost. She is not at all what he imagined, not in any way. And yet, as she stands up and lifts her eyes, he has no doubt, no doubt at all. If only she will have him.

They shake hands, and that's it for a while; there's so much to do for the meal, bringing tables and chairs out of the house, and his uncle Stávros monopolizes him, relating a problem to do with boundaries for a new road. Stávros keeps leading him away, he keeps looking over Stávros' shoulder, and bachelor Stávros' round blue eyes are laughing at him. His father, having filled carafes from the wine barrels in the storehouse, joins them, leading Stávros out to the vineyard. "Come cast an eye on my young *rhodítis*; it's not doing so well." As though anyone other than his father could think of grapes!

But finally the long meal is set, is eaten; his boarding school discipline keeps him from stuffing or starving, though Stávros puts a hand over his about-to-be third glass of wine. He looks at her, away from her, and consequently seems to pay more attention to Stavroúla, his elder, simple sister. Sensitive as a child, selfless as a saint, she brims with love for him, rises and goes to lean her thirty-two-year-old head with his same red-gold hair on his shoulder, stroking his arm. The go-between is a little alarmed; the subject of Stavroúla has been skirted, more emphasis placed on the lack of a dowry to be met by himself and his brother. But he is grateful for her comfort, this frail woman who is every day filled with the wonder and confusion of a child.

The meal is cleared away. The girl sits, talking with his mother. (She is a small brown girl, neither beautiful nor ugly: no dress will ever really become her, nor ever make her ridiculous.) She is shy, but neither emboldened nor embarrassed by the attention, leaving the go-between to answer questions about her family, her *papadiá* sister. And still she sits, as the elders stretch and yawn, peel off to cots brought out from the storehouse, pallets laid under the arbor.

"Walk?" he manages to croak, who got top marks in oratory.

"Yes," she nods, oblivious to the arch looks that follow them into the orchard.

He doesn't know where to begin, asks several silly questions about her native island, and then suddenly, "My sister . . . some say she had a fever when she was a baby, but . . ." A priest himself must be mentally and physically perfect, but genes . . .

"You love her very much, don't you?"

"Yes."

"I will love her as you do." She has said "will," not "would!"

He walks on in silence, then pulls an apple from a tree. "You want one?" She nods. He reaches for his knife, but he's wearing the suit. "*Gamóto!* I don't have a knife! This suit!" Now he has cursed in front of her, but she laughs. Another thing: "You know, I may not be chosen. I think I will be, but . . ."

"I know."

"You'd be just a farmer's wife then."

"I understand." She takes the apple and bites into it. Silence, more walking. Then she asks, "What sort of a priest do you want to be?"

He hasn't had his mind on that for some time, having just finished two harvests. But he turns to face her. "Well, Christ said, 'Feed my sheep.' He was a shepherd." Passed long, dull hours (cold or hot) on the hills, tending the flock, watching out for their stupidity, their willingness to entangle themselves in rusty wire, to fall off cliffs. "But – when I look at my villagers, I don't see sheep. Perhaps we have evolved some in two thousand years. Anyway, I'm not a shepherd but a farmer. All I can see to do is . . . cultivate."

She's surprised. "Cultivate?" then thinks. "Yes, I see. Prepare the ground, fertilize?"

"And hope for good weather!"

She laughs, then blurts earnestly, "I want my girls to be educated, just like the boys."

He takes her hand. "The girls, and the boys, will be whatever they want to be – doctors or dressmakers or fishermen. You know, we have a woman fisherman in our village. I – " surprising himself – "am a feminist. *E*, sort of!" His wedding gift from his old schoolmate. Without ever having given it a thought, he suddenly blurts out, "I want – if, you know, and God willing – what do you think about having girls in the psalmody class?" He feels himself burning.

Mouth full of apple, she stares at him, open-eyed. She is quite silent, staring at him. Suddenly, she sees him, top to toe, inside out. The image she had – the dark, reserved, pedantic middle-aged patriarch her sister is married to – disappears in midair. They are standing in the vineyard, waist high in grape vines, under the bright afternoon sun. A long snake uncoils itself from beneath a vine and whips away. She is shaken, staring at him. She feels herself taken up into a chariot of fire; wings are sprouting on her back, damp from their natal waters.

"How long do you want?" he says.

"Six . . . six months," she stammers.

At Easter, they were married. The soft voice of the old priest circled like doves above the wreaths on their heads. As the white-bearded old man took Ilías' hand and led him in the dance around the altar, Ilías felt (rather than thought – he was too filled with emotion to think) the passing of the mantle of priesthood and knew he would be chosen.

In the halcyon days of the following winter, those days so sunny and peaceful it is said a bird may nest on the sea, their first child was born. It's a good thing Ilías declared himself so early a friend of girls, because soon (or so it seems, the years pass so quickly) they have five of them, clustered around one boy.

As his uncle predicted, the village has changed; the houses are all full now, repaired, rebuilt. New ones (and villas, hotels, and *pensións*) climb the hills, spreading over pasture and fallow land. Some of the social changes worry Ilías: the discos and bars and *bouzoúkia* separate the young people from their parents and grandparents. Staying up late, they don't make it to church. But he takes himself to them, blessing the bars (and sharing a whiskey afterwards), dropping in for an ouzo, a little dancing. He knows some disapprove; there is *koutsobolió*, gossip, but it doesn't bother him. If he worried about keeping the skirts of the *ráso* out of the mud, how could he plow? And if the young don't come to church much, they come to him with their problems.

"Pápa," calls a young bartender, as he's sweeping out a disco one morning. "Pápa," says this fellow who would call him "Ilía" in the *kafeneío* or the street, "can I make a confession?"

"I'm not a confessor," the priest says, "but you can talk to me."

"Do we have to go to the church? People would talk . . ."

But Ilías' church is wherever the people are, and the two sit down in the morning-after dankness, the stench of old cigarettes, to talk over the problems of the disturbed young man.

Ilías has a vineyard, inherited from his grandmother, so small and so high up a steeply terraced mountain that no tractor can reach it. He climbs a dry riverbed six times a year to hoe and prune. The vines were too old to be very productive – neighboring vineyards had been abandoned – but he's replanted. While he's there, he can see, especially in the winter, far out over the sea almost to Pátmos. Below, he can see the whole valley of his parish: the newly greening fields, the outlying farmhouses, the water glinting off the reservoirs, the chapels standing alone in fields or vineyards, the clustering houses of the village, the old church on its hill, the grave-yard. He almost cannot believe that so many souls depend on him, but he wears the burden lightly as he returns to his hoeing, humming a *rembétiko* song about a *hanoúm's* deceptions.

September, festival of the Holy Cross. Barreling along a dirt road in a red VW minibus filled with old people and children to celebrate at a mountain chapel. When the engine finally refuses, the children run to fetch donkeys to take the grandmothers the last half-mile. The chapel owners are poor farmers, so there will be no laden tables for the hundred or so guests, but the relatives are already unloading from their donkeys the baskets of fresh rolls and wicker bottles of homemade cherry drink. The chapel is brilliantly whitewashed, of course, and the family has decked the fading paper ikons with garlands of sweet basil, grown in the summer for just this day, and has placed baskets of the herb in the windows. The air is spiced with it.

There is no place for Ilías to robe, so after greeting him the family leaves him alone in the church. He robes, then lights a candle and says a prayer for his sister Stavroúla, dead three years now, whose name day it is. He misses her terribly, her death the only drop of sorrow in his cup.

He reflects that next year at this time (if God wills) he will be back in Pátmos for the nine hundredth anniversary of the founding of the mon-astery. He remembers the ancient riches, the gilded ikons and bejeweled chalices, the manuscripts bearing words older than the church, the ex-quisite psalmody. Breathing in the fragrance of basil, eyes wide open, he extends his arms as wide as Christ's, then brings them together in an em-brace, touching his hands palm to palm in a prayer of thanks. He crosses himself, blows his nose, strides to the door, and calls out, "Everyone ready? Let's begin.

V

Spring

Spring is Ánixi, the Opening. The earth opens gradually, imperceptibly, as the plowed earth is pushed aside by delicate blades of new wheat, but the earth respects no calendar. The greening begins in December, even before the solstice. In January, high on the north-facing mountains, anemones rise from stony rubble to flourish in the bitter wind. In February, small green nubbins appear along the gnarled black stumps of grapevines. The vines stretch and twist over a fine mat of silene, rose-colored flowers small and flat as a coin. The ground seems stained with them, as with wine, as though a great unseen hand, holding a glass of last year's vintage to the sun (that color, sun through wine), had splashed a libation on the vineyard. The flower's going to seed may be the signal to plow the vineyard. Plowed, the earth is tan, bare, grooved, scraped clean. The vines sprout leaves, blurring the dark, knotted wood with pale green fluttering translucence.

Winds

The earth is still cold. The wind is still cold. The plants are waiting, roots and seeds poised beneath the surface. Sun comes closer, but it cannot warm the dense cold soil alone. It must have help from the winds. And while the sun is dependable, the winds are capricious and cannot be timed. Some years, punishing Voriás keeps howling down from the glacial Caucasus mountains until April; other years it gives way to Gharbís, the sweet air that blows in from Morocco and wraps every plant and chilly human in a shawl of soft light wool. A warm spring wind that also wafts in from the west, Zéphyros is delicate enough not to blow the blossoms off the trees. In late May, Óstria, a hot dry wind, comes up from the south and ripens the wheat. One south wind that is never welcome is Sirókos: teasingly, it hops from side to side, banging loose shutters on first this side of a house, then another: bang, bang-bang, bang-iti-bang. Hoodlum Sirókos lifts up trash and seaweed from the shore and scatters it through the village streets. One year, just before Pásca, Easter, when the whole village – houses, churches, and streets – had been newly whitewashed and shone white as an Alpine peak, Sirókos blew in from the Sahara carrying half a desert of red dust and half a sea of rain. It dumped this load on the snow-white village, and within an hour the streets were inches deep in rust-colored mud, the houses were streaked with red ochre, and the ivory cups of newly opened calla lilies in my garden filled with a slurry the thickness of blood. After defacing the beautiful village, the wind scrambled away like a gang of graffiti painters.

Summer winds are more tractable. In July and August, Meltémi, a north wind now gently warmed by the summer sun, blows in three-to-five-day spurts, cooling hot sands and bodies; it kindly takes a rest in the evenings, so nights are warm for the evening *vólta* – that slow parade from one end of the village to the other – for al fresco dining, for dancing under the stars. This gift of the north slows the transpiration of the leaves of trees, protecting the growing fruit. The sailor's favorite, Meltémi blows strong and steady and its skies are as clear as a blue diamond. Occasionally, it can get as wild as a maenad, blowing to eight or nine Beaufort.

Beaufort is the measure of the wind's power. A sailor can judge the force of the wind by looking at the surface of the sea. He judges from the whiteness of the waves, referred to as horses, presumably those of Poseidon. At four Beaufort, the waves are small with frequent white horses riding the crests. At five the waves are moderate with many white horses galloping and rearing. At six Beaufort, the horses leap high in a great white herd, and at seven they are blown into foam, in streaks along the direction of the wind, the waves then becoming dangerous. Seven is near gale force and eight gale force, when the sea is white with spindrift. At eight the passenger ferries don't leave port, and at nine all shipping is stopped. Especially vulnerable to strong winds is the strait opposite the village, between Páros and Náxos. Small trading *kaíkis* have been stranded on one side or the other for three days, the sailors staring longingly at their visible homes, normally less than an hour away.

Between bouts of Meltémi comes the fisherman's favorite, Bonátsa, a calm spell which mysteriously sends fish leaping into the nets in silver thousands. But no human can predict when the winds will come and how strongly. They obey no laws and honor no wish of man or god, which is why Odysseus' host Aiolos, supposedly the master of the winds, had to stuff all the winds but Zéphyros into a bag and tie it tightly with a silver cord. Sadly, in sight of Ithaka, their home island, the crew, suspecting Odysseus was hiding treasure, opened the bag and . . . whoosh! . . . out came all the winds all at once, smashing the ship and drowning the crew. Odysseus, cast adrift, was not to feel the sands of home beneath his feet for twenty years.

The winds of Greece were first observed and charted by Aristotle; he drew a wind rose, rather like a compass rose, with Athens at the center surrounded by the horizon divided into twelve directions of winds. It was he who noticed that the north and south winds were the strongest, a true observation which misled him into thinking that every wind had a twin of equal force and opposite origin. Subsequent observation has established that the winds are by no means so symmetrical and vary greatly from season to season. The winds in the ancient time were considered semi-deities, usually portrayed as winged, flying anthropomorphs. The Tower of the Winds in Athens, an early weather vane, boasts a frieze of eight winds sculpted along with their attributes. Apeliótis, the east wind, holds a tunic full of fruit, while Skíron, the northwest wind, is overturning a ship. Looking at the sculptures, sailors would know to avoid setting out when the vane atop the tower was pointing to Skíron, but would do so gladly when it indicated that Lips, or Lívas, the southeast wind, was exhaling sweetly and steadily across the Mediterranean.

Flowers

Anthistíria, the blossoming, is one of the ancient names for March, probably referring to the flowering of the fruit trees. Clouds of pink almond blossoms back the white mass of the mountain monastery of Áyios Andréas, and most farms have a tree or two. Almond is scentless, but the fragrance of lemon flowers in Anna and Pantelís' orchard, only a few weeks later, was almost dizzying, sweet but freshened by its citrus edge, bringing memories of the scents of other white flowers: magnolia, jasmine, black locust, mock orange, gardenia.

March in Greece is as willful and unpredictable as elsewhere, blowing cold and warm in no orderly way. One of its epithets is March of the Five Opinions. "March snowed seven times and regretted not having snowed again" is one axiom, and another is "Crazy March freezes the donkey to death in the morning and rots him in the evening." Lovers wish that their "love not be like the snow of March, which falls at night and melts by morning." The sun is as strong in March as it is in August, burning pale skins that have been covered all winter. Some people wear a red thread on the wrist to protect them from the sun.

March sees a joyful occasion: the return of the swallows. Every year the sleek, busy little birds return over the sea and find their last year's nests, tucked up beneath balconies and under arches. To and fro they fly through the farms and fields, gathering new twigs and grasses. In the evenings, they come out in droves to hunt bugs to take home to their chicks, acrobats without trapezes swooping over the twilit sky. Children sing a song to welcome them:

269

They've come, they've come,
the swallows and other honey things.
Stay and chatter, and sweetly warble.

In late March, the earth opens more, and more quickly. Suddenly there is stock—white, violet, dappled—big bushes of it growing in pots, at corners of fields, by Bárba Níkos' well, in forgotten gardens. It has a spicy and luxurious scent, like soap in a Turkish *hamam*. Soon the edges of the *monopátia* and cracks in the village streets are springing with chamomile, a tiny daisy with feathery foliage. On a walk to the country I see, tucked into the corner of a rock wall, small arum lilies – green, tinged with maroon – and their large spade-shaped leaves. On the road to the *hóra*, the bus passes a hillside covered with the butter-yellow *spárto*, Spanish Broom, and its honey-like fragrance permeates the bus. We passengers breathe it in. Spring is finally coming.

April is true spring. *O Anixiátis*, the old ones called it – the Opener. In mid-April he land explodes. Sun and wind work together and, almost overnight, in the fields outside of the village, every inch of earth not covered with sea, sand or bedrock bursts with flowers, layer upon layer of bloom. Close to the ground crawl and twine vetches, tiny brick-red and yellow sweet-pea-like flowers. Above them, flat mauve agrostemma, pink flax, and rose-veined Cranesbill geraniums stretch upwards toward the light. Through them pass the knee-high stalks of wheat, their beards barely surfacing through a flood, a deluge of brilliant scarlet corn poppies. Delicate as silk crepe, the power of the poppies is in the unimaginable number of their host – millions, millions of millions. And in their color. Hold a poppy up to the sun and see the blood that courses through your own veins. All the poppies are scarlet with black velvet centers; here and there a black or white cross splotches the inmost petals. On the margins of the poppy fields wave wispy blond naturalized grains – sesame and barley, sown by birds or plow animals – and pulses escaped from the vegetable fields: yellow flowers of chickpea, striking black and white blossoms of fava beans.

Like holiday fireworks, the florescence explodes: Tch-tch-tch, the tiny vetches. Ssssss, the grasses (ants climbing the stems). Pop-pop-pop, the agrostemma, flax, and geranium. Bam! Bam! Bam! Boom! – a crimson shower of poppies. Coming upon a scarlet vista of poppy fields, we catch our breath and exhale: Aaaaahhh!

In these brilliant days, the sky is a wash of *louláki*, the sun golden and glorious, the winds soft as cat's fur. To walk through the fields is to experience a kind of madness, the senses dislocated, overwhelmed by the sheer abundance, the assault of the intense color, a strong scent that is not the fragrance of the flowers but of the opening earth itself. On a walk, I gather one of every flower to take home. I must use both hands to carry the bouquet. The poppies don't last in the terra cotta bean pot. Their petals fall quickly, liquify, and stain the light-blue window sill with red ink.

Slowly with the warmth, then the heat, other flowers open. Climbing up to an abandoned monastery atop a small mountain, I find myself all but submerged in acres of dark blue lupines. From the summit, the green of the lacy foliage mixes in the eye with the blue, creating a land-bound sea of aquamarine.

In a couple of weeks, the wheat rises to peek out around the poppies, the green mixes with the red and, from afar, the fields glow with the color of drying blood. The farmers say a wheat field dense with poppies is a poor field, but the symbiosis has existed for millennia. Dímitra's crown is a *stephání*, or wreath, of wheat and poppies. Poppies follow poppies; as the corn poppies fade and drop their petals, small orange ones appear. But they are overshadowed by the vigorous *mandilíthes*, white chrysanthemums with a golden corona around the yellow center. They shove through the other flowers like a rowdy crowd rushing a football field. The *mandilíthes* are strong flowers that endure both drench and drought. Their cheerful heads nod and wave in the warm wind. When they have completely crowded out the poppies, the fields look like cream-colored wool blankets spread to dry.

And then suddenly it is over. The south wind comes, ripens the wheat, and dries all the soft field flowers. The wheat fields are ochre-gold, the fallow fields straw-blond, veiled with Queen Anne's lace.

Months

Despite the beauty of the weather and flowers, spring months have their dangers. March and May are two of three months (August is the other) that begin with a three-day period called the *Drímes*. These times are wrapped in superstition: on these days, do no work, do not begin a project; clothes washed will dissolve, wood hewn will rot, and hair washed will fall out. In August, even bathing and swimming should not be done, for during that month a *neraída* called *Aloustína*, or She with the Unwashed Hair, seeks out mortal men and dances them to death.

April is called the hungry month, sometimes the Tilter, because last year's wheat and oil may be running out and people need to tilt the *pithária*, the storage jars, to get the last grain or drop out of them. May – called the Green One, the Flowery One, the Month of Roses – is so dangerous one curse is, "May the evil hour of May find you." Marriage in May is to be avoided because "the donkeys marry in May." Sometime during April and May occur one or more than one *Psychosávato*, a day for honoring the dead. Relatives may decorate graves with flowers or offer mourners *kólyva*, a mixture of wheat, almonds, and other "first fruits." It is said the dead souls leave the underworld and mingle with the living from *Pásca* to Pentecost.

The explosion of life in the spring, followed so quickly by its virtual disappearance, echoes the mythologies of the area: passion followed by death and resurrection, not only of Jesus but of Adonis and Persephone, and even Osiris. Adonis, the human lover of Aphrodite, was gored by a wild boar and bled to death. The pure red anemone is named for him, and in other eastern Mediterranean countries people sow Adonis gardens of quick-growing, quick-dying grains and greens in large, shallow pots. Now is the time also of the rape of Persephone, seized while picking flowers and dragged to the underworld. Desolated, her mother Dímitra wanders the earth in search of her, oblivious of her charges, the new vegetation, which withers and dies. Is Hades the hot wind that blasts the springing softness? All the flowers and the legends are saying, "Youth blooms and dies. That is its nature and its fate."

In the heat of May, everything tender succumbs to dryness. Thyme persists for a while into the summer before retiring as leafless humps of scratchy twigs. Only in a round dip in a green field, on the cool side of stone-walled ditches, a few lupines, a clump of *mandilíthes*, a mat of papery purple statice survive. But other flowers have learned to draw their strength from, it seems, solid rock and arid dust. I lived one late spring and summer in a (barely) converted chicken house on the farm of Kikí and Yiórgos, an elderly couple who spent the winters in Piraeús. On the dirt road up from the main one, bushes of cistus, rock roses, white and pink flowers of wrinkled crepe blossomed throughout the summer with no evident source of water. Beside the equally dry footpath to the farm sprang a huge clump of flat, green-and-yellow blooms on blue-green stems, semi-succulents later identified as euphorbia. Asími, Kikí's niece who looked after the chickens when aunt and uncle were away, called the plant *kaliánthropi*, "good people." She picked a small conical floweret from the complex blossom and showed it to me. "If you dry this," she said, "you can use it as a wick in an oil lamp."

The chicken house itself was built right on the sandstone bedrock. For acres around, the dry, gravel-strewn rock was blanketed with thyme, thorny burnet, and other ankle-scratching scrub. But also growing out of the hard-packed stony soil were tall, lush, fragrant sages: there were purple and white sages, tall spikes with furry olive-green leaves, and sage-like *siderítis*. The flowers of this, called "mountain tea," climb the stalk in hemispherical clumps of green honeycomb; from each hole hangs a saffron yellow "bee," a little like a snapdragon flower. The flowerets of white sage are shaped the same but organized differently. The scent of all the sages lingers on your clothes if you brush the leaves as you pass.

A short walk uphill from the chicken house, straddling a stone wall, was a large caper bush. Long, lithe stems, grass-green and smooth as lacquer, arched up from the ground. Their leaves, oval and flat, were graduated along the stems like a necklace of jade beads strung on silk. The flowers, born in the dawn and by sunset wilted into a forlorn tangle, had white soft petals from which emerged long silken tufts of purple stamens. Studded along the stems were the tiny oval buds that, soaked and brined, were a delicious addition to tomato salad.

Once, while walking across the seemingly barren waste, I nearly stepped on a great circular clump of orchids, half a meter in diameter. The soft, rose-pink, columnar flowers, delicate as pink chiffon, soft as baby's skin, sprang straight out of the flat, gravel-strewn moonscape. I was struck dumb, stayed gazing at them for a long time. When I told Kiki about it, she said, "Oh yes, we call them *salép*. We used to make a hot drink of the roots." She had never seen it growing, she said. I went back some days later, but couldn't find the magical orchids. I felt like someone in an old tale who had glimpsed fairies dancing in the moonlight, and was never, ever after, the same.

But even when dryness settles in for a long stretch, there are flowers. Statice, called locally "sheep's food," winds around the sandy edges of fields near the sea. There also grows beach poppy, *skiláki* or "little dog," a large yellow, poppy-like flower with light blue-green leaves. *Mandragóra*, with its flat rosette of deep green leaves, often hugging a stone wall, offers a bouquet of pretty mauve blooms and, later, little fruits like cherry tomatoes; *mandragóra* is so witchy-looking that I had trouble believing it isn't poisonous, but the berries are said to be edible. Queen Anne's lace, faintly purple while still uncurling from its ball, spreads a scrim of white over the straw-colored fields.

Under the banks of the roads, where what little runoff there is can collect, the willowy stalks of chaste tree spring from a round clump, the flowers the color and shape of lilacs, but softer. On the dusty shoulder of the road, stately acanthus, its white and violet flowers clustering on stalks tall as a man, rise from the generous rosettes of the deep green, lobed and notched leaves which, in marble, have graced the capitals of Corinthian columns and all their inheritors for two millennia. Asphodels, small brown and white striped blossoms clustered on bare, wire-like stalks, are the flowers that Achilles strides through, returning to the Elysian Fields after speaking with Odysseus at the mouth of Hades. The flowers are a small grace in the desolation of the underworld.

Perhaps the most astonishing flowers of later spring and early summer are the sea daffodils, or Pancratium lilies. These foot-high lilies, with three white, fluted flowers to each stalk, push their way up through the sands of beaches where nowhere in sight is there any fresh water or soil. On an unfrequented beach, I once came across a colony of about a hundred, their complex heads nodding in the sea breeze. The scent, sweet as orange blossoms, pervaded the air for perhaps half a kilometer. A small clump of them shoved up between the flagstones on my terrace. I found it completely magical to sit there in the moonlight, breathing in the sweetness of the ghostly white lilies.

Among the wild flowers of the island are dozens and dozens of the species, the originals of garden flowers familiar to me: chrysanthemum, stock, yarrow, lunaria, love-in-a-mist, columbine, and gladiolus – these last being slender, tall, half-closed magenta trumpets, more delicate than their bloated hybrid sisters. Where I throw out my wash water, a rose-striped mallow grows. Purple-and-white convolvulus climbs over everything, lush and strong, its leaves heart-shaped.

Other plant ancestors or parallels are wild vegetables and fruits. There are many kinds of *hórta*, edible greens such as dandelion and mustard. *Agriosélino*, "wild celery," is a thick "tree" of heavy rounded heads of bright yellow. *Pikrangoúria* is wild cucumber, called *pikró* (bitter) to indicate that it is poison, because its yellow blossoms and ragged green leaves are almost identical to those of the domestic variety, the name and its characteristic of "squirting" when touched are the only warnings to would-be gatherers. The herbs – borage, sages, oregano, rosemary, fennel, and of course thyme – grow in dry places; wild mint grows near wells and springs. Wild pear is a shrub rather than a tree, its fruits virtually inedible but its wood often used for grafting. Wild olive, the great-grandmother of the generous gift of Athena, is still found on rocky hillsides. The same is true of wild fig, which plays a vital role in the fertilization of the edible fig by harboring a little wasp that carries the wild fig's pollen to its domestic cousin.

Here wild flowers are never cultivated, and there are few garden beds. Instead every house boasts water-saving pots and cans of exotics. Many people grow lilies, white for *Pásca*, red for Ascension. The ubiquitous five-gallon cans are culled from the grocery stores, where they are used for everything from olives to oil to kerosene. Painted white or blue, they are the most common planters. Marigoúla the dressmaker tended a dozen or more cans of pink carnations climbing a double set of stairs and falling over her doorway beneath them. Another householder lined up half a dozen blue-painted cans of white vinca, with its shiny deep-green leaves, on the *pezoúli*, stone bench, outside her house. Pots and cans of multi-colored portulaca grace balconies, and everywhere – on windowsills, *pezoúlia*, and the streets themselves – grow pots and cans and barrels of the most prized and most common flower, the small-leaf, doming basil. Basil is called *vasilikós*, the royal herb, because a plant growing in the area of Calvary led Ayía Eléni to the true cross. Basil is considered both holy and a flower, and is never eaten. A pot of basil on the windowsill is said to keep flies away, and tubs of it outside the church doors invite those who enter to brush their hands over the leaves, releasing the fragrance. Tucking basil behind the ear is a habit of men. Yiórgos the dowser, a trim, dark-skinned man, was often seen riding his Vespa in white shorts and T-shirt with a green sprig of basil stuck behind his ear; its delicate scent was far preferable to aftershave.

The village is bright with vines which spring from a soupçon of soil between the cracks of flagstones in the streets or courtyards. In spring and early summer, the village streets are fragrant with the sweetness of jasmine and ailanthus, Tree of Heaven. Thanásis' *avli* is overhung and perfumed in spring by the soft purple blossoms of a *meliá*, chinaberry tree. Farther along his street, a large shrub of angelica in front of a little chapel is always in bloom on the church's springtime *yiortí*. The small, white, sweet-smelling flowers resemble orange blossoms, both in their waxy appearance and inviting fragrance. When almost everything else is dust, bougainvillea blazes out against whitewashed walls. Mostly bright purple, sometimes rose or copper, it defies drought and blooms from May to October. Although a definitely foreign plant, it is so widely planted it has become a naturalized citizen of floral Greece. Other adopted shrubs that brighten the summer landscape are *pikrodáphni*, a rose-flowered oleander with a scent like a baking cake, and two spiny succulents: the lobed and thorny prickly pear with its sunny yellow flowers and the New World agave, with its rosette of spiky,

275

fleshy leaves from which springs a single, five-meter flower resembling a branched candelabra. The pale ochre, empty summer landscape is a perfect background for the blue-green lobes and leaves as they rise from piles of tan rock.

Panigýria

The most ancient, most holy, and most pagan of all the Greek celebrations are the *panigýria* of spring. In March comes the Annunciation of the Panagía. May begins with *Protomaiá*, May Day, a celebration of love and fertility that ends with a summer solstice celebration on St. John's day. In late May comes the joint *yiortí* of Saints Konstantínos and Eléni, so revered that they are called the Equals of the Apostles. But the keystone of the Orthodox ecclesiastical year, the culmination and renewal of it, is the celebration of *Pásca*.

Although it is truly the keystone, *Pásca* (or rather the date of it) is wildly unstable, as it can happen anytime from late March to early May. Attached to *Pásca* are the fifty days of Lent, beginning with Clean Monday, and the fifty between *Pásca* and Pentecost, so it is possible for the season to begin as early as the first days of February or end well into June.

These movable feasts and fasts are unstable not only in date but also in significance. Although it celebrates the death and resurrection of Jesus, *Pásca* is not an original Christian celebration but a fusion of the celebrations of archaic Greek vegetation deities, such as Adonis and Persephone, and the Jewish Passover, itself an Egyptian festival of the beginning of the harvest adopted by the Jews when they were slaves in Egypt. *Pásca* (sometimes spelled *Pascha*) is Aramaic for the Hebrew *Pesach* or Egyptian *Pisach*. Both mean "sacrifice." It was and is traditional all over the Eastern Mediterranean to slaughter a lamb on which to feast on *Pisach/Pesach/Pásca*. Since Jesus was crucified on *Pesach*, the imagery of the "sacrificial lamb" has clung to him. Joined to the role of sacrificial lamb has been that of the scapegoat, an actual goat on whose back were symbolically loaded all the sins of the community and who was chased away into the wilderness to cleanse the sins of the people.

Pesach itself is relatively stable, occurring on the fourteenth (the first full moon) of the Hebrew month of Nisan. However, the Hebrew calendar, a lunar one, is variable if compared to the solar calendars. Every four years an extra "month" is added to the Jewish calendar to keep certain dates, like that of *Pesach*, congruent with the seasons. Early in the existence of the worship of Jesus, some Eastern Christians, who certainly thought of themselves as Jews, commemorated the death of Jesus on *Pesach* and his resurrection two days later. As it did (and does) in Jewish practice, *Pásca/ Pesach* could fall on any day in the week.

Roman Christians followed another model. Because the *Pesach* on which Jesus died fell on Friday, the day of the resurrection was Sunday. This day, the Sunday after Passover, previously only the first day of the week, became the day of the celebration of the Resurrection. Calculated according to the Julian calendar, which became common throughout the Roman Empire in 40 B.C.E., *Pásca* is the first Sunday after the first full moon after the spring equinox. However, the date of the equinox itself was not as certain as we now know it, being for some time observed in Rome on the twenty-fifth of March and in Alexandria on the twenty-first.

For four hundred years before the Greek revolution, the lands we now know as Greece were part of the Ottoman Empire, using the Islamic calendar for civil purposes and the Julian for religious ones. When newly free Greece converted to the Gregorian calendar, the church wished to keep the day of the celebration of *Pásca* the same throughout the Eastern Orthodox countries. Therefore, it was decided to calculate the date of *Pásca* according to the Julian calendar only. Thus all the holy days dependent on the date of *Pásca*, from Clean Monday to Pentecost, are common to all the Eastern churches, varying some thirteen days from the holy days of the Western churches. Every seven years, Orthodox *Pásca* and Western Easter coincide, and all of Christendom celebrates this great holiday on the same day.

Holy Week and Pásca

Pásca in Náousa was astonishing. At the time I lived there, with the exception of a few tourists and myself and one family of Jehovah's Witnesses, everyone in the village of about fifteen hundred people was a Greek Orthodox Christian. That is not to say that everyone was pious – by no means. Many people were indifferent or even hostile to the church, its practices, and its priests. But the celebrations – *yiortés* and *panigýria* – are so woven into the fabric of life that they would be hard to ignore. The *Pásca* services particularly are so beautiful and exciting that very few would stay away. At the climax of the liturgy, midnight on Saturday, the entire village, including visiting and returning relatives, perhaps two thousand men, women, and children, would be crowded together in the dark street leading up to the church, lit candles in their hands, kissing and wishing each other "*Hrónia pollá!*" There is something so beautiful in this unity that one can almost understand why some people are willing to fight and die to achieve or maintain it, though often as not it is a mirage, a fantasy born of its lack, "the dream of a shadow of smoke."

The Orthodox celebration of *Pásca* is so much written about that it is hard to find a way to convey the heights and depths of emotion that characterize it. Like other commemorations of Christ's death and resurrection, Orthodox *Pásca*, over the course of eight days, retells and re-enacts the narrative of Jesus' last days. Day and night over the long week, priest and *psaltes*, cantors, and a shifting crowd of lay people sing, chant, and pray during thirty-nine hours of liturgy. Unlike other public performances, such as passion plays which employ actors for all the parts – Pharisees, Sanhedrin, Apostles, Pilate, and even Pilate's wife and may include parades of penitents – the Orthodox commemoration is accomplished through words, song, and ikons.

On the first day, Lazarus Saturday, the miracle of Jesus raising his dear friend from the tomb anticipates his own death and resurrection. It is this miracle, performed reluctantly by Jesus out of love for Lazarus and his sisters Martha and Mary Magdalene, and witnessed and acclaimed by many, that causes the Pharisees to decide to have Jesus killed "for the good of the nation" lest the Romans notice his growing following and "take away our place and our nation."

The next day, Palm Sunday, recalls Jesus' courage in coming into Jerusalem to celebrate Passover. Hiding out in the wilderness for fear of the Pharisees, Jesus remembers the prophecies and, accepting his fate, decides to reveal himself. He enters the city riding on a donkey, a sign of humility. His followers welcome him by strewing his path with palm fronds and flowers.

Monday and Tuesday are dedicated to two analogies. One is the metaphor of Christ as the bridegroom marrying his Church. Here the priest tells the story of the unwise virgins who did not prepare for the coming of the Bridegroom, and were therefore left in the dark (Jesus is often referred to as Light, for instance, the Light of the World). The other analogy is the story of Joseph, who, like Jesus, is betrayed, buried, "resurrected," and, avoiding the temptations of Potiphar's wife, becomes a king.

Wednesday is a day devoted to holy substances, especially chrism or *myron*. Jesus is called the Christ, or the one anointed with chrism, a holy oil still in use, though oddly nowhere in the Gospels is there any mention of an anointing other than that by Mary Magdalene. In an echo of Magdalene's acts, on the evening of this day the Orthodox confess their sins, ask for forgiveness, take Holy Communion, and are anointed with holy oil. In this church, unction or anointing with oil is used for healing, both physical and spiritual, and not only at the deathbed as in the Roman rite. Anointing with chrism is also done at baptism and at the ordination of priests. On this day the story is told of Mary Magdalene, who brings a precious aromatic ointment – some say myrrh, some say spikenard – in an alabaster box and, after washing Jesus' feet with her tears and drying them with her own hair, breaks the box. The disciples are angry, asking, "Why didn't the woman sell the ointment and give the money to the poor?" But Jesus replies that, anticipating his death, she has washed and anointed him as is done with the dead, so that he can be buried. The word "embalm" comes from this custom of anointing the dead with spices and unguents, perhaps to mitigate the odor of corruption, since it was customary for mourners to visit the tomb on the third, sixth, and ninth days after the death. On the third day after Jesus is taken down from the cross and laid in Joseph of Arimathea's rock tomb, Mary Magdalene comes a second time to wash and perfume the body of her teacher. She does not find his dead body, but, standing in the dark of the rock tomb (according to which Gospel one reads), either a Jesus almost resurrected or an angel announcing, "He is not here. He is risen." In any case, Mary is the first of Jesus' companions to witness the Resurrection.

Mary Magdalene, called "The Equal of the Disciples," is a much neglected personage in the story of Jesus. Often referred to as a prostitute, nowhere in any of the Gospels is she so characterized, though she herself confesses to sinfulness. Perhaps we simply associate women with sexual sin, when, in fact, women may engage in the full range of sin from sloth to wrath. Avarice was not Mary Magdalene's sin, however, as she is often said to have supported the disciples from "her own substance." A thoughtful woman, she is the one who sits at her rabbi's feet and engages in discussion while her more conventional sister Martha goes on, grumpily, with the housework. Legend has it that after Jesus' death she went to Rome and preached, carrying out her mission as an apostle, "one who is sent," even speaking to the Emperor Tiberias and bringing him a red egg, the symbol of rebirth. Later, when aged, she is said to have joined the apostle John in Ephesus, a sanctuary for women under the protection of Artemis (where another legend has it that he had brought Mary the mother of Jesus, whose life was in danger). There Mary Magdalene is said to have collaborated with John on the Gospel that bears his name but not hers.

The Magdalene's story exemplifies that of all unusual women. The discovery of the so-called Gnostic Gospels reflects the post-crucifixion attempts to exclude women from significant roles in the new church. The Gospel of Phillip describes Mary as the companion of Jesus, who, the disciples complain, loves her more than he loves them, often kissing her on the mouth. She is accused by Peter of lying when she describes finding a risen Jesus in the tomb, and again when she reports words and ideas of Jesus the disciples seem not to have heard. Peter frequently grumbles about her presence and authority. The apostles' jealousy peaks in Judas, whose anger at Jesus' acceptance of Mary's gift of the ointment spurs him to the fatal betrayal, and eventually to his suicide. Peter's misogyny, allied with Paul's and mixed with the patriarchal Jewish culture of their converts, would finally (in the third century) exclude women from roles in the church they had previously held as evangelists, priests, and even bishops. Even at this time, bishops, while men, were expected to be married and be fathers to their own children as well as their flocks. Later, this role would be designated for celibate males only.

Perhaps the most beautiful hymn in the Orthodox canon, sung on Wednesday of Holy Week, commemorates Mary Magdalene's washing of Jesus' feet. Written by Kassianí, a ninth-century abbess, poet, and composer – the first woman composer in history whose work survives today – the hymn, in the voice of Magdalene, is unusually emotional and lyrical for Byzantine hymns:

> *Sensing your divinity Lord,*
> *I, a woman of many sins,*
> *take it upon myself*
> *to become a myrrh bearer*
> *and in deep mourning*
> *I bring before you fragrant oil*
> *in anticipation of your burial; crying*
> *"Woe to me! What night falls on me,*
> *what dark and moonless madness*
> *of wild desire, this lust for sin.*
>
> *Take my spring of tears*
> *You who draw water from the clouds,*

bend to me, to the sighing of my heart,
You who bend the heavens
in your secret incarnation,
I will wash your immaculate feet with kisses
and wipe them dry with the locks of my hair;
those very feet whose sound Eve heard
at the dusk in Paradise and hid herself in terror.

Who shall count the multitude of my sins
or the depth of your judgment,
Saviour of my soul?
Do not ignore your handmaiden,
You whose mercy is endless.

The Last Supper is also remembered on Holy Wednesday. At the Passover supper, Jesus is aware that his death is near, that there is a traitor among the disciples, and that many are afraid and will not stand by him. Still, he washes their feet, an act of humility and kindness. As they dine, he offers them bread and wine, which he calls the "true food," his own "body and blood." Following the supper is an incident that shows Jesus at his most human. Full of sorrow and foreboding, he goes into a garden to pray. Again and prophetically, he is deserted by his disciples, who fall asleep, leaving him alone. In his anguish, he implores God, "Father, let this cup pass from my lips." And yet he adds, "Nevertheless, not as I will but as thou wilt." It is to this garden that Judas brings the crowd of Pharisees, who come with clubs and swords to arrest Jesus – who chides them, saying that they could have taken him peacefully any day while he was teaching in the temple.

On Holy Thursday night, the priest and the *psáltes*, along with the congregation, re-enact the events leading up to the crucifixion, reading twelve passages from the gospels relating to the Holy Passion and Jesus' last instructions to his disciples. The priest "acts" all of the parts: Pilate trying to avoid crucifying an innocent man; the Sanhedrin who call for Jesus' death; the Roman soldiers who crown the "King of the Jews" with thorns, mock him, scourge him, and nail him to a cross.

The cross is not the large, heavy one of other re-enactments, but a slender wooden one to which the priest "nails" a nearly life-size ikon of Jesus, cut out like a paper doll. In the old church in the *hóra*, a very old ikon has moveable arms, so that the priest indeed drives nails into the hands and feet, but this is unusual. The crucifix is adorned with a *stepháni*, a wreath of flowers, and carried in procession around the church and set down in front of the ikonostasis. All the ikons are draped in black. Even Nature is moved:

> *The whole Creation mourned, seeing Him suspended naked upon a tree.*
> *The sun hid his rays, and the stars gave not their light; the earth quaked*
> *with great fright, and the sea ran away; the rocks were split asunder; and*
> *many graves were opened, and the bodies of holy men arose.*

On the next day, Great Friday, the ikon is "unnailed" from the cross. A *psáltis* stands with outstretched arms covered with a white sheet, while the priest, acting as Joseph of Arimathéa he who claimed the body of Jesus, removes the ikon and tenderly folds it into a shroud. He then takes it to the "tomb," in this case, the altar. There he exchanges it for the *Epitáphios*, an embroidered cloth ikon representing Christ enshrouded, and places it in the *kouvoúklion*, an open bier lavishly decorated by the village men and women with roses, carnations, lilies, and leaves. On Friday evening, the *Epitáphios* is carried in procession around the village, the villagers following with lit candles, and then returned to a stand in the front of the church. Back at the church, the priest sprinkles the worshipers with rose water, symbolizing tears.

On this day also are sung the Lamentations. Most of these are psalms expressing the singer's despair at the depth of his or her sinfulness and the loss of the Light, but some beautiful stanzas express the agonizing grief of the Panagía:

> *Oh my sweet springtime, my most beloved Child,*
> *whither hast thy beauty sunk down? . . .*
> *Oh Light of my eyes…how art Thou now hidden in the grave? . .*
> *Who will give me water and a fountain of tears . . .*
> *that I may weep for my beloved Jesus?*

So affecting is the sorrow of the Panagía that her lament has become a folk poem in the form of the *moirológia*, a traditional dirge sung by women. In this tradition is the modern poem of Yiánnis Rítsos, *Epitáphios*, a lament of a mother for a son slain in a political uprising:

> *Where did my boy fly to? Where did he go, so far away?*
> *The cage is without a bird, the spring is without water.*

It is considered an especial blessing to pass under the bier holding the *Epitáphíos*. I remember seeing, one Holy Friday, a rather large and ungainly young woman pass several times, on hands and knees, beneath the flowery "tomb." When I returned to the village a few years later, I heard that, although only in her late twenties, she had died of heart disease, and I wondered if she had known of her illness and hoped for a cure.

On Holy Saturday women keep vigil in the church. The first time I entered a church on this day, I was astonished to find a group of women neither prostrate nor weeping nor praying, but sitting companionably, knitting and chatting while their kids played around and under the flower-bedecked bier, reined in from time to time by a scolding. This behavior, I would find, was not impious; the same people would behave as casually at a vigil for a deceased neighbor, though possibly the more personal grief would quiet the chat somewhat, and kids would be banished.

This all-day vigil replicates the whole long, wretched day that Mary Magdalene and the other Marys had to wait before returning to the tomb with materials to "embalm" the body. Jesus died on a Friday. From sunset on, the day was the Sabbath, and, as observant Jews, none of the mourners could do any work until dawn, though it is said in one of the Gospels that Mary rose before dawn to collect the spices and unguents. It is the darkness before dawn that calls into question Mary's meeting with (depending on the account) an angel or Jesus himself. Interestingly, the newly discovered Gnostic Gospel of Mary claims that she saw him "in a vision," so that darkness would have no effect. The disciples seem always to have insisted on material evidence of Jesus' divinity, urging him to do miracles, for instance, and they seem to have lost hope and faith at his corporeal death, failing him at Gethsemane and deserting him at his crucifixion, with only the women and John keeping Jesus company at the cross and the grave.

But the long day comes to an end. The Matins, held in the Jewish way after sundown of the eve, begin in mourning and end in joy. As the day darkens, the villagers slowly fill the church, then the churchyard, then the half-mile street that climbs from the *agorá* to the church. Each person is carrying a white candle. Some carry *lambádas*, thick white candles often as tall as the donor, votives for favors asked or received. As well, men, women, and children carry in their pockets red-dyed eggs, symbol of the Resurrection, ready to crack them in the "egg war" after the service is over.

As the twilight turns into evening, the chanting and reading in the church reach the event of the death of Jesus. In honor of the darkening of the Light of the World, lights in the church are extinguished, and for a while the service continues in darkness. Only the small flames of the ikon lamps flicker, glinting off the gold of the saints' haloes. Then suddenly the black-clad priest emerges from the sanctum, holding a candle he has lit from an ever-burning flame. "*Défte lavéte phos!*" he cries, "Come and receive Light from the Light that is never overtaken by Darkness!" He lights the candles of the near worshipers, who light their neighbors' and on and on. A river of flames flows out the church, into the churchyard, and down the street.

I remember the tremendous excitement of my first *Pásca* in the village . . . or was it the first? All the *Páscas* flow together – the music, the chanting, and the rituals all the same, the same gathering of the villagers, the slow spread of light from candle to candle, and then the voice of the priest calling to the villagers, as the Magdalene did to the disciples two millennia ago, "*Christós anésti!*" "Christ is risen!" and the musical cacophony as two thousand people reply, "*Alithós anésti!*" "He is risen indeed!"

I remember that always a hymn was sung, but it was almost drowned by cheers and greetings: "*Chrístós anésti!*" said the woman one step up the stairs from me. (Was it the *mamí*? I think so). "*Alithós anésti!*" I replied and accepted her kiss, and passed both greeting and kiss on to the neighbor on the other side.

Suddenly crackling through the night were the deafening explosions of homemade firecrackers being thrown against the stone walls by small boys. The boys had been hiding in the cemetery next to the church, where they had brought a great straw-filled effigy called the *Ioúdas*, Judas, which they gleefully set on fire. One dry year, the boys not only burned the *Ioúdas* but set fire to the cemetery, an act unnoticed while everyone else was cracking their red eggs, kissing, and wishing each other, "*Chrístós anésti!*" Fortunately the sexton rushed to the scene with a hose and buckets and kept the fire from attacking the great dark cypresses which might have gone up like gigantic *Pásca* candles.

A few Roman candles (set off by the high schoolers) traced hissing, golden arcs through the dark blue sky, but most people were already on their way home, the lights of the candles flowing through one *stenáki* or another as everyone peeled off, going home quickly, first to make the sign of the cross on the ceiling above the front door with the smoke of the candle, and then to fall upon the long-awaited midnight feast. The centerpiece was always *mayerítsa* , a delicate soup made from the innards of the lamb that would be roasted the next day. When one has fasted, even for a week, *mayerítsa* seems the most delicious food on earth: its light velvety texture coats the starved stomach and yet does not glut, so that one sleeps well and comes next day to the *Pásca* feast with plenty of appetite.

On Holy *Pásca* there must be more services, but I never knew anyone to go. All our minds were on the spring lamb, whether spit-roasted or, more traditional in Páros, oven roasted with potatoes. Our friends Okeanís and Mímis always spit-roasted in their yard in Santa Maria. Their men friends would come early in the morning to dig the pit and start the charcoal. Slowly other friends would come, twenty or thirty or more, bringing *mezédakia*, such as *moussaká*, *pasticcio*, or *dolmádes*, salads of cabbage and lettuce with fennel, *tsouréki*, a rich bread nestled around a red egg. And of course desserts and wine. It was always my pleasure to make a giant yoghurt and almond cake, whipping twelve egg whites by hand, and rushing it to the bakery the day before, so that it could soak in lemon syrup overnight.

For the very observant, the celebration of the Ascension lasts another fifty days, until the feast of Pentecost. The entire thirty-nine hours of liturgy are repeated. But truly, the people have embraced spring with all its blossoming and warmth. They throw themselves into their duties to the earth: plowing, pruning, and transplanting for summer vegetables; careening, caulking, and painting *kaíkis*; airing heavy winter blankets and mattresses in the light dry breezes.

Zoodóhos Pigí

The Friday after *Pásca* is the feast of the *Zoodóhos Pigí*, the life-giving spring, which was celebrated on the land of Panayiótis and Stylliani Anagnostópoulos in Lággeri, where I lived when I first came to Náousa. It was one of only two *panigýria* celebrated in the old way (the beheading of John the Baptist in late August being the other). Trestle tables were set up in the fallow field next to the little chapel. Panayiótis would have decanted numerous bottles of his amazing wine, which everyone looked forward to all year. The celebrators came and brought donations to the feast – a *touloúmi* of cheese here, a gourd full of olives there, a jar of *piktí*, marinated fish. To balance her husband's wine, Stylliani was sure to have baked three ovens full of her famous black bread. This *panigýri* was special to the farm families scattered throughout the hills and back country because, being busy and living remotely, they rarely came to the village. There was no electricity for a phonograph, but usually old Bárba Iosíf, who played the bagpipe, would come and bring his nephew to keep the rhythm on the *toumbeléki*. Despite the rarity of their chances to dance, the country people did so with more grace and joy, and more elegant restraint, than the village young people, who tended to introduce untraditional flourishes and leaps. As the *panigýri* at Lággeri seemed to be pretty much a farmers' holiday, my friends and I would walk out, greet the family, drink a toast, and then hike over the hill to see Okeanís and Mímis, who, living in the parish so to speak of the little church, would also be celebrating.

Four other important celebrations occur before and after *Pásca*: three saints' days and a pagan festival (or perhaps two): the Annunciation on March 25, and on May 21 the *yiortí* of Ayios Konstantínos and his mother Ayía Eléni. *Protomaiá*, May Day, is an ancient fertility festival while the *yiortí* of Ai Yiánni, St. John on June 24 is half holy and half pagan.

The Evangelismós

The *Evangelismós* celebrates the Annunciation, when an angel appeared to Mary to tell her that she would conceive the son of God. The Annunciation is so sacred that ordinary people must be careful not to conceive on this day; some say that children so conceived and born on Christmas turn into *kallikántzari*. This *yiortí* is special to Greece because it was on this day that the first shot was fired in the revolution that freed Greece from the Ottoman Empire. The holiday is both religious and national, celebrating Greek independence and the formation, after two thousand years of division and occupation, of a Greek nation. The school children parade around the village and present patriotic pageants. One I saw was largely dedicated to Cyprus, which had been invaded the summer before. A fifth grader read a stirring poem he had written, a call to the world (at least, the village) to come to Cyprus' aid and free her from the invaders. It was well received despite a certain difficulty with his *s* sounds.

Ayíou Konstantínou and Ayías Elénis

Even though there is no church in Náousa for the mother-and-son saints, Konstantínos and Eléni, May 21 is a day of wide-spread celebration, since so many villagers are named for the emperor who made Christianity the state religion of Rome and for his mother, who is credited with converting him. For their work in spreading Christianity, the mother and son are called the Equals of the Apostles.

Protomaiá

Far and away the most glorious holiday, after *Pásca*, is *Protomaiá*, the first of May, a thoroughly pagan day dedicated to flowers and young love. In the city it is "Labor Day," with parades and flags from all the unions and political parties. But in the country it is the day when people are flower-mad. The weather is almost always warm and dry, so every family or *paréa* packs a picnic and heads for a country house. The stores open only long enough for shoppers to stock up on bread, new tomatoes, cheeses, salami, olives, herring, and the first strawberries.

From the time the young people awaken, they are out gathering flowers, and on May Day no garden is safe, no rosebush, no pot of carnations or lilies. Thievery is law! Thanásis' Aunt Eléni had a vine of red and white roses that made a lovely arbor of her front entry. On May Day, she would sit on the porch with a large butcher's knife and threaten anyone who even thought about stealing her cherished roses. Still, she generally lost a few blooms to early risers, and she would always give Thanásis a single rose for his own wreath.

The scarce roses and carnations are the thieves' prizes, but the field flowers are the staple of the wreaths people make to celebrate the day when spring is at its peak. One glorious May Day I walked out with Thanásis and his neighbors, Asími and her sister Mersiniá and their daughters Stélla, Frangíska, and Anna, and others of the *paréa* to their summer house on the bay of Ambelás. We filled our baskets and arms with flowers from the fields along the way: lots of *mandilíthes*, yellow and white daisies; stalks of wheat; purple statice, mallow, geranium – anything we could find. The women had brought a few roses, some carnations, and a lily or two from their gardens. We dragged all the tables out of the house and dumped our armloads of blossoms on them. While Asími and Mersiniá busied themselves in the kitchen, making us a feast, we began to make our wreaths. First round and round we twined grapevine – new shoots saved from the February pruning and soaked overnight. This grapevine is called the *maióksilo*, the May wood, and has obscurely erotic connotations: A man to a young woman, other males attending, on the day before May Day: "You have your *maióksilo?*" (Sniggers.)

"Yes."

"You've soaked it in water?" (Giggles and nudges.)

"Yes."

"Is it strong and flexible?"

"Oh, yes!" (Whoops and tears of laughter.)

May Day is clearly a celebration of youthful love and fertility. A wreath, *maí*, if hung on the door of a single young woman, may be stolen by a young man in love with her. "To take the *maí*" means to fall in love, but the thief may not reveal himself until Ai' Yiánnis' day, June twenty-fourth.

On my first May Day, Stella showed me how to make my wreath. Taking a little handful of *mandilíthes*, she made a small bouquet, bound it with string, cut the stems short, and tucked it into the vine. We alternated flowers. Soon we had four large wreaths – one for each household. When we returned to the village, we would hang the brilliant wreaths on our doors. Against the blue or green paint, the colors of the flowers would glow.

The wreath of flowers, *stepháni*, is a very old custom: people wearing them are pictured in classical mosaics and Koptic tapestries. The ancient Greeks were so devoted to flowers and wine that the great gastronomical text, the *Deipnosophists*, tells what flowers to wear when drinking which wine. The *stephánia* come down to the present as the garlands wreathing the ikons in a church on a holy day and as the means by which people are married: both bride and groom wear crowns of white flowers joined by a ribbon.

Ai Yiánni

Although May Day is a joyous holiday, it is not strictly a *panigýri* because it is not a saint's day. But the wreath of courtship begun on May Day finishes on June twenty-fourth, the Nativity of St. John, Ai Yiánni to the villagers, called the Baptist or the Forerunner because he went before his cousin Jesus and proclaimed his coming. How odd that youthful love and fertility should be celebrated on the *yiortí* of this very ascetic saint (although its proximity to the summer solstice gives us a hint)! In his ikons, Ai Yiánnis is pictured as gaunt and disheveled, wearing rags of animal hide and climbing sheer broken rocks, with not a rose, a leaf or a twig in sight.

Doubly oddly, the day is popularly called Ai Yiánni Klythoná, St. John the Fortuneteller, for a custom Sophía told me about. She remembered that, when she was a girl (at least fifty years ago), on the eve of Ai Yiánni, the girls would collect water from three fountains (no talking allowed!) and then decorate apples or maybe cucumbers with carnations, stuff verses in them, and cut their names on them. The fruit or vegetables would go into a tub with, she says, a "big masculine key." They would leave, all overnight to "see the stars." Usually, they did this in Sophía's family's large, walled, vine-covered garden. "I don't know if they do this still," she said, looking a little sad. "Everything is so different . . ." But the young ones still do what Sophía did the next night: lift the dried May wreaths from their doors and run to the *platía* to throw them on bonfires. When the wreaths are ablaze, the young people jump over the flames. "If a girl had a secret lover," Sophía said, "he would reveal himself at the fire jumping."

After the bonfires, the boys and girls would go to Sophía's garden and choose their vegetables. After reading the little poems (unseen blushes, squeezings of hands in lovely terror, giggles, always some chagrin), the girls would whip the covers off the food – salads of early tomatoes covered with capers, oregano-scented *souvlákia*, strawberries – and after the food, they would dance. "We didn't have a pick-up," she says, meaning a phonograph. "To dance, we made music with our voices. We all knew all the songs, and sang them beautifully." All the songs, then and now, are about love:

> Your eyes are telling me,
> If I died, they'd cry for me.

A little wanderer I am, my lady.
Take me! Take me in your arms!
To an island harbor, take me.
Take me!

I love a fisherman.
Take me in your boat,
Let me set the hooks,
Pay out the line,
And catch your little fishes!

Willowy, willowy girl,
I'm going to steal you some evening.

They sang, and sing, songs to boys who are carpenters and fishermen, and to girls named Myrtó, Garoufaliá, Lemoniá—Myrtle, Carnation, and Lemon Tree—names which themselves waft fragrance into the velvet air, like perfume on the wrist or between the breasts.

Did anyone draw your name?" I asked Sophía.

"Of course. Lots."

"Who?"

"Ha!" she said archly, patting her very black hair. "I'm not telling!" In the end, she never married, but stayed home to nurse both father and mother into old age and death. Perhaps her apple slipped off, fell to the bottom of the tub, eluded the shadow of the key, never saw the starlight.

The Miracle

"Have you seen the miracle?" asked Dímitra, the *kafetzís'* daughter, when I came in for a late morning coffee. "Come on, I'll take you." It was March 25, the day of the Annunciation, and I was in the *hóra* to shop.

She led me through winding streets to a little church, which did not stand alone but was joined to houses on either side. That it was a church was discernible only by the formality of the double doors in the blank wall and the cross on a small marble plaque over them. Branches of myrtle, fastened above the plaque and strewn in the street, announced that it was the church's *yiortí* .

The doors were open, and people were streaming in. A considerable crowd was gathered, mostly women and children with a sprinkling of men. The adults were standing behind some ropes tied to chairs forming a rough circle in front of the altar. Three or four children were standing on the plain, high-seated pews against the walls. The simple but elegant little church was filled with the buzzing of loud and excited whispering. Dímitra elbowed her way up to the front, looked, and crossed herself. On the black-and-cream tile floor, lying diagonally to the ikonostasis – old, heavily carved and gilded – was a long, cruciform puddle of tan beeswax.

"That old woman," whispered Dímitra, pointing with her eyes at a stooped white-haired woman in shabby mourning who was surrounded by other women caressing and comforting her, "takes care of the church. Because it was the Eve of the Annunciation, candles – big ones, *lambádas*, were left burning all night. When she came in the morning, one of the candles had fallen from its candlestick." Dímitra motioned to a tall, smooth marble pillar carved with crosses standing in front of the ikonstasis. "The wax had melted, just in that shape, see?" Indeed, the four- or five-foot candle had melted into a shape very like the gilded foliate cross that topped the ikonstasis.

Dímitra continued in a whisper. "The wick was still burning and the old woman rushed to stamp out the flame. When she picked up her foot, where her heel had pressed – see there, near the top of the cross? she saw the face of Christ." A smooth rounded indentation in the wax, clearly the heel print of a soft slipper, was at the point on the cross where Christ's haloed head is usually seen.

Dímitra's whisper became excited. "The old woman ran to tell the *pápas* and the *pápas* telephoned the bishop on Sýros. He s just got off the boat. The bishop will tell us if it's a real miracle." A miracle would be desirable,

Dímitra said, because this island could then attract pilgrims, like neighboring Tínos, where a nun's dream of an ikon buried under a ruined church had come true, a great church had been built, and thousands of miraculous cures had resulted.

More and more people were squeezing in, shoving their way to the front, crossing themselves. Children, brought in to see the holy phenomenon, were growing restless. Two little tots escaped their mothers and ran under the ropes. "Come back here!" a mother shrieked. "Don't step on the miracle!"

A gray-haired man opposite – a fisherman from his cap and *fanélla* – laughed. "Miracle? Ha! It's just a puddle of wax!"

A dispute ensued, adherents of both sides of the issue loudly debating it. Bored children were crying, and whatever miraculous effects on them witnessing the phenomenon was supposed to have were clearly not immediate. Then the crowd stirred. A wave of voices announced, "*Erhete O Despótis!* The bishop is coming! Sssh. The bishop..."

A tiny, frail, white-bearded man in black *ráso* and *kalimáfki* covered with a long black veil paused in the doorway. As he entered, several women and one man curtsied and reached out to kiss his ring. The bishop looked around, making the sign of the cross, as the crowd parted to allow him and several accompanying priests to advance. The bishop stood looking a few minutes at the wax cross spread out over the floor, seeming to pray, and then murmured something to one of the local priests, who called over the elderly woman Dímitra had indicated. The bishop took both her hands in his own and spoke to her very quietly. Her old, lined, lashless eyes were brimming with tears.

"What did he say?" I asked Dímitra, as everyone else was asking a neighbor. Dímitra shook her head. The *pápas* asked everyone who was not there to pray to go home, and most did.

In the street, we learned what the bishop had said: the elderly lady had been "personally blessed" with a vision for her devotion to the church.

"So much for miracles," laughed one of the men.

Some of the women looked disappointed, even angry. One huffed, "That looked like a miracle to me. The bishop is biased in favor of Tínos."

Back at the *kafeneío*, sipping another coffee, I asked Dímitra. "What does it mean, 'personally blessed ?"

"There was just a vision, not a miracle. Anybody can have visions. A miracle has to be . . . well, more people have to see it, maybe. Or maybe there has to be something – a lost ikon, a saint's bones . . ."

"Curing a blind person?"

"That usually comes after."

"So we don't have a miracle, after all?"

"No, but . . . think of that old lady. How nice for her that Christ would do that. Now she can die happy."

Koúla's Wedding

Pásca, or rather the week after, is one of the best times for weddings. The weather is usually perfect—warm but not hot, and generally dry. All the relatives who can have come back to the village from Athens and Piraeús, New Jersey and Melbourne. To house the overflow, hotels are open but not full. Students of schools and universities are free for the week. The musicians, the band of five from Piraeús who play at all the island *panigýria*, may already be booked to play at one in a neighboring village sometime that week. Everyone is in a festive mood. Any night, singing floats out from the open doors of the *ouzerí* in the harbor. *Opa!* and *Eis ygeía!* overlay the music from the juke box in the *taverna*, along with the click of glasses, as families celebrate not only the resurrection of Christ but that of their family unity, often a casualty of emigration. The ready-made *kéfi* all but guarantees a joyous celebration for a wedding and a lively start to the marriage, and every marriage must start with joy.

Just after the New Year, Kyriakí (called Koúla) found she was pregnant and was faced with a dilemma. She and Arghíris had been engaged for nearly seven years. Neither was well-to-do. Although Arghíris was a partner in a pastry shop, he was paying off a loan he had taken out to buy into the shop. Koúla's father was a fisherman who had for a long time not owned his own boat. His two daughters were both much older than his only son, so the boy could not help amass dowries for the sisters. Koúla herself, working hard and long hours, was saving to finish her house, while Arghíris was doing the same to clear his debt.

"I'm not getting another abortion," she said, lifting her firm but delicate chin.

Arghíris agreed; he was more than ready to take up domestic life. This sneaking around and finding empty houses to make love in was getting old. "We'll just have to rent," he said. "Manólis is nearly finished building that four-plex. Maybe we could afford one of the flats."

Koúla's fine dark eyes filled with tears. A baby started before the wedding was a little embarrassing – some old gossips would tch-tch – but renting was thought to be shameful. So strong was the idea that a couple should start off married life in their own house that the most pitiable thing the gossips could whisper was, "They're renting, you know."

Time was another consideration. Of course they wished to get married as soon as possible, but the Christmas season had gone by, and even if they bustled about, it would be Lent before they could make all the arrangements, and weddings are forbidden during Lent. In practical terms, even if they were allowed to have a Lenten wedding, at the reception they would have to serve only fasting foods, which would not be productive of *kéfi*. No, they would have to wait until *Pásca*, now three months away.

The most important reason for waiting was that their *koumbáros*, who happened to be Arghíris' brother Lákis, a maritime officer, was at present somewhere in the South China Sea. When they reached him, by a series of interconnecting ship-to-shore radios, he confirmed that he would not be able to arrange immediate leave. "I can be home just after *Pásca*," he said. "Is that in time?"

The *koumbáros*, or if a woman, *koumbára*, is a position unique to Greek Orthodoxy. Not merely "best man" or "matron of honor," the *koumbáros* or *koumbára* takes on a wide range of duties and privileges. The man or woman does indeed stand up with the couple at the church, but this is the smallest of the many responsibilities, which include being the godparent to the first child, and in some communities, sponsor to that child's wedding and the baptism of his or her own first child. These duties are not taken lightly. They involve a lifetime bond consecrated by the church. A *koumbáros* or *koumbára* is in effect tied to the new family for at least two generations, and to his or her own family as well: if a *koumbáros* dies before the wedding or the baptism, his child is obliged to shoulder the responsibilities. The relationship between the couple and their *koumbáros* or *koumbára* is so intimate that marriage between the children of the couple and those of the *koumbáros* is prohibited as incest.

There is a practical aspect to the tradition. Married people may take problems with their spouses, which they might not want to discuss with their parents, to the *koumbára*, who can act as intermediary or Solomon. In relation to the baptized child, the *koumbára* is literally the parent in God, responsible for the child's spiritual education, but also an alternate parent, sharing with the birth parents in the child's upbringing.

For the most part, this relationship is taken very seriously on both sides, although the benefits of having a wealthy or well-connected sponsor are a temptation. A well-to-do *koumbáros* may contribute to the dowry of a girl when she is of marriageable age, or provide job training for a boy, perhaps taking him into his own business. Politicians are infamous for accepting sponsorship for dozens and dozens of constituent families who hope the politician will deliver a government job for the grown child – a unique form of baby-kissing. The parents are expected to support the politician's re-election.

In Koúla and Arghíris' case, Lákis had long ago, at their engagement celebration, offered sincerely to stand *koumbáros* for his brother and Koúla – and, not unusually, to pay for the wedding. "No stingy wedding," he had said. "I'll have plenty of time to save money for a blast."

Koúla and her mother could make all the arrangements for a big wedding, but they couldn't spend Lákis' money without his approval, which, considering the itinerary of his ship, took time. So *Pásca* it had to be.

"I'll be five months gone," Koúla said, patting her tummy.

"Do they make wedding dresses that size?" Arghíris asked. She hit him with a pillow.

Koúla's mother Asími and her aunt Mersiniá had taken on the planning of the wedding so that Koúla could continue to work extra hours at the sweet shop, trying to save against the day the couple would have to pay rent. The sisters had just had an interview at Liggéris' and Zambétta's new hotel, trying to get an idea of the cost of the *gléndi*, or reception. This was so astronomical the two sisters could hardly speak. They were walking along a back street toward their homes when Mersiniá, the elder, broke the silence. "One thing we don't have to worry about is the *príka*. Between your girls and mine, I've been hem-stitching sheets and spinning wool for blankets for ten years. And they have enough embroideries among them to open a museum."

"The cost," Asími said. "That much money . . ."

"Well, Lákis must know what he let himself in for. People his age have been getting married these last five and ten years. Besides, we can check out everything for him. They don't have to ask the entire village to the table." The marriage ceremony at the church and a short reception afterwards are open to anyone to attend, but special guests are invited to the *trapézi* or table, where musicians play all night and into the next day (traditionally for three days), and food and drink flow freely to fuel the dancing.

"No," said Asími, fanning herself with a sheet of paper, though she wasn't hot. "Just three hundred."

"Three hundred?" said Mersiniá. "When did the village get that big?"

"While we weren't looking," answered her sister. "And the expense!" Asími repeated. "Remember your wedding? And mine? Our relatives saved up for years; they set aside this *touloúmi* of cheese, that barrel of olives, so many barrels of wine. 'Your wine,' Uncle Nóntas used to say when we visited, pointing out the barrels in the barn. I always imagined it was aging away. I was afraid it would go sour before I could find a husband. What a relief when I found out he just meant he'd promised two barrels for each of us."

Mersiniá smiled. "Weddings then were a community affair. Everybody chipped in: a sheep, a pig, chickens, vegetables. And bread! Every oven in the village would be smoking for days! The aroma! And we did it for everyone. Weddings and *yiortés* and *panigýria* were our only entertainments."

Asími's brow was still furrowed. "Still, I'm so glad they aren't going for a three-day affair, like we had. Zambétta's sister had that last year, and an *andígamos* a week later as well. Imagine how much *that* cost."

"Well, they own the hotel and all the cooks are family, so it's cheaper for them. I wish we didn't have to have Koúla's in a hotel. Remember when all the weddings and *panigýria* were held in the church courtyard? Did we have three hundred people? We might have – which was half the village then."

"Yes, and do you remember the band that came?"

"Of course, Yiórgos Konitópoulos. That whole family of wonderful musicians sailed over from Náxos on Bárba Gavrilis' *kaíki*. We didn't pay them anything. We fed them, they slept somewhere the next day, and they played all that night and the next. They couldn't have made much money. It was just after the war and everybody was poor."

"Now they're so famous the King couldn't afford them! And they played at our weddings!" Asími sighed. Was it so long ago, her own wedding? Yes, nearly thirty years, and times had changed so much.

"Speaking of the band," said Mersiniá, "I suppose we're stuck with that Kóstas who usually comes. He's no Konitópoulos, worse since he added those American drums. But we can't afford anyone better. Should we try to telephone or write to him?"

"Write. You do it. I'm not so good with the letters." Like many villagers her age, Asími had grown up during the war, when there was no teacher in the village. She could read and write but always felt unsure about it.

"Whatever you wish. Now about the *bonboniéras* . . ."

For weeks the two mothers and their three daughters discussed and planned the wedding. "The *kreváti*," Asími said, meaning the Ceremony of the Bed. "Vangelió's supplying the sweets, her mother's making tea. Who's going to ask Sophía to sing? Koúla, you should do that."

Koúla groaned. "Oh no. I can't bear it. She's always digging for gossip.

It'll be all over the village about . . ." She patted her tummy. "And I bet she'll hem and haw and say she really can't sing it unless the bride's a virgin." Koúla looked meaningfully at her sister Frangíska, who was giggling. "Can't you do it, *mána?*"

"I could," agreed Asími. "It would be less embarrassing, that's true. But then, you know Sophía. She'd be so insulted she'd bad-mouth us all over the village. We'll go together, all of us. Now, what's next?"

"I'm worried," said Koúla, "that Arghíris is going to drink too much waiting for the band to come and get him, then show up at the church drunk. Can we appoint someone to keep him sober?"

"Your father will do that."

"*Mána*," interrupted Asími's thirteen-year-old son Yiannákis, who had slipped in the door, tossed his schoolbooks on the divan, and gone to the kitchen to see what was for dinner. "Can I take the band around to the houses to collect the guests? That would be fun."

"Good idea, son. You know what to do: take them to Arghíris' first, then to the church, then all around the village, and at last come back here for Koúla. But no drinking until the *trapézi.*"

"No, *mána.*" Yiannákis looked at his mother with an angelic expression, but big sister Koúla wasn't fooled.

"You do it right or I will slaughter you," she said, focusing on her little brother the black lasers of her eyes.

Koúla's main worry was how to furnish the new apartment. Usually, a bride's dowry furniture was accumulated piece by piece, as she could afford it. But Koúla had to get it all together in a few months. That meant going to stores in Athens, buying most of the things, and having them shipped out. The biggest piece, though, had to be made in the village, and she thought her dear friend Thanásis the cabinetmaker would make her what she wanted and give her a good price. "I want a big cabinet, you know, with shelves for the glassware, a place for the television. Glass doors – you know, modern."

"No problem," said Thanásis.

"Can you do it on time?" Thanásis was known for high-quality work but also for taking forever, and Koúla was asking him to build cheaply and quickly. "It's got to be ready before the *kreváti*," she said. "Thursday of Holy Week."

"It will be." Thanásis, who had no helper, was sweeping the floor of his shop.

"You're sure?"

"*Lógo timís*," he said. "My word of honor. And the *stephanothíki* will be my gift. You want mahogany or Swedish pine?"

Still, Koúla was nervous. If the cabinet wasn't ready, where would they display all the dowry – the china and glass, the embroideries – and the wedding gifts?

Finally the day arrived – or not quite. The wedding was scheduled for the Saturday after *Pásca*. Lákis had wangled leave and would fly into Piraeús on the Friday. Some weeks before, Koúla had been to a bridal shop in Athens, chosen a dress with a high waist, and paid the rental fee. One of her aunts, who worked in a hotel and so couldn't come to the island for *Pásca*, offered to pick up the dress as well as the *bonboniéras*, the wedding favors, and bring them with her. She would take the same boat as Lákis, who would help her with the unwieldy boxes.

Because the Friday of Holy Week was a significant *yiortí* in the village – the celebration of the *Zoodóhos Pigí* – the *krevátí* ceremony was scheduled for Thursday. Sophía had agreed to sing the song blessing the bed in which Koúla and Arghíris were to consummate their marriage–and presumably sleep in for the rest of their lives. As predicted, Sophía had tried to make Asími squirm about Koúla's expecting, but Asími stood up for her child. "Of course, if you don't want to do it," she said to a snooty Sophía, "I think I can do it myself – piece together the words. I've heard them often enough over the years."

At this, Sophía breathed through her nose and sat up straight. "Piece them together? No, the words must be right, or the blessing won't work. I'll do it. Still, girls are not what we were. None of this . . . fooling around for us, *E*? We were all virgins."

Since as far as anyone knew, Sophía at sixty-some was still a virgin, Asími kept her mouth shut and helped herself to one of the *baklavás* she'd brought.

The Thursday after *Pásca*, then, all Koúla's friends and relatives assembled in the new flat. Traditionally, mostly women, especially unmarried girls, attend the *krevátí*, but tradition has relaxed quite a bit, so the crowd was mixed. Along with the two Katínas and other girlfriends, mothers, aunts, and cousins, were a few young men friends, among them Thanásis, who had dark rings under his eyes. He had worked long hours all week and well into last night finishing the elaborate cabinet, coat after coat of lacquer followed by sanding. At dawn, finally satisfied, he had broken it down, loaded it on a truck, and, with Arghíris' help, hauled it up two flights of stairs, where together they reassembled the showpiece.

Arghíris was sporting serious whiskers.

"How long have you been growing them?" asked Thanásis, accepting the beer Arghíris handed him.

"Oh, about six weeks. I might as well make it worth the barber's time," he laughed. "Drives Koúla crazy. I've told her I'm growing a beard for the wedding."

Koúla, coming into the room with a box of china, didn't take the bait but stood and admired her cabinet. "Oh, Thanásis, it's beautiful."

"Not bad," he said proudly. "On time, too."

The next time Thanásis saw his cabinet, at the *kreváti*, it was filled with china and glass, and figurines, all resting on embroideries and crocheted doilies. The friends were already assembled in the bedroom. Sophía, her jet-black hair newly permed for the occasion, cleared her throat to hush the chattering women and began, in her still-lovely voice, to sing the strophes of the blessing of the bed. "My bride," she sang, "I wish you from my heart . . ."

The assembled women sang in response, "My bride, I wish you from my heart . . ."

Sophía moved on, each strophe echoed by the women: "May your bed be a golden treasure of love and joy!" Then, nodding to Arghíris' mother and to Asími, she sang,

> Come, mother of the groom,
> and you mother of the bride,
> Both of you together
> throw sheets on the bed,
> And wish your children
> Love and joy!

Asími and Arghíris' mother, on opposite sides of the bed, and with some help from Aunt Mersiniá and sister Frangíska, spread and tucked in the wedding sheets, white with cut-work hems that Koúla's grandmother, *Yia-yia* Frangíska, had been working on since the engagement. Over them they spread a white *hrámi* Mersiniá had hand-spun from her own sheep's fleece and had given to the nun Andonía to weave for her niece; *Yia-yia* Frangíska had added the deeply crocheted edges. "Koúla will want more modern things for her new life," Mersiniá sighed, "but the wedding bed-clothes should be traditional."

The bed made, the guests should have bounced a baby on it to wish Koúla fertility, but none was available, and the half soccer ball under her pretty print dress made it unnecessary. So all the guests threw money and *kouféta*, sugared almonds, on the bed and repaired to the *salóni* to drink coffee and eat pastries.

"Too bad Lákis couldn't make it," Katína said.

"Couldn't get an earlier flight from Bangkok," Koúla answered. "He called from Piraeús. He'll be on the boat tomorrow, with my aunt Eléni and the wedding dress."

Perhaps Koúla, all her friends and relatives around her wishing her every happiness, forgot to add, *"Ama théle o Theós,"* "If God wills," because the next morning, the day before the wedding, Koúla's fisherman father woke her with the words every mariner fears: *"Halaí o kósmos !"* ("The world is in ruins!") Koúla rushed to the kitchen window, which looked out on the bay. The white horses of the waves were rearing and leaping over the midnight blue water. Koúla looked at her father. "How many Beaufort?" she asked, pleading with him to say, "Not so much. It will be all right. The ships will sail. Lákis will come."

Instead, he put his arms around her and said, "Today, tomorrow. What does it matter? There, there, *mátia mou, chrysó mou! Min klés!*" But of course she cried, and cried more when Lákis, captain of ocean-going ships, telephoned from Piraeús to say that no ship was leaving the harbor and, in his opinion, "We're in for a gale – two, maybe three days." The best he and Aunt Eléni could do was hole up in a harbor-side hotel and be ready day and night to jump on the first ship out.

"Halaí o kósmos !" Liggéris greeted me that morning as I entered the dining room of his and Zambétta's new hotel. Living and teaching in Athens, I had come back to the village for *Pásca* and Koúla's wedding. My school was in recess for Holy Week, and I didn't have class until Tuesday evening, so it had seemed safe – spring storms being rare – to plan to leave on the Sunday ferry, or if not Sunday, then Monday. There was even an early boat on Tuesday. So, though I felt for Koúla, I wasn't really worried about my own situation. The storm would abate, the wedding would go on tomorrow or the next day, and I would be back in time to teach my Tuesday evening class. In the meantime, as I sipped my Nescafe, I noticed I was not the only guest concerned about the weather. The band – Kóstas the gypsy who played *bouzoúki*, a woman singer, and three other men (the violin, the guitar, and "those American drums")– was seated around a table, talking across the empty dining room to Liggéris behind the counter.

"*Halaí o kósmos* !" Kóstas called. "I gotta get outa here Sunday. Got a gig in Kíthera on Wednesday."

Liggéris grunted. "Storm better be over before that. Do you know how much food I've bought for this wedding? The meat alone . . . Well, I can freeze that, but the vegetables . . .We'd all better pray."

"And pray the bride doesn't deliver before the storm's over!" laughed Kóstas, but Liggéris didn't answer. Koúla was his folks, and Kóstas, even if a customer, was a stranger.

"*Halaí o kósmos* !" Thanásis greeted me when I met him in the *platía*. The wind was whipping our cheeks, pulling my hairpins out and tangling my hair, and actually blowing some of the sawdust off Thanásis' sweatshirt.

"What's going to happen?" I asked.

"Nothing to do but wait," he said, unfazed as usual. "When the storm quits, the ferries will sail, Lákis will come, and we'll have a wedding. In the meantime . . .you don't have to work. Make the best of it! It's Koúla who's in the dumps."

"Pity Alíki isn't here." Our friend Alíki's father had recently been diagnosed with an aneurism, so the family had not come from Athens to open their hotel for *Pásca* as was their custom. Alíki was always the moving spirit of the *paréa*, the circle of friends that included Thanásis and Koúla, and a number of other cousins and friends. Wherever Alíki was, there was *yélia*, laughter and joy, and she would have had Koúla laughing in a moment. We all did our best. We played cards, watched the television weather news four times a day, went to the sweet shop to eat pastries. There one of the loafers in the *platía* called out to Koúla, "Where's the *koumbáros?*"

"In Piraeús," Koúla answered.

"If the storm lasts much longer, he should bring a bigger-size dress." General laughter. Koúla was not amused.

"*Halaí o kósmos!*" Day after day the world fell apart. The sun shone brightly, the sea was the blue of a sailor's uniform, and the snow-white spume spread over the waves, the most dangerous kind of stormy sea. A large white ferry which had been on its way north from Santoríni was sheltered in Náousa harbor. Across the strait we could see another hugging the dock at Náxos. Passengers, stuck for days, must have been subsisting on cheese toast, chips, and candy bars from the ship's bar. In the village grocery stores, spaces began to appear on the canned goods shelves. The day passed when I should have returned to Athens, but the storm raged on. There wasn't a boat – ship, ferry, or *kaíki* – on the Aegean Sea. Luckily, my boss was realistic: "This is Greece," she sighed. "Get here when you can."

Finally, after five days, we awoke to a calm sea. When I went down to the dining room for breakfast, Liggéris gave me the news. "Ships are sailing! Lákis is on his way! Wedding tomorrow!"

"What about the band?" I asked, spooning honey on my bread. "Kóstas said he had another engagement?"

Liggéris shrugged. "Hot air." Liggéris had hoped that, while they were waiting, the band would play for free at the hotel and help him sell some of his overstock, but Kóstas had refused and the musicians waited out the storm playing cards. Already two days overdue at my job, I had to decide whether to catch the next boat for Piraeús or, as I wished, to stay for the wedding. I phoned my boss again, who, fortunately, was kind as well as pragmatic. "Of course you must stay. I'll teach your classes."

"I'll be back on Friday," I said, and added, remembering Koúla's omission, "if God wills."

The next afternoon Thanásis and I waited at his house for the musicians to pass, gather us up, and take us to the church. In the distance we could hear them circulating through the village, picking up the groom's people. The walking band consisted of one violin and a clarinet, which strictly speaking is not an island instrument, but Demosthénis, the harbor café owner, loved to play and was included in every *panigýri*.

"Listen," said Thanásis. "They've brought Arghíris to church. Now they'll come for us." And soon they did. We joined a throng of bride's people and half-walked, half-danced to the church. The church was already packed, but people kept pushing me up toward the front, where Koúla, shining in white satin, and Arghíris, serious, shaven, and sober, stood before a table on which were a pair of white candles and a large silver cup. Behind the table the young priest, Pápa Ilías, stood reading from a huge silver-covered missal. Lákis, splendid in his captain's uniform, stood behind the couple. As I watched, he handed a small packet to the priest, who removed two gold rings and, making the sign of the cross on first the groom's and then the bride's forehead, declared that Arghíris, the "servant of God," and Koúla, the "handmaid of God," were betrothed.

The service was long, with many mentions of Biblical marriages – Adam and Eve, Abraham and Sarah, Isaac and Rebecca. As usual, hardly anybody was listening. All around me people were talking, commenting on how beautiful the couple looked in the flickering light of the white candles, on what a lovely strong voice Pápa Ilías had, on how Arghíris looked as though he were going to faint. Children wound in and out of a forest of adult hips, boys with their hands in their pockets and glints in their eyes, little girls shoving up to look at the bride. Only around the table with the four participants was there any peace, as Pápa Ilías spoke of the beauty of marriage and asked God to bring the couple "a peaceful life, length of days, the joy of grateful offspring. Let them know their children's children," he intoned, as he spotted one of his own little girls stroking Koúla's satin dress.

Soon, taking up the *stephánia* – wreaths of white paper flowers linked with a long ribbon – Pápa Ilías touched them to each of the couple's foreheads three times, and placed the wreaths upon their heads. Koúla's wreath was tilting to the side, so she reached up and seated it more firmly on top of her white veil.

After more lengthy prayers and references to the marriage at Cana, where Jesus turned water into wine, the priest offered the couple a drink of wine from the "common cup," and then led them in the "dance of Isaiah," three times around the table. Lákis as *koumbáros* held onto the ribbon joining the *stephánia*, signifying his promise of a lifelong relationship with the newlyweds. As they danced, the onlookers pelted them with rice and sugared almonds.

After more prayers for their happiness and fruitfulness, the priest removed the *stephánia*, the chattering crowd parted, and Arghíris triumphantly led his glowing bride out of the church into the church courtyard. There they greeted their guests, who swarmed to kiss them and wish them "*Na zísete!*" "May you live!"

Crack! Zap! Bam! Bam! Bam! The young boys celebrated the happy couple with homemade cherry bombs, while mothers and fathers chased after them, trying to grab the firecrackers before some kid blew off a hand or set fire to the bride's dress. Asími and Mersiniá distributed to all the *bonboniéras*, little tulle bags filled with sugared almonds.

The crowd dispersed. My *paréa* drifted down to the sweet shop to drink an ouzo, getting a start on what would be an all-night party. Fortified, we wound our way to the hotel, where the band was just warming up, waiting for Koúla, Arghíris, and the priest to arrive. The first hour or so of the reception was focused on the *horós tis nífis*, dance of the bride. Perhaps according to the old tradition that a bride leaves her own family, and even village, to become part of her husband's, the bride dances with anyone who wishes. First she dances with her *gambrós*, groom, and then they together with their close family members, and on and on into a widening group of well wishers.

The first dance is a *syrtos* ; the line dance integrates the new couple into the community. The next dance is a *bállos*, a couple's dance of flirtation that completes itself in the wedding. The songs are lovely and traditional. From the time they are wed, the *nífi* and *gambrós* are referred to in song as *pérdika* and *aetós*, partridge and eagle:

> *Today let the sky be clear!*
> *Today let the day shine forth!*
> *Today are being wed*
> *An eagle and a partridge.*

As the dancers took the *nífi*'s hand and danced, the bride's mother sang of how her partridge was flown from her nest. Other people contributed lyrics, some traditional, some inventive, some–as the time wore on – bawdy, or *sókin*, shocking, as they say here. Many instructed the groom:

> *Groom, groom! Love the bride!*
> *Do not scold her.*
> *Like the flowers of the garden*
> *Be proud of her...*
> *Admire her like the sweet basil of the earth.*
> *Love her and do not scold.*

Others asked the blessings of the Panagía:

> *O Panagía of Náousa with the hundred candles,*
> *May the couple that has become live a thousand years!*

A much repeated favorite was the *gambrós*' song. Appropriately for this village, he compares his *nífi* to a boat:

> *Like a swift boat*
> *you are, my darling.*
> *You rule the sea.*
> *Should you wish, take my life.*
> *Should you wish, give it to me.*
>
> *Many boats I fitted out*
> *Just to come and find you.*
> *If you don't want me, my darling,*
> *I'll come some night and steal you!*

Of course, Arghíris had done the "stealing" some time ago, but no one was churlish enough to remind the family and friends of this fact.

The greeting and ritual dancing accomplished, the wedding soon became a party. To allow Koúla to change her dress, and Liggéris and his crew to set up tables for the *trapézi*, a hundred or so of the guests, led by all the musicians – violin, guitar, bouzoúki, and clarinet – trooped down to the harbor, where Demosthénis, happy to be playing his clarinet, treated us all to ouzo as we danced in the twilight, circling around the little *platía*. Winding through the village, we passed Arghíris' sweet shop where his partners stood with trays of ouzos. Soon, light-headed and gay, we returned to the hotel for hours and hours of food, wine, music, and dancing.

The wedding guests danced *syrtós*, *bállos*, *kalamatianós*. We danced in lines, in couples, in groups of three or four. In the beginning we danced with dignity, but as time wore on the hilarity triumphed over propriety. Then people began to dance show-off dances like *tsámiko* and sexy dances like *tsiftetélli*. They climbed on the tables and danced amid the salads and *souvlákia* and spilled wine. They smashed plates and even bottles. Dodging dancers, Liggéris and his crew kept a steady stream of plates of salad, stew, cheese, and steak issuing from the kitchen. From time to time, some one would dash in with broom and pan to try to keep up with the breakage.

The dancers were tireless, stopping only to snatch a bite of bread or *souvlaki*, drink another glass of wine. The *violiá* never took a break, playing continually. I knew this madness would last at least twelve hours, and I had determined to see it through, but around four o'clock I could not eat another bite, drink another glass, or dance another step. I slunk away to my room upstairs in the hotel, where I dropped fully clothed on to the bed. The music was still so loud I could hear every word, all my favorites mixing in my dreams:

> *Maria in the yellow dress*
> *Who do you love better –*
> *Your husband or the neighbor?*
>
> *A little wanderer am I, my lady!*
> *Take me in your embrace!*
> *To an island harbor, take me!*
>
> *I love two black eyes*
> *Today there is a wedding*
> *In these lovely surroundings*

So much a part of my dreams was the music that when it stopped, I was instantly awake, knowing that the guests were on their way to wake up the *nífi* and her *gambrós*. I slipped on my shoes, ran down and outside, and caught up with the happy throng passing from house to house, where sleepy relatives of Arghíris and Koúla stood outside with trays of ouzo and cognac or sweet cakes. Through the village streets we wound, the thirty or forty remaining guests, Lákis at the head of the line. We danced wherever we found an open place, and soon arrived at Koúla and Arghíris' apartment building. By this time Kóstas the *bouzoúki* had found himself a donkey, which he rode right up the front steps, and proceeded to sing the awakening song:

> Get up, white eagle
> and shake your feathers!
> Aman! Bring out that partridge
> You hold in your embrace.
>
> Get up, O groom
> and treat us,
> so all of us can wish you
> "Live long and grow old!"

Nothing happened. Kóstas repeated the song, some guests joining in on "Get up!"

Nothing. White Eagle was apparently not in fine feather. "He didn't leave the hotel until three," Thanásis whispered. "Koúla had to drag him out."

A third time Kóstas sang the verses, then, slyly, added some of his own:

> Get up and tell us, Arghíris,
> Was it warm?
> That is, the blanket?
>
> Get up and tell us, Koúla,
> Was it hard?
> That is, the mattress?

At this, Koúla appeared on the balcony and announced that Arghíris was a bit under the weather but was now up and dressed, and we were welcome to come up. And so we did, trooping into the apartment and into the bedroom where we pretended to examine the bed for signs of deflowering. Everyone admired Thanásis' *stephanothíki*, mounted over the bed, now with the two wreaths of white flowers inside. We crowded into the *salóni* where Arghíris, pale, red-eyed, bewhiskered, offered us yet more glasses of ouzo with which we drank the health of the eagle and his partridge, over and over: "*Na zísete! Eis ygeía!*" The singles among us were also toasted: "*Sta diká sou!*" "To your own wedding!" Perhaps it was to ensure that the pitifully unmarried would not bring bad luck to the newlyweds.

After sleeping most of Sunday, I caught my boat back to Athens and my job, leaving behind a life of unimaginable warmth and gaiety. All went well with Koúla and Arghíris. The first child was a boy, baptized by Lákis and named for Arghíris' father. The next time I saw Koúla, a few years later, she was living in her own house, a duplex she and Arghíris and their two children shared with her sister Frangíska and her family. I met the two sisters in the street by Thanásis' house, the street on which they had been born and lived until they were married. The snow white of the houses, the brilliant magenta of the bougainvillea, and the shining onyx eyes of the sisters, each with an infant in a stroller and a toddler clinging to her skirt, reminded me of the wedding songs we had danced to:

> I love two black eyes!
> I wish for two sweet black eyes
> that you be proud of each other
> In these lovely surroundings.

The Mamí and Her Husband

The *mamí* lived at the top of a white marble road: not a laid road of cut slabs but a natural outcropping of the marble core of the island released from its crust of country rock by erosion of water, wind, shod feet, unshod hooves. The road rose from the surrounding gray rock like a spring of immortal water, a cataract of foam metamorphosed into milk-white stone, polished as smooth as an archaic statue. It descended from the *mamí's* modest snow-white house down, down between high banks of garden walls. Obstructed near the bottom of the hill by a house-high boulder of black gneiss, the marble river veered, dropped, and finally disappeared under the paving of the main road into the *platía*. Where winter rains left pockets of earth along the edges, in spring red poppies, chamomile, and wild mint blossomed.

I loved to climb this road and visit the *mamí*. In the summer I would go barefoot, to feel the cool of the marble beneath my feet. The smooth, curving stretch of marble seemed to me a part of the naked body of the island itself, which drowsed beneath its coverlet of rock and soil, dreaming of the beginning of time. Every once in a while, I imagined, as it shifted in its sleep, a slab of the gray, mica-spangled country rock would split, fall away, and crumble, baring a thigh, a shoulder of pure white marble.

The *mamí's* house was the only one in the village that opened onto the marble road. An elbow of the marble, jutting into her kitchen, supported the hearth. The *mamí* loved the road, swept and washed it every day.

The hill was so steep that the *mamí's* kitchen was built below the level of the paved cross street, while the other rooms – *salóni*, bedroom, washroom – dropped as the road dropped, matching its descent. Each stepped-down room had its own veranda, lush with rose and coral balsam, vining geraniums, green basil – all in blue pots, beautiful against the sheet-white walls, the doors and windows painted green as water.

The *mamí* had all these years refused the offers of the *koinótita* to cut or build steps along the steep marble road, which, polished by thousands of years of rainfall, was as slippery as satin. To visit her, one could either descend from the upper road, stepping carefully a few meters to her kitchen door, or, as only she and a few brave souls cared to do, ascend the whole length from the *platía*. Most people, those who came to call her out to give an injection of insulin or penicillin or to attend a woman in labor or a child with a temperature, stood on the upper road and called into her kitchen window: "*Mamí? Ela, mamí!*" She would come to the window, her head framed in green at the level of the seeker's knees, then listen to symptoms or fears, dry her hands or turn down her soup, get her medical bag, and, climbing sure-footedly on the silken marble, join the caller on the upper road.

This was her way – to walk to the home of the patient – even when she was still the government nurse-midwife with a nice, clean surgery, located on the second floor of a building in the *platía*. No elderly woman in rheumatic pain, no injured workman, no over-term young mother needed to climb the long flight of stairs to the surgery for an injection, a change of dressing, or daily palpation. The *mamí* herself walked – downhill to the harbor and the *platía*; uphill to Alónia and Ai Yiórgi; out to the farms of Phíkia to the south, Campos to the east, Ksifara to the west a dozen times a day and, before she retired from birthing, all hours of the night. She had entered, in its turn, every house in the village and the surrounding countryside.

There was nowhere the *mamí* would not go, no matter how remote the house, hiking kilometers up a dry riverbed in the blaze of summer or, in winter, scaling the rock walls along the banks of that same river now rushing with ice-cold runoff. To every corner of the parish she shared with the priest, she strode on her neatly shod feet – an elegant figure with her green overcoat buttoned around a gay scarf, her eyes ever moving over the landscape, alert to a bush of new-leaved sage (for bronchitis), oregano (for stomach ache), or a patch of chamomile (for bathing newborns). Since she had arrived in the village some years before the war and the Occupation, by the time I knew her there was scarcely a living child or adult who had not come slithering and yelling into her deft, red hands, and few of those now only bones and memory who had not closed their eyes under those same hands, gentle and dry as tissue paper.

After a birth or a death, she would stop at one of the small chapels which dotted the landscape. There she would light a candle to the Panagía, kiss the hand on the ikon that clasped the Babe, and refill her own well of spirit. Returning home, she would walk clear into the center of the village, perhaps for shopping or a little gossip, but most probably so as to end her journey climbing upwards, as though touching that white shoulder was as necessary as making her cross or kissing the hand of the Panagía.

In appearance, the *mamí* was ageless. Her movements were lithe – *ligerí*, as they say, like a willow – and her skin soft as rose petals; her hair was shining with a little henna; her clear eyes changed with the weather from hazel to gray, around them the faintest of lines. Her age? You would say thirty, thirty-five, possibly forty, but feel . . . puzzled. She had passed through certain events – had arrived on the mainland, an orphan, in an exodus from Asia Minor. But which exodus? She had done her hospital training in Athens and before the War had come to the village as the government nurse. Adding up probable numbers this way resulted in an age that seemed impossible for the youthfulness she displayed. And the modernity: she was opposed to all forms of superstition, no matter how linked to religion, unless she felt they were good for the patient. Thus she refused to let her new mothers and babes lie in their blood for three days, as some deemed necessary, but washed them clean immediately with chamomile tea for the infant and a good alcohol rub for the mother. Also, she dismissed the idea that for forty days after birth the new mother, a *léchona*, should not leave her house. "Nonsense!" she urged. "Up with you if you want! A walk, a little company will only do you good. Sweeten your milk!" She had no objection to a friend or neighbor of a patient dropping oil in a glass of water to remove the Eye, and certainly none to herbal teas, but kept her own good eye on the patient's symptoms, and when the time came that she thought a shot of penicillin necessary, she insisted on it. She encouraged, even taught, the use of *vendoúzes*, cupping glasses, to alleviate cold in the muscles, but she discouraged the corollary practice of cutting and letting blood, since the danger from infection was greater than the possibility of a cure.

More than anything, the *mamí* believed in daily palpation for the expectant mother. She would listen to the heartbeats of both mother and child with her stethoscope, but it was through her hands that she kept track of the baby's progress. Softly over the mother's belly they would move, her fingertips telling her how the fetus was growing, when and where it was shifting. She always knew when a birth was going to be as easy as pitting a ripe plum, when labor was going to be long and stubborn, and when there was danger. "Athens," she would say then, maybe weeks ahead of the due date, her hands moving from the mother's belly to stroke her cheek. "You have to go to Athens." Few wanted to go; they knew her skill, had seen her deftly turn breech babies, unwrap strangling umbilical cords. But when she said go, they went.

The *mamí* cared for her patients not only with hands and medicine, but with the example of her own active, involved, and exquisitely clean life. She was known as the cleanest woman in the village; however, her cleanliness was not a caustic scouring impelled by phobia but a belief in the healing power of, say, sheets scrubbed in pure water with green soap and hung to dry on sage shrubs or above a pot of carnations.

To birth, to bind, to cure, to comfort, she had visited everyone in the village. There was nothing she had not seen: the priest's backside, the young wife's cancer, the incestuous father's rage, the child in convulsions, the botched abortions, the contagion of poverty, the misery of wealth – and yet nothing drew from her contempt or despair. Only on those walks back would she sometimes stop and consciously bring up in her mind the new wheat or the pink cistus, or count like beads on a *kombolói* the red-faced babies of the decades: Aspasía, four now, just learning to ride a trike; Yiorgákis, ten, a lisping and bespectacled honor student. Yiánnis, a breech birth, had just bought his own *kaíki*, and Katerína was going to marry him. Counting their mothers and, in time, their own babes, God willing, that would make three generations born into her hands.

Before the arrival of the exclusively male government doctors, most of whom served out their required two years stoically, counting the days to when they would be released from this backwater of a village to begin practices in Athens or Thessaloníki, the *mamí* had held the health of the villagers in her own hands. She had resources; in the *hóra* less than half an hour away by taxi, there were two doctors, both French-trained, al- though no clinic. Only a little farther away by tractor or mule, near the mountain church of *Tou Stavroú*, lived a seventy-year old bonesetter, who had learned the skill from her mother, and she from hers. The *mamí* stood between them in many ways. For so many years, so few of the benefits of modern medicine – x-rays, surgery, sophisticated drugs – were available on the island that she had had to use what came to hand, find the good in it, weed out the bad. She educated the villagers about modern practices and the French-trained Athenian doctor in the *hóra* about local ones. When he first arrived, he was shocked at the paucity of scientific resources, at having, for instance, to do his own lab work in a converted toilet, and at the people's dependence on herbalists and faith healers, including the priests. The villagers came to him after the herbs had not worked and be- cause he was cheaper than the priest, who had to be tipped for anointing and praying. However, the *mamí*, who was proud of having been hospital- trained herself, gradually introduced him into the blend of traditional and modern medicine she had herself learned to practice.

Once a ferocious storm blasted the lighthouse keeper off his catwalk onto the black rocks of the promontory. Rescued and brought to the village by *kaíki*, he was improbably alive but had multiple compound fractures. The storm that had toppled him kept in harbor any ship or he- licopter that might have taken him to hospital in Sýros or Athens. Even had he been able to be removed, he would not have been out of danger: he was bleeding profusely and the open wounds invited gangrene. The *mamí* telephoned the doctor only to find him out, then sent a tractor up a mountain for the bonesetter. When the doctor finally arrived, he was horrified to find a wispy old woman with blue-filmed eyes, praying aloud and manipulating the bones visible and invisible. He opened his mouth to castigate the *mamí* for overstepping her bounds. But as he watched the old hands at work, probing, pushing, pulling, he fell silent. Later, after stitching the wounds, administering antibiotics, and plastering, the doctor confessed quietly but with conviction that he had never seen a better job. "Quick thinking," he praised the *mamí*, "sending for her. Still, without antibiotics, we would have lost him." The *mamí* blushed, and never mentioned the penicillin in her own bag.

Six months later, the lighthouse keeper was walking; six later still, without the shadow of a limp. He attributed his recovery neither to the bonesetter, the doctor, nor the *mamí*. "I was drunk when I fell!" he'd laugh. "God protects drunkards and idiots!"

"The *mamí*" the villagers always called her, as though there were no other–although after she retired from government service a dozen or more others came and went. She was so universally admired in the village that she had passed through the fire of not one but two scandals that would have driven another woman to take either her life or at least a boat for Athens, where she could live with her shame in anonymity. Newly arrived and single, lissome and red-haired, the young *mamí* had had her choice of husbands. As it happened, the one she chose, a scion of a large landowning family, did not work out. Five or six years after the wedding, they applied for divorce. Divorce in those days was in the hands of bishops. The grounds were few, and one would expect the curious gossips to have circulated, not to say expanded upon, any hint of adultery but in fact, to this day no one but the old priest knows the grounds. They had no children, the gossips said, straining their memories, so perhaps the husband was impotent. The *mamí* could not be at fault – not the *mamí*! And yet, she was a foreigner and he a native! It was he who slunk off to Athens and she who stayed, living chaste and single for more than twenty years, dedicating her life to birthing and healing, until she married her second husband.

Now *there* was a scandal! He too was a foreigner, another Asia Minor immigrant, from a family that had been resettled in the refugee quarter of the *hóra*. As he grew up, he hired out to farmers all over the island, bit by bit learning their skills, though he had been born a city boy and occasionally went off to live with relatives in Thessaloníki. Perhaps it was there, in the *tékes*, the soon-to-be famous dives of the *rembétes*, the despised hashish-smoking refugees from Asia Minor, that he discovered a gift for music, learning to play both *baglamás* and *bouzoúki*, developing a repertoire of the sad and bitter songs called *rembétika*. When, back on the island, he began to dance, he danced only the *rembétis' zembékiko* – tough, lonely, jazzy, and world-weary – rather than the sweet, smooth communal *syrtós* and *bállos* of the islanders. A man's man, when he came to the village he was the star of the *ouzerí*, bringing shreds and patches of the sharp and tragic underworld of the *mánges* and the *hanoumákia*, the tough guys and loose women, to the naive, resigned monogamists of the village.

To tease them, he would sing about a little *hanoumáki* walking through the alleys in red Turkish slippers, or a pair of the little sluts smoking hashish on the beach, or a whole harem swimming in the Pasha's pool. Seeing the villagers sigh with longing for sensuality not dampened by fathers-in-law, snotty brats, and grocery bills, he would switch and, scraping his *bouzoúki* harshly, evoke their misogyny. "Murderess," he would sing:

> *Why do you poison my heart*
> *With so much cruelty*
> *And take away my soul?*

He played and sang not only in the fug of the *ouzerí*, but after work, after supper, in the houses of the farmers he worked for. Where there were daughters in the house, instead of the tough songs of the *téke*, he would sing about "green eyes" or, depending on the girl, of "black eyes and black eyebrows."

> *Your eyelashes shine*
> *Like the flowers of the field…*
> *You lower your lashes*
> *And take my mind and reason away.*

If the daughter showed signs of softening, he would be quick to snatch her sympathy:

> *Rain, thunder and lightning*
> *And someone in pain*

Cries in his narrow room
And sighs deeply . . .

Loneliness shoots arrows
Which pierce his heart.

Stealing a look at her, he might dare to sing, to repeat, the last soulful lines:

Who can I find now to tell
Of my great despair?

Such a man, though he may pretend to wider experience than he actually has, stirs violent passions among innocent young girls – the more innocent the girl, the more violent the passion. Still, although landless, he was a hard worker, so when the daughter of a farmer whose vineyard he was planting fell sick unto death with longing for him, and it was clear to her parents that objection would be futile or dangerous, they were married. During the engagement – not long, just enough for her to finish embroidering her dowry sheets – he would tauntingly sing to the love-struck girl:

Crazy girl, you want to marry me
And stand beside me as a bride.
You'd better know you'll regret it bitterly
And soon find yourself on the streets...

With a chap like me who's a rembetis and broke
You're sure to come to grief.

But he wasn't really a *rembétis*, and he didn't stay broke for long. He worked her land, worked others', gathered a bit of money and bought a field or two, worked those. He sang in the *ouzerí*, danced in the *taverna* – always the tough, lonely *zembékiko*, never the sweet *bállos* with the wife or *syrtós* with the villagers – but still, whenever he danced, all eyes were fastened on him. He drew attention as a trawler draws a net.

And yet . . . I never heard anyone call him *levéndi*. It is one of those words, one of those concepts that defy translation. *Levendiá* is the greatest quality a Greek man or woman can have. "Charisma" comes close and the *mami*'s husband (not yet her husband) certainly seemed to possess that. Only rarely were songs or stories not bubbling up from his throat. Woven into the idea of *levendiá* is generosity, and he was generous though not extravagant in the *taverna* and was always willing to lengthen his own long working day to help out a neighbor, always willing to sell a pig on shaky credit. And yet . . . something held the word back in the throats of the villagers.

I met the *mamí* one fall day when her husband and I had been picking olives. Despite his gray hair, he was a fast and agile worker, climbing the trees and shaking down a hail of blue and green. Although we had started working before dawn, the stingy farm wife had fed us next to nothing: a couple of eggs poached in potato water and some fly-crusted *mizíthra*. "Come to my house this evening," he had whispered as we returned to the grove. "The *mamí* will feed us up!"

And so she did, not only with a nourishing fish soup and wild greens but, later, as I got to know her, with stories. She had a wealth of them. As well, she knew the complex genealogy of the village and would explain to me who was whose third cousin or brother-in-law, who could or could not marry whom, and why this had caused trouble. She had for decades visited every corner of the whole *koinótita*, not only the village proper but the isolated mountain farms and the tiny valley settlements of four or five houses. Bit by bit, she pieced together for me an overview of generations of relationships. My own friends never spoke of these things, so sometimes I was astonished to learn that, for instance, Thanásis was a third cousin of Annoúla, or Stávros a nephew of my landlord Yiánnis, or that Dimítris had never married because he had been in love with his second cousin Maria and the bishop would not approve a marriage. The *mamí* told the stories, but she never judged – but no, that is not quite right. Cruelty and stupidity, so many instances of which she had seen over the years, evoked from her a deep sadness, but she never spoke angrily of anyone.

The first evening at supper, however, the *mamí* had been friendly but quiet. Her husband had brought me as something of a trophy, and she had been pleased. But his behavior at dinner was . . . disturbing. He laughed, he sang, he poured the wine – but there was an edge to the attention. He was not just flirtatious, but somehow challenging. As I became more friendly with the *mamí*, I began to think he was, perhaps, jealous – but of whom? If I saw him in the village, he would call me over and, laughing, always laughing, quiz me on what we talked about when he wasn't there. Then one day while I was waiting for her to return from a patient visit, he came home, and finding me alone, lunged at me and, attempting to kiss me or worse, literally ripped the bodice of my new dress. I managed to escape, but too ashamed to explain the tear to the seamstress, I took it to be repaired in the *hóra*, and ever afterward was careful not to be alone with him even for a moment.

When her neighbors and mine saw me going often to the *mamí's* house, they began little by little to tell me her own story. "Ah, the poor thing!" whispered Pagóni, who lived just up the hill. "Some days she dares not leave the house, her face is so bruised and swollen. Only if someone comes and calls her out for a sick person will she go."

Adrianí, a fisherman's wife with a bad heart, said, "I saw her trying to hang a sheet with one hand, the other tucked into her body. I wanted to help but I dared not . . ."

And then finally, Marína came out with it: "He killed his first wife."

I don't know if it was true. He was certainly never indicted. But in those days . . . They say he beat the poor young woman, not often but badly. The first few years of the marriage seemed to pass calmly, but soon things changed – though never when he was drunk. Drink brought out the smiles and songs, the charm. And if she may have, in the beginning, objected to his evenings in the *óuzeri*, soon she was grateful for them. He would come home singing, hang up the *bouzoúki*, and lie down to sleep like a baby. Why or when he would fall into a rage, no one could guess. He broke her cheekbone once, they say, and another time knocked out two teeth. Where were those who could have defended her? It would not in those times have been a police matter, but where were her family, her father or brothers? Dead, perhaps? Disgusted, maybe? They might have excused their inaction, saying, "She had been mad to marry him, hadn't she? She must have done something to provoke him," and adding, "Anyway, a woman who stays with such a man deserves what she gets."

In the end, after fifteen years of marriage, one night he beat her so badly that she ran away and broke into a warehouse down at the harbor, spending the night hidden among the nets. There, alone, they say, she had a heart attack. The next day the doctor, summoned by the fisherman who found her, put her on a boat for Athens, but when the husband heard about it, he took the children out of school and sailed to her on the next boat. She died in the hospital. Within the hour he left to return to the island. Said Marína, "Strangers washed her, strangers buried her. She was not even brought back to the village. Who knows where she lies, and if anyone goes to clean the grave?"

He told it differently, omitting the beating, emphasizing the wife's long illness, his being left alone with two young children. "I knew what I wanted to do. I got on the boat and came straight to the *mamí*. 'Will you marry me and care for my children?' I said, and she said yes. And so . . . I tied my donkey."

"What?" I gasped.

The *mamí* laughed. "It's just a way of saying, we got married."

The neighbors were shocked. "Married not much more than forty days after the death," said Pagóni, and crossed herself. "Too soon. Against God."

Why did she take him? Since the whole village knew, she must have known: she must have dressed the wounds, rubbed the bruises with arnica. Was it for the children? To have children to care for, after a childless marriage, after years and years of bringing others' babes into the world? Or had her admired chaste singleness never been so much her own choice as her defense against the stigma of divorce, against becoming, in the eyes of the village, a woman dishonorably available? It was possible, in such a small village, that in all these years there had been no other suitable man; he would have had to be a widower, for no one else would have married a divorcee.

Or was it for none of these reasons, but simply that she was as vulnerable as any young virgin to the charm, the trace of bitterness, the angry sensuality?

If she married him for the children, her heart was soon broken. The girl, by then high school age, refused to live with them and went off to relatives of her mother's on another island. The boy, somewhat younger, proved wild and intractable, oblivious to the *mamí's* love, and finally was sent to America to live with his uncle. And the great-hearted, irreproachable *mamí* was left to live out her life – of birthing, healing, and consoling – with the man they never called *levéndis* in the house at the top of the marble hill.

Shortly after her marriage, the *mamí* retired from the government service, some said to avoid having to go out so much in public. But as the country recovered economically from the long effects of the war, things were changing. The village was now getting young government doctors, most of whom were proving less educable than the doctor in the *hóra*. They wanted a more up-to-date midwife, one who would convince the village women to go to hospital in Athens rather than birth at home, and who felt no need for daily palpations. (Once a week, the government said, and once a week it was.) With her husband's income, the *mamí* could afford to reduce her practice, concentrate on those of her patients who were aging or who lived far from the village clinic. Her small feet were as strong as ever, carrying her surely up dry stream beds and across stony fields, but the added leisure allowed her, after an examination or a change of dressing, to sit a little while, drink a cup of sage tea, and deliver the news of the village to the mothers of emigrant sons or to the lonely survivors of marriage waiting for death to reunite them with their mates.

I had been away from the village for five years when I came back for *Pásca*, arriving the evening of Good Friday. I decided to visit the *mamí* on the way to church to join the *Epitáphios*, the procession that reenacts carrying Christ to the tomb. It was raining and so, instead of climbing the marble road as I loved to do, I ascended by a surer path. As I rounded the corner of the *mamí's* house, I looked down the road, expecting the pale luminescence of white marble in the semi-darkness.

Instead I saw stairs: gray concrete stairs descending from the upper street. My first thought was that she had died, left the house, the road. Puzzled, I knocked at the door. No answer. But I had forgotten island ways. I opened the door – as usual it was unlocked – and called into the kitchen, "Mamí!"

"Who is it?" shouted a voice from deep inside the house – her husband.

I stayed by the door and called my name, asking, "Where's the *mamí?*"

"Gone out to give an injection. Come in."

"I'll come back," I said into the emptiness.

"Come on in," he called. "I'm sick, laid up. I can't hurt you, *putána*," he said, as though reading my mind. Leaving the outside door open, I advanced to the door of the *salóni*. He was lying on a sofa, smoking, and beside him leaning against the wall was an artificial leg. "Can't even get up," he laughed. "Come in. Sit and visit a poor cripple."

Still wary, I sat on the stairs between the kitchen and the *salóni* and heard the story. In his field south of the village, he had been harrowing with his small tractor. "You know how long it took me to pay off that devil machine? And then it turns around and eats my leg!" A rope had become wrapped around the wheel, stalling the machine. He had jumped down to untangle the rope, forgetting to turn off the motor. Free of the rope, the harrow had begun to whirl, and cut off his leg at the knee. "I took the same damned rope and tied it around the leg, what was left of it," he said, "and passed out." Luckily a passerby found him, and then: "Helicopter, Athens, hospital! Don't remember much of it. And then the wooden one." It wasn't wooden, of course – it was a hideous pink and tan plastic thing with chrome joints. "No more *zembékiko*!" he laughed, "but – *Dóxa to Theó* – it wasn't a hand; I can still play *bouzoúki*." The scarred, long-necked *bouzoúki* was leaning against the sofa, near a table with cigarettes, a bottle of pills, and a glass of water. "A song to welcome you?" he asked, reaching for the instrument.

At that moment I smelled rain and felt rather than saw the *mamí* come in. I got up and embraced her. She was as quick and lithe as ever, her cheeks as rosy, her hazel eyes as bright.

"A little coffee?" she asked, untying a rain-sprinkled scarf, and repeated the question into the *salóni*. A strong stroke across the strings answered her.

"You'll read my cup?" I asked, reminding her of the rainy afternoons we had passed with this fortune telling.

"Ah, the cup does not tell us everything," she sighed, measuring out coffee and sugar into a *bríki*. "You saw?"

"Saw what?" I asked. "Him? The leg?"

"*E*! Those two. No, I meant the steps."

"Yes," I said. "The marble's gone."

"Not gone. It's still there. I wouldn't let them dynamite, just build up the steps. So he can go down to the *ouzerí*," she said, and after a second added, "He'd die if he couldn't."

From the *salóni* came the familiar sounds, bitter and sorrowful but alive. It seemed to me his playing had improved with loneliness:

> *In the deep midnight*
> *There's a knock at my door,*
> *But no one appears.*
> *Who can it be? What do they want?...*

> *Wasting away on my bed*
> *I wait for Death,*
> *And the clock on the wall*
> *Leads the funeral dirge.*

Lifting the foaming *bríki* from the flame, the *mamí* looked straight into my eyes. There was no sorrow in her own. "At last," she said, smiling a little, "I have him where I want him." She took him his coffee, but we drank ours in the kitchen, chatting. The insistent music, however, and the ironic voice wound their way into our conversation.

> *Save me, my little Panagía,*
> *Have pity on my youth;*
> *Drive Death out of the yard*
> *So I won't have to meet him.*
> *And the clock on the wall*
> *Leads the funeral dirge.*

After coffee, I went out. It was still raining. For a moment I stood on the veranda, looking through the iridescent rain at the little road. At the edges of the gray stairs, patches of white marble gleamed under a street-light. I covered my head and headed uphill to the church, meeting halfway a stream of villagers bearing on their shoulders the coffin of God.

Dímitra's Path

Now is the time of the mourning mother. The light is at its strongest. Noon lasts all day, beating on her head, her shoulders, her feet which are treading, treading the stony paths, the stony fields. Stiff thyme scratches at her ankles and calves, tears at her skirt. Rude seeds cling to the hem, hitching a ride to elsewhere, seeking. And she is seeking – who? The daughter, the gay one, the soft spring light; her lost clarity, hope too soon scythed down, swallowed up by this dryness.

Even now the absence scrapes like thistles. She bleeds, from wherever blood is left. Drained. Wept out, eyes dry as old wells, cobwebbed, catching flies. In her heart she cries again, "Why? Why?" She feels again her terror, as night drew in, as the child – she thought of her as a child – didn't come home, the meal on the table untouched, gelid. Walking all night, calling, searching. "Where?" The waking nightmares – vipers, vampires. The terrible quiet of absence. In the morning, the evasiveness of the policeman: "Gone? A girl, *kyría*. A young woman . . ." Shrug.

"My child!" she screamed. And they looked, they said, but nothing. Driven, wild, she walked from house to house. Nothing. Blank faces.

Nothing for two weeks until Póppi, the daughter's bosom friend, came, shamefaced, hauled out to the farm by her grandmother. "I promised not to tell, *kyría*. I saw them, walking on the beach."

"Who?"

"A man, a man from a yacht. She left her shoes. . ." Shame-faced , the girl produced a pair of plastic sandals.

She snatched the sandals, screamed at Póppi. The grandmother screamed at *her*. Again to the police: more shrugs. More going from house to house, now weeping. Doors closed.

Then the letter came. She keeps it in her pocket – keeps all of them now, years of them – carries them everywhere, though they're shapeless, dry, crumbling in her pockets like last year's leaves.

> *We are married, dear mother – and in church, not that that makes any difference; we were married from the moment he extended his hand from the white boat, and I sailed away with him, leaving my shoes on the beach.*

Cheated. Cheated of a wedding, of placing the wreath on her head, of giving her to a groom. Cheated of a groom. She hates this man who stole from her the fruits of her labor.

The winter was too warm, too dry. Everything came on early, the trees bloomed too soon, and then, early March, weeks of unceasing north wind. Blossoms blew down like snow, dried, became dust. Now, a few small apricots cling to inner branches – so few, and not as sweet as last year's – and a few almonds, hardly enough to make *kólyva* to lay on the graves.

She will not walk through the orchard, averts her eyes from the memories: hands filling a basket with apricots, fat little hands grasping windfalls, small brown arms pulling lower branches, strong brown hands steadying a ladder.

When she was growing, every day, every minute, I looked at her and saw a new face, new worlds, new languages stirring. I was thrilled, I was terrified – such awareness, such beauty – but she evaded all the perils: croup, measles, vipers, busy roads. And just as I was sure, she was gone – gone in a day, a hot wind and gone.

After I knew, I closed up the farm. Slaughtered the pig, sold the chickens, left the doves to themselves, put the fields to wheat. Where, these days – after wars, after hunger, with the cities calling – are there hands, young or old, to hoe beans and tomatoes, pull and braid onions, prune vineyards? And where is the rain? Not for years the rains of my youth, the fine, sweet rains, August to March, that nourished us slowly, slowly brought us to ripeness.

All winter I stayed in the village, away from the farm, tended an old woman, once lovely, once a poet. As a child, I had sat with my head on her knees while she sang the world into being, taught my eyes to see. I owed her at least a quiet death. But, oh, the decay, the illness, the lapses of memory, the shuffling among yellowed papers for a poem, a poem about poppies. Pity, irritation, and terror pulled me down, pulled me away from the daughter, from the spring. Maybe I feared to force myself on her, maybe I was mourning. I tied a black kerchief on my head, observed all fasts to deprive myself of hope. It must not be I who remains.

I meant to go up Ayíou Andoníou on a chill, bright day (January? February?) to see the anemones nodding in the winter wind – pink, violet, ice blue, the rare fuchsia nodding around cool marble boulders. On such days on the mountain, the air is like diamonds, the far islands are so close and clear, you can almost see the spots of fuchsia on their hills. I meant to go, but this year . . .

I knew the winter was too warm, the anemones were passing, and yet day after day I didn't go. They passed quickly without the cold. I knew, yet didn't get out of the village – shopping, talking, breaking, mending – didn't get out on the cold road inland, go up the white path with its flat marble flags, cut and smoothed out of memory; I didn't see them blowing, the delicate anemones, in the north wind.

In February, old Lýsandros came and said, "Your wheat's stunted." And still I didn't get out – passing, fretting, carrying, cleaning. Then he came, only March, and said, "It's gone. Thresh it – animal food."

"Take it," I said, "I have no animals to feed." And I thought, it's my fault. I didn't slow her down. No, I didn't let her grow. Gone too soon. Blown away.

A year later, another letter. The postman begged for the stamp: "From so far away, *kyría.*"

> *Remember how we dreamed of going to the city? How innocent we were! When people say to me, "Paris is beautiful," or maybe it's Johannesburg or San Francisco (we go all over), I look in their eyes to see if they're mad. They say this when, here and there among these gray abysses, enough light has filtered down to grow a leggy and feeble tree, or where sooty water pumped into a basin creates a shadow of a spring. The water is death to drink.*
>
> *The only natural life is rats.*

Winters passed, and springs, and I didn't get out. The lupine grew gray and the winds blew out the poppies, and the *mandelíthes* dried to straw, and finally, when the old woman died, I shut up her house and went back, dreading every step.

Nothing left, no color but dust, only the white and green acanthus on the roadsides – a male flower, too tall, too stiff, thorny – and over the dry dearth, a white veil of *staphilinós*, like cataracts on old eyes. Up a dry road to an empty farm, centipedes and scorpions, feral cats that eat their kittens, fields of stubble. All dry, old paper, dust.

The letters still come, every few years.

> *All day, I do nothing. He is out, buying and selling his stones and metals. I wait. It takes all day, this waiting: vacuuming, putting the dishes and the clothes in machines, buying and cooking frozen food. We eat ten-month-old peas and years-old fish.*

At night we go and watch colored lights on a screen. The others laugh or cry. They are like the dead: they want to remember life, when or if they lived, but they can't, so they are moved, as much as they are ever moved, by these shadows.

Nothing planted, nothing to do, so she walks: walks the stony roads, dusty paths, and stubble fields, mourning her dead spring. Everything scratches, her legs run with blood. Where she walked yesterday she found a patch of, oh, hundreds of tan, tissue-paper orchids, what had been orchids, polyanthus columns of coral pink. Never had she seen more than two together, and she had missed this wonder. But she hadn't known, hadn't passed this way, hadn't broken out of shopping and chopping, indignation and fear, and now . . . Nothing crumbles in the hand as dry as regret.

The old woman died vomiting blood, shitting the bed. There was no love in it. Without me, she would have died alone, but with me, we both died alone. She hated it, my cleaning and carrying, feeding and wiping. As though nothing – not sight, not words, not memories – remained, only pride and pain. As I stood at the grave, I saw my womb, saw yawning nothing but a full grave and an empty house, and in three years the grave too would be dry and empty. Too soon, too soon. And my child in Hell. If she had flown from this small dovecote to circle the mountaintops, I could have been glad, but this . . .

It is only his life I hate; him, I . . . love does not seem to be the word. I love you, Mána. I love our land, our island. For him, it is beyond love. I did not want to grow up to marry some Tzanís or Arghíris, and spend my life cooking his dinner, acceding to doltish desire, becoming another strígla screaming at the children. Perhaps if I'd known a father . . . But all I knew was a ring in a drawer, and a mother, who sometimes slept with gypsies. I hated you for this. I wanted – I thought I wanted – a kind of convent of the two of us, our gardens, our kitchen, our interior worlds. But no, as the flame broke out in you (poor Mána, I understand now), so it broke out, a holocaust, in me.

If you could know him, you would understand. There are not a dozen people in the world as powerful as he, and this power – you would not believe it – reaches into every corner of the world, even to the deserts and the veldts and the little farms of our island. And yet . . . He was my savior, but now I am his. He says I am his link with life.

Don't think that I have for him this long face I show to you; no, for him I am all smiles, caresses, jokes. And his private sibyl – all his plans he lays before me, and waits for my answer. And I am always right, he says. For this reason, I cannot leave him, not even for a short visit. He needs me so desperately, he would replace me in a week. And then I should be nothing.

When I look in the mirror, which I do rarely, there is a face I don't know, not mine, not hers, not even my mother's. Flesh beginning the melting, bones shrinking. I won't need a tomb: they can slough off this dried skin, throw the bones straightway into the ossuary, build them into a wall. Too soon half dead, too long waiting to die.

Thank you, Mána, for offering to send pomegranates by Kapetán Vangélis. But they would be confiscated at the border. And really, it is not so much the fruit I miss, but the budding, the flowering, the swelling of the smooth green belly, the reddening of the full womb, day by day. I remember jumping out of bed at dawn to see which buds had flowered, shriveled, swelled, ripened. The black tree was like a village (not a crop like the almonds and apricots), every bud in her own time flowering, coming to term, bursting, offering her brilliant fruits, her seeds, her children, to us and the birds and the earth.

It is not things but Time itself I miss. Here there are only symbols of change: in the monotonous flow of imperceptible seasons appear tokens of life, but never at the right times: pomegranates and grapes appear in spring, grown in another hemisphere; in summer, anemones cut and wrapped in cellophane, come from God knows where, someplace where there is, presumably, spring and earth to grow them in. Like votives on ikons, the fruit and flowers here are only commemoratives of miracles occurring elsewhere. I pity them, I buy them, but they are already dead. They taste of ashes, they smell of death.

We are to have no children until he makes his mark, whatever that is. I cheat but nothing happens. Pray for me. My life seeps out like gas under the door of a suicide.

The farm is dead. Around the cistern, the flower pots are long since smashed or stolen, the earth spilled, the water green with algae. The coops and the cote are littered with decomposing feathers. In the bedrooms, the mattresses are bitten open, the cotton on the floor peppered with rat shit. The mirror reflects nothing.

But there is nowhere else to go. She has trodden every path, and everywhere met death. Yesterday she walked up to the beehives beyond Roussos'. Twenty terra cotta hives built into a stone wall, and all empty, spiders webbing the openings. "What happened to the bees?" she asked Roussos.

"A sickness, kyría. Five years ago. Didn't you know?"

"No," she said, "it's seven years since I lost my daughter. I noticed nothing."

When will I come? When will I come to you, Mána mou, our fields, our stones, our old friends? That it should depend on money, and on a man, drives me almost mad. Here there is money, money, money! You would gasp, agápi mou, you so happy with so little, if I told you what it's spent on: metals – gold, silver, steel (so much steel); certain bright stones to catch what little light there is; machines to do our work and leave us free to stare out the window at the walls of glass, glass which walls us in so the ones on the other side may see us but not hear our cries; clothes and clothes and clothes to keep us from a chill that has nothing to do with winter. And yet somehow there is never enough, and the mills and their manikins toil all night in a blaze of light, and he says, "Later, next year, when I've made my pile." Every day he carries enough in stones in his pockets to buy all the farms on the island, but somehow it is not enough even for a boat ticket.

I hold my head, remembering how little we lived on, how busy we were, our brown hands always busy, rubbing the green soap into our few clothes, spreading the sheets on the fragrant skinári, stripping the small blue olives, dropping apricots into a basket, raising the bucket from the deep, deep well. I remember the faded clothes we wore (here everything must look new) and the fierce beautiful chill of the wind, the blackness of night, and how we sat, silent, watching for hours no shadow on a screen but the moon, the real moon, red as a heart cut in two, rising huge behind the ragged black mountains.

Still it's not really money that drives him, but Time. Here Time means not stopping whatever you are doing: running, running, buying and selling. If you stop, you are dead, he says; someone else gets ahead of you. I remember another kind of time.

It is the trees that first call her back. They went unwatered so long, she thought they must be gone, but here a pistachio, there a pear, has put out new growth. Suckers only, but growth. She gets the saw and prunes them – not the right season, but it's so dry now it can't matter. And something must be done to fill these hands, still these restless feet.

Alone on the hilltop, alone but for lizards skittering over gravel, she feels a cool breeze, recalls Póppi, her daughter's friend, coming last week, showing off her small son, her new red car, driving them up a new road to the very top of Prophítis Ilías. "And up we went," she says to the lizards, to the *mandragóra*, "up the near-black mountain, beyond any villages, above ancient terraces and suddenly before us, under the indigo sky, whole faces of the mountain covered with broom, golden blooms thick on thorny green stalks, releasing into the high pure air such scent!" The air was pure fragrance, a joy to breathe, to stand still and breathe honey on the top of the world, looking down and out to the islands scattered around the blue-green sea. A place she'd never stood, and a joy to stand with her, Póppi the foolish, boy-crazy flirt now herself blooming quietly, ripened but blooming and the wide-eyed child, among the last blossoms, censed by the honeyed air.

Póppi asked her to stand godmother to the child on the way. She knows it's a girl. She talked of . . . her. "Ten years now," she said. "Will she ever come back?"

Back, dear mother? I doubt I could come back now. I have become almost accustomed to this semi-darkness, where night is never dark and day never bright, shadowed by smog. I go to the cinema with the others, and I, too, confuse the shadows with life, and life with shadows. I've grown used to the distances: meat invisibly killed, cut shapelessly, frozen; dried flowers ('How colorful!' I said the other day of a wreath of moribund roses, like something forgotten on a tomb); tasteless fruit from halfway round the world; letters.

I doubt I could do it now: gut a fish, eat an apple off the ground, follow an open casket. I am not sending you a picture; it would

*worry you how oddly I've cut my hair, but he says it makes me
look younger.*

Her hair, her beautiful dark hair, which I plaited every day of her life for fifteen years.

At the baptism, she thought she would cry a font of tears, but the baby, slick with oil and yelling, was so hard to hold safely, so needful of soothing, she forgot and laughed out loud. "Do you renounce the Devil and all his works?" the priest said, and "Yes, yes, " she said, "of course she does," but the little squirmer already had her mother's eyes, and come fifteen years the Devil would have his hands full.

The child is a comfort. Spends days at the farm, chases the chickens, pulls little fistfuls of flowers. Calls her "aunt." "Aunt, tell me a story." "Look, aunt, I found a dolly!" And she adopts the dolly as though it were born to her, and they make daisy chains together and knead bread, and she strokes the fine dark curls and waits for them to grow so she can brush and plait.

> *One day, in a gallery, staring at dead images painted by dead
> painters, I saw you, Mána. Seated, hands resting on knees, a
> dress with roses covered by an apron, an old-fashioned kerchief
> you never wore but your shape, your enormous dark eyes. The
> dead artist's dead mother. But it was you, Mána, alive! and I
> knew you, knew you alone were alive, alone could bring me
> back. I rushed home – home? To a hotel in a city stranger than
> most – and I flew at him. "Years," I screamed at him, "the best
> years of my life!" We have a bargain now: he's going somewhere –
> Africa maybe – some trouble in his mines. This time I will not follow,
> this time I will come. I will come. You will not know me, I am so old.*

She watches every day, standing on the hillside greening now with winter rains, with her tears of joy. She takes the lisping child and, holding the tiny hand, walks up the hill where the hives are once more buzzing, slowly in the chill, but full, their honey stored against the winter. And holding the child in her arms, telling her a story, watches for the taxi.

She will not be the same, I mustn't expect it. Fifteen years . . . a woman now, not the child who ran down to the beach on a day in May, her hair in a braid. Will it be cut, gray, gray like mine? Her eyes . . . what have they seen? What will I see in them? How will they see me?

She hears the crunching of the gravel on the road before the grinding of the motor. Shouldering the child, she descends the rocky path, treading carefully not to stumble, but around her every tree is scattering its golden leaves, every plant is shaking loose its seeds, every newly plowed field is censing the air with the fragrances of the earth.

The taxi stops at the bottom of the path. "Aunt," the child whispers in her ear, "who is coming in the taxi?" She can see the driver struggling with bags, ducking back to accept his fare, turning at the sound of pebbles rattling down the hill.

She emerges from the taxi. Her hair is cut and, yes, silver-streaked. She is thinner, paler, pale against the blackness of her dress, against which gleam cold gems. "Aunt," the child cries, "who is that lady?"

Squeezing behind his wheel, the driver calls, "Eh, Kyría Dímitra, your daughter's back!"

"My daughter," she murmurs to the child. "My daughter who was lost. Come greet her."

As Dímitra and the child approach, the dark woman's eyes are blank, black without irises, but in an instant they flood with light, the green of the wheat, the brown of the earth.

She is just the same. There is no strangeness. In a whirring of wings they are in each other's arms, all three of them, the hair of each tangling in the other's, the tears of one flooding the cheeks of the other. And who's to say where one ends and the other begins?

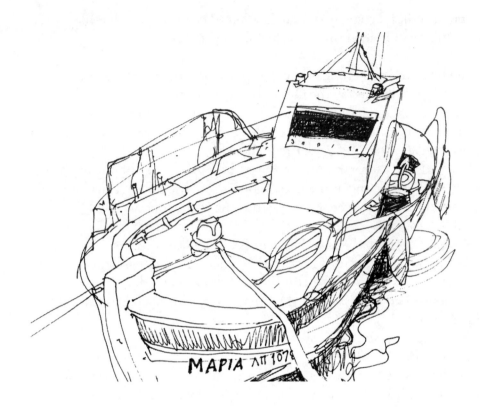

Bárba Stellios and the Mermaid
A Paramýthi

The old man was painting a boat. The small *kaíki* was resting upside down on weathered boards held up off the beach by piles of rocks. On an up-turned fish box, he had set a half-dozen rusty tin cans, a plastic bucket of casein medium, screws of newspaper holding powder pigment, a bunch of sticks, and three or four stumpy brushes caked with old paint.

The foreign woman was painting the same boat, or wanting to. It was to be her first venture in egg tempera, the famous medium of Byzantine painting, suggested to her by one of the other foreign artists she hung out with. She had a block of wood neatly surfaced with gesso, a plastic egg carton containing a dozen yolks, a varnished wooden box holding tubes of water pigments, a dozen sable brushes in various widths, and a folding easel.

As she was setting up the easel, the old man was bending over his fish box, shaking first cobalt blue and then emerald green pigment into a couple of cans, sloshing water from a bleach bottle into them, dribbling a little of each into the other, then following with a glop of medium and another sprinkle of red or yellow, and stirring all the messes with the same stick. He took the cans to the boat, and across a matte sky-blue hull he slopped first a slash of emerald, then one of bright light blue. He stood looking at them, covering up one eye and then the other. Finally, he turned around, showing he'd known she was there all the time, and said, raising his eyebrows, "*E lipón?*"

She was shifting from irritation to panic. She had sketched the boat yesterday and, to paint it today, had just spent half an hour setting up and cracking eggs. And here he had come, scrambling down the embankment by the bridge with his basket full of paints. Now he was not only blocking her view but was about to change the very color scheme that had inspired her in the first place. She must have looked miserable, because he grinned and, lifting his shoulders, twisted one hand, meaning, "What's up?"

He was a short, brown, weathered old man. You would say old because he had an untidy thatch of pure white hair on top of his sunburnt face, and because around startling light blue eyes there were lines etched as though onto copper. But his body was as lithe as an eel's, and his brown hands and bare feet, shiny as glace kid, were smooth and unknotted.

"I like the other blue, the *ouraní*," she said in halting Greek.

"*E*, but I've had her that way three years. 'I'm gonna change my song,'" he laughed, whistling a snatch of the song that says that. "What's it to you?"

She showed him the sketch. "The boat's so beautiful. I wanted to paint it, just as it is, in this light." The bottom of the tubby, saucy little boat was pure yellow to the water line, then sky blue with the double gunwale cypress green and orange. It stood on pale buff sand, and at just the right distance and proportion was a cream-cheese chapel whose blue dome –

"Your eggs are baking," he said, picking up her water bottle and squirting a few drops into each shell, laughing at her surprise. "Monastery," he said, tapping himself on the chest and chopping his hand off toward the mountain. "Monks up there, ikon painters. They almost got me!" He picked up her block of wood and looked at the sketch. " Okay," he said in English, then reverted to Greek, "*En táxi*. Today, I paint the bottom always yellow anyway. Tomorrow, the rest. But in the ikon, me! Stéllios! *Bárba Stéllios* now," ruffling the white hair. "Foreigners paint ikons, take photographs: Greek sea, Greek boats, Greek churches—no Greeks! You put Bárba Stéllios in the ikon with his boat. *En táxi?*"

"*En táxi!*" Oh, easy assumption of a bargain struck! They spent the rest of the morning on the hot, brilliant shore beside a demure sea, the artist painting Stéllios painting the boat, and Stéllios alternately slopping paint on the *kaíki*'s bottom and undertaking her artistic education.

"I hope that wood's old; otherwise, it's gonna split on you."

"It's old."

"What is that?"

"A shadow."

"Take it out."

"What?"

"It's a lie. Don't paint anything that's gonna change that quick."

"But . . ."

"You want that, take a photo."

Despite his promise, he started painting the hull dark blue. She protested, "Stéllios!"

He countered, "Church too small, and only the dome."

"That's all I can see from here."

"You lazy! Get up, go look! Church very important to Greeks. Make bigger."

"But perspective . . ." She couldn't say that in Greek, so she lost that round, too.

"Put in more houses. It's a village, not a desert island." She put in more houses.

"Good sea."

"Thanks."

"Pretty color, but no fishes, no octopus."

"But I can't see any fish!"

"You *know* they're in the sea, don't you?"

"Yes, but.."

"You foreigners! All eyes, no *nous*," tapping his brain. "Fishes. And some waves. Your sea looks like blue cement."

It was noon, the eggs were "baked," and anyway, egg tempera doesn't take much fooling with, so the painting was pretty much a mess. Exasperated, she packed up and left. Stéllios called after her, "Where are you staying?" but she didn't answer him.

Still, the next morning, as she was breakfasting in the harbor, he was sitting with a group of cronies. He waved to her and then came over. "You gonna paint today?"

"Yes," she said, hesitantly. And brought out the block, scraped clean and with a design penciled on it. "More church," she said, "and fish in the sea. And you painting the boat."

"Not bad," he said, after a bit. "But you need more going on. A priest at the church, people on the bridge. This is a village – *póly kósmos*, lots of people." And he left to go back to his cronies.

When she went to pay for her coffee and yoghurt, the *kafetzís* smiled and said, "Paid for. Bárba Stéllios." So now she was under an obligation she didn't understand. Perhaps that was why, despite irritation – who had been to art school and who hadn't? – she took her block home and sketched a scene: the beach, the boat, Stéllios, the church, the bridge with a couple of loafers hanging over the parapet and criticizing Stéllios. What had been a study in light and shadow had turned, she thought, into a cartoon.

But Stéllios almost approved. The next evening, although she had changed cafes, he found her. She had avoided the beach and harbor, working in the shade of the eucalyptus trees in the village park.

"Work on your ikon?" he inquired, sitting down and signaling for a coffee. He seemed in a mood and said nothing for a while. Reluctantly, she showed him the block. "Better," he said. "Still, it's not art. Painting, but not art." She was affronted by this so they sat in silence for a few minutes.

"There are no shadows," she said, angling for a compliment.

"This life," he said, "is a shadow. It passes. Some day . . ." He sucked in his coffee. "You know what is art in Greek?" he asked in English.

"*Téchni*," she said, proud of her vocabulary.

"*Tch*," he said, raising his eyebrows in that negative gesture. "Art is *zographikí*. *Zoí* means life. You gotta paint life."

The waiter came near and Stéllios flagged him. Then he got up to go, taking money from his pocket.

"No, please," she begged, "Please don't pay."

But he had already done so. Turning to go, he said, "Tomorrow, I'll take you to see real ikons. Harbor. *Proí-proí*."

The painter stowed her block and headed back to her room in the house of a lady named Marína and her husband Michális. She loved this room; it was a kind of salvation. After two years of saving and planning, including taking classes in Greek, she had come to Greece, as all artists do, for the light. The light was there, the kind, generous, ivory-colored light, and she painted what it illuminated: whitewashed walls with blue door-ways, fields of poppies, vineyards. These, watercolors mostly, were lovely, but so were all the watercolors of the other foreign artists – some nice, some loutish – who inhabited the cafes. Every night she would go back to her ugly cement-block *pensión* with a sense of loss, a sense that something, Greece itself perhaps, was eluding her. She was thinking about going home when she was approached one day in the market by a white-haired woman with amber eyes, wearing a pale gray *róba*, who had a small boy in tow. "Ask her in the foreign tongue if she wants to stay in your mother's old room," the grandmother said to the little boy, who was squirming with terror.

"Never mind, child," the foreigner said, "I speak Greek . . . some anyway." The old woman, Marína, was delighted, and the two women chattered as they walked to a house on the edge of town. When the visitor saw the room, with its ochre-painted floor, white iron bed, white cut-work curtains, and hand-woven bedspread – every surface elaborate with crochet and cross-stitch – she thought she'd finally found . . . if not all of Greece, at least a real part of it. Paper ikons and a *kandíli*, vigil lamp, guarded the bed's head, and tacked around the mirror were Christmas and Easter cards in which battleships and airplanes sailed through garlands of roses and ribbons held up by white doves, while the Panagía, the mother of Christ, hovered in the corners. Although she could see at a glance that the mattress was lumpy and sagged like a hammock, when she opened the double doors into a sunny garden full of fruit trees, she just said, "Sýmphoni," which was not quite the right word, but Marína understood. "I thought you'd like it," she said. "You're an artist."

Since Marína and Michális had gone to the country for a couple of days, she couldn't ask them about Stéllios nor how early in the morning was meant by proí-proí, so the next day she was at the harbor at seven-thirty. She sat around drinking Nescafe until ten, chatting with the fishermen, who exchanged bawdy looks when she inquired for Stéllios. "Bárba Stéllios, zoirós, E?" Much laughter.

Stealthily, she looked up "zoirós in her dictionary: lively. She was sure there was another meaning. When Stéllios finally showed up, he had a big key in his hand.

"Where were you? Lazy, sleep til ten. Foreigners! Come on!"

"Where're you taking that girl, Bárba?" called one of the fishermen.

"To church, loudmouth!" called the old man.

The church was a tiny chapel dedicated to St. John, about twenty feet long, with a barrel-vaulted ceiling only ten or twelve feet high. Walls and ceiling were covered with frescoes, some pale and flaking, some clumsily restored. The stories of the Bible stretched in panels, like comic strips, from wall to wall across the vault.

"Na!" Stéllios said. "Ikons! Real ikons! You see any boats without people, houses without people? See any shadows?"

She didn't. She stared and stared, at Jonah in the whale's mouth with the citizenry of Nineveh lined up at the dock to greet him, at Noah and the tiny ark bristling with creatures, at Jesus dragging his cross through serried ranks of Judeans. As Stéllios' finger pointed here and here, she saw, yes, fish and octopus and sea urchins in the sea, snakes in the earth, and birds in the air. And angels with two wings, with six wings, all in converse with people.

"Now that," Stéllios said, "is art."

"The fish," she said, "isn't big enough to swallow Jonah."

"But you know it did, said Stéllios.

"And the ark is too small for all those animals."

Stéllios huffed. "Small? It was big enough. You know that. You've got to paint what you know, not just what you see. These ikons . . ." he scratched his white head. "They talk to us, to people. They tell stories. Who cares about boat on beach with shadow? See that any day. But stories . . . they help us live." He pointed out more stories – Cain and Abel,

Ruth and her mother-in-law. "Stories," he said again. "Ikons more than art. They have *simasía*."

"Meaning?" she said. "They have meaning?" Not something she'd learned in art school.

As they left, he said, "What did you do with your ikon?"

"I'm working on it," she grudgingly admitted.

"*Kalá*," he said, and went off whistling.

Later that day she got the key from a neighbor and went back to the church for another look. She could see Stéllios' point: for instance, when Jonah arrived at the dock in Nineveh, probably there was no one around – a few dockworkers, a loafer or two, the customs inspector – to witness his emergence. But people in the millions, since Biblical times, have believed in the miracle of the god-forsaking man saved by a whale (or maybe a dolphin, though it looked more like a mullet). So these ranks of men on the dock, of women peeking out windows, were representing, say, themselves as they would be, after being changed by Jonah's words, and also their descendants in the succeeding millennia. It was a lot of weight for a six-inch square of plaster to carry.

She couldn't see exactly how these ikons related to her painting. But certain techniques she found charming, so the next day, reverting to her familiar acrylics, she repainted the scene: boat, Stéllios, houses, church, loafers, donkey, waves, fishes, octopus, sea urchins all outlined in various colors from vermilion to black. She rather liked it.

Stéllios liked it much better. "Pretty," he said. "Good fishes. But . . ."

"I know," she said testily. "Not art."

Stéllios shrugged. "You're still painting what you see," he said, "not what you know. *Nous*," he said, tapping his head. "Remember *nous*."

"What about my fishes?"

"Your octopus has seven legs."

In the next few days, she made several visits to the little church. "What am I looking for?" she wondered, trying to put herself into the place of the anonymous artist. "How his arms must have ached, painting over his head." And what was he painting? People, buildings, mountains, animals, sea creatures, waves. Stories. And . . . meaning? Something beyond . . .the invisible made visible?

Why did he paint? Why did she paint? And what was Stéllios' interest in her painting? *Zoí* . . .

She wandered around the village, away from the *platía* where the foreigners sat drinking retsína. She walked through all the back streets and up the three hills. She watched women washing clothes in the little river, was nearly knocked down by children racing home from school, saw a priest go sadly to toll the death knell, stepped around the golden nets of the fishermen spread out on the docks to dry, bought peaches from the *manávis* with the donkey.

A few days later she prepared a block, a much larger one (she had to use plywood), and began sketching a new painting. In the middle ground appeared the boat again, and Stéllios, and the church beyond, now with a priest pulling the bell rope. On the bridge above the beach was the *manávis*, with his donkey laden with vegetables and a housewife poking through the baskets. On the parapet leaned a couple of idle old granddads. Under the bridge, two women washed sheets in the river, while a couple of kids played marbles. Beyond them all, the white cubes of houses stair-stepped up a hill and, in the foreground, the blue sea teemed with fish, octopus, cuttlefish, sea urchins, and seaweed, above which a red *kaíki* cast its golden nets. She couldn't see all those things from where she had stood, so to get in all the people and animals and so forth, she had to give up on perspective and just crowd everything in. She wasn't sure what she had done, not sure what it meant, but it pleased her. She went off to market and bought another dozen eggs and settled to painting.

She hunted for Stéllios for several days before she found him, one morning, sitting in his usual place in the harbor. When she showed him the painting, warning him that it was not quite dry, he burst into a brilliant smile. "Now this this is art, Greek art. Only thing: you forgot the sun. But never mind." He called all his cronies to come and look.

"Zoí," he said to them. "Life, isn t it?"

"*Nai, nai, i zoí mas,*" each of them said, admiringly. "Our life."

"*Zoí mas,*" she said to herself.

The oldest of the cronies, a tiny bent old man with an enormous white mustache, pointed to the *kaíki*. "That's my grandson's boat. Only red one in the village. But," he said, squinting his eyes, "his masts are blue."

As she left the harbor, Stéllios called after her. "When our boats are dry, we'll go to Donkey Island to gather capers. You can give them to Marína."

"How did you know where I live?"

"This is a village. Everybody knows everything," he laughed. "Everything!"

That evening, she was invited to eat with Marína and Michális in their garden. The foreigner's duties as a tenant included dining occasionally with the old couple and reporting on her days. So that evening she dutifully said, "I'm going to gather capers with Bárba Stéllios."

"Which Stéllios?" Apparently it was a popular name in the village.

She brought out a charcoal sketch of him. "That one!" Michális exclaimed. "Her old lover!"

At which Marína giggled, "Yes, he loved me, but he was too old for me!" Marína was getting a pension, so Stéllios had to be at least seventy.

"You watch that one," she twirled her hand in a circle. "He's still *zoirós*!"

"And . . ." said Michális, tapping his head.

"Oh? How?"

"He's a vegetarian."

"And that's not all," added Marína, widening her amber eyes. "He talks," she whispered, "to dolphins."

"Sings," said Michális.

"Really?" The foreigner breathed.

"*E*," said Michális, "that's not unusual. Lots of fishermen whistle to the dolphins, and they come. They're the fisherman's greatest friend; they've saved many from drowning. But they're his greatest enemy, too; they leap in the nets, you see, when they're hungry, or just to tease, and there goes a whole day's catch, and an expensive net."

"But what Stéllios does," said Marína eagerly, "he sings them away from the nets. The fishermen know when they're going to cast the nets in the dolphins' waters – Philízi is one place – and Stéllios goes out in his little boat and sings to them, draws them *away* from the nets."

The foreigner couldn't tell if she were being put on or not. "What sort of songs do they like?"

"Sea chanteys, of course."

"Is Stéllios a fisherman then?"

"Well," said Michális. "He was . . .once. But then . . ."

"Then what?"

"Ah!" said Marína. "I will tell you the story, but first I'm going to get my spinning."

Michális pulled a pipe and tobacco out of his pocket. "Are you going to start, '*Red thread* . . .?'"

"No, because this is the truth. I heard it from his own lips."

Michális recited it anyway, the beginning of all *paramýthia*.

Red thread bound, on the spindle wound,
Kick the wheel to get the tale
A-spinning!

"This is no *paramýthi* but truth that I'm telling you. It was a long time ago, in the twenties I suppose, because we'd just had our first batch of refugees. I was a little girl, twelve maybe." Michális rolled his eyes. "Yes, twelve. Maybe fourteen. Stéllios was a young man, very handsome, small but, well, lively as I said. And with golden hair, and blue eyes. *Oraíos.*"

"Get on with it," said Michális. "Forget his blue eyes. Get to the mermaid."

"Mermaid?" the painter gasped.

"In my own time," said Marína, attaching a white fleece to a piece of cane and tucking it under her arm. "Where was I? Well, he was a fisherman, only a small boat, and of course nobody had engines then, *ohi*, only oars or sails. Now, most people, they fish in a group, usually a family, four or five boats, but Stéllios always went alone. He hadn't any family, only old Loukás, the coffin maker. Maybe because Loukás too had been a refugee from the first troubles in Asia Minor, he had adopted Stéllios. But Stéllios never liked making the coffins. When Loukás died, his was the last coffin the boy made. Then he built a little boat and went out fishing. From the first, he had phenomenal luck with octopus. He'd take his glass-bottomed bucket and his *kamáki*, trident, and what they use – some hooks and a piece of white cloth – on the days when the sea was calm, and he'd come back with twenty, twenty-five octopus. Soon, he was leaving the *kamáki* on the dock; he learned to just slip in the water, waggle a bit of cloth around the rocks, and grab the creatures with his hands. He fished only octopus at first, because he didn't have a woman to make nets for him."

"A woman?"

"*E amé*, then we made all the nets by hand, the women did, and we'd boil them in pine bark in big cauldrons. You know where? In the port, where Arghiró's grandson has that bar." She expressed her opinion of the bar by removing from her armpit the piece of cane holding the fleece, and scowling at it as though it were the grandson.

"*Lipón*," said Marína, continuing to spin white wool with a drop spindle. "Stéllios made enough money to buy nets, and out he went. His favorite place was out beyond the lighthouse. There he'd cast his nets, then go in near the rocks for octopus. Probably that's where he first met

343

the dolphins, because that's where they're seen the most, and probably he whistled to them, as many do, and being alone, he would sing as well. However it was, they never seemed to jump into his nets as they did into everyone else's."

"Luck," said Michális.

"What about the mermaid?" said the painter.

"Patience. Shall I make some coffee?"

"No," the visitor said quickly, "thanks."

"Broke my thread," said Marína, and the audience had to wait while she unraveled a bit and wound in the broken end.

"Well, he was doing all right, making ends meet, but not, with only his little boat and a bit of land Loukás had left him, making himself rich. He was, of course, looking for a wife, but he couldn't afford a poor one and the ones with dowries wouldn't look at him."

"There were many who more than looked," said Michális. "The *kape-tánisses*' delight, he was then. Wives of ships' officers," he explained, "poor lonely women!"

Marína tch'd. "Stéllios, though, unlike a dolphin, if he leapt in another man's nets, he was careful to leap out again without damage."

"*Les?*" said Michális, eyes twinkling. "What about that blue-eyed boy of . . ."

"Runs in the family," said Marína. "Her uncle Níkos had blue eyes."

"Go on."

"Well," said Marína, "one day and this he told me with his own lips – he had cast his nets out beyond the lighthouse. There was a pretty stiff *Voriás* blowing, so as soon as he cast the net, he headed back to haul it in. But, oh! heavy!! He pulls and strains, dreaming of a big catch, a ton of fish! He'll sell them, and treat all around at the *ouzerí*! Then he notices the dolphins swimming around close to the boat, leaping, poking their heads up. '*Gamóto!*' says he (I'm sorry to tell a foreigner that Stéllios curses, but it's the truth). 'I've netted a dolphin!' Away drain his hopes like fish escaping from a torn net. His new net is in shreds, a poor dolphin entangled, which is often their death. And he'd come to love them, never having suffered from their rowdiness. Well, he hauls up, hand over hand, and the net gets heavier and heavier, and the sea boils silver with little fish, and suddenly, towards the end, he sees a big tail thrashing among all the leaping *melanoúria, barboúnia . . .*"

"We don't need a fish catalogue," said Michális.

"Silence, husband! Now this tail – did I say it was a big tail? – was very strange, not a dolphin's, nor any fish he knew. It could be, maybe, one of those big *palamídes* they had in Asia Minor, because it was that sort: sleek and silvery. Whatever it was, it was going to finish his net. So before he hauls in the last bit, he ties up the net, strips off his clothes, and leaps in to have a look. Down he goes, and as he's coming up alongside the net, he opens his eyes, and what he sees almost makes him swallow the sea."

"The mermaid!"

"Indeed. And what do you think she looked like?"

"Why," said Michális, "we know what they look like: green tails, sometimes two, yellow hair, little pink breasts . . ."

"Tch. Not in the least. More fish than human, he said, a human head, with the almond-shaped dark eyes of a seal, and for hair, long diaphanous golden membranes, he said, like you see on tropical fish in the market in Athens. And from her arms, which were short and with webbed fingers, floated more membranes, like a *hánoum*'s veils. And as for breasts, she hadn't any, really, because, as he saw instantly, she was very young."

"Ten?"

"Not that young. *Lipón*, there she lay, jammed amongst panicked fish, drowning, and staring at him with huge, dark, pleading eyes. He burst up to the surface, very confused, *vévaia*. But, losing not a moment, he rolled into the boat, grabbed his knife, dived back in, and started immediately cutting his brand new net from around the membranes of her hair and hands that had caught between the layers."

"He must have had the lungs of a sponge diver," grunted Michális.

"Perhaps, for it took him at least a quarter of an hour to cut her out, and he only came up once, bringing her with him, still partly entangled, and she stuck her little nose just above the surface like a seal . . ."

"It probably *was* a seal, said Michális

"I think I'll just go put the beans in to soak." Marína put down the *róka* and rose from her chair.

"Sit down, sit down. I'm teasing you."

"You're still jealous. You know I only married you for your fortune."

"Hnh. Go on."

"*Lipón*. As soon as she was free, the mermaid gently wrapped one of her webbed hands around the boy and pulled him back down to where the destroyed net was floating in the sea, and panicky fish were darting this way and that, trying to escape. She swam to a little pink *barboúni*, snagged by the gills, gasping and wriggling. Stéllios cut it out, and it swam to the mermaid, darting in and out of her floating hair, like a kitten. She soothed and teased it. Then Stéllios felt a bump from behind, and *na!* there was a great dolphin, looking at him and smiling. The other dolphins were chasing after the fish, rumpusing, but just as one was opening his mouth to chomp a *melanoúri*, the mermaid turned her head and sang . . ."

"Sang?"

"*E*, made a sort of singing noise. The dolphin veered away, looking like a dog after the chickens being reprimanded by his master. Stéllios, having gotten the message, began removing the rest of the netted fish; some survived and some didn't. The mermaid was hovering all around, getting in his way. She looked sadly at the dead fish floating to the surface, but then she hummed, sang, or whatever to one of the dolphins, and they cleaned up the lot. Then she swam over to Stéllios and embraced him."

"Of course," said Michális, "he's now been underwater for half an hour."

"So he said. Anyway, he was embarrassed, being no cradle robber."

Michális again rolled his eyes heavenward but said nothing. "But it was just a friendly hug. Then the mermaid suggested they swim out to the rocks off the lighthouse, and talk."

"Talk? She could talk?"

"In a way, like the dolphins."

"*Etsi?* They can talk too?"

"Tsss! Doesn't it say so on the television?"

"That's true," the visitor interrupted, "scientists . . ."

"Never mind scientists," said Marína, putting down her spindle and sitting up straight. "Mermaids can talk because they are descended from the sister of Alexander the Great."

"So they speak Macedonian, no doubt." Michális, relighting his pipe, spoke in puffs out the corner of his mouth.

"They speak," Marína huffed, fire in her amber eyes, "Greek – pure, archaic Greek! Anyway, he rowed the boat to the rocks, and the mermaid with her *barboúnia* and the dolphins swam alongside, and they spent the whole day swimming and talking."

"Talking? So this *fantasía* isn't even a *románza?*"

"Sex!" she snorted, "Is that all you ever think about? Forget it. It's late and I'm sleepy."

"No, no," the visitor pleaded. "Please go on, Kyría Marína! What did they talk about?"

"E! Nobody ever knew! But from that day, Stéllios was a changed man."

"He gave up the *kapetánisses?*" Michális puffed on his pipe.

"Not *that* changed."

"Is that when he became a vegetarian?"

"No, that was later."

"When he went to the monastery?" the artist put in.

"What monastery?"

"Well, how changed? He stopped fishing?"

"Not really, but he stopped using a net, or a *paragádi*, you know, the line with many hooks."

"If he wasn't using nets, how did he catch anything?"

"His hands, or a *tsírtos*."

"A sort of wire basket," explained Michális. "Woven so the fish swim in – you put cheese or sardines in it and then they can't swim out.

"But Stéllios cut out the trap part, so the fish could swim out if they wanted to. Everybody thought he was crazy, but . . . he caught fish. He'd go out, always alone, and he'd come back with a catch, always a small one, very few fish but those the most valuable: lobsters, octopus, *barboúnia*, *scórpios*, *mougrí*, that sort. Never more than a handful of little bony ones, which he'd boil up for his own *kakaviá*. Soon the other fishermen began to be jealous of him. They watched him on the dock: day after day, a perfect catch. They spied on him at sea, and saw him not paying out nets and hauling them, all day and all night, like a proper fisherman, but swimming! Swimming everywhere! And wherever Stéllios was, there were the dolphins, leaping and smiling, playing around his boat or swimming in mid-channel towards Náxos."

"*A-de*! expostulated Michális. "You're as crazy as he is. No one can swim to Náxos."

"Crazy? In '23, thousands of people swam from Asia Minor to Sámos and Lésvos. And that's farther."

"*Télos pándon.*"

"Doesn't sound like he was making a living, though?" the artist ventured.

"He was doing all right. He'd started working Loukás' little land, but it wasn't enough to support a wife."

"So you took me instead," laughed Michális.

"Oh, Mr. Wide-acres! See," she said to the artist, woman to woman. "Fifty years ago and he's still jealous."

"And besides you were only twelve!" Michális brown eyes sparkled.

Marína was placidly mending another broken thread. "As I said, there was a lot of grumbling down at the dock. Stéllios was a foreigner, after all, a refugee. And a lot of our people resented them. In the *hóra*, the government had built houses for them, ones with tile roofs, which it had never done for us. They were very poor, having no lands, but many of them claimed to have been rich, and complained a lot. And then, many of them were, well, Oriental. Some women wore veils, even, and dressed gypsy-like. So there were whispers about magic and . . . stupid, of course, but then there was Stéllios, with his wonderful fish, like something out of a *paramýthi*."

"Which this is not?" Michális puffed on his pipe.

Marína inhaled sharply. "Are you going to let this foreigner go back to Nea Yorki or Londino or wherever she's from saying that Greek men don't let their wives speak in their own houses?" Silence from Michális, with a look like St. Sebastian full of arrows.

"Anyway, Stéllios goes down to the *limáni* one morning and his boat's sunk. He hauls it up quietly and mends it, then he's gone for a few days. When he comes back, he's empty-handed. I forgot to say that times were getting bad. We'd just lost a war, the government was squeezing us hard, and also there was a drought. One who was in a bad way was Battístas; he'd lost a brother and a leg in the war, was trying to support two families fishing, with a wooden leg and only a six-year-old kid to help. Well, one morning Stéllios stops by to help him empty his nets – almost nothing in them – and the next day Battístas goes out and comes back up to the boom in fish. 'Course, everybody else is spitting three times – *ftou, ftou, ftou* – over their shoulders to keep off the Eye, but nobody's really jealous because they pitied the poor old peg-leg. Then the same thing happens to this one, whose wife is dying from a new baby, and then to that one, who's also in trouble, and another, and so on.

"This was strange. Once in a while, there's been someone who was bad luck; if a fisherman caught him looking at his boat, he'd quick throw a knife into the mast but this was good luck. Of course, the greedy ones start to smarm up to Stéllios, but he's not having any. There was one family, they owned about five boats and the *psaropoúla* that took the fish to Athens. The only thing Stéllios would do for them was, he would go out in his own boat alongside them, and sing away the dolphins, if they took part of the catch to the refugees or other poor."

"What happened to the mermaid?"

"The mermaid? Well, I don't know. 'Bout that time, I cast my eyes on a certain person, and he finally made up his mind, so I stopped being able to talk to Stéllios. Things were different then. People watched a girl like hawks."

"How did you talk to him before, then?"

"There were ways."

"Do you think he ever saw the mermaid again?"

"*Lipón*. My uncle Damianós was out fishing by himself one day, off

Santa Maria, and he swears he saw Stéllios in a cove, diving in the water with a seal. Except that they, the fishermen, know all the seals – they even have names – and where they live. And there're none at Santa Maria. And no one has ever gotten close to one."

"You think it was the mermaid?"

"*Epísis*, in the summer, in the dark of the moon, Stéllios would make his torches and go out *pyrofáni* like everyone else does, to call the fish with light, but he always went, alone, to a place where everybody knew there were no fish. But my uncle Damianós . . ."

"Let me tell you," Michális broke in softly. "Her uncle Damianós would drink the sea thinking it was ouzo !"

"*Sópa!* Anyway, one dark still night (for *pyrofáni*, the sea must be like oil), my uncle's boat had drifted quite far from where he had started out. For some reason, he hadn't noticed – "

"The reason used to come in demijohns."

" – and suddenly he heard singing, beautiful singing coming from this cove – "

"By the time he finished telling about it at the *ouzerí*, there were three violins, two lutes, and a clarinet." Michális by this time was trying so hard not to laugh, tears were brimming in his eyes.

Marína paid him no attention, winding her thread into a ball. "And he swore, on the Panagía, that in the torchlight he saw Stéllios, naked, and a beautiful, shining woman, silvery and rosy like a *barboúni*, with golden hair like moonlight, sitting in the shallows and playing. And, flashing blue and silver in the torchlight, a whole school of dolphins! And the singing was not just Stéllios,' but a beautiful, high clear sound like a choir of angels."

"Not too long after, Uncle Damianós himself joined the angels, helped along by his liver."

"Oof! You do," said Marína, throwing him a venomous look, "love to destroy my stories!"

"Ah, my eyes, my gold, my heart!" said Michális, leaning toward her and grasping her hand. "From the day you took me, I have never wanted to hurt the smallest hair of your darling eyebrows!"

At that, they looked so fond, white hair and all, that the visitor thought she'd better go to her room.

The summer dawn was a wash of peach and pale gold. Stéllios' boat was painted and dry, and he was rowing it out of the harbor, standing up in the stern, holding the oars in his hands and guiding the tiller with his foot. He glanced down at the foreigner and smiled. "So you live at Marína's?"

"*Amé.*"

"Talk to you about me?"

"*Amé.*"

"*E, lipón?*"

"She told me you sing to dolphins."

"True. Many do."

"And that you're a vegetarian."

"Also true."

"And that you're friends with a mermaid."

"A mermaid?" he laughed. "Ah, ha, ha, ha! That Marína! Ha, ha, ha! She didn't, I suppose, tell you about my goat whose milk never stops flowing?"

"No."

"Nor about my granary that fed the entire village during the Occupation?"

"No."

"Nor how I married the *neraída* of the peach tree?"

"No. You tell me."

He laughed again, tears rimming his blue eyes. "Ah, Marína, Marinoúla!" He began to sing, words she couldn't catch except, occasionally, the name.

They had been sailing now for a while, the offshore wind spreading a faded, rust-red sail, angled on its gaff, across the brightening sky. Stéllios struck the sail and glided onto the rock of the island. She passed out the baskets for the capers, her sketching things, their lunch, and a couple of straw hats for the sun. Stéllios knotted the painter rope to an iron ring set in the rock.

The little island was a massive, tipped block of rosy-tan rock, worn, split, rising in tilted steps from fragmented boulders on the landward side to steep, sheer cliffs on the open sea. There the gulls nested, and here, from every crevice, sprang the exquisite caper bushes. Their long, lithe stems, grass-green and smooth as lacquer, arched up from the ground. Their leaves, oval and flat, were graduated along the stems like a necklace of jade beads strung on silk. The immense, fragile, watercolor flowers – white soft petals from which emerged long silken tufts of purple stamens – were fresh and upright now, just after dawn, but by afternoon they would droop and wilt into a forlorn tangle. Studded along the stems were the tiny oval buds they had come for.

"It seems a shame to pick the buds," the artist said. "They will never become flowers . . ."

"*E!* We take a few, here and there, we don't hurt the plant. The buds, well, we don't all have to have children!" Stéllios laughed.

They lined their baskets with leaves and picked for a while, Stéllios singing. Then they sat down to eat a little bread and cheese, and drink some of Stéllios' golden wine.

"I'll tell you about Marína."

"Yes?"

"When she was young . . ." Here he popped a raw caper into his mouth, and crunched it with white, strong teeth. "She was the most beautiful girl in the village. And very religious."

"Really?"

"*Vévaia!* She'd go, oh, twice a week to sweep out the little church of Ayí Anárghiri, you know, on the beach outside the village, down a path behind a clump of tamarisk? Such a clean little church! And Marína, always spinning, spinning, with the *róka* in her little hands. Spinning and talking and spinning ! Little Marinoúla!"

He laughed, pulling himself back to the present, the ruffled aquamarine sea, the rocks, the capers, the foreign woman. "You want to pick capers, or paint capers? Or paint me picking capers?"

She had brought water colors, thinking to capture the fragile caper blossoms. But she had another idea, an idea for an ikon. "I thought," she said, "I'd paint the mermaid."

Thanásis and Chernobyl

When Ingrid told him she was pregnant, Thanásis could only look down at the blue and white checked tablecloth, the loaf of bread he'd just brought in and set on the table. If he looked at her face, he saw in it too many emotions rearranging her eyes, mouth, and cheeks, changing the color of her skin. So he looked at the tablecloth, then up but away from her expectancy out the kitchen window to the street. The window was blue, too, with a square of white wall across the narrow street, and suddenly he felt his house – his own little house so dear to him – to be a prison.

He had to get out, go – do what? Talk – to whom? His friend Alíki, most likely. But he couldn't leave, couldn't just walk out, not until Ingrid and he had talked. But he couldn't talk. He could hear her talking, saying, over and over it seemed, the same words – September, job, Stockholm – followed by silence, a vacuum of silence.

Her silence was so wanting. The wanting filled the house. It drew in the walls, sealed off the doors and windows. No, he couldn't go out now, and it was hot in the kitchen, the oven on, both leaves of the door to the courtyard closed. She'd asked him to latch it, saying (with such intensity) that she had to talk to him, the minute he'd parked the motorbike and stepped into the courtyard. Puzzled, he'd laid the bread on the table, doused his head under the tap and scrubbed his hands, and was lighting a cigarette when she just blurted it out.

He felt he'd said nothing, but indeed a self he recognized (wearing the same sawdusted shorts, sweaty T-shirt, plastic sandals) had asked question after question: "How do you know? So soon? Are you sure?" She'd answered with a lot of details while he stared at the tablecloth and lit another cigarette and felt the ghosts of all the wanting of him move out of their tombs and back into the house, and his infant freedom open its mouth to scream.

This is what I imagine when I think about my friend Thanásis and the crisis in his life – in all our lives, since in Greece no one has a life utterly private from family or *paréa* – during the spring of Chernobyl, 1986. Chernobyl comes into it because Ingrid, Thanásis' Swedish *gómena* – something between girlfriend and lover – found she was pregnant in April of that year. During the weeks following the explosion, Ingrid was some of that time in Greece and some in Sweden. Both countries were irradiated by the same cloud, whose effects no one knew for sure and about which there were frightening and conflicting reports from every source. So, the whole issue of baby or no baby was clouded not only by the emotions of the two perhaps-lovers and probably a dozen other people, but by the terror that any decision, or advice affecting a decision, could result in tragedy.

Confounded and confused, Thanásis, after a strained and largely silent dinner, left Ingrid and walked up to the hotel to talk to Alíki. Spirit of the *paréa*, *bon vivant* she might be, but Alíki was also bedrock practical. Whenever any of the *paréa* was mired in a problem, a talk with Alíki would set him or her on the right track.

There were guests in the hotel lounge, so Alíki took him out to the balcony over the sea, poured him an ouzo, brought him a little dish of olives, and then sat quietly as he talked. When he finished, she asked him one or two questions, and then came down immediately and definitely on the side of abortion. Unconventional in some ways and liberated in others, Alíki was Greek to the core in the matter of children: you don't have them unless you have a strong, loving, and supportive family. Alíki had been married then for two years after being engaged for three, and she had been trying for a year to get pregnant, disappointed and anxious month after month. And here was this "on-again-off-again, boiled-squash of a *gómena*," as she called Ingrid, pregnant and clearly wanting Thanásis to get married and make a happy little family. Alíki was indignant.

"She wants him to marry her," she said to me a day or two later, when I dropped by the hotel on my way into the village from the country. "It's nonsense! They hardly know each other. Besides, how many times has he said he's never going to get married?" We were folding towels in the linen closet of the hotel, a place we could be private.

"Dozens," I answered.

"And how does she imagine he can support her? He can barely support himself," she said, as she stacked a pile of towels on a trolley.

This was certainly true. Although he had recently been able to buy, on time, the carpenter shop he had worked in since he was a youth, Thanásis never had a drach to spare. He was always sought after by builders or friends for special jobs—a round window or a carved door, or the furniture he preferred to make: dowry wardrobes, beds, and sofas. But the money for the time put in was a pittance. The lucrative jobs were the standard doors and windows he disliked cranking out. And in fact such jobs rarely came his way, partly because his equipment was old and liable to breakdowns. If he had married a village girl, she would have come with a dowry, a house or a shop, or even a job. Ingrid held an important and well-paid position in the Swedish government arts organization, but there would be little she could do in the village to earn money—give English and German lessons maybe, hardly a substitute for a career.

"So, what do you think?" Alíki asked me, blue eyes snapping.

"I think," I said, "I ought to go talk to Ingrid. She's all alone here."

"Well, talk some sense into her." Alíki pushed the linen trolley out of the closet and locked the door.

"I'm not taking sides," I said. "I just think there are things she ought to know about Thanásis, things he might not have thought to tell her."

"Like what?"

"Like about his parents."

"His parents? What does that have to do with anything?" Alíki said, puzzled.

"Everything," I said.

For over ten years, Thanásis had cared for his elderly, invalid parents, rushing home from his carpentry shop several times a day to cook, spoon feed, clean up, and launder (by hand) soiled sheets and nightclothes for, first, his mother, dying from kidney cancer, and then—with a brief respite—for his father, paralyzed by a stroke. All those years he had been devoted, uncomplaining, and competent. But the care had taken its toll. After he buried his father, he was finally able to live a quiet bachelor life. And, yes, as Alíki said, he had reiterated many times, sincerely and firmly, that that was the way he wanted to live—single, alone in his house.

Thanásis' house was precious to him. He had been born in it, the youngest (by ten years) of four brothers, and it was his only inheritance from his parents – from his mother really. Most of the houses in the village were owned by women and passed, usually, from mother to daughter. The older brothers, as strikingly handsome – well built and with strong features – as Thanásis himself, had not grumbled much at his inheriting the small family home. They had all married women with houses of their own. Also, it looked increasingly like Thanásis would not marry and the house would sooner or later pass to one of his several nieces.

Since he had inherited the house, Thanásis had worked very hard to repair and improve it. He had a strong feeling for Greek tradition and did not, as many villagers did, destroy the beauty of the old house with "modernization." The new windows and doors he made were copies of the old ones: small shuttered windows, two- and three-leafed doors with hand-forged metal hinges and handles. The new woodwork was painted the same color as the old: a medium blue. "When you're next to the sea," he said once, "the color should be blue. Green is for the country."

"And red?" I asked. "On Ios they paint the woodwork red."

"No taste," Thanásis said firmly.

The walls of the *avli*, the courtyard, he built up with stone just enough to give a little privacy from passing tourists without cutting himself off from neighbors. Over the entrance, he raised a stone arch around which he trained a brilliant purple bougainvillea. Religiously, once a week, he whitewashed the joints of the slate flags in the street and an outcropping of rock opposite, and, the week before Good Friday, as is the custom, he whitewashed the entire house, inside and out. When others began to use a chemical substitute for whitewash, Thanásis continued to use the real stuff, applying it so thickly that the edges of the street curved into the house. It became the most photographed house in the village. "Just think," he said to me one evening, as tourists clicked away outside, "there are pictures of my house all over the world!"

Thanásis' traditionalism was conscious and not confined to architecture. He treasured every Greek custom, pagan or Christian. Each New Year's his door boasted a sea squill bulb, each May a wreath of flowers. He hired as a sometime housekeeper the most slovenly woman in the village because she was a *podáriko*, that is, she was always the first to set foot (*pódi*) in his house on the first of every month and, according to tradition, brought in a stone and a glass of water, all of which was supposed to bring him luck. Though not particularly pious, he still visited all the village churches on their festivals, especially the little chapel of Ayía Ekaterína on his mother's name day. He never missed walking up the mountain on the autumn festival of *Taxiarchón*, when the monks of Longovárdas chanted the liturgy so beautifully in the empty chapel of a deserted monastery.

Thanásis' house was important to him not only because it was his inheritance, but because it was the *stékki* of the *paréa*. It may have come to be the meeting place of the *paréa* when he was housebound, caring for his parents. In any case, the house was fairly central, and there were no children or (after his last parent died) old people to disturb or be disturbed. After work the friends would check in, sit around the kitchen table, maybe drink an ouzo or a beer, nibble a *mezé* or two, and make plans for the evening. They might decide to go for a walk, take a taxi to a *taverna* in another village, or just amble down to the harbor for an ouzo. Many times indecision would win and they would just hang out in the kitchen and watch television or play cards. In the summer, the kitchen was too hot to sit in, especially if anything were cooking, so the *stékki* moved to the *avli*, cooled by sea breeze, shaded by a chinaberry tree in the day, dark and sweet at night, open to the street. The friends would sit there in the dark, drinking, eating, greeting passers-by.

When Thanásis and Ingrid first got together in the summer before Chernobyl, that is where and how they would spend their evenings, with or without company, sitting outside in the dark or moonlit courtyard, eating leisurely dinners, drinking wine and talking. As the neighbors passed, maybe taking the kids to the *platía* for ice cream or returning home late after closing a shop, the greetings would flow out of the dark: *"Kalispéra! Kalispéra sas!"*

If Alíki was the life force of the *paréa*, Thanásis was its still center, what held it together. *Paréas* are almost lifelong associations, but they do change with marriage. As the years passed, one and then another of Thanásis' friends married, and although they remained friends, with children and spouses to care for, they had little time to spend idling and drinking with the singles. There is a saying in Greece that if a man isn't married by the age of thirty-three (the age at which Christ died), he should go to a monastery. What women of that age do is not even mentioned. By the time Thanásis was in his mid-thirties, the *paréa* was considerably diminished.

However, as tourism increased in the village, Greeks from other areas began to arrive and open shops. Chrístos, an Athenian architect, and his partner Tom opened a boutique and then the first fashionable restaurant in the village. Both Katínas went to work for Chrístos and introduced him and Tom to the *paréa*. Truman came back from Athens and opened a shop. About this time, Thanásis began to do some remodeling on the old family house of Násos, a successful dentist who had been born in the village but lived in Athens. In the course of the work, Thanásis and the rest of the *paréa* got to know the hospitable Násos and the friends he often entertained. Both Chrístos and Násos recognized and encouraged Thanásis' nascent aesthetic sense, which was beginning to show itself in what he was doing on his own house. And so the *paréa* expanded again.

Once Thanásis recovered from his grief and exhaustion after his parents' deaths, in his early thirties, he began to have summer affairs with tourist women. European, especially Scandinavian, women were descending upon the village in increasing numbers, looking for sun and love for their summer holidays. Thanásis' quiet bachelor life was brightened and in no way threatened by these casual affairs. Since many in the *paréa* were now working in restaurants, bars, and other tourist establishments, he was often without company in the summer evenings until the workers could close up shop or restaurant – often after midnight – and join him for late-night drinks. He would usually offer hospitality to the *petite amie* of the moment, sharing with her not only his bed but the homely pleasures of his excellent cooking and his lovely courtyard. And sometimes, on a temporary basis, the company of his *paréa*.

When the European women first began to come to the village seeking summer lovers (within the limits of their round-trip tickets), the young men did not, as it might seem, swarm to taste this honey. Although invisible to tourists, the villagers have more eyes than Argus. Goings-on would be spotted by this sweet baker or that *pensión* maid and relayed to the mothers or fathers either of the young men or of the marriageable girls – who, strange as it may seem, held the high cards in the wedding game. Reports of a young man's promiscuity could easily nip in the bud a possible marriage–and marriage, according to village ethos, was the only way to live.

Thanásis, however, was in many ways the perfect Greek lover; he had no parents to worry and no intentions of marrying, and on top of that, he lived alone in a very charming, very Greek house by the sea. When he did take a *gómena*, either the *paréa* would include her or Thanásis would separate from his friends for the duration of the affair, usually two weeks. The members were willing to accept Thanásis' fooling around with tourist women in the summertime – when the village was flooded with exoticism of all kinds – as long as he returned to his character as bachelor-host-to-all in the winter, when the village reverted to its own character, and *paréas* that had been split or enlarged by the inclusion of off-island relatives or foreigners contracted again, became native.

Ingrid, although single and typically Scandinavian – tall, slender, and flaxen-haired – was not really one of the sun-and-sex brigade. She had come to the island with friends, a couple and their baby. I don't know how she and Thanásis met – perhaps swimming off the rocks at Ai Yiánnis, perhaps in a bar, maybe in the somewhat rickety outdoor theater where we sat on droopy canvas seats and watched movies too new to be old and too old to be new. At any rate, they met and began to keep company. She moved into his house and, after a week or so, extended her vacation a couple of weeks. But at the end of August she left. Summer came to a close, and the village threw away the sun tan oil, shut down the travel agencies, moved the kids back into their bedrooms, and got down to work--its own ordinary, rightful work – once more.

But, it seems, summer wasn't exactly over for Ingrid, or for Thanásis. During the autumn they talked weekly on the telephone. How did they communicate? Ingrid spoke a little Greek and Thanásis had by this time picked up some very elemental English. Somehow, the conversations led to her coming to the island for Christmas. That is when I met her.

In the winter of 1986, I was back in the village. I had a Fulbright that year, but after spending four miserable months in an expensive, unfriendly town in Crete, where all the books of the new university's library were still in boxes and where there was for me no *paréa* – no one to eat with or talk to, no one to even have coffee with – in a fit of homesickness I had bought all the books I needed, packed up my computer, and returned to Náousa. There, people leaned out of stores to shout, "*Yia sou! Kalós ilthas!*" There, people were dancing and singing in the *tavernas* and *ouzerís*. And there, for the first week at least, every coffee or ouzo I drank was quietly paid for by someone – a farmer I'd harvested for, a fisherman whose child I had taught. The old friends, now grown older but only a little more sober, welcomed me back in that casual way the Greeks have that makes it seem you left only the day before yesterday and are not likely to leave again, so making a fuss is superfluous, because what is important is that you are here now.

I was delighted that Thanásis had a girlfriend, and I liked Ingrid immediately. Not that she was particularly charismatic; in fact, she was quiet, intelligent, and mature, in her late thirties. A university graduate, she spoke seven European languages and worked in the film section of the Swedish national arts organization, all of which made for common ground with us. If I was surprised or dismayed in any way about the relationship, it was by the very fact of her intelligence and competence – and by the fact that they were getting along so well. They were not visibly "in love," with public petting and cooing; they were simply comfortable together, happy but not euphoric. To me that meant the relationship was real and that it would demand a future, which would be difficult if not impossible. No man from the village had yet married a foreigner, and, as I knew myself, no woman used to an intellectual life and professional work could survive there for long.

Such marriages would happen eventually. As tourism increased, as Greece became a full partner in the European Economic Community, more and more off-islanders – natives who had emigrated to Sydney and New Jersey, non-native shopkeepers and artisans from Athens and Germany, retirees from all over the world – would come and settle, bringing with them habits of thought along with business acumen, and they would create as it were a miniature, cosmopolitan, middle-class world. As the village grew, a middle school and a high school would be built, and the teachers – some native, some not – created, along with the teachers of the private language schools that sprang up, an intellectual world within the new bourgeois one.

But that had not yet happened.

When Ingrid returned to the village for several weeks at Christmas, the members of the *paréa* were nervous. When she returned for *Pásca*, some of them – Truman and Katína – were, not to put too fine a point on it, furious.

The *paratsoúkli* or nickname of one of the Katínas was the *Mouní*, which does not translate well into English, which has no neutral colloquial words for the pudenda, so "cunt" is too harsh and "pussy" too cute. The irony of the nickname was that, already at thirty-some, Katína was pretty definitely a y*erondokóri* or "old maid." She'd taken to doing little housekeeping jobs for Thanásis – his laundry and occasional shopping or cooking. He accepted it as kindness offered, appreciated it certainly, although he had for over twenty years managed on his own, doing all the cooking, cleaning, shopping, and washing. So I wondered whether Katína's anger at the reappearance of Ingrid in the "real time" shattered an illusion she'd created to protect herself: that Thanásis was unmarriageable for her or any woman. The *Mouní's* anger broke through one night shortly after Ingrid arrived, when she and Tom had been drinking (and no doubt gossiping) and had decided at one in the morning to wake up Thanásis and get him to make them coffee.

Midnight visits were not unusual in the village. I'd been hauled out of bed in the wee hours many times to make coffee for friends who desired to both sober up and share with me the last of their high spirits. But Katína, not to mention Tom, knew enough about Northern Europeans to realize that Ingrid would not greet them – as Thanásis would have normally – laughing and cursing at the same time, groping for cigarettes and putting the *bríki* on to boil. And they didn't, as many of my callers did, bring a song, perhaps rehearsed over and over in the snugness of the *ouzerí*, but instead a madness about the laundry.

Once into the house, whose doors were never locked, Katína – with Tom standing by, laughing helplessly – began yelling about dirty underwear and misfolded sheets. Then storming past Thanásis, who was heading sleepily for the coffee cupboard, she burst into the bedroom and began ripping open drawers and wardrobes, throwing shirts and bras and pillowcases on the floor. Thanásis stopped in his tracks. Ingrid cowered in bed, naked under the blanket. He got rid of them somehow. But they left behind an emotional chaos greater than the scattered clothes.

If Katína had been furious at Thanásis for taking a lover, Truman seemed to have been driven mad by the news of the pregnancy. As I've said, Truman's place in the *paréa* was tenuous. He had a tendency to pick fights with people, once throwing some tourists out of his shop for claiming he'd copied his paintings from postcards. (He hadn't; they just looked like copies.) Only his childhood relationship to Thanásis, and Thanásis' tolerance of him, allowed him a place in the *paréa*. Many times the others would get sick of him and want to shun him, but Thanásis always stood up for him. Thanásis' sudden acquisition of a steady winter girlfriend, and then the alarming possibility of a marriage, threatened Truman's already shaky social acceptance. Truman expressed his fury, or perhaps terror, in a bizarre way.

Thanásis' house, built out over the rocks of the secondary bay of the village, had only a wooden floor between the *salóni* and the *apothíki* or storeroom below, which itself was closed more or less by a wooden door rotting and falling off its hinges. The planks of the floor had shrunk with age and, through the gaps in the *apothíki* door, sea-light and occasionally the sea itself penetrated into the *salóni*. A few days after the news of the pregnancy ran like wildfire throughout the *paréa*, Truman went into the *apothíki* under Thanásis' *salóni* and shat. Shat what must have been an incredible amount. Perhaps he had planned this protest and saved up his shit for days. With this ordure, Truman plastered the underside of the *salóni* floor, forcing the mess up into the cracks between the planks. Ingrid must have been out while this singular protest was in process, but when Thanásis returned from work, he found her sitting in the courtyard crying. She could hardly tell him what had happened, just choked out "*salóni*" and retched. Thanásis opened the door and reeled. The stink was . . . there are no words for what it was like. He stood as though paralyzed, overcome with grief.

When Thanásis had gone to lay his troubles at Alíki's feet, he had been confused. Alíki was adamant that Ingrid had to abort, and quickly, as she was already more than three months along. Alíki telephoned immediately to a doctor friend in Athens and actually made an appointment. At that time, Thanásis felt she was right: Ingrid must have an abortion. He would put it to her forcefully but kindly.

Yet something about Truman's scatological attack challenged Thanásis. Not being Greek, that is, having some compunctions about involving myself in people's private business, I delayed going to see Ingrid for a couple of days, but then I ran into Thanásis in the *platía*, and we sat down for a coffee. He was still undecided about what to do but in some way clearer about his feelings. He cared for her, he said; he just didn't want to get married – to anyone. Then he told me first about Truman's attack, which stunned me, and then, as he was leaving to go back to work, about

Chernobyl. "Some nuclear plant in the Ukraine blew up. Made a big cloud of chemicals. You know where the Ukraine is?" he asked.

I was vague. "North, I think. Pretty far away."

"They say the cloud is drifting west."

"Towards Greece?"

"Can't think so. This time of year, all our weather comes from the south and west," Thanásis said. Since it hadn't crossed my mind that Greece would be in any danger, I was not so much relieved as puzzled.

I went off to see Ingrid.

Although Thanásis had told me about Truman's assault, I hadn't really taken it in. But when I arrived at the house, I found Ingrid sitting in the *avli*. Thanásis had sealed off the interior and exterior doors with plastic sheet but the stink was still palpable. We could smell it even outside where, despite the chilly spring weather, they were spending most of their time.

"Thanásis says there's nothing to be done until the hot weather comes and dries the *scatá* enough for it to be chipped away," Ingrid said, "a task he's not looking forward to. Let's go for a walk." We headed out of the village along the sea and she talked, haltingly at first, more strongly as she found her voice.

Ingrid was one of those slender women who often skip periods, so when she went to the village clinic, she said, she thought her slight morning nausea was the usual adjustment to island water. She was impatient when the nurse-midwife, wiser than she, ordered a pregnancy test, but when the test was positive, she was, of course, in a very basic way thrilled. Nearly forty, and for some years without a partner, she had long ago given up on becoming a mother, given up on even thinking about it, how a child would impact her life. And suddenly here was the answer to a long-forgotten prayer.

Dazed, she left the clinic and kept walking, through the village, along the sea, and into the country, out towards the farms of Ksifára and Lággeri, where in the summer she and Thanásis had walked to go swimming. Then the land was completely arid; the sea dominated their every thought and desire. Now it was April, nearly May. Every field, every roadside, indeed every crack in the flagstones of the village streets was exploding with life. In the narrow lanes, patches of chamomile sprang up from pockets of soil a child could cup in her hand. Out in the country, new wheat was thrusting up though fields of blood-red poppies. Along the edges of the rough road bordering the sea, lupines, sea lavender, and fennel blossomed, rising from soil even now so hard-baked it was impossible to imagine from what source it found water. In the pastures calves nursed greedily, while lambs and kids leapt the stone walls only to be called back by the bleats of their mothers. In the orchards tiny green lemons sprouted among the fragrant blossoms.

And she, Ingrid, was pregnant.

Ingrid had been on the island in the summer, and summer had been an idyll – the sun, the sea bathing, the wonderful food, the happy drunkenness, the love in Thanásis' large bed with the gentle waves swishing outside the window. And then she had come in winter, and winter was different. The village seemed much smaller, the people friendlier and yet more alien. Surprisingly, to a Swede, it was cold. But she and Thanásis had stayed close in the small house; they cooked, talked, ate, drank, made love. Friends came by . . . well, she thought they were friends . . .

And now she was here in the spring, and nothing had prepared her for this explosion of fecundity. She sat on a stone wall and gazed at the sea – a demure sea, calm and sweet, neither the dazzling sea of summer nor the cold, intimidating one of winter. And for a while she thought about nothing – just sat quietly at the center of all this fertility, fertile herself, finally fulfilling the promise all women are born with. She was so full of awe, of wonder at herself, that for a long time she did not even think about Thanásis.

At the end of the road, at a place they used to swim, she turned back. And only then, returning, stooping to gather a bouquet of flowers for the kitchen table, did she start to think what Thanásis would say, what he would do, what he would feel. She found she could not even guess—they had after all, known each other for (unless you count telephone calls) cumulatively less than two months. And so, for knowledge, she substituted hope.

I'm trying to keep the dates straight. *Pásca* was the fourth of May that year; the meltdown at Chernobyl was on the twenty-sixth of April, but we didn't hear much about it for a while. The cloud of cesium 137 and strontium 90, drifting west and south, did not reach Greece until May first, which that year was Holy Thursday. It should have been May Day, when usually we would go out to someone's country house to plait wreaths of flowers, eat, drink, and dance, but I can't remember whether we celebrated or not, or whether the lack of celebration was because of the holiness of the day – the day before Christ's crucifixion and a severe fast – or whether it was because the *paréa* was split into factions over the pregnancy issue, or simply because everyone in the village was in a panic.

The news of the explosion had been announced on the radio the day after it happened, but it was a couple of days before we learned about the magnitude of it – a hundred times greater than Hiroshima, the scientists ultimately decided – and another day or two before we heard that the cloud of radioactive debris was headed for Greece. The announcements from the government, as I remember, reflected the general confusion. The cloud was headed west; the cloud was headed south. We should stay inside or cover up; no, covering up wouldn't protect us. Foods were safe; foods were not safe. This last was true, or true for a while: the dust, by this time, was falling onto fields where plants were growing and animals were grazing. It was, they said, nothing you could wash off. When the animals ingested this dust, the cesium, strontium, ruthenium, and radioactive iodine did not break down but passed into the animal's flesh and milk. There was a run on Noúnou, the popular canned milk; supplies in the village were exhausted mere hours after the government advised mothers to neither breast-feed their infants nor feed their children fresh milk.

What were we to do? What were we to eat or not eat, with a great feast coming up in days after six weeks of fast? What of the spring lambs set aside for *Pásca*? They were being fed on milk – was it contaminated milk? What of the farmers? Could they sell their peas and lettuces? How about the yoghurt and cheeses being made from the freshened cows and goats? The orchards were filled with budding fruits. Would they be edible? Saleable? At this time, very little food was imported from other countries, and those were nearby, Israel primarily. Would the cloud extend to the southern islands, to Israel?

I don't remember what we did. I remember the doubts, some fear, much denial. Such a thing could not happen, or, something so far away – Russia, for heaven's sake – could not affect us. Even when instructions came down from the government, many did not believe them. (In Greece, hardly anybody ever believes what the government says anyway.) Even when the farmers were prohibited from selling milk and cheese made during the days the dust fell, many did not believe they could be poisoned.

Those who did believe, and who panicked – rightly, as it turned out – were pregnant women. I cannot be sure, but I think one or two I knew quietly went to Athens and aborted within weeks of the contamination. They were not alone: all over Europe women afraid of the effects of radiation on their unborn children terminated pregnancies. Their entirely intuitive fear – who knew in those days exactly how a fetus could be affected, that the radiation would be found to alter DNA? – was many years after justified by high rates of childhood leukemia, of thyroid cancer, of children born without limbs and brains.

And yet, fifteen years later some reports denied any effects at all beyond the immediate neighborhood of the meltdown.

What I discerned that day Ingrid and I talked was confusion, her lovely hope spoiled by Thanásis' dismay and his ambivalence. I told her what I meant to, about Thanásis and his parents, and she took it with, I thought, understanding. Her own mother, she said, was crippled with rheumatoid arthritis. She spoke of the effect it had had on her own life. When we returned to the house to make coffee, I asked, "What would *you* like to do?"

"I think," she said thoughtfully as she measured coffee into the Melita she had brought with her from Sweden, "have a baby. Look after it. Live with Thanásis."

"Where?"

"Here, or at home in Stockholm."

"What does Thanásis say to that?"

"He doesn't say anything."

"Do you want to marry him?"

"I don't know."

I tried to speak as gently as possible. "Ingrid, this isn't Sweden or the States. It's a tiny, unsophisticated island village. To not marry would be a scandal here. People would shun you. Thanásis' family wouldn't take it kindly." *Whew*, I thought. *The sisters-in-law would descend on Thanásis like wolves on the fold. His aunt Eléni, his mother's sister, not known for a pleasant temperament, would scavenge the carcass.* I tried another tack. "Do you love him – love him as a husband? "

She turned and looked at me. "It's more than in love," she answered surely. "More than a summer romance. I knew that." She dumped the filter, poured out two cups and asked, "What does he want? Did he say?" Her long, pale hands wrapped around the cup. "Pity you can't get cream here."

"No," I said, "they don't use cream in coffee or in anything else. Probably they make cheese out of it." I took a deep breath. "Ingrid, what are your options? If you don't get an abortion, what will you do? How will you raise a child?"

She hadn't thought much about it, she said, but as she mulled it over, it seemed that something in her head or heart had been doing some private thinking. She had sometime realized that a house in Greece with a handsome carpenter, a mommy and daddy and baby, might not be in the stars. She could support a child, she said. She had savings and income from an inheritance, would get maternity leave from her job, had friends and a mother who would rally round. Of these she was sure, and sure as well that her heart was breaking. She was not a woman who just wanted a child, who had used a man to get one, but a woman who all her life had longed for a soul mate. She thought that in Thanásis she had found him, was at least finding him . . . and now, that which should be a symbol of that finding, the treasure at the end of the journey, was tearing them apart with the journey barely begun. And yet, she was nearly forty, her own journey half over.

After listening to her, I took a deep breath and said, "Ingrid, I think you should leave the island. Too many people here are in your business. Go home where you have friends and family. Talk to them. If, in the end, you decide to have an abortion, it's better to have it in Sweden. Here, you'd have to go to Athens and then come back, and if there were an infection, you'd be eight hours from competent care." She shuddered, but for what reason I wasn't sure. "What's important is that you make this decision on your own, without any Katínas and Trumans and old ladies, including me, poking their noses in." She sighed.

I added, "But one thing I feel I have to say: don't depend on making a family with Thanásis. I've known him for a long time, off and on. I would trust him to do the best, most honorable thing possible, but not anything against his nature."

And so, days before *Pásca*, on the day after the radioactive cloud reached Greece, Ingrid flew through it back to Sweden. My well-meant advice had sent her right into the densest cloud of radiation in history. It was symptomatic of our general confusion about the threat that I hadn't even considered the danger, either to her or to her unborn child.

The *paréa*, on the other hand, sighed with relief. "She'll get an abortion and poor old Thanásis will be off the hook. And we'll never see the bitch again," said the Mouní.

Strangely, I don't remember anything about where I celebrated that *Pásca*. I remember from previous years going up to the church at night with my candle and my red egg, gift of a neighbor, in my pocket; I remember the crowded street, abuzz with gossip and horseplay; I remember the children, boys mostly, waiting impatiently to explode their firecrackers, burn the Ioúdas, and smash their red eggs together. Do I remember that it was chilly or that it rained? No, I never knew it to rain on *Pásca*, though often a few days before. But it did rain then: the rain passed through the cloud and washed all the radioactive elements into the soil, the stony but

fertile soil that is the skin, the life, of Greece. And though I cannot remember where I went after the cries of "Christ is risen!" and the thousand
candle flames flooding down the street, where I went to eat *mayirítsa* or,
the next day, to eat lamb, I do remember that the day was not so exuberant
as other *Páscas*, that people were quieter, as though avoiding the subject
of what was happening to us, trying to concentrate on the idea of the
Resurrection, of the return of spring.

That year, as though to echo our worry and sorrow, there was no celebration of the *Zoodóhos Pigí*. I had arrived in the village just in time to
attend the forty-day memorial for Panayiótis, and there I learned that
Styllianí had also passed away in my absence. So that year, with the young
couple in mourning, there was no *panigýri*, which might have lightened
the heaviness of the atmosphere. A week or so later, I went out to Lággeri
to swim and stopped by to pay my respects. It was late afternoon, and
the children, whom I had wanted to see, were still asleep, but Lélla and
Aristídis were sitting in the *avli*, once the domain of old Styllianí, where
she would sit cutting up vegetable scraps for her chickens. Behind the
couple were stacked dozens and dozens of their round *mizíthra* cheeses. The
cheeses, famous all over the island, were their most important source of
cash. And now . . . "The government says we can't sell them," explained
Aristídis mournfully.

Lélla added, "Now's the time the cows are giving the most milk. What
are we to do? They must be milked, they would ache so, and get mastitis if
we didn't. The calves are already weaned. We could feed the milk to them,
but . . . they say the milk is poison. And the pastures are poison, too. The
wheat will be poison." Her dark eyes held incomprehension. His, worry.

It all looked so normal: the wheat fields and pastures, now drying to
a golden haze; the citrus orchard with its deep shadows; and the tomato
patch sprouting small green fruit. I thought of my old landlord, their uncle
Minás, and his bees. "And the honey?"

"I harvested what was there," sighed Lélla , "before the bees could bring
in the dust, but it's little, so early."

I looked at them. I had always thought of them as solid, prosperous,
amazingly competent. They did everything by hand, plowed and threshed
with mules, even refused to put a pump in the well, a quarter mile from the
house, hauling water in buckets for themselves and their animals, watering the vegetables and orchard by gravity from a *stérna*, or reservoir. They
raised all their own food, ground their own wheat, made bread in a beehive oven. And now . . . they were at a complete loss to understand this
reversal of natural order. How could such an incident out of science fiction

touch, contaminate, and destroy this holy simplicity? There was nothing I could say. I offered my condolences for Panayiótis and Styllianí and left them sitting in the *avli*, their hands unaccustomedly idle.

A couple of weeks after Ingrid left, I went round to see Thanásis in the evening. Since all in the *paréa* were working in restaurants and shops, he was alone, for which I was thankful. I went out and fetched a supper of *souvlaki* and a bottle of ouzo, and we sat in the *avli* in the dark and talked. He and Ingrid had been on the phone almost every night, Thanásis said.

"And . . .?"

"She's decided to have the baby."

"And how do you feel?"

"Good. I feel good. It's... I never thought I'd have a child. I'm getting used to the idea."

A nearby small church was having its *yiortí*, so, after we finished our *souvlákis*, we walked over there. Outside the church a huge angelica shrub was covered with waxy white blossoms, censing the air of the whole neighborhood. We went in; Thanásis made his cross, kissed the ikon, and lit a candle. Then we walked along the rocks by the sea.

"She wants me to go to Sweden," Thanásis said suddenly.

"To live?" I asked.

"Yes," he said.

We were standing on the rocks at the end of the bay, looking out over the dark water to the village, the harbor, the lights. Music played in the distance – from a restaurant, a disco, someone's party.

"Not a bad idea," I said, trying to be upbeat. "For a few years anyway. They make a lot of furniture in Sweden. Good stuff. You might learn some useful techniques."

Thanásis lit a cigarette and said nothing.

I tried a new tack. "You'd be able to save money, do the things to your house you want to." I started to say "new flooring" but decided not to raise the issue.

Thanásis stood, looking out over the sea. Beneath our feet, the water swished quietly into and out of a hollow in the rocks. The village was a black silhouette against the lights of the harbor. "I don't want to leave here again," he said quietly. "If you love a place, you have to be there every day. You have to keep up with what's happening – the weather, the trees and flowers, the festivals, the lives. When I was in the Navy, on Crete, I missed the village every day, every hour. When I came back, I felt like a stranger. This life," he said, groping for words, "is like an embroidery; every day the design is worked out. Being away – it's as though moths eat holes in the fabric. Pieces are missing. The life is not whole."

There was nothing I could say, I who had left rags of lives all over the world.

A couple of weeks later, I left. Back in the States, I heard from Alíki that she was pregnant, and then that she had had serious complications but the baby was fine. I heard nothing from Thanásis, but that was not surprising. In seven years away, I'd had one postcard from him.

Two years later I came back for the summer. I was staying at Alíki's hotel, and so heard all the gossip. Much had happened in my absence. Alíki's father had died and she and her brother had taken over the hotel.

"And the babies? Yours and Thanásis'? About Chernobyl?" In the years I was away, more and more horrors about the explosion had been revealed.

"God be thanked, both are fine. Ingrid is here--staying with Thanásis," said Alíki. "She got eighteen months maternity leave. Paid. Do you believe it?"

"Sweden! Well, good for her. And the baby?"

"*Koukla*! A doll! An angel! Thanásis is crazy about her. You know she is named Katerína, for Thanásis' mother?"

" And are you friends?" I asked, tentatively.

"Oh yes. Little Katerína is the same age as my Aghis."

"And the village?"

" There was a lot of muzz-muzz but she is so precious everyone falls in love with her. Anna's little girl Mersíni cherishes Katerína like a doll. Even Thanásis' Aunt Eléni, who, you remember, is not famous for a charitable disposition..."

"The one who accused me of witchcraft?"

"Yes," Alíki laughed. "Well, she has been talking about leaving her house, the one next door to Thanásis'–to little Katerína." In fact, years later, on her death bed, Eléni would sell Thanásis the house for a few drachs, to prevent the relatives from trying to cheat him out of it.

"And the *paréa*?"

"The *Mouní* is still pissy, but she has gotten very odd anyway." The *paréa* had closed ranks again. The rifts were healed.

I went round to Thanásis' and was so happy to see *them* happy. They were sitting in the *avli*, Ingrid glowing and Thanásis cuddling the pink and gold baby and feeding her a bottle. I found a temporary niche as babysitter, so Ingrid and Thanásis could get out in the evenings and join the others to drink in the harbor.

They worked it out this way for years. Whenever she could, Ingrid would bring Katerína to the island, Every Christmas, Thanásis would go to Stockholm for a few weeks. They talked on the telephone once or twice a week. Seven years later, back in the village, I went round to Thanásis' house one evening to lure him out to dinner, and he was on the phone with Ingrid. When Katerína was old enough to travel on her own, she would spend all the months of her summer with her father.

I have on my study wall a photograph of the two of them, the tall dark man and the leggy, pale blonde child, whitewashing the street in front of the house. She is holding a dripping brush and laughing. In the photo, she is probably twelve. Now she must be twenty. I have not seen her since she was three or four or Thanásis for almost ten years. The last time I visited the island for a few days, he was away on a rare trip off-island. I used to write but he would never answer letters. I cannot afford the international phone calls – too much to say for infrequent ones – and I have been so involved with describing what is becoming past that the present slips away, day by day, year by year.

In the last decade or so, alliances between islanders and foreigners, some resulting in marriage and some not, have become common. Mostly these arrangements are between island men and foreign women, who are no longer looked upon as loose and immoral. With the settling in of the socialist government, the status of women has been raised greatly, which in turn has contributed to a greater understanding of liberated women from other countries. Still, when an elderly neighbor asked me why Thanásis would not marry Ingrid, I spun a falsehood, one I thought she might understand. "She would lose her citizenship," I lied, "and not be able to work in her country and care for the child. Besides, she is not Orthodox, and says she cannot become Orthodox while her mother lives." Fortunately, the old lady seemed not to have heard of the European Union and Greece's own newly instituted civil marriage.

T. S. Eliot wrote, "Humankind cannot stand very much reality." I think he did not know Greeks. Everything about Thanásis' and Ingrid's situation was destined to isolate them from village society. A village woman in Ingrid's position would never have borne a child out of wedlock. She would have had an abortion or, even against her will, married the child's father. If she were a minor, the father would have married her or gone to jail. But times were changing. Not only the leftist government, but also the influx of foreigners – no longer tourists but residents as well – and their "foreign ways" were influencing the behavior of the villagers. It was their own humanity, however, their loyalty to family and friends, that colored their perceptions of the changes. One young fisherman, having built his own flat on top of his mother's house, moved into it with his girlfriend. "Of course," said his mother, Mersiniá, "in my day, a girl had to be a virgin. Had to be, no exception. But things are different now. It's good to know that," here she motioned towards her lap, "is all right. In the old days, it wasn't always, and that made trouble. We hope they marry, but it's up to them." And so in time it came about that Ingrid and Thanásis' unusual union was only the first of many.

The reality we couldn't face was Chernobyl. There was no room there for change of perceptions: the air, the soil, the plants, and the animals were contaminated – that was sure. Scientists all over Europe were measuring the levels. Governments all over were wringing their hands and promulgating half-truths or downright lies. The half-life for the strontium and cesium was three hundred years. People with their three score and ten cannot think in terms of three hundred years.

Besides, we had to eat, we had to drink water and wine. Farmers had to feed and milk cows, had to irrigate, gather, and sell produce. Fishermen had to fish and tourists to swim.

So what did we do about the danger? We denied it. After a few weeks, when the government – with no reliable information – said it was safe to resume normal life, we did so. We sold and bought and ate contaminated cheese, irradiated meat, poisoned fruit. What else were we to do? Could half of Europe emigrate to Australia?

I spent time in several places in Greece that summer, on islands and the mainland, and after the first couple of weeks I never heard the accident, the cloud, or the radiation mentioned. Chernobyl was our new Apocalypse, a silent, colorless, gradual one borne on the summer winds. And like the barefoot fanatics who roam the streets with flags and sandwich boards proclaiming the end of the world, sooner or later we all realized that our fear, however rational, was useless. Knowledge would not save us. And so we threw away the signs, furled the banners, and walked backwards into the future.

VI

Summer
Frosini

Summer

Day

Summer in the Greek islands is not a gentle time. It is called *kalokaíri*, the "good weather," in the same propitiating way that the Furies were once called Eumenides, the "beneficent ones." They used to say that summer began in March and winter in August, but as the level of the sea has risen and fallen over the millennia, so has the weather changed. Now summer begins in the middle or end of May, whenever a hot, dry wind from the distant Sahara blows steadily for a week, parching and bleaching the green wheat, the cream and yellow daisies, scarlet poppies, and purple lupine to an even straw color, a blond crispness. After the wheat has been reaped, the sloping and terraced fields seem covered with heavy, faded golden velvet, like old curtains from a noble house – fringed with pale plumes of *kalámi*, embroidered here and there with the glossy dark green of *skinári*, and the gray-mauve of stones hazed with flowering thyme.

What winter is to Scandinavia, summer is here: the land is dead, unresponsive, dangerous. Only the lowest forms of life – lizards, scorpions, vipers – survive exposure to the arid heat. This is the season the goddess Dímitra treads the earth dry and sharp as shattered pots, mourning for Persephone. Dímitra's glances wither every growing thing but *mandragóra* and asphodel, flowers of death and dryness. Only the herbs – thyme, oregano, sage – carry a hope of solace, of renewal.

Day is a blaze of near-white light. The summer sky is not blue: the fissioning sun permeates the sea mist, fractures into billions of shards of looking-glass shifting and flashing over the sea's surface, reflecting back pure, undyed brilliance. The old word for this blinding near-colorlessness, *glaúkos*, survives as our name for the ophthalmic disease characterized by unbearably painful flashes of light. Here, going around with the head uncovered or eyes unshaded, especially in the sheet-white alleys of the village, invites sunstroke: fever, a galaxy of pinprick suns dancing before the eyes, unconsciousness. Heat radiates from whitewashed walls, shimmers over fields, slides up mountains. To move quickly is to be drenched in sweat the minute one stops, finds shade, or enters a house. To do any work outside, one rises in darkness, works until midmorning (tilling, gathering), eats a meal, retires to the dark coolness of a shuttered house or a bed made up under an arbor, and sleeps until the sun abates. In the relieving twilight, cows are milked, orchards are watered, gardens are hoed, shopping is done.

The sun draws water from every leaf, every rivulet, every well – and from the sea. The horizon hazes over, closes in, becomes imperceptible; its edges blur, removing from certainty the existence of limits. The adjacent islands disappear, become rumors of Elysia. Perhaps somewhere out there is another world, but this one is all-consuming, like a demon lover, beautiful to the point of pain. Life becomes a struggle, a sacrifice excluding, forever and ever, all sight or thought of other.

Sheltering behind brakes of cypress or cane or walls of stone, in the dusty *perivólia*, are peaches and almonds, eggplants and melons, struggling towards ripeness. Their success depends now on water – not rain (for rain at this time of year, say the farmers, is poison), but on whether it rained enough during the winter, whether the veins of the mountains are full, whether the ground water seeping into wells and reservoirs will last, will this year keep the vines and trees from arid death.

With the sky remote and glaucous, the land dormant and baked to the color of bread crust, the sea – the vivacious, charismatic sea – spreads its colors like a titanic peacock. Homer called the sea "wine-dark," and out on the open water, under the ship of Ulysses or the *kaíki* of Kapetán Linárdos (on his way to Crete with wine to trade for olive trees), it can be dark as sweet island *mávro*, and under a wintry sky, its slate-gray may hint of burgundy. But in summer, in the bays and coves, it is a sea for which Homer had no epithet. Perhaps, blind, he had never seen or could not imagine jade, aquamarine, chrysoprase, emerald, tourmaline, sapphire, lapis, even amethyst – all of these mined out of the darkness of mountains and brought up into light, becoming light, liquefying, spilling, flooding round this rough tan rock – transmuted not just into liquid but into the natal medium of all life, this soft salt element in which all is born, nourished, sustained, cured, reborn.

In the gold satin calm of afternoon, a small *kaíki* hangs upon pellucid water, a blue and orange brush stroke on the green. Diving from it, one swims through a limitless jewel. Seen from beneath the silken surface, the sun is a pale candle flame, the sky a weak twin who cannot sustain the frail weight of a human child, even with feathery wings beating, beating.

Undersea the light is aventurine, pale green sifted with gold dust, billions of mote-like creatures moving in a stillness. Around the diver's flowing body (every gesture of hand or leg, or strand of hair, a ballet) rush, flicker, and flash silver flecks of fish. Over the ivory bottom, heaped with tan rocks, wave white flowers of seaweed; between ivory and tan hover the pale, shy tentacles of octopus. The sand shifts, clouds, resettles for a moment disclosing, camouflaged among the rocks, shapes of white-crusted terra cotta: amphóras, slipped off the deck of a wine-trader or gone down with the pottery boat from Siphnos (which still comes, bringing jugs and ewers with the same rims and handles that emerge from the misting sand). Slowly, delicately we trace the shards, feeling the potter's thumb, his knuckles. Our own are losing power, becoming soft as fins. Alongside squid and cuttlefish, we propel our boneless bodies, grazing the sea floor, looking for something deeply our own: a white arm or shoulder, a face half-buried in the immortal sand.

More than light and shards surrounds us – also legends, and the awareness of legend. Swimming in the blue-green mist of the source of stories, shall we find here our lost city? Swimming farther and deeper, shall we see at last, shining through the light-struck green, roofless temples and columns of white marble crowned in white leaves (almost waving); mosaics of dolphins, octopus, fish, and urchins (flickering); sealed jars of wine two thousand years old? Somehow, still ourselves moving weightless in the natal sea, we will unseal the jars, drink the wine . . .

What holds us? Is it the wine or the light or the mitral water? We are able never to leave again, forever swimming and waving, through cities not built on land and sunken, but founded here in this element. We become one of the myriad of its creatures; like dolphins, otters, seals we slide, leap, dive upward into the sun, shaking our heads (scattering pearls), becoming, after a thousand years, ourselves a legend.

There is a myth among tourists that "Greeks don't swim." But nothing could be further from the truth. What they don't do is lie about on the sand like pods of mating walruses courting third-degree burns. But look in the coves near the farms, in the early morning or late afternoon, and you will see whole families, parents and grandparents, perhaps unloading a donkey laden with children and pots and pans. With a quick dip, the tired farmer and farm wife cool down from the hot work of picking tomatoes, boiling milk for cheese, firing ovens. Their children, well protected with hats and chemises, play in the shallows, while the grandmothers scour pots with sand and warm their old bones. For the sea in summer is not so much a recreation as a tonic every doctor prescribes: for arthritis, hot sand and sea bathing; for dermatitis, sea bathing; for being born English, sea bathing; for all the aches that winter has left, for nerves, for veins, for edema, for pregnancy, for cough – sea bathing. And every huge-busted, black-suited grandmother with oyster-white legs and turquoise veins arises from the foam a young Aphrodite, for She is not youth and beauty, but our feelings of youth and beauty, our feeling, leaving the sea, slicking back our streaming hair, that all our scars of skin and soul have been washed clean, that eternally young we rise from the foam to face a world, itself newly born, which waits for us to embrace it.

Threshing

The climax of the agricultural year, towards which all anxieties accumulate, is the threshing of the wheat. In December the farmer worries about rain, since too much can wash the germinating seed downhill into the sea; in February, when the fields have sprouted sweet and green, he worries about too little. In April he dreads too much heat too soon; in May he fears the African winds will not blow hard and dry. By June (called in the old times *Therinós*, the hot one), all possible disasters not having eventuated, he paces the golden fields of heavy-headed stalks, trembling with the fear of a mother in the weeks before her daughter's wedding. One thunderstorm now, and all his sweat and care – a year's food – will lie rotting in the earth like a girl buried in her wedding dress. Even if it storms once a decade or less, still the farmer crosses himself with every hopeful thought, makes no plans (or tries not to) until the precious wheat is safely reaped, dried, threshed, and stored.

Threshing used to take place in July, once named for it: *Alonáris*. The poet Odysséas Elýtis calls it "July in its luminous shirt," perhaps thinking of a gleaming shirt of sweat on a brown back as the farmer, a handkerchief tied on four corners covering his head, forks wheat into the thresher with his strong, scarred hands. In the golden fields, wheat has been reaped and stooked or loosely stacked for weeks now. Slowly the thresher, a clanking red monster like an old-fashioned railroad car, rich with gears and pulleys, levers, belts, and smokestacks, makes its way from farm to farm, where its mechanical maw is stuffed with wheat from towering stacks, and its other end spews out pure grain.

Though sickles hang on every stable wall, only a few farmers still reap by hand: walking the rows, gathering a sheaf with the left hand, cutting with the right, twisting a few stalks around an armful to make the sheaves. Old Leónidas does, for his steep terraced fields (once vineyards) reach high above Sarakínika, a crescent here and there behind huge boulders, atop bare cliffs of basalt or limestone – no way for a machine to pass. Nearly ninety, he's shrunken to less than five feet, and so, he chuckles, he doesn't have to bend so much: "The shorter I get, the easier it is!"

Most farmers reap by tractor now, but many still bind the stalks into waist-high sheaves, and most gather them (heads down to defeat the canny crows that caw overhead) onto the stone threshing floors, *alónia*. After a week or so in the baking sun, the wheat is dry enough either to be fed to the red thresher or to be trodden by a donkey or cow ridden and guided (perhaps by a child, scarved to the eyes against the dust) around and around, slowly, heavily, in the parching heat.

The *alónia* are round, stone-flagged, and ringed with low stone walls. Before the wheat is brought to it, the *alóni* is thickly whitewashed to burn out of the crevices moss, lichens, ants, scorpions. The *alóni* must be in the path of a good wind: north and west winds are steadiest, will blow the chaff from the tossed grain straight out into the surrounding fields, while the flighty southern *sirókos*, bouncing from side to side, will stir it all up, puff the chaff back into the circle or into the faces of the threshers.

Perhaps the most beautiful *alóni* on this island belongs to the family whose farm nestles under the north-facing summit of the mountain range south of the village. Home, stables, and barns stair-step down the slopes in cubes and rectangles of white stone. Most blessed, the farm is backed to the west by its own chapel, neighbored to south and west by monasteries, and to the north – down the slope in the valley – by a blue-domed, cypress-ringed roadside church. This large *alóni* is at a crux of spiritual influences as well as being the one most accessible from neighbors' mountain wheat fields.

Despite the farm's nearness to a surfaced road, the hill farmers abjure machines and thresh only with animals and humans. When the grain is dry and the wind blows steadily from the north, hill farm families – men, women, and children – walk or ride their mules down dry riverbeds, carrying wooden forks, shovels, and quantities of burlap sacks. Shortly after dawn, Longínos and his grown son Márkos have emptied the *alóni* of a small mountain of sheaves which have been drying for nearly a month. Now two newly arrived neighbors harness and yoke the animals – a mule to an ox, perhaps – tying bags over their haunches to prevent soiling of the grain. Then a young boy jumps on the outward animal and, riding sidesaddle, kicks it with his heels. *"Ah na! Ah na!"* Longínos and four or five others begin tossing in sheaves, giving them a hard bat on the stone curb of the *alóni* to loosen the grain. Under the hooves of the animals go the bundles of stalks. And the treading begins.

There are far too many helpers at the moment, so the talk is easy. The children tease and run about, waiting for their turn to ride and guide. A couple of women follow Kyría Ipapandí to her house and bring out straight-backed, straw-bottomed chairs for the older neighbors. Men light cigarettes and chat while watching the animals step round and round, occasionally adding a sheaf or two to the circle.

The sun rises slowly over the mountains, heating the stony land; the animals tread slowly, beating down the pool of wheat. The day advances; the piles of wheat diminish. Before midday everyone is sweating, less from exertion than from the pitiless heat radiating from the unshaded earth. Faces are wiped with handkerchiefs. About noon Ipapandí calls from the farmhouse that dinner is ready. The mules are unhitched, watered, and set to graze, and the neighbors repair to a meal in the cool farmhouse. But there will be no midday siesta today. For who knows whether tomorrow the wind will blow from the proper quarter?

As the grain separates from the straw, it falls to the floor of the *alóni*. One of the women steps in from time to time and sweeps it toward the rim of the circle. The farmers remove the straw with smooth, three-pronged wooden forks, always giving them a shake to dislodge tenacious grains. Soon the grain at the edges is nearly up to the curb and the piles of sheaves have disappeared. The animals are led out, relieved of their harnesses, and tied under a shady tree up the slope.

It's time to winnow. Every man, woman, and child takes a broom (short, handleless) or a shovel. They sweep the wheat into the shovels and toss it high in the transparent air, making showers of gold in the afternoon sun. The wind blows, the chaff eddies and disperses. Over and over, golden fountains spurt into the air from the basin of the *alóni*, fall back into a golden pool. The light chaff sparkles in the air, gold dust blown from the palm of a god careless of his wealth.

Above in the blue sky circle a hundred or more white doves. For weeks they have been tediously gleaning the mown fields, but now they catch the flash of a golden treasury of grain. The birds loop and circle, hoping that for a moment the wheat will go unguarded. But no, the grain is being swept into sacks, tied up, loaded on donkeys and mules, shut up in Longínos' barn. The doves give up hope, fly off down the valley in a great wave of foaming white.

Tomorrow, weather permitting (with farmers, it's always "weather permitting"), the neighbors' grain will be threshed in the same way – round and round will go a mule and an ox, in and out the yellow straw, up into the blue air the golden rain of chaff and grain. Sun, wind, sun, wind: growing, ripening, drying, threshing.

After threshing, the grain must be stored in a cool dry place with an even temperature, since moldy wheat is deadly poison. In ancient times, it was poured into huge terra cotta *pithária* sunk into the ever-cool earth. That is why Persephone descended into Hades to rise again in winter, green and young, sprouting from her own seed, the "first fruits" which were always saved from each harvest. Today's wheat may thus reach back to the beginning of time. More recently the grain, sacked in burlap, has been stored in stone bins inside the house (unheated except for cooking fires) on top of which, in the winter, on rafts of cane, beds are made. The wheat gives off warmth, relieving the pitiless chill of island winter, but keeps cool and dry itself. Nikodímos has another way: "We clean a room, a stable, and fill it, stuff it to the ceiling with straw. Then we burrow into the middle and tramp, tramp, push, pack! we make a hollow space, and there we store the grain."

Man and mold are not the only beings that thrive on grain; so do birds, mice, rats. Against these, in archaic times, the farm wife would make a pet of a snake, *phidáki*, any but the deadly viper. With a saucer of milk on the hearth and a little hole cut low in the kitchen door, she encouraged it to spend its winters hunting their common enemies, resting curled upon a warm hearth when replete, and perhaps, in their shared solitude, whispering in her ear the secrets of Earth. The coiled snake, often carved on the hearth or door post, was the symbol of Hestia – goddess of the hearth and of settled, agricultural domesticity. At some time, Hestia's *phidáki* was first appropriated as a symbol by Zeus and then replaced as a hunter by Psipsína, the domestic cat, who is now to be seen on every farm trotting purposefully towards the granary, her family tumbling after her. Though the modern farm woman now (like many of the rest of us) fears snakes, the cat has never captured her real affection. It is fed in the courtyard, and never allowed inside the house.

Wheat is the center of agricultural life, and its growing marks the year: plowing, sowing, reaping, threshing. Bread is the center of human life. The grinding, mixing, rising, and baking of bread is a cycle that cannot be broken. Each batch of bread is baked from the *zímos*, starter, of the previous. Yeast is never bought; if one is absent long enough for the *zímos* to die (perhaps a few weeks in Athens for shopping or an operation), one gets more from a neighbor or the bakery. Twice or three times a week, the dome-shaped oven with its chimney in front is stuffed with brush (thyme, oregano, sage among it) and fired. When the stones are hot, the ashes are raked out. Into the hottest oven goes the bread; when it is finished, it is slid out on a long wooden paddle. Then into the cooler oven go pans of roasts, stuffed vegetables, *mousakás*.

The Junta that controlled Greece from 1963 to 1974 passed a law prohibiting the use of home-threshed and ground wheat. No one knew why, and almost everyone defied it. The Colonels, village boys themselves, should have known better: for a farmer to buy bread, or even flour, from the village is a shame amounting to a scandal. (The Junta also outlawed the home distilling of ouzo, *soúma*, and cognac, thereby losing any credibility they might have had among the village and farm people.)

Bread is simply the main food. The loaves are thick, crusty, round as the oven; the best are gray-brown in color. The flour may contain barley or rye as well as wheat, and perhaps (despite careful sifting and sorting in wooden drum sieves) the seeds of wild grasses, poppies, naturalized sesame. Of course, there are other foods: the *dimitriaká*, named for the goddess of agriculture – beans, lentils, and chickpeas; eggplants, green beans, and okra; the "new" but beloved potatoes, tomatoes, and peppers; the *horta* (wild and domestic greens), the orchard fruits, and the birds and animals. But bread is the center. When Stamatoúla's son came back from teacher's college in Athens, where he had learned to eat more meat and less bread (he had some reason, for the bread was a pallid shadow of hers), she regarded him quietly for a time from her still, black-olive eyes, and then spoke: "O kós-mos trói kai psomí." "People also eat bread." *Kósmos* – all the world, all the proper world, the common and logical world, us. *Psomí* – bread, the food that most nourishes us and that, like pottery, requires only the humblest materials, which least drain the resources of Earth, yet require the most knowledge and art. "O kósmos trói kai psomí."

Bread, since Christ and even before, in spite of Abel's fate, has replaced meat (except at Easter) as the food of sacrifice. On any *yiortí* , the round loaves are brought to the church. Whether made at home or in the village bakery, they have been pressed with a wooden stamp bearing ecclesiastical symbols. In the church, they are piled in a pyramid on a little table before the altar, blessed by the priest, then cut up and distributed to the people as they leave the church – not a symbolic wafer but a good hunk of nourishing bread to be taken home and eaten with coffee or milk. The bread is transformed only in its effect on spiritual well-being and in its name, from the time of blessing being called *ártos* in the classical tongue rather than *psomí* in the demotic.

In other religions, bread used for ritual purposes is unleavened, but *ártos*, like everyday bread, is leavened. As in the process that turns grapes into wine, the putrefaction of the original element symbolizes the death of the human body, and the metamorphosis of simple wheat and grapes into bread and wine presages the promised Resurrection.

In the plain, honest bread is Christ the carpenter, the villager, the friend of fishermen, who strove so patiently to present aspects of the spirit in simple, understandable words and images: all people brothers, a family with God as our father and our mothers each somehow a Panagía, a stainless Mother; our life a humble one of working and breaking bread together in thankfulness for Life itself, which is every minute both matter and spirit, made so by our awareness, our love; and death no end but a familiar beginning, not a cycle but a spiral: sowing, ripening, reaping, threshing, grinding, fermenting, rising, baking – seed becoming wheat, wheat becoming bread, bread becoming spirit, and spirit sowing seeds in heaven as well as earth.

When the threshing is done at last (Ach! the heat, the sweat, the itching of the chaff!) and the year's grain is safely stored, the threshers go off to rid themselves of their rank and prickly clothes, douse themselves with buckets of cool well water, or throw themselves into the July sea, orange-lacquered by the setting sun. Then the threshing floor is swept, tables and chairs brought from the house, and many dishes – bread, of course, as well as cheeses, tomatoes, meat, eggs, olives – are carried out. Everyone is working: the smallest child just managing a chair a little too big for her, the mothers and aunts hurrying with copper pans full of chicken and potatoes, the fathers and uncles filling green bottles with black wine from the barrels and arguing about the quality: always one's own is the finest; the argument is really about whose is second-best. And, in the cool of the evening, there is a little celebration: food, wine, song, dance.

Is the dance round because the threshing floor is round? Or is this idea inescapable, the round and round of the seasons, the cycling that, like the dance itself, never quite comes back to where it started but lifts off in a spiral? The same threshing floor, the same wheat (but not: this is the seed of last year's seed, and last year was wetter or hotter), the same people but, no, this year, uncle Iakoumís is missing. An old man wipes his eye and sighs: "O *kamménos*! What a 'strong glass' he was! And a great liar! We shall not see his like again!" Another voice rises, a woman's: "Is Tzanétta making a match of it with Arghíris, Matoúla's boy? *Eh!* We'll see." Each leader dances his or her brief moment of figures, all the same but with individual graces, and then retires, but the line moves on, around and around

– threshing floor or world itself – season after season, year after year. And every day, bread is baked, sanctified, broken, and eaten, and thanks are given.

Cyprus

July, 1974. Golden days: the wheat reaped and stooked, threshing barely begun. Like crows scattering crazily from a farmer's shotgun blast, the village was panicked by news and the lack of it. Frozen in panic, we gathered tensely around radios which only intermittently gave out confusing scraps of information. Right-wing militarists, fanatics for political union with Cyprus, had assassinated Archbishop Makários, president of independent Cyprus. He was dead. He wasn't. He had escaped to Malta. Within days, the army, finally fed up with the Colonels, surrounded Athens and Thessaloníki, and toppled the government in a bloodless coup. But in the chaos, Turkey had leapt at its chance, first bombing and then invading Cyprus.

Junta or no Junta, coup or no coup, Greece was committed diplomatically and emotionally to the defense of Cyprus. With one radio broadcast, every able-bodied man in Greece under forty was called up. They went: Chrístos the long-faced humorist from the *kafeneío*, with his rifle that had not shot even a hare for twenty years; Yiórgos the bridge-playing bank manager (surprisingly, the commander of the island militia) in a uniform smelling of naphtha ; Chrýsanthos the taxi driver, one month shy of exemption; Takis, the mechanic on holiday from New Zealand; all the farm workers. They went, white-faced, dark-eyed, stoic, frightened. On the bus, a boy in tears held tightly to the hands of his grandfather who whispered, "You'll be all right. It will pass. *Pouláki mou*, it will pass." No words of patriotic bombast, no exhortation to bravery. The mothers, weeping, filled canvas bags with food – bread, rusks, olives, cheese, wine – and pressed them on their loved ones. And a good thing they did. "There was nothing for us at the armories," Pantelís said later. "There wasn't time to mobilize. They gave us amphetamines because there was no food." Nor guns, nor ammunition. "Only boxes filled with rocks," the legacy of the corrupt Junta.

The *hóra*, the port town, swarmed with men waiting for boats to take them to Piraeús, and with frantic tourists screaming for places on boats any islander would almost have cut off his foot to give up. The tourists were wild with fear at having to stay, the islanders desolate with having to leave. Kyriákos the playboy, an underwater demolition expert, was the only one to show any enthusiasm or excitement; for him the war was a change from the tedious seduction of tourist girls. Donning his Navy uniform, he commandeered gasoline and drove his speedboat to Piraeús.

Bombing in Cyprus, chaos in Athens and in the *hóra*, but in the countryside – stillness, silence. Windless, sun-drenched days. The wheat stood in the fields, heaped on the threshing floors, waiting, but nothing was moving, not tractor nor thresher nor animal. Were there ever such beautiful days? Peace, serenity. Over the golden fields, across the azure sky, like sheets freed from a clothesline, flocks of white doves undulated. Descending, they settled to gleaning the unguarded grain.

That summer, I was living in a small house on a high hill east of the village in Santa Maria, among the several farmsteads of the hospitable Anagnostópoulos family. The day after the invasion, I walked over the mountain to the farm of Panayiótis and his wife and married children. Although it was their baking day, Stylliní and Lélla had not even lit the oven. Instead, the whole normally busy family was sitting on the terrace, listening in silence to the broadcast of the general call-up. Looking down at their own half-reaped fields, suddenly I realized, "This wheat lying ungathered and unthreshed is next year's bread." By the very broadcast we were listening to, the men who knew how to run the threshing machines were being drafted to go to war. Of those who would remain, few – mostly old men without the strength – any longer knew the skill of threshing with animals. Grandmother Stylliní rocked back and forth in her chair like a *moirologístra*, a professional mourner, lamenting the departure of the owner of the mechanical thresher:

> When, when will come again
> Young Nóndas to thresh our wheat?

"I thought you did your own threshing," I said.

"Of course we do," she snapped, and began again. Both Panayiótis and his son were too old for this draft, so she was not mourning for them. Here the word "our" ripples outward, farther than the threshing circle, farther than the village, farther even than Cyprus . . .

Beneath the lushness of midsummer lurked the threat of hunger. Ungathered tomatoes rotted on the vines; apricots fell with quiet thuds to the ground, where mice ate them. And gliding after the fattened mice went the snakes – the "blind ones," pit vipers, little silver bracelets of death as small as three rifle bullets, and surer.

In the village, it was too quiet. There were suddenly only children, women, and old people. In the greengrocery, instead of tall, handsome and stormy-tempered Pípis, sat his gentle white-haired father Pantelís, like a ghost of his son. Manólis with the bad leg manned his shop (arranging and rearranging his sparse stock) almost in shame, worried about his son Andréas, called up just as he had won a place at university. In other shops sat wives and mothers; some were simply closed.

Silence. In all of Greece, no sound made by motor: no hooting ferries, no chugging fishing boats, no buzzing motorbikes, no gear-grinding trucks. In the usually bustling morning, it was quiet enough to be *mesiméri*, sleepy afternoon.

Except, there was always a radio playing. It said nothing, though, gave no news, only occasionally reiterating the general call-up, and, after the coup, playing folk music. "It must be a good government, this new one," said Eiríni, my landlord's wife, grave in her rusty mourning, "to play such beautiful music." Yiánnis and I looked at each other, both thinking, *Is this the kind of folk music a rightist or a leftist government would play?*

"Is it very authentic?" I asked.

"Yes," said Yiánnis.

"Leftist then?"

"Centrist," said Yiánnis, "because of the army."

The previous fall, I had been living in Athens when dictator Colonel Papadópoulos had been quietly toppled and replaced by a general. The radio then had played only martial music. Locked in our houses by curfew, we listened to an entire week of *Dum, dum, da-dan-ta-da*, interrupted only by warnings that anyone violating the curfew would be shot on sight.

Now everything on the island was upside down. Tourists were refusing to stay in hotels, instead camping at the port. Mariánthi, the supreme broody-hen mother, cried, "If the Turks come, I will kill first the children and then myself." A famous journalist, posted to Cyprus but hiding out on this island writing a novel, having previously demanded anonymity, was futilely pulling every sort of rank to use telephone or telegraph, to get off the island. Later, when we could laugh again, we read aloud, in *Newsweek* or *Time*, his eyewitness account: ". . . bullets ricocheting off whitewashed walls . . . keening black-scarved women." Imagined bullets and our walls, but it could so easily have been true.

Silence, and darkness. The island, all the islands, and all Greece were blacked out. Five hundred miles on every side, not a light was showing, nor a motor sputtering or drumming. The electric plant had shut down. No moon. By midnight, no glimmer of light was left to define, with a slightly bluer or grayer darkness, mountain from shore. No horizon. No light: not the weak headlights of Stamátis' truck wavering along the road from the village, not a flicker of a lantern tracing a nightly round from stable to hencoop to outhouse; only, somewhere in every house, a *kandíli* burning low before the ikons.

Outside: soundless, opaque blackness. But it was a stillness that hid desperate fear: less than three hours away by air, ordinary people – men, women, and children just like these, in villages and towns just like these, doing these same jobs (fishing, gathering eggs, drawing up contracts, studying fractions) – were being bombed, burned, and strafed. There, the blackness was slashed with violent color – red of tracer bullets, citron of explosions, vermilion of fires. Three hours. Less than a boat trip to Athens. Death, neither dark nor silent, waited behind a black curtain.

A year later, an exhibit of Cypriot children's art would show us the colors as we saw them with our hearts' eyes: red splashes on whitewashed stones, blue faces with white eyes, black scarves against blood-orange fire.

In the end, it was over in a week, or two weeks – for us. For the Cypriots . . . a life ended, with thousands dead and thousands in exile. But a small genocide, a week or two in the press.

Here the threshing began again. The men came back and got to work, laboring day and night (by tractor light) to retrieve the losses. The boys came back and strutted before their juniors with stories of the war they had experienced in the Piraeús armory. The only ones who had gone to Cyprus were the playboy frogman, who had done no diving but sat on a destroyer watching the American Sixth Fleet "monitor" the bombing, and little Pantelís, the schoolteacher, who, an infantryman, had actually fought, but would not talk about it. Ever.

Gasoline still being short, harnesses were dug out of storerooms, mules hitched up, the sheaves piled on the *alónia*, and the wheat threshed in the old way, round and round – cycle after cycle, bloodshed and peace, famine and plenty, fear and release. Round and round they trod, with a round dance at the end, and a round loaf for the altar. "*Dóxa to Theó,*" thanks be to God that this year we break bread together, once more, at our own tables.

The folly of Cyprus toppled the Junta, and once more, after so long, Greece was free – not just alive, but free! No longer was there need to speak in whispers, to fear the cowardice of spies, suspect the motives of neighbors.

Free! There were never such *panigýria* as that year's. In every village, the violins played with more verve, the dancers twirled and leapt with more skill and joy. The black wine was sweeter, too, strong as brandy and light as champagne, but it was freedom that went to the head. Fingers snapped like crickets; glasses clinked like tambourines; feet flew like eagles. Plates were smashed for the first time since the Junta's prohibition. Even the old people stayed out nearly to dawn. And all through the night we heard singing.

Once, during the dark nights of the Junta, lying in my bed, I had heard, beautifully, tragically, and defiantly sung, the Resistance anthem:

> When, when will there be
> A clear, starry sky?

To sing it, and many other songs, at that time had been to court arrest and imprisonment, and I never heard the songs without a rise in the heart, a catch in the throat. Now, in the giddy summer nights, along the streets all the forbidden songs rang, but riotously, raggedly. The exquisite white doves of the hope-beyond-hope had begun their quarrelsome nesting. The prisons were emptied, the exiles returned, war was averted; the dance of normal life resumed. But the music, the beautiful, brave, difficult, broken-hearted spirituals of political oppression, would never be the same.

Night

Night rescues us from the fevered dreams of day. The night sky in the islands is a theater like no other, and all beings attend the performances. Cattle in a field drift toward the setting sun, its gold reflected in their eyes. People at the same time drift toward the little harbor from the tables of whose *ouzerí* they watch and toast the *iliovasílema*, the "reign of the sun." They watch the whole hour or so of it, commenting on each swathe and shift of clouds, each explosion or shrinkage of the fiery disk. *To perivóli tou ouranoú*, the slow sippers will sometimes call the sky, "the orchard of heaven," where cloud trees bloom peach, apricot, or pomegranate, and cast plum-colored shadows.

When the afterglow has flared and fled, after an intermission for an-other carafe of ouzo, a saucer of tomatoes or grilled fish, the watchers scrape their cane-bottomed chairs around to face the east. Still sipping slowly, they wait patiently for the second act, the rising of the moon. Here the moon comes up behind Náxos, the neighboring island, and summer sea mist often magnifies the full moon into a brilliant slice of blood orange that seems to span twenty miles of violet mountains. As it rises, the moon shrinks and distances itself, leaving the human world for the celestial. Still, at *pansélino* – full moon – she sheds a light by which one can read (if that is all one has to do in the magical brightness) or, more likely, steer a safe way home after a night of wine and dancing.

On moonless nights, the stars are so diamond-bright, and so many – millions and millions, one thinks, fizzing against the blue-black heavens. They seem so close, so very close, it's hard to believe that with a ladder and a basket you couldn't gather them, that the smaller ones wouldn't sprinkle down and entangle themselves in your hair. The brightest stars, Venus and Jupiter, throw pencil-thin lines of light across the sea. *Pénte asterinós*, Elytis calls this sky, intensely starry. And if you can't read books by starlight, you can read faces: eyes white and dark, teeth flashing a smile.

When neither moon nor stars are visible, the total darkness is a gift of infinite compassion, calming the senses, revealing the qualities of lesser lights: the tiny yellow flame of a lantern moving slowly towards you along a country road three kilometers away; an aquamarine cone of sea glowing back to the blue-white carbon lamp of a night-fishing *kaíki*; a ridge of orange flame racing along the black mountains of the opposite island. Each has its story: the lantern is Yéro Nóntas coming back from his grandson's name day in the village, drunk and singing; the light-fisher is not finding any octopus because he's looking in the wrong place; the flames are Naxian shepherds setting fire to the *phrýgana* to improve grazing. ("Barbarians! We don't do that here!")

In the village, night is the social time. People, rested and showered, dressed in clean clothes, gather in families, in groups of friends to walk up and down, do the *vólta* between bridge and church: to greet and be greeted, encourage encounters, inquire after relatives or business. "How is your grandmother? Ah, the poor thing! And Evdoxía s new baby? *Na sas zísi!*" "Look, President, the permission for my daughter's house still hasn't come through, and costs are skyrocketing daily. Can you do anything?" And, of course, there are politics, though these must be discussed sitting down, over an ouzo , a coffee, even an ice cream. The young girls are walking three and four abreast, arms linked; the boys, as it happens, are walking the other way, but the mothers and the younger children are keeping watch from the roadside tables of the pastry shops. This is not as easy as it used to be; tourism has clotted the streets with unknown faces, enlarged the *vólta* to include window-shopping at the boutiques on the market street. "Where is your sister?"

"Oh, uh, she's with Frangíska; they were at the ice cream place . . ."

"Get her. Now!"

Night provides cover (the deep shadows between street lamps and under the eucalyptus trees), veils blushes, obscures closeness not tolerated by day. Assignations are made, leaves rustle, doors creak, sighs come out of nowhere. A distant motorcycle starts up, sputtering. Whose? Where? Night confuses sounds. Voices come over water as clearly as over the telephone – but whose motorcycle? Where?

More than anything, night teaches us the use of our senses, to walk a familiar road with no other light than the stars or, when even these are dark, to navigate by smell and touch. A warm sweet fragrance, sand underfoot, light wind: the cove at Ayí Anárghiri by the tamarisk trees, just past the spring (turn right in five minutes). Uphill from that, snuffling and a rich odor: the field with two mules and a cow (dip coming up). Downhill, going into Lággeri, a cooler breeze, the growl of egg-sized pebbles grinding together (keep right until you feel beach grass, then left).

Blind people know this sensory aliveness. Elsewhere, the seeing are sunk in light, civic light, twenty-four hours a day. Reason: fear. But here there's no fear, and so, resting sight, we are sensually free to smell, to hear, to touch the sphere of night with all parts of ourselves.

When Cyprus was being invaded, all Greece was in a state of emergency. Blackout was ordered, the use of gasoline was prohibited, and the village electric plant shut down. There was no moon. I was living on the top of a tall hill from which I could usually see half a dozen islands, even see tiny lights from neighboring Náxos. But those nights, for three or five hundred miles on every side, not a light was showing, not a motor coughing or drumming. The stifling black silence seemed to wall me up in a cell. It beat at my ears, made them hum. Was I hearing my blood pump? One night I crept out into the rocky *phrýgana*, terrified of vipers, and gathered handfuls of pebbles which I threw out one by one into the deadness to create some kind of depth. Suddenly, from far away floated the creak of oars, muffled voices. Someone, some defiant one, heedless of law or danger, was fishing. My ears relaxed, and I slept.

Panigýria

Summer nights are filled with *panigýria*. Each celebrates not only a holy event or personage, but an aspect of human life or nature, an end or a beginning. In June, a riotous Ai Yiánni with its bonfires welcomes summer and lovers; at the end of August, another, quieter Aí Yiánni gathers the people together before they go back to work or school or leave for distant shores. In between is the second greatest *panigýri* in Greece, the *Panagía*. It celebrates both the Dormition of the Panagía, her going to sleep, and the Assumption, the rising of her body to join her son in heaven.

It is no accident that the two great *panigýria* – Easter and the Assumption of the Panagía – celebrate the only instances of flesh ascending to spirit. Christ of course was already, through his father, half spirit. But Mary, who was not, made it the hard way (an inspiration to us all), by being perfect in virtue – not a nun locked away from the world but a human mother, one who birthed and labored (cooking, cleaning, washing), lost her son (to politics, jealousy, and conspiracy), then lived in exile, grew old, and finally closed her eyes to this tiresome, heavy world. She did not die but went to sleep, and her spirit, free at last and followed by her stainless body, ascended to heaven.

Christmas in Greece is not a great miracle. Isn't everyone born, causing his or her mother great pain, giving the midwife anxiety, leading the father to drink more than enough ouzo to quell the misgivings about what he has done to this sweet girl who only yesterday was making dolls of rags and flowers? Yes, all have been born, but only these two have truly and permanently passed beyond gravity.

There is no real belief here in the afterlife. Christ's message was of community, continuity, living life so as to leave it in hands you have helped to be good, healthy and happy, free of envy, free of vengeance. If I am you, and you are she, or he, and on and on in a widening circle, then none really dies. But the individual body achieves its rest and the individual soul closes its eyes, having done and seen and eaten and danced. Of course, if one could be perfect – but Christ himself met his match in the politicians, against whom even divinity is helpless, so we are stuck with the existing world, and for elevation from it we have religion (not too much), wine (just enough), and a dozen or so times a year, dance. It is no wonder that so many *tavernas*, the alternative to the church courtyard or the village *platía*, are named Paradise.

The Panagía goes to sleep at a time, mid-August, when the land and all Her creatures are themselves slow and drowsy in the heat of the year's *mesiméri*. The cycle of the Mother, all of Her aspects, is at its nadir. The wheat's in, the hens are laying few eggs, the cows giving little milk. The calves, weaned, do not seek the udder. The *meltémi* blows, a heavy wind, steady and warm. Sleep, deep but with a consciousness of light, a longing for dark, is the desire of all.

Many centuries past, the Panagía (old, old, not the blooming young mother of the ikons, but a frail, old woman, dry as paper) lay alone in her small whitewashed house in Ephesus, her pale blue-veined hands folded over her only faintly beating heart, praying for release. Alone? No. She is tended reverently by women, some of them converts to a way of thinking that will not for decades be thought of as a religion, some of them the devotees of Artemis (herself a woman, immortal), who has given Maria, all these lonely years, sanctuary in her city. But still the old woman is alone; none of the ones who matter – her son, her husband, even John – is beside her. The holy vitality ebbs, the skin becomes transparent, and, in a sigh, the soul escapes.

At this moment, the ikons show us, the long-lost Son appears, cups the tiny soul in his hand, and then from the corners of the earth (Rome, Damascus, Smyrna, Antioch), flying in an instant, come the Apostles. The body is wrapped in white linen, coffined, laid in a rock tomb. But three days later, when the tomb is opened, the wrappings lie limp and empty. Her body has gone to rejoin its spirit, so that year after year into eternity the Mother may give birth to life and hope.

The Panagía thus became the first purely human being to redeem her Son's pledge of Resurrection. Pure and perfect, she had no need to wait until the last trump. And yet for all less perfect beings, she is the *Odigítria*, the guide, the one who shows the way.

Perhaps this, the incredible hope she embodies, is why the going to sleep of the poor life-worn mother is celebrated with such noise, such blare, such chaos, such tidal waves of people. For days before the fifteenth of August, ferryboats crowd into the harbor of the *hóra* in such numbers that collisions are frequent. The navy complicates the situation by claiming a berth at the too-small mole for a gray cruiser, full of white-clad sailors running up blue and white pennants. Each arriving ferry, like a self-contained tornado, opens its maw and releases a roaring deluge of cars, trucks, motorcycles, people. Expatriate islanders from Athens or Australia employ more awkward and temper-trying transportation than the Apostles', defying death on overbooked airplanes or oversold and overscheduled ships to get home for the celebration. Along with them come tourists (rose pink and peeling); gypsies (brown, brilliant, spangled); peddlers and hawkers of ikons, underwear, and bouzoúki tapes; pickpockets and prostitutes.

Struggling through the chaos, held and wheeled by loved ones, are the crippled, the cancer-ridden, the palsied, the schizophrenic. The Eve of the Panagía is a time to hold vigil all night in the church, to burn candles, pray, hope for miracles: the re-knitting of severed spines and damaged nerves, the resurrection of buried wits. This church is not the great thaumaturgical one of Tínos, is not hung with votive ships fully fashioned of silver and gold, or with Cartier watches and emerald *colliers*, but with small, flat *támata* of nickel silver – arms and eyes, legs and hearts – and *stephánia* of all the flowers that fleshly arms, strong or atrophied, can hold.

Early on the morning of the day, three bishops (tiny, ancient, white-bearded, high-capped and crowned, coped in cloth-of-gold like living Infants of Prague) sail in like the Magi from the capital island; they are met by local priests holding black umbrellas. The Sea Scouts squeeze chubby thighs into uniforms bought in the fall; their sisters drape themselves with some teacher's version of classical dress (blue rayon cross-tied, not too tightly, over the breasts). Lyceé students, boys and girls, don various versions of traditional costume: short jackets and long skirts, tasseled caps, dark blue knee pants. Here and there struts a proud boy child in a grandparent's gift of full Attic dress: red tasseled cap, black embroidered vest, full-skirted white *foustanélla*, white stockings and low-heeled *tsaroúhia* with pompoms like red geraniums.

As the time of the procession approaches, at the docks, in the school-yards, and outside the church, there swirl little counterclockwise eddies of frenzy provoked by a burst zipper, a no-show deacon, a fainting navy bandsman. Some adults streak through the streets on urgent missions; others sit blank-faced and stolid (having too early claimed a seat at a café or window), waiting and waiting.

Finally, as happens every year, the chaos resolves itself, in the square in front of the great church, into a recognizable parade: first acolytes swinging censers; then bishops and priests (gold, all gold, reflecting back the glory of the sun); then the great, dark, de-framed ikon of the Panagía herself, steadied on the shoulders of six or eight dark-suited, sweating men; then more priests and more censers; then a long file of worshipers (dressed soberly, but to the nines), then the sailors and the brass-flashing Navy band; the blue-clad virgins; the Sea Scouts; the dancers in costume; and finally the school children: high school students in white blouses and dark blue skirts and pants, littlest children in their baby-blue smocks, all herded (butted as by goats, nipped as by dogs) by nervous and overdressed teachers.

If the spectators are first struck by the image of the Panagía swaying through the sun-bright streets (crossing themselves as she passes), piety soon gives way to patriotism – the drums and blaring off-key horns of the band, the tight smart uniforms of the sailors – and then to parental pride, unless it is indeed one's own son whose zipper has popped or one's own little daughter who is inexplicably in tears.

The lyceé students dance in the squares, the little ones are treated to ice cream, the men gather for an ouzo or two, and soon what is on everyone's mind is dinner. Everywhere, in *tavernas*, dining rooms, kitchens, courtyards and streets, the tables are loaded with pans of roasts (perhaps kid or pig) and potatoes, carafes of wine white and black, plates of melon and peaches and surrounded by crowds of relatives. Repletion and the heat of the day demand naps; in every room on every veranda, cots made up with cool white linen hold bodies in sleep as deep as death. But the waning of the sun and heat resurrects the *makarítes*, the "blissful dead." They rise, wash, dress, and in the cool of the evening commence the *vólta*, up and down the sea front, surging slowly with ten or twenty times the number of strollers of any other holiday. By ten or eleven o'clock, when night has truly fallen, the revived spirits flock to the transformed little woods beside the church or to a *taverna*, for, unbelievably, more food and wine, *violiá* and dancing.

But all this happens in the *hóra*. The villagers go, many of them, but it is not their festival, and most are content with their own brief procession led by their own priest past their own houses and shops, and the dancing of their own children – in simpler homemade costumes and to scratchily amplified taped music – in their own *platía*. Their great celebration is, oddly, not the going to sleep of the Virgin, nor her assumption three days later, but a noncanonical day, the *Enniámera* – the "ninth day," once the first formal memorial of a death.

Is it a coincidence that on this day, long ago, the village fishing fleet routed a foreign invasion? Of course not, and so the Panagía is thanked in the morning, her ikon encircled with *stephánia* made mostly of basil and marigolds now in this searing sun, with a few treasured roses. Just before dark, the present *kaíkis* sail quietly out of the harbor and return ablaze with torches and crammed with present heroes and heroines who debark to dance victoriously in the harbor *platía*. Nobody really knows who the invaders were. ("Turks, *vévaia!*" "No, Venetians!" "Maybe Russians?") The young people are dressed in such fanciful scraps of costume (red head scarves and cummerbunds) that they are popularly known as pirates, although why such marauders should be so joyously welcomed is as much of a mystery as the clamor and cacophony accompanying the going to sleep of the Virgin. Since the *Enniámera* is special to the village, there are celebrations everywhere. Dimosthénis plays the clarinet for dancing in the harbor *platía*; elsewhere, juke boxes are blaring loudly enough for dancing outside the *tavernas*, which, like the *ouzerís*, are packed with visitors from other villages and from the farms.

The *Enniámera* is the one *panigýri* that will draw the farmers to the village. Their duties are few in August; they can afford to stay up until almost dawn. By the light of the morning star, they lead the cows to pasture, scatter feed for the sleepy hens (surprising the rooster), and take water to the mule. Then they fall into bed in their clothes and sleep until twilight, when the chores call again.

Frosíni

In the August sun, the courtyard of her house is a cube of light as white and hot as molten steel. On the stone steps inside the massive, iron-banded wooden front door, Kyría Frosíni is sitting in a small triangle of shade cast by the facade of a large church. She creates a deeper shade, dressed as she is completely in black from headscarf to, even in this heat, long-sleeved *róba*, thick black stockings, and slippers. The only touches of color, of movement, are her pale downcast face and brown hands. Beside her slumps an open sack of wheat; on her lap rests a large wooden and wire drum sieve with which she is sifting and sorting newly threshed grain. Her fingers swirl the wheat, picking from it tiny stones and bits of stalk. Now and then she throws a handful of grain onto the marble flags, and a dozen or so white doves flutter down from the pointed stone corners of the roof and the cross atop the church to peck and coo at her feet.

The church is not a family chapel but a large domed structure which can (and does on its name day) hold two hundred people. The facade, taller than the two-storied house, is pierced by narrow windows and rises to a flat stepped belfry topped by a stone cross. The house that encloses the courtyard is three-sided and two-storied: an upper veranda of arches supported by Byzantine half-columns shades a ground floor of *apothíkis*, storerooms, with dark wooden doors set behind an echoing row of arches.

The house is locally called "the Monastery," as though there were not several dozen on the island, inhabited and deserted. It was built over three hundred years ago, they say. A devout and wealthy man built it, high on a mountain above terraced fields and overlooking a deep bay, to house his monastic son. Alas, the son died before the monastery was consecrated, and so the builder dowered it upon his daughter, and it passed down century after century in the female line, from grandmother to granddaughter, until the line ran out some four generations ago, and the building and lands were bought by the ancestors of the present occupants.

The once-magnificent church is now empty, bare of anything but the pale ghosts of frescoes, one or two mildewed ikons on canvas, the effaced, worm-eaten remains of a carved and gilded ikonstasis. At present, its only gold is a mountain of wheat, which the marble floor is keeping temporarily cool against the August heat. Kyría Frosíni's son and another young man, handkerchiefs tied about their heads, are bagging the wheat, fairly quietly, their usual converse dampened in volume and spirit by the presence of both the church and Kyría Frosíni herself, an austere figure in her unrelieved mourning.

She sifts and sorts the wheat, and her thoughts, despite her necessity to concentrate, scatter themselves, flutter away. She is lightheaded from fasting: twelve days now without flesh or milk or egg or oil or wine, two days to go before tomorrow evening, the Eve of the Assumption of the Panagía, when she will, for the third time, take Faní, her crippled twenty-four-year old daughter, to pass the night in the great church in the *hóra*, praying and asking for prayers, hoping and begging for hope.

She must focus her thoughts on Faní (her broken back, her shriveled legs, her girl's life of dances, flirtations, marriage, and children blighted like a frozen vine) and send them straight to the Panagía, the Sorrowing Mother, so that with the dawn of the festival day, Faní will rise (tired, of course, her eyes violet-shadowed), rise (even though stiffly), and walk haltingly perhaps, since it's been six years, but . . . walk! Hand in hand, they'll walk out of the church, take the bus as she used to, arriving home from school and swinging off the high step, books in hand. But no, the poor thing will be tired, so they'll take a taxi. She'll find Chrýsanthos and bespeak the car tomorrow. It will be chaos in the *hóra* with thousands of people milling about: worshipers, tourists, boy scouts, priests and bishops, hawkers and gypsies. Yes, it won't be easy, with the muscles all but atrophied. It will take time. She can't expect a miracle.

But a miracle is what she does expect – a major reversal of the flow of life. What she grieves about is why it has not occurred before; this will be the third year they have kept vigil. Why didn't the Panagía hear the first time, or the second? Perhaps, perhaps because Frosíni was still in deep mourning: first for her husband, dead of cancer the year after Faní fell from the olive tree, then for her brother, whose tractor rolled on him during that winter's plowing. Was it perhaps indecent to have prayed for Faní, for Faní only, so soon after these deaths? Her mind tells off the tragedies like beads on a *kombolói*: the child's fall, the brother's death, the husband's illness and decline with his refusal of the doctors and the treatment. Why? Because Faní was his little bird, his heart, his gold? Had her blighting so disheartened him that he cared nothing for his life, for the rest of them – not Frosíni, not the other children, not even his son Ianákos, his heir?

She sighs. It must have been the Eye. She had been too lucky: her marriage, the Monastery, the four beautiful children . . . well, three . . . . why could she not protect them? Was she not herself the most effective remover of the Eye in the village? Hasn't she taken away Lemoniá's headaches and the Málamas baby's fits, speaking over them the words learnt from her own uncle, dropping oil into glasses of water, oil that didn't rise until she prayed over it? Hadn't her words and acts turned away envy and admiration – curing earaches and menstrual cramps, slowing rapid pulses, bringing on labor for this one and that (so many, dozens), for indeed everyone but her own?

When the children were small, she had pinned the blue beads on them every day. And every year called the priest to come to sprinkle holy water, cast the devil out of the houses, the village house and the Monastery. But the priest, the priest is a man, and besides . . . She sidesteps the issue of the priest, with whom she has a quarrel, but the Panagía is a woman, a mother, whose neglect Frosíni feels keenly. "If she does not sympathize with me, why? why?" Her mind ranges over her sins, bouncing, deflecting, fluttering. She was a faithful wife, if not . . . A devoted mother, if perhaps too . . .

She wrings her hands, shakes her head, unties the black silk scarf over her black, gray-streaked hair, stands up (to a small spell of dizziness), and calls into the church, "My son, will you drink coffee? And you, Kóstas?"

"Yes," they call, "almost finished for today."

She crosses the courtyard and, despite her griefs, her weakness, is dazzled by beauty, color, pride. Climbing upward along white marble balustrades and half columns, echoing the arches, are vines – magenta bougainvillea, purple passion flower, blue bonnet, convolvulus, jasmine. From shallow bowls are flashing, like lights on water, the trembling spots of orange and fuchsia, lemon and pink portulaca. Climbing the stairs are blue-painted cans from which sprout domes of green basil and white vinca, and from which plummet tangling cataracts of wine-red carnations and blue Star of Bethlehem.

All of these are hers, her children too, raised from slips, from seeds, patiently and lovingly over forty years. And these flourish like the green bay tree, while the children of her body wither . . .

Ascending the unrailed marble steps, she steadies herself, picks a leaf of basil to crush under her nose. Worry haunts her like a scent. She enters her bedroom and changes her dress for another, still black but thinner. On a wooden peg plastered into the stark white wall, she hangs the black róba. Changing her stockings, she sits on the foot of a white iron bed. In this bed, she gave birth to all the children, four living and two stillborn. Now hers is the last room in the Monastery to keep its original floor, and she had to fight her son for it: "When it falls in, then cement it, but not before or when you marry, and it's your room." She also fought him about the generator, and later about the reservoir he'd wanted to install, ejecting her pigs and chickens from their sties and barns, the doves from their cote.

Ianákos! always full of plans, changes . . . his father dying too soon to settle the boy down. Frosíni crosses herself at his memory.

This room, which for so many years she shared with her husband, is itself a cube, four white sides rising from the earth floor to a ceiling of cane. The tall white walls are unadorned, except for a space above the bed, where against a black cloth hang the family ikons, some old, some new: her husband's Áyios Yiórgios, his father's Áyios Ioánnis the Baptist, those she brought with her: her own Ayía Efrosíni, and the one she values the most, her grandmother's Panagía – old, dark, cracked, the hand holding the infant Christ covered with silver, a *táma*, an offering of thanks for some miracle long forgotten. The only window pierces the west wall: framed in marble, double-arched and columned, carved with a cross, it is deeply recessed and so high that beneath it is a worn marble step. Aside from the bed, the only furniture is a dark wooden trunk, which holds her few clothes, all black, and five meters of white cloth for her shroud.

She sits a moment on the trunk, then rises and mounts the marble block beneath the high, narrow window. Resting her head on her folded hands, she gazes at the beloved scene: down terraced fields now golden with stubble, here and there dashed with the green of a fig tree (doll-sized children picking figs); down farther to the winding ribbon of road (toy tractors red and blue, a white bus passing silently); down yet farther to the sea, now green as basil and still as oil. It is this she has loved most about the Monastery, this poise between heaven and earth, this distance from the embrangling busyness and clash of life. But what was once a dream fulfilled is now an illusion of retreat, one she clings to as she clings to, steadies herself on, the marble sill.

South from the sea, dipping from a hill crowned with a windmill, is the wide, orchard-spotted, vineyard-furred valley where lie the lands of her own family: there the house she was born in, now her brother's; there her own dowry vineyard of black grapes. Rich land, decent houses – but for as long as she can remember, the Monastery on its mountain has been the home of her heart.

Tall, white, buttressed, backed in the spring by acres of pink-flowering almond trees, it had shone in her mind, a castle from a fairy tale. From her first visit (five years old? six?) on its *yiortí*, she had desired it deeply. Little by little, she saw, like a series of revelations, what she would do here – nothing very different from what she did at home, what all girls did: baking, cooking, cleaning, spinning, weaving, knitting, raising fowl, making cheese – but she knew that, done at the Monastery, each act would be transmuted. There would adhere to it – no, emanate from it – a certain

. . . romance? piety? She was never able to say exactly what it would be. Perhaps nobility, though not in the class sense, because only fools concerned themselves with such things. They, her family and the family of the Monastery, despite its ghostly splendor, were peasants, farmers. But it was possible to be thus with a difference, with a passion.

So even as a child, learning, for instance, to sift flour into sponge, knead it, shape it into small balls and set them to rise in a long, latticed wooden form, to cover them with a fresh white and blue cotton cloth – or perhaps it was to make *mitzíthra*, or *moustalevriá* – even then she saw herself doing these acts in the Monastery, sliding the loaves not into her family's outdoor oven but into the great beehive oven at the end of the second-story corridor. Her passion so informed her work that even as a girl she was famous for her baking, her cheese, her preserved fruit, her weaving, her white cut-work embroidery.

The only way to achieve this dream was, of course, to marry the heir to the property. This was by no means unthinkable: the families held adjoining lands, always a benefit, and were certainly social equals, and they were nearly so in the matter of holdings. The obstacle was that this heir, a strong if wild youth named Manólis, was fifteen years older than she, and from the time of her realization, she lived in dread that he would marry another before she grew up. Indeed, she was scarce twelve when he, with a great *gléndi* to which all the neighbors were invited, announced his engagement. A matchmaker aunt had been busy, all this time, and had come up with a bride from a mountain village who would add her acres of olives to those of almonds and grapes.

Frosíni's despair was numbing. Not even to her mother had she confided what were not so much "hopes," which all girls had, but assumptions as set as baked bread, so her parents were puzzled about her sudden loss of, almost, life itself: her long silences, idle hands, white face, red-rimmed eyes evidences of sleepless nights passed in suppression of tears.

And then, quite suddenly, the boy's father died, kicked by a mule. The "bride" declined to wait three years for the mourning to pass, having other fish ready for the frying. And Kyría Frosíni, somewhere between joy and terror, after discussing the matter with the Panagía, simply approached her mother and stated her wish. There wasn't any difficulty. Some months after the forty-day memorial, her father took the opportunity of an exchange of labor, spoke to the young man (still smarting from his jilting), and that was that.

Although no rings had passed, she entered into the status of bride. Two or three days a week, she would ascend, on her own white mule with its blue saddle and beaded bridle, the long steep path to the Monastery, to grind and milk, bake and make cheese, keeping the widow company, becoming her daughter, the sister of Manólis' sister, and, as she grew into womanhood, becoming bride, wife, and (with the equally untimely death of the widow) the mistress, center, life force of this extraordinary place, bringing to it something of a fulfillment of the destiny it had been waiting for through centuries.

Not without cost. Her own mother did not like the close deaths, her accession (at twenty) to such glory. She came herself to speak the words and drop the oil, brought priest after priest to sprinkle with a twig of basil dipped in holy water the corners of each room, the barns and sties, the animals. But for so long, they were blessed, it seemed, with luck as golden and benign as September weather. For so long. Until Faní fell . . .

"*Mána*! Where's our coffee?"

She starts, gasping, calls, "Right away! Right away!" and hurries through the room to the veranda and then the kitchen where her son and his cousin Kóstas, both dark-tanned, black-haired brawny young men, are sitting on straight chairs, wiping their sweat-streaked faces with the knotted handkerchiefs just removed from their heads. "Ugh! Go wash yourselves!" she exclaims, lighting an alcohol burner, and spooning sugar and coffee into a brass *bríki*. "There's a bucket on the veranda! You want *paximádi* ?"

"Yes, and some *mizíthra*. We're not fasting!"

"Of course not! Working men don't fast."

"Your mother's fasting?" she hears Kóstas saying. "They're going to the church again?" Silence. "Come on, Ianáko! She's right. *E, Kyría Frosíni*! If you're taking Faní to the Panagía, I'll drive you in the truck. More comfortable than the tractor, and the taxis will be jammed."

"I don't ride on tractors. And neither does Faní."

From a terra cotta casserole, she scoops sour *mizíthra*, white cheese, last night's milk scalded and thickened with rennet. She sets the rusks, a bowl of the *mizíthra*, and a saucer of dried olives on the table.

"But at the *panigýri* in Alykí . . ." says Kóstas, puzzled.

Ianákos hushes him with a gesture.

"What about the *panigýri* at Alykí?" Frosíni asks, holding the coffee over the gas flame.

"Nothing," says Ianákos. "I went, Kóstas and me, that's all."

"You're a good boy, Kóstas," Frosíni says. "Here's your coffee, all foamy. Money's coming!" The men sip the coffee, holding the small cups daintily with their thick and callused hands, dipping the hard rusks into a bowl of water. She eats a rusk herself, to still the dizziness.

When they've left, she covers the *mizíthra* with a clean cloth and carries it downstairs to a dark, dry cool room built into the north corner. In this *apothíki* are stored barrels of wine, of oil, of olives in brine, of cheeses in brine or oil; cane baskets of *throúmbes*, sun-dried olives; grass baskets and hairy goatskins of cheese; crocks of preserved pork and fish; sacks of wheat, almonds, walnuts; bunches of raisins. There would usually be baskets of eggs too, but now, in August, the hens are not laying a dozen a day amongst the fifty of them. The cellar seems chaotic: cane shelves and baskets swing from the rafters, sacks sag here and there, barrels stand upright or lie sideways on trestles. On the walls hang old tools; a wooden plow leans along one wall. But the room has its own order, that of use, and she picks a path surely through the dark to a shelf with other cheeses stacked on it.

She runs her hands and eyes over every item, counting, recording. She knows to a liter, to a kilo, the contents of her stores, notes that a *touloúmi*, a goatskin of cheese, is missing. She frowns, remembering how Ianákos, a few evenings ago, took the tractor to go out, and, with a slyness in his eyes and some excuse on his lips, avoided taking his sisters and a visiting cousin with him. She decides he has taken the *touloúmi* to a *taverna* owner, a bribe against or payment for the breakage he causes in the wildness – drinking, dancing, smashing plates and bottles – she hears about from her gossips and relatives. She sighs. Of course, the *touloúmi* (and the Monastery, the fields, everything except the girls' dowry lands) are his to use or give away – but the waste, the waste! It's time he was married and settled down.

In a box in the corner are the *lampádas*, pure white candles the height of a person, which the family will carry with them to the church. There are five, one each for herself and Ianákos and the three girls. Despite the expense, Frosíni has bought one for Voúla, the married daughter living in Piraeús, though she has not promised to go to the vigil. She refused last year, after a quarrel over Fani's treatment, and broke Frosíni's heart. Exercise, therapy: what good were they? The doctors who prescribed them had no hope, no faith. To trust in them was to despair. "Atheist!" Frosíni had called her, and in anger Voúla had bundled the children into the car and taken the ferry. The acrimony had been soothed over but the issue remained, like the subtle stink of a rat in a storehouse.

Emerging from the darkness of the *apothíki*, she reels from the white blast of noonday sun, holds her apron to her face, and steps blindly across to the stairs, where she sits. Noon. No food to fix, Ianákos will take Kóstas into the village to eat a meal cooked by Arghiró, the second daughter: glory be to God for this steady, normal girl – pretty, too, with her auburn hair, but twenty-six already and no groom in sight. Faní's hair too was auburn, deeper than Arghiro's. She had been the prettiest of the girls, poor Faní, but now . . . . Frosíni crosses herself and spits three times against the Eye, that which envies you your good fortune, your fertile lands, your healthy children, your auburn hair . . .

A cup of coffee – no, better chamomile tea; after so long a fast, coffee is too strong, makes her heart beat too hard, as it is beating now, as she ascends the stairs under the weight of heat. A little tea, some bread, some bread with jam, and then . . . rest, she must rest. She needs to rest and be strong, strong to carry her child in her arms – but what is she thinking? Faní is too heavy for her now, and Kóstas will take them in the truck, and help with the wheelchair. Take them from the village house. Frosíni must rest now, go down to the village in the evening coolness.

She hates to leave the Monastery. Leaving it, having to make their home for the most part in the village, was a terrible blow. For almost a year after the accident, she had clung to the idea that the Monastery itself would heal the child with its air, its beauty, its quiet . . . What need had Faní of a wheelchair? Where she needed to go, her father could carry her, without shame. But then he too sickened and the boy, barely strong enough himself to do his father's work, could not carry them both, carry them all with their burdens of grief.

Worse, the children and her husband united against her. They would not even agree to live in her own village house, her mother's, left to her, with its tall ceilings and wooden floors, its balcony high over the harbor, its sunny rooms open to the light from long casement windows. They insisted on making a new one out of the storerooms beneath, a series of rooms without light, on the level of the public street. Against her cries and then her wounded silence, they remodeled the basement rooms, pouring (over the ancient earth) garish terrazzo floors and a ramp like a badge of shame, and electrifying everything. The older girls, excited by spending money, went up to Athens, came home with a truckload of electric things: lamps and water heaters, a refrigerator, a cooker with an oven. "Look, mána, you don't have to cut brush or rake out ashes!" But she said nothing, continued to do her baking in the Monastery. Since Ianákos acquired the tractor, there was not enough work to justify feeding a mule, so she walked, ten kilometers up and back, carrying, when her son forgot, bundles of brush on her back.

And so they made their home in the noisy, prying village. "Faní needs company," they had said, but was this company – these thoughtless girls chattering about flirtations, engagements, and weddings with poor Faní lying there white and helpless, listening silently and crying afterwards?

Not only Faní; Frosíni cried herself. Other women's daughters would follow the violins through the streets, proud in white dresses, to meet grooms at the church, but her Faní never, and Frosíni longed to be away from the triumphs, away from her envy, away alone with her grief and bitterness.

The Monastery had failed her. No, it must be she who had failed . . .

After drinking her tea, she returns to her bedroom, where she stands before the ikon of the Panagía, crosses herself and repeats the prayer: "My most gracious Queen, my hope, Mother of God, shelter of orphans . . . I know no other help but thee." As she prays, she thinks of the Panagía that, as the priest said (before she quarreled with him), "We venerate her because she not only gave life to our Lord but, being His mother, She understood His mind, His very thoughts." But Frosíni does not understand *her* children. Yesterday she had had a little, a very little dizzy spell, had sunk down on the stairs, unable to move out of the punishing sun. Thus her daughter Arghiró, coming up from the village to collect the milk, found her. The young woman dashed across the courtyard, scattering pigeons, fussing and scolding. "*Mána! sto Theó!* Madness to fast at your age! And in this heat!" She helped Frosíni up the stairs into the coolness of her bedroom, where she stripped away the black scarf and black stockings, and, wringing a towel out in a basin of cool water, wiped her mother's face, arms, feet. Then she went to the kitchen to dip a glass of water, put lentil mush into a bowl. "Here, drink this! Eat this!" Dashing into other rooms, she returned with pillows plumping, propping, scolding, repeating herself. "*Mána!* Foolishness to fast . . .no need . . . And making Faní fast too!" Scolding her, Frosíni, as though she were the mother and Frosíni the child!

"Hush," sighed her mother weakly. "Don't tell me again. I cannot take her to the Panagía if I don't fast, you know that. And this year . . ."

"This year will be just like any other. Nothing will make her walk again, nothing. Not faith, not fasting, nothing!"

"You don't know . . . You don't believe . . . I suppose you won't come, like Voúla."

"*Mána*, of course I'm coming. And I do believe. And haven't I been fasting, too? But . . ."

"But what?"

"*Mána*, the Panagía . . .she chooses so few to heal . . . And no one we know, or even know about."

Frosíni raised herself from the pillow. "Didn't you read the paper to me yourself? Where this one and that one, crippled, stood up and walked? That the blind could see? Haven't you seen the *támata*, the silver arms and eyes, the golden legs?"

Arghiró did not answer but wrung out another cloth.

"Are you stealing from your poor crippled sister her only hope?"

"Her hope?" answered Arghiró shortly. "Forgive me, *Mána*, but this hope is yours. Faní has her own."

"What are you saying? Her own? What other hope could she have than to be whole again, healthy, able to walk, to love, to marry, bear children?"

"She . . . She hopes to live, as she is, without grief. To . . . make her own life."

"Never has she said such a thing!"

"To me, yes. And to Voúla."

"Ah! Voúla, the atheist! She and her doctors!"

"*Yia to Theó*, *Mána*! Voúla is not an atheist. She just thinks that Faní should take better care of herself, should do the therapy, the exercises."

"Will the exercises make her walk? No! Didn't that doctor say himself?"

"They'll improve her health, her circulation. Hasn't she already lost a toe to gangrene? Next it could be a foot, a leg."

"She should take care of legs that will never walk? Oh my child, my poor little bird, my broken one!" Frosíni fell into weeping and lamentation. Arghiró stole out, the untouched bowl of lentils in her hand, and closed the door.

Frosíni has stopped praying now and, sitting on the bed, is talking to the Panagía as mother to mother. "My children are becoming foreigners," she says. *Atheists*, she thinks, but does not say so to the Panagía. "Arghiró and Voúla, the married one who lives in Piraeús? They are always at me to take Faní to some new hospital or doctor. Doctors!"

Kyría Frosíni's opinions of doctors has worsened since the departure – none too soon! a of a young government service doctor. She had liked him at first – handsome, polite, unmarried, a few years older than Arghiró. Frosíni opened her house to him; he ate with them three or four times a week; they played cards and laughed. Such a disappointment, when one evening he announced his coming engagement. To whom? A stranger, another medical student. Secretive, deceptive! And cruel of him to have put ideas, not only in Arghiró's head (though she had seemed unconcerned), but in Fani's. Surprisingly, it had been the younger daughter he paid more attention to and towards whom he had assumed such authority that Frosíni had surmised . . . well, of course, a doctor . . . it was not impossible . . . so she had done what he ordered, cut off the cotton garment she had sewn Faní into, that she might not be wounded by the sight of her poor atrophied legs. And, although horrified, at his insistence, Frosíni allowed Arghiró to take her sister to the beach! To swim! To expose her body to everyone, all the evil-mouthed gossips in the village! But the worst was when, even after the engagement, he would take Faní in his car when he went to visit in the country! The two of them, alone! And she, her mother, could say nothing – or *said* nothing, anyway. Engagements can go away, can't they?

But this one didn't, though he did, leaving the family divided and Faní full of strange ideas.

Frosíni directs her eyes to the Panagía, whose own seem always to be looking beyond her. "Panagía, what am I to do with these children? She'll go, she says, and she'll pray, she says, but she does not believe . . . and you do not hear me. A life of her own? What life?" And yet, snatches of recent scenes and words come to her. Faní and her brother, talking, figuring. Faní wanting to swap her dowry house, the one in the harbor, Kyría Frosíni's own house that she has deeded to Faní, passing over the elder sisters, for Arghiró's land on a rocky promontory.

"Why?"

"Too many stairs."

"After the Panagía, stairs will be nothing."

"Anyway, *Mána*. We've agreed. Write the paper, please."

"Why do you want this land?"

"Ianákos and I, we want to build a hotel. I give the land, he the capital."

"Hotel? Are we hoteliers or farmers?"

"I am going to need money."

"Your husband will give you money."

Ianákos, slier, more patient: "*E*, that land won't make a nice house for Arghiró. It's going to be all hotels in ten years. Noise, discos, drunken tourists. Such a place to raise children? Not even ice plant will grow there."

"And Faní s house?" Silencing his sister with a look, he wheedled, "Better she build close to the Monastery. Peace, greenery, and we can be closer."

Baffled, Frosíni put off signing the paper: "After the Panagía."

Another torture (and she turns in the bed): the shop. Fani's idea. A tiny tobacconist's in the harbor came vacant. Shock! "You want to sell cigarettes?" Only the unfit, the disabled, are licensed to sell tobacco.

"No," said Fani, disarmingly. "Our handwork: lace, embroidery, knitting. Arghiró's and mine, Voúla's. We can work all winter and sell in the summer. You know we need the money. We shouldn't sell any more land, to pay for me. And we still have the death taxes . . ."

"But who will sit in it?" Frosíni's mouth went dry.

"Well, Arghiró, or maybe cousin Marigó. *Ela!*"

She gave in, and was betrayed, for wasn't it Fani who sat there, in the chair, without even a shawl over her legs, chatting and visiting? But it was true they needed money, for the doctors, the trips to Athens, the taxes.

And to sell land was to cut off a piece of the body. So much land they had sold in the last few years! The rocky outcroppings they had let go to foreigners to build villas on – well, the land was good for nothing, now that they ploughed by tractor. But in the weeks before his death, her husband had, without telling her, divided a good-sized field, just walking it in the old way and selling it without a survey. They thought the land was dry, but the buyer had drilled and found water – rare in those parts. She was sure the water was on her land, so she was suing to get it back. She *would* get it back, her land, her water. Everyone steals from a widow; there was the farrowing sow Nikiphóros hadn't paid for, and then the ikon.

Sometimes in confusion she dates her ill luck from the disappearance of the ikon, although that was after Fani's fall. The priest had brought an "art expert" to see the remaining ikons in the church, seventeenth century, painted on canvas and sent from Constantinople. Flaked and ragged, yet still there: the Anárghiri, the "without-money" saints, Damianós and Kosmás, doctors who treated the sick without fee. Saints, indeed. And the ikon went with the "expert" for "restoration" and never returned. The priest said it turned out to be not restorable and was burned. But didn't his son, that Athens lawyer, build a great pretentious villa just after that? Since then, she has refused to see the priest, never goes to liturgy, does her praying by herself, calls another priest from the *hóra* to bless the houses. Were they taking their revenge, the saints? Sometimes she has dreamed the ikon was calling to her; then she was sure it existed still, but despite her prayers, it would not locate itself.

This is Frosíni's grief, her guilt: that what the Panagía has granted to others – true visions of lost ikons, healing of broken bodies – she does not grant to her, she who has lived in love and reverence of Her all her life, whose body has been like a censer, whose faith has been like a flame before the image of the Mother.

It must be the Eye. Someone was eyeing them. Who? She went to her sister-in-law, who claimed to be a good remover of the Eye, but she was a fake, Frosíni was sure. She even asked the priest in the *hóra* for an exorcism, but he refused. "You must accustom yourself. Life has its ups and downs," he preached at her. What did he know, a foreigner from Athens?

The girls made money with the shop, but what were they doing with it? She pried, asked in for sweets a girl not so friendly with Faní, who might tell secrets. "So what are my rich daughters going to do with their money?"

"Buy a car," said the girl, less well off and jealous.

"A car? We don't need a car. Voúla has one she brings in the summer. She likes to drive to the beach. But we don't need a car. No, I'm sure it's for her furniture; she has a boy and is not telling me! In fact," Frosíni exclaimed slyly, "I know who it is!"

The girl shrugged, said nothing more.

A car! She can't walk and she wants a car? But Frosíni is sure of it: what did she find the other day under the pillow on the wheelchair? A *táma*, a votive offering, of real silver! Not to be bought in the village; a relative in Athens must have gotten it for her. Who? Probably Voúla the atheist. But the shock was not that Faní would offer a votive to the Panagía – all supplicants do – but that the metal was impressed not with the image of legs, as were those Frosíni herself had ordered from Yéro Yiánnis, the village goldsmith, but with a car! A car! To Frosíni such a thing was sacrilege.

The sun is now streaming into the room, two barely slanting columns of golden light stretching across the white space, falling on the earth floor and turning it as orange as a moon. Frosíni wipes her eyes with the ends of her scarf and looks again at the ikon of the Panagía, wondering whether to tell Her about the car. The ikon is so old, so cracked and dark that the face of the Mother can scarcely be seen; only the gold of the background and the silver of the little hand gleam faintly in the western sun. Just as Frosíni begins again to speak, she starts. The little silver hand . . . it moved . . . didn't it move? She opens her eyes wide: surely it moved, though it is not doing so now; surely the hand moved from the Child to the face, the lips of the Panagía. Frosíni holds her breath, all her senses alive, her eyes glued to the ikon.

And she hears what she had been dimly aware of but ignored: noises outside, downstairs a rattle of iron, the scrape of the great wooden door against stone, laughter. Laughter? Shaken, she climbs down from the bed, peers out through the door: it must be Arghiró coming for the milk. The milk! She has forgotten to milk! Where are her shoes? She hears the poor cows lowing, then hears, as well, more laughter not Arghiró's: Fani's! "*Mána!*" the young voice calls. "*Mána!* Where are you?"

"Faní! My child! What are you doing here?" Over the balcony she sees Faní being lowered into her chair by Kóstas, Ianákos returning to close the door.

"I've come to stay the night with you. So has Arghiró. We've brought supper. Voúla's coming tomorrow with the children and then we'll go together to the Panagía." Frosíni starts to descend, but Faní has already wheeled herself to the stairs and is preparing, with Kóstas' help, to mount. "No, don't carry me. I'll go up on my *kólos.*" And so she does, bumping up step by step on her bottom. "Didn't know I could do this, did you, *Mána?* I've been practicing. Now Kósta, bring the chair." Faní, sitting on the flags of the veranda, lifts her face to her mother; her light brown eyes are sparkling, her normally pale cheeks rosy. "Well, are you glad to see us?"

"*Vévaia,* my little bird, but . . .why did you come? I was about to leave." But she had not been; she had forgotten to milk, to slop the pigs, to sweep the wheat off the flags, to . . . . She had been lost the whole afternoon, sitting on her bed . . .

"Well," says Faní, smiling, brushing back her long auburn hair and re-clipping it with a barrette, "we thought it would be good luck to sleep here tonight together. And tomorrow Arghiró will wash our hair. Then, in the evening, Kóstas will take us down in the truck and Voúla will meet us on the road. Much nicer than struggling with the crowds in the village. Is there any tea?"

Frosíni is amazed. They've thought it all out, without her. "Tea? Of course, but . . . I have to milk . . . feed the pigs . . ." But she's thinking, "Voúla's coming . . . and, we're here together, in the Monastery, almost all together."

"Argiró's milking now. Ianákos will feed the animals. Let's make tea." Faní wheels toward the kitchen, where she dips water from a bucket into a pan and sets it on the cooker. Frosíni, too weak to protest, sits in a chair at the table.

"*Mána,*" Faní turns her eyes on her mother. "You will keep your word, won't you, *Mána,* and sign the papers for the hotel?"

"Ach," groans Frosíni. "That hotel!"

Faní cuts her off. "Listen, *Mána,* I have to tell you something. It's not good to have secrets, going to the Panagía." Faní lights the gas with a striker. "Before I had the idea for us to build the hotel, Ianákos was talking about selling the Monastery to foreigners."

"What?" Frosíni feels a shock as though she has jabbed her finger on a poisonous fish spine. "What?"

"Well, you have no idea how much money they were offering. And Arghiró's afraid no modern bride would live here, you know, so far away with no road and no electricity. And the farming – it's not as profitable now, since Father died, with less land and having to hire help. But a little hotel – he can build his own house into it, and we can all help Arghiró and his wife when he marries. And the Monastery we can keep the way you like it."

"Sell? To foreigners?" Frosíni is not over the shock. Of course, the place, the land, is Ianákos' own; he could sell it if he wanted but never had she thought he would not want to live here, with a wife, children . . . "Foreigners?" It seems like sacrilege. What would foreigners do here? "The church . . ." she gasps, "what would foreigners do with the church?" But it is not the sanctity of the church that possesses her.

"Exactly." Faní is smiling but behind the smile hovers anxiety. "So, don't you think I was clever? He's excited about it, already talking to builders. But you must sign the papers."

"Of course," Frosíni answers as though in a dream. "Of course . . . after the Panagía . . ." Faní takes a breath and opens her mouth, but Frosíni hastens to say, "After the Panagía. But I promise." She notices the water is boiling and sifts a handful of dried chamomile into it.

"And another secret, Mána." Faní reaches under the cushion of her chair and pulls out the silver táma of an automobile. "I'm sorry I kept it from you. This is what I'm asking the Panagía for – a car, a special car, fixed up for me, so I can go wherever I want all over the island! to the mountains! the beach! and take my friends without having to ask and hope and wait."

"But the Panagía will . . . I'm sure . . . ." But Frosíni is not sure, not sure of what she's seen, if anything, nor what it means.

"Sure?" says Faní, crossing herself and spitting : ftou ftou ftou. "Don't bring the Eye on us! Anyway, let's call it insurance!"

Before Frosíni can answer, Arghiró enters with the milk and climbs the stairs. She bends down and kisses her mother, then reaches down a big pot. "We'd better make mizíthra with this milk since we can't drink it and can't refrigerate it. How are you, Mána? Have you eaten anything? This tea is ready."

The sun has reached the corner of the kitchen window and gleams on the dark copper of the pots and the girls' hair. Frosíni looks at them with love as they chatter. From time to time, she lifts her hand toward her face, stiffly, trying to interpret the Panagía's gesture. Suddenly she realizes the girls are silent, staring at her.

"What is it?" Frosíni asks, bewildered.

"You want us to be quiet?" Arghiró asks.

"Quiet? What . . . I don't understand."

"You did this," Faní raises her hand to her mouth, "*Siopí*. Quiet. Didn't you?"

"Did I?" asks Frosíni, "E, I was just... Never mind. Do we want some green olives for supper?" She sits down again as Arghiró leaps to the door. She sits and sips the tea, and when Faní has wheeled around to unpack the groceries, Frosíni's hand steals again to her face, her lips. *Siopí*, the Panagía gestured . . . and in the quiet she heard . . . girls, even crippled girls, even unmarried girls, laughing, planning. Heard them taking care of themselves, of each other, of their brother, of her. Turning the flame down under the milk, she walks into her bedroom, now a blaze of golden light. Above the bed the dark ikon hangs, its colors barely discernible. Only the little silver hand clasping the Child glows in the western sun.

"*Siopí*," Frosíni sighs. "*Siopí*." Tears well up in her eyes, she is so ashamed. These past six years, she thinks, I have done nothing but weep and complain and pray. When all I had to do was listen. When all the time, my children were growing out of their griefs, making their lives. As I made mine. As I made mine.

Suddenly, Frosíni sees that her children are indeed her children. Their visions, their wills, are as strong as hers. She does not truly approve of these visions, but then, she remembers, her mother did not approve of hers. I have done well, she thinks, E! Well enough. And she lifts her eyes to the ikon. She recites, without tears, her little hymn of praise.

Supper passes in quiet conversation. No mention is made of hotels or papers or even the coming vigil. Leaving the girls to clean up, Frosíni retires early. In the after-light the white walls retain the day's luminescence, seem to be waiting for the moon to find them, to cover them with silver. Exhausted but sleepless, Frosíni lies straight on her bed. She is thinking about tomorrow, how the church will look: the white marble columns cool and pale in the darkness; the painted and gilded ikonostasis garlanded with flowers and basil; vases of lilies and roses crowding the floor beneath the ikons; and the flames of hundreds of tall *lambádas* and smaller candles, and oil lamps dancing over the gilded ikons, bringing the saints to life.

Shuffling, stumbling up the aisles, filling the chairs and the spaces before the altar will come the sick and the crippled, the palsied, the blind, the insane, and their families. Frosíni, surrounded by her children, will sit close enough to hear the beautiful voice of the priest, but not so close as to seem pushy. All their family and friends will come in twos and threes to say a prayer for them. And she and Faní and Arghiró will bed down on pallets to wait the night through. They have done it so often, hoping and hoping, but always, the next morning, in sorrow and disappointment, they have gathered up their belongings and gone home to another year of grief and shame. But tomorrow will be different. Tomorrow . . . She will take the *táma* of the legs – E! Why not? She has already paid for it. But this time she will not be begging for a miracle. She will be giving thanks for the one that has already occurred

VII

The Last Panigýri
Leaving

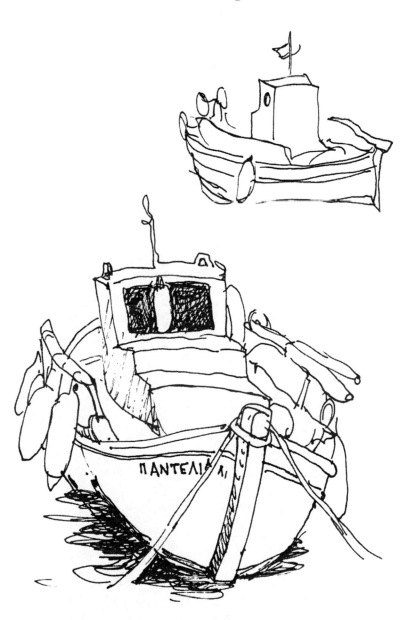

The Last Panigýri

Suddenly, overnight it seems, the tourists are gone, the children are in school, the farmers start worrying about the grapes, and another summer passes into history. But just before it does, the village throws one last *panigýri*. The date is the twenty-ninth of August. The locus is an uninhabited monastery across the bay from the village. The *yiortí* is that of the Beheading of John the Baptist, the ascetic saint whose name is so entwined with Eros. The ikon of this event shows the raggedy ascetic with great feathery wings, holding his own unkempt head in a golden dish. It was on such a dish or platter that, Salome, the daughter of Queen Herodias, presented to her mother the head of John, who had bravely accused the queen and her husband of incest. Herod, after watching Salome dance, had offered to grant her any wish, and though not pleased when she asked for the head of the prophet, gave orders for him to be killed. To honor the poor prophet, it is an Orthodox tradition to fast strictly on this day, and avoid using plates and knives, reminders of the instruments of John's beheading. But this is one day that hardly anybody fasts, except perhaps the ghosts of the monks of the nearly ruined monastery.

This second Ai Yiánni of the summer is also celebrated at night. All afternoon the fishermen, on a busmen's holiday, have sailed back and forth in their red and yellow or blue and green *kaíkis*, carrying tables and chairs (indeed, entire cafés-worth), barrels of wine and boxes of food, and later, people – girls and youths, men and women, grandparents and small children. By twilight, the entire population has vacated the village, packing into boats – cargo *kaíkis*, dinghies, sailboats and speedboats – debarking people with their baskets of food in a grand chaos on the rocky shore. A quick visit to the saint (light a candle, kneel, make the cross, kiss the ikon), and everyone is ready for the all-night, out-of-doors celebration: feasting, singing, and dancing – not to the glorious *violiá* (now departed to night clubs in Athens) but to Dimosthénis' clarinet, Bárba Iosíf 's bagpipe.

Isn't it strange that the poor saint's beheading is so joyfully celebrated? Perhaps it is not his pain that is the inspiration but the beauty of the rocky peninsula on which the half-ruined monastery sits, its new coat of whitewash glowing softly behind the flickering lights of the little lanterns and oil lamps people have brought. At the shore, a crescent of white sand sifts down to the bottom of a dark blue bay, where, as night deepens, it sparkles in the starlight.

Around the small group of crumbling buildings is uncultivated, barren land, springing with the plants that need no water. In the warm August night, the scents are intoxicating: yellow sage and purple sage, oregano, thyme, the amazingly fragrant thorny burnet. The villagers breathe them in, for they are the last of this summer's growth, and winter is coming.

This is not only the last *panigýri* of the summer, but also the last of the warm, maternal nights, so the people, even old people and toddlers, stay late, very late, putting off the end of summer – the return to school for the children and students, embarkation for the captains and engineers, the grape harvest for the farmers. It is a *panigýri* that always ends quietly, just before moonset, with a slow whispering walk to the jetty (small children heavy and limp as sacks of wheat on their fathers' shoulders) and a sail home in darkness. The quiet celebrants, deeply tired and deeply at peace, lean on the gunwales and on each other, watching the black wake for the last glow of phosphorescence.

Leaving

I am leaving again, this time by plane. The old ferry boats, whether rusty or sleek, have been replaced by huge ships with supermarkets and discos in them, floating malls. Sailing in them is hardly a nautical experience. Standing outside the tiny airport – a legacy from the German occupiers – Thanásis and I engage in that sort of waiting conversation. Did I get everything? Yes. Can he do anything for me? No. I should say something more meaningful but I am thinking, I am leaving for the last time. I will never come back. But I always think that and yet I do, time after time. Something makes it possible to return, makes it impossible not to. *Nostalgía*, the Greeks call it: the ache to return.

But I dread returning. Each visit is like walking into a movie whose film has been burnt, perhaps, or cut up and spliced, so that I do not know what has happened in the lost fragments, who those people are, what they are doing in my Náousa, a place which now exists, it seems, only in my memory. I am like the sea captains, away for months, for years, who on return wander around not recognizing children who've grown, going to visit people who've died.

Finally as the tiny plane skids to a halt and passengers debark, I embrace and release my friend. We have no more to say. I am off to the *ksenitiá*, the foreign lands, out of his life again, though he is somehow never out of mine. He wishes me "*Kaló taxídi,*" a good journey, and catches a ride with the taxi, back to his life, the life of the village.

That life, in the years I have come and gone from it, has undergone many changes. "Some forever, not for better," as the song says. Certainly the village, with all its new buildings, has lost its previous plain, modest beauty. The white walls are covered with graffiti-like advertisements for travel agencies and hotels. In the *platía* an open fast-food restaurant violates the darkness with its walls of orange Formica, stainless steel counters, and fluorescent lights. The government's architectural protection has done little to even soften the effects of over-building; its so-called regulations (for whitewash and blue paint) mere tokens, its ignorance of island style inexcusable. "The first mistake," Okeanís, an architect, said once, "was not to regulate the materials. If it were required to build in native materials, for instance, stone, whatever new buildings went up would harmonize with the old ones." But only a few areas were protected, resulting in a proliferation of brick-and-concrete block constructions looking like characterless city apartment buildings. Nor were any limits placed on height, so that, building story upon story, turning houses into hotels, neighbors were blocking other neighbors' views of the sea and access to sun. What was so beautiful about the architecture was the strict geometry softened by the uneven textures of stone beneath whitewash and the varying heights and angles of buildings dictated not by a government but by tradition, landscape, and human necessity.

And the noise! In the old days, when people would ask me why I loved living here, they would always answer their own question with "*i isihía, e?* the quiet. And it was quiet, day and night, with the exception of housewives calling to each other; children racing home from school, yelling out their glee, *kaíki* engines sputtering, and the occasional song leaking out from the *ouzerí*: Was it Sarándos singing his old-time pop songs? Or Nikólas the forbidden songs of Theodorákis?

This visit I had stayed in an apartment on the *agorá*, through which trooped every night crowds of drunken tourists, yelling and vomiting, until four or five in the morning. It had been late October; the season now extended from April until November. How could the *koinótita* have done this to the people living in their ancestral homes on the *agorá*, the *platía*? The noisiest thing in Náousa used to be the quarter-hour in the early morning when Pantelís drove his old rattle-trap down into the *agorá* to deliver the day's vegetables and fruit to his son's *manáviko*.

There was some light at the end of the tunnel. After years of terrible pollution of the bay, when even large fines could not prevent hotels and yachts from emptying their toilets directly into the sea – resulting in floating islands of fermenting human waste – the *koinótita* finally decided to build a treatment plant. The excavation of the sewer crossed the bedrock in front of Thanásis house, an irritation because he had just built a little seaside *avlí* there, so he could get away from the gadfly tourist-paparazzi who invaded his privacy with their day and night snapshotting of his beautiful house.

But perhaps the most heart-breaking change I would only learn about four or five years after I left for the last time. Fish, fishing, and fishing boats are so characteristic of the Greek islands that I was astonished to hear that most of the fish being consumed in Greece now comes, frozen, from Vietnam. "Not that fish," *taverna* owner Liggéris used to say to me, indicating a gray mullet a little dull of eye. "That was caught yesterday. Leave it for the tourists. Here's one for you – caught this morning." No more.

The news that brought tears to my eyes was that the EU's solution to the overfishing of Greek waters, particularly those around the islands, was to subsidize fishermen not to fish, provided they destroyed their *kaíkis*.

Hundreds, perhaps thousands of the old wooden boats, with their saucy hulls and masts and cabins painted in brilliant blues and yellows, oranges and reds, greens and white – products of a centuries-old folk craft – were burned or bulldozed. Some few were sold to collectors in European countries. It was these boats – emblematic of the islanders' relation to the sea and to a shared and vibrant, inherited sense of beauty – that had brought me ten thousand miles to experience the life of island Greece.

Leaning against the chain-link fence, I tell like beads on a string the rare experiences Náousa brought me: perfect quiet, perfect darkness, perfect beauty, unshadowed land, sun pouring down upon it like melted platinum, moon rising red as a blood orange, sea like a pool of liquid aquamarine. And man's touch manifesting a shared vision, the corners of a street rounded, softened by centuries of weekly whitewash. Beyond this physical beauty, the beauty of the community, the unriven commonalty of one culture, one language, made infinitely rich not only by millennia of history but by the variety of personalities. Three Greeks, four opinions, they say. What an astronomical number of opinions would there be in one small village – thousands at least! And yet I think of the unity of *paréa*, of food and wine shared, of dancing *syrtós* in *tavernas* by the midnight sea, in the streets during a wedding, on the blond sands.

As I wait restlessly to board my plane – the debarking passengers seem to be quarrelling over the luggage – I wonder if my nostalgia is not only for the place but for the times we lived (an eye blink in the history of the island), for the people we were, and are no more. So many gone . . . but then, I remember the children: Thanásis' white-blonde daughter, Alíki's two lively sons, and Koúla's and Katína's babies. For every tomb in the graveyard, there is a bright-eyed boy with dark curly hair, a girl arguing for her first high heels. They will have a different life, will begin a new millennium. But I am glad I lived here when I did, saw what I saw, knew whom I knew. Those times were for me, as the islanders say, *káthi méra panigýri* – every day a celebration. But like the sea, life is ever-changing. The village itself has changed in my absence, will continue to change. I will never again know it the way it was, however I understood it to be.

Squeezed into a miniature seat in the thirteen-person plane, I look out over the land as we lift up and circle into the wind. I catch a glimpse of Lággeri, the enormous bay, Panayiótis' farm, the little church, the islet with its ruins – and then as we climb I can see the whole *koinótita*, from the monastery of Longovárdas perched in the mountains of the south to the village harbor, still crowded with *kaíkis*, to the *manávika* of Ksifára with their brakes of cane and cypress. Now we are heading east, toward the strait between Páros and Náxos. The autumn air is so crystalline that, as we pass over Sánta María, the still-mysterious troughs, parallel lines stretching across the bay like staves on music paper, are visible beneath the jade water. Beyond the bays, the sea is sapphire and there are tiny white-caps but not enough to keep the *kaíkis* in harbor. Could that large red and blue one belong to Panayiótis and Stávros, the cousins who feed dolphins? That orange one with no mast, heading for Náxos, is surely Sarándos and Eléni's?

Now we are high over the island, and I see its entirety – the village, the *hóra*, the other villages – and soon, as the plane gathers speed, the next is-land, and the next. All the same, all rocks in the sea, encrusted with white villages. I think of the villages – the houses, the lives in them, the people, the songs, the ideas and stories I will never know.

As we near the mainland, I try to comfort myself. Whether I return in the body or not, the village will endure for me as a place and time when life was all it should be: as common as bread and wine, as various as the moods of the sea, as austere and joyous as a dance.

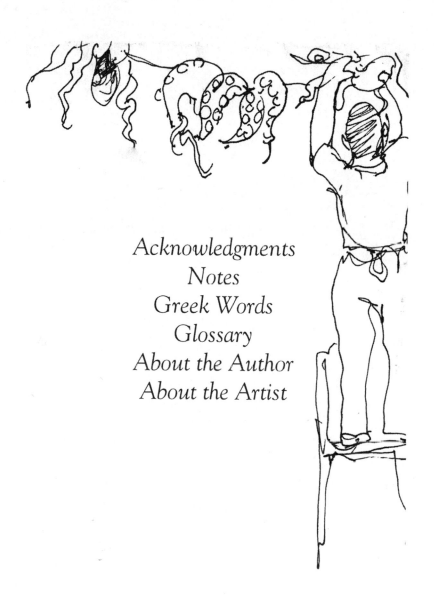

Acknowledgments

This portrait of the village of Náousa on the island of Páros, Cyclades, Greece, could not have been written without the help of hundreds of people. Over a thirty-year period, numerous village people shared their stories with me over cups of coffee or *fascómilo* or glasses of ouzo. Primary among these were members of several families: the Maroulídis family, especially Alíki; the Petropoúlos family, especially Mersiniá, her sister Asími and their daughters; the Anagnostópoulos families of Lággeri and Santa Maria; the Zoumís families of Kámpos and Ayíou Andréa; the Kortiános family, especially Stávros, my *piatikí paréa*. Pétros and Marilyn Metaxás housed and fed me extravagantly. Individuals who were generous with time and patience include Pápa Pétros Kortiános and Voúla Skandáli, Anna Kassaliá, and archaeologist Demetrius Schilardi. These are only dozens who taught me about the village; there were hundreds. I thank them all sincerely.

What Thanásis Tantánis contributed cannot be briefly acknowledged. His presence throughout the book (in his own name though sometimes in imaginary contexts) is evidence of my gratitude for friendship and *paréa*, for hours and hours discussing customs and people, for listening to and commenting on my stories.

In addition, I received enormous help from members of the Modern Greek Studies Association listserv (MGSA-L) and that of the archaeology of the Aegean (AegeaNet). Especially many thanks to Sabine Beckman, archaeologist, who lives, works, and botanizes on Crete, for identifications of plants, photos of native flowers, and homely as well as learned information. Thomas Doulis and the late Father Elias Stephanópoulos kindly read and commented on chapters concerning priests. Except for those quoted and noted, books consulted are too numerous to mention, but three not specifically cited were especially helpful: for folk beliefs, Alki Kyriakidou-Nestoros, *Oi Dodeka Mines* (Malliaris: Athens ND); for history of fishing, Thomas W. Gallant, *A Fisherman's Tale* (Ghent: 1985); and for history of wine, Miles Lambert-Cocs, *The Wines of Greece* (London: Faber 1990).

I have been lucky to have generous and knowledgeable readers. Póppi Kazamía Cottam has been for years my friend, expert reader, and oracle; it was a happy day when she picked me up hitchhiking. Catherine Siskron's insights were always amazing. Susan Garfield shored me up when I flagged; she is deeply appreciated and greatly missed. A class with Maxine Hong

Kingston opened windows I didn't know were there. Four writing groups shepherded me through the long years of writing; especially patient were the last: Polly Bowman, Seda Collier, Doe Tabor, and Andy Traisman.

Long-time Náousa resident Alice Meyer-Wallace contributed the cover painting and sketches. Margaret Matson and Annie Frangeskos, artists in their own right, translated them into appropriate technology.

O Prophítis Ilías, the prophet Elijah, was fed by ravens in the wilderness. My ravens have come in institutional and human form. I am deeply grateful for two faculty research grants from Golden Gate University, a National Endowment for the Arts fellowship, and an Oregon Literary Arts award, the Leslie Bradshaw Fellowship. Throughout her lifetime, my mother, Alice Ball Nilon, put up with my obsession and many times rescued me from the effects of it, mostly getting stranded in Greece with no money; she would be proud to realize that something came of her generosity. Lynn Bowers frequently provided shelter on her Fox Hollow farm. Penny Sabin, who often shared Greece with me, Vic Sabin, my always willing reader, and Tracy Lord all know why they deserve heartfelt thanks.

Last, Stephen Corey, Editor of the *Georgia Review*, delayed the writing of poetry to edit my manuscript; his eye is like an eagle's but his touch is like a feather.

Versions of several chapters appeared in the *Missouri Review, Ascent*, and, most frequently, the *Georgia Review*.

Notes

Lággeri

p. 35 From *The Odyssey*. Trans. Robert Fitzgerald. Vintage: New York, 1990. Ll. 484-488.

The Village and the Sea

A note on Greek popular music: Three different musical traditions are everyday parts of the lives of Greeks: demotic, rembetic, and pop. The first is folk music in a living tradition, embedded in a locale; the music of the islands is called *nisiótika*, after *nísos*, island. *Rembétika* is the music often called *bouzoúki*, café music brought to mainland Greece by refugees from Asia Minor. Popular music or *laiká* derives from both traditions and from European-American pop. Much Greek classical or semi-classical music also derives from these genres.

p. 51. "I've told you..." Traditional. My translation.

p. 51. "If I die..." A version of this is found in Gail Holst, *Road to Rembétika: Music of a Greek Subculture*. Trans. Holst. Denise Harvey & Co. (Limni, Athens: ND) Third Edition. P. 85.

p. 71. Information on smuggling in Sými comes from William Travis, *Bus Stop Sými*. London: Rapp and Whitney, 1970.

p. 72. "Oh sea..." from *Songs of Greeks Far from Home*. CD. Domna Samiou: Athens. ND.

Laundry

p. 161. "A little water, Kyrá Vangelió mou..." Traditional. My translation. *The Odyssey*. Op cit. LI. 191-193.

All other songs in this chapter are found in Ellen Frye, *The Marble Threshing Floor: A Collection of Greek Folk Songs*. Austin: University of Texas Press, 1973.

The Schoolteacher

All songs can be found in Holst, op. cit. except "I *Mána sou i ponirí*." Traditional.

The Eye

p. 223. I heard that knowledge of *ksemátiasma* is handed down from woman to woman, but Kalliopi says it is transmitted from man to woman and so forth; she learned from her uncle. Also, she says that the oil must form one unified puddle, not disperse as I thought.

Spring

p. 280-281. "Hymn of Kassiani." From *Greek Orthodox Holy Week and Easter Services*. Compiled by Father George L. Pápadeas (Daytona Beach, FL: 1987).

P. 282. "The whole creation mourned." Op. cit.

See Elaine Pagels, *The Gnostic Gospels* (Vintage: New York, 1979).

Koúla's Wedding

p.301. "May your bed..." can be found in Marilyn Rouvelas, *A Guide to Greek Traditions and Customs in America*. 2nd edition. Nea Attiki: Bethesda MD, 2002.

All wedding songs except the following may be found on Náousa Páros Folklore Group. Tape recording. 1995.

p. 307. "Maria in the yellow dress..." Pop. Composer unknown.

p. 307. "A little wanderer I am, my lady." Traditional. My translation.

p. 308. Get up [Arghíris], and tell us... Improvisation. Singer unknown. My translation.

The *Mamí* and Her Husband

All songs can be found in Holst.

Dímitra's Path

This story is based on the myth of Persephone and Demeter. Kóri (usually spelled Kore) means daughter or young girl. In Modern Greek, she would be called (for short) Foní and her mother Dímitra.

Bárba Stellios and the Mermaid

A *paramýthi* is a folk or fairy tale. For the story of the Gorgona or Mermaid, see page 162.

Greek Words

Spelling
Many Greek words are familiar to English readers, but Greek is a language with many forms and cases. To ease the path of the reader, I have used English plurals, as in *agorás* and *kaíkis*, but left the Greek accents. As well, I have not represented cases, except vocative, as in "Yiánni!" As well, unless the usual English spelling is seriously misrepresentative (Lycabettus for *Likavitós*), I have left well enough alone, as in *néreid* and amphóra. However, I have used *k* rather than *c*, *as in Akrópolis* and *ikon*.

Translation
Greek words are translated the first time they are used. After that, the reader is referred to the Glossary .

Pronunciation
No standard transliteration represents the actual pronunciation of Greek. To help the reader "hear" the words as well as possible, here are some clues:

Accents: All stresses are marked with an acute accent. Náousa, Lággeri.

Italics: Greek words are italicized. When Greek words are common in English (amphóra, agorá), they are not italicized but the accents are left in to indicate pronunciation.

Vowels: A as in Java: *Akrópolis, Anna.*
    E as in eh: *Evángelos* (except in *paréa*, where it is A as in *paint*).
    I as ee as in sweet: *Alíki, Ilías.*
    O as in home: *Horió.*
    OI as in keen: *Koinótita, noikokyrió.*
    U is always ou as in pouffe: *Náousa, Koúla.*
    AI or AY as in aye: *Ayios, Ayía, Ai'.*
    Medial Y as ee in sweet: *Kýrio, Kyría.*
    Initial Yi as in Ye, pronounced very quickly Yiánnis, yiortí

Consonants: as pronounced in English except:
    D should be pronounced Th as in *then – Despótis.*
    Th should be pronounced as in thing: Thanásis.
    H is aspirated as in A-Ha: *Horió.*

Initial Y (without i) as in youngster: *Yéros*.

Initial G is sometimes aspirated and sounded as Y: *gymnós=yimnós*
        and sometimes hard: *gigantes* as in great.

Medial G is softer: *panagía*, almost *panayia*.

Glossary

All Greek words are italicized and defined in the text on first appearance. The following list is for words that are often repeated without definitions. The reader should keep in mind that Greek is an inflected language and that in addition to case endings for nouns and adjectives, there are masculine, feminine, and neuter endings as well as singular and plural. When these are clear, I use them. When they are not, they are anglicized.

A

agorá: market
amé: sure, indeed
amphóra: large ceramic jar for wine (Ancient)
ánemos: wind
Apókries: Carnival
apothíki: storehouse
árchon: village elder
áyios: (m), ayía (f) holy, saint. Shortened to Ai. The possessive is used for the holy days: Áyiou Ioánnou, Ayías Varváras, Ayíon Apóstolon (m. plural possessive). The plural is Ayi (m) and Ayíes (f)

B

bállos: island couples dance
bárba: uncle, old man (affectionate)
bonboniéras: wedding or baptismal favor, also called kouféta.
bouzoúki: lute-like instrument played in rembétika
bríki: long-handled Greek coffee pot

E

E lipón: Well . . .
Eis ygeía!: To your health!
en taxi: okay
Yiortí: saint's day
Éyia móla!: Way haul away! in sea songs
exohí: countryside

F

fanélla: hand-knit undershirt
phíkia: ribbon weed (sea weed)
flokáti: thick, fleecy blanket or rug of sheep's wool
fortoúna: howling gale
foúrnos: bakery

G

gamóto: curse word
glaúkos: glaucous, pale blue-gray
gléndi: party
gómenos: (m), gómena (f) lover (crude)
gymnásion: high school
gýra: religious procession around the village

H

halál: (Arabic) ritual slaughter, koshering
hánoum: (Turkish) harem woman or loose woman
hárika: pleased to meet you
Háros: Charon
hasápiko: butcher shop, butchers' dance
hasápis: butcher
Hiérete!: greeting.
Hóra: the main village. On Páros this is Parikía, the main harbor town
horió: village
horós: dance
hrámi: bedspread
Hrónia pollá!: Many Years! holiday greeting

431

I

ikóna: picture, ikon
ívris: hubris, over-weening pride

K

kafeneío: (n) café
kafetzís: café owner
kaíki: large wooden fishing boat
kakaviá: fish stew
kalá: well, also All right!
kalámi: reed or cane
Káliméra: Good day!
Kálispéra: Good evening!
kalimáfki: priest's stovepipe hat
kallikántzari: demons who rise from
   the underworld at Christmastime
Kalo drómo: "Good Road!"
kalós: (m), kalí (f), kaló (n) good
Kaló stin'e!: Hello (to a female),
   kalo ston'e   (to a male)
Kalós ilthas: "Welcome"
kamáki: trident
kambána: church bell
kapetánissa: captain's wife
kofíni: tall basket
koinótita: community, political unit
   of village and environs, township
kólyva: wheat and fruit dish offered
   to the dead
kóri: daughter, young girl
kóritsi: young girl
koroidema: practical joke, leg pull
kósmos: people, the world
kouféta: Jordan almonds
koumbolói: worry beads
krío: cold
kyría: (f) respectful address
kýrio: (m.) respectful address

L

lambáda: tall votive candle
levendiá: charisma
levéndis: (m), levéndisa (f) one with
   charisma
líra: old gold coin
louláki: woad, bluing

M

mai: May, May wreath
makarítis: the blissful dead
málista!: I agree!
mamí: nurse-midwife
Mána: mother (affectionate)
Mánaviko: truck farm or greengrocery
manávis: truck farmer or seller of produce
Máti: the Eye
mátiasma: Eye-ing
matiasmén-os: (m) -i (f) affected by the Eye
mávro: black, "black" wine
mezés: mezédes, mezédakia appetizers
mitzíthra: fresh cheese
monopáti: narrow path
mousakás: baked vegetable (and meat) casserole
moústos: grape must, juice after pressing

N

Na zísete!: May you live (said at weddings)
Na sas zísi!: May [a child] live!
Na!: There!
Nai: yes
neraída: fairy, water sprite
neró: water
nífi: bride, daughter-in-law
nisiótika: island music
nisiótiko: island style
noikokyrió: thriftiness, husbandry
noikokýris: (m) -ía (f) householder, housewife
nostalgía: the ache to return
nóstos: return
noús: mind, brains

O

Opa!: "Ole!" Exclamation of encouragement
oraío: (n), -a (f), -os (m) beautiful
ouraní: sky blue
ouzerí: drinking place
ouzo: thrice-distilled grape liquor

P

pallikári: brave young man
Panagía: the All-holy One, mother of Jesus.
panigýri: festival
pápadiá: priest s wife
pápas: priest, Papádes priests

papoútsia: shoes
paramýthi: folk or fairy tale
paréa: circle of friends, company
patitíri: stone vat for treading grapes
paximádi: rusk
pensión: rooming house
perivóli: farm, orchard
pipína: olive seed remaining after crushing
píthos: pithári huge terra cotta jar
platía: town or village square
pnévma: spirit, breath (Ancient Greek)
póly: many, much, a lot
ponirós: (m), ponirí (f): canny, cunning, sly
prássino: green
príka: dowry
proí: morning
psáltis: cantor
psári: fish
psarás: (-ades) fisherman, -men
psaropoúla: fish broker's boat
psomí: bread
pyrofáni: night fishing with torches

R

ráso: cassock
rembétika: (also rebetika or bouzoúki) music
    of Asia Minor refugees
rhódi: pomegranate
rhodokókkino: rose-red
rhódo: rose

S

salóni: living room
sapoúni: soap
simasía: meaning
siopí: silence
sirókos: south wind
syrtós: (syrtos) line dance
skáfi: wash tub
skína: skinári mastic bush
spa!: hush!
soúma: local distilled grape liquor
souvlaki: meat grilled on skewers
stamní: terra cotta jug
stéki: hang-out
stenó stenáki: narrow street
stéphani: wreath, garland
stérna: reservoir
strophe: verse (of poetry)

sýmphoni: agreed!

T

Ta Phóta: the Lights, another name
    for Epiphany
tapsí : round baking pan
távli: backgammon
téchni: art
teláro: fish box
télos pándon: never mind, anyway
témplos: ikonostasis:
tsírtos: fish trap
Theophánia: Epiphany
touloúmi: goat-skin full of cheese
tsámiko: Epirote dance
tsiftetélli: belly dance

V

Voriás: North Wind

Y

yéros: old man (respectful, affection-
    ate)
ygeía: health

Z

zographikí: art, painting
zoí: life
zoíros: lively

About the Author

Alison Cadbury's stories and essays about Greek island life have won her a fellowship from the National Endowment for the Arts and another from Oregon Literary Arts. They have also won a Pushcart Prize and many honorable mentions from *Pushcart* and *Best American Essays*. An essay, "The Folitsa," appears in *Greece: A Love Story* from Seal Press, edited by Camille Cusumano. A translation of travel writing by Greek author Ilias Venezis appears in *Greece: A Traveler's Literary Companion* from Wherabouts Press, edited by Artemis Leontis. She lives and teaches in Eugene, Oregon.

About the Artist

Alice Meyer-Wallace, who created the cover painting and black-and-white sketches for this book lives in a converted goat shed and teaches painting in Náousa, Paros, Greece. She also spends time in her house on Majorca. In winter, she lives in Pennsylvania, where she teaches and shows in various galleries, including the Plastic Club. She works in many media – oils, watercolor, collage, as well as pen-and-ink and has issultrated children's books and books of poetry.